Three Exemplary Novels

Tres novelas ejemplares

A Dual-Language Book

Miguel de Cervantes

Edited and Translated by

STANLEY APPELBAUM

DOVER PUBLICATIONS, INC.
Mineola, New York

Copyright

Bibliographical Note

This Dover edition, first published in 2006, contains the unabridged Spanish text of three stories ("La gitanilla," "Rinconete y Cortadillo," and "El coloquio de los perros") from *Novelas ejemplares* (first printed in Madrid in 1613 by Juan de la Cuesta for the bookseller Francisco de Robles), together with new English translations by Stanley Appelbaum, who also wrote the Introduction and the footnotes.

Library of Congress Cataloging-in-Publication Data

Cervantes Saavedra, Miguel de, 1547–1616.
[Novelas ejemplares. English & Spanish Selections.]
Three exemplary novels = tres novelas ejemplares : a dual-language book / Miguel de Cervantes ; edited and translated by Stanley Appelbaum.
p. cm.
ISBN 0-486-45152-6 (pbk.)
I. Appelbaum, Stanley. II. Title. III. Title: Tres novelas ejemplares.
PQ6329.A6A27 2006
863'.3—dc22

2006046278

Manufactured in the United States of America
Dover Publications, Inc., 31 East 2nd Street, Mineola, N.Y. 11501

INTRODUCTION

Cervantes

Biographers of Cervantes have often been romancers, clutching at straws of evidence in a natural desire to flesh out their account of Spain's most honored author, especially with regard to his early formal education. Some recent reference books still repeat as gospel assumptions that have been seriously questioned by scholars. The following sketch, of necessity already brief, generally omits dubious or disputed matters.

Miguel de Cervantes Saavedra was born in 1547 in the Castilian university town of Alcalá de Henares, east of Madrid. His ancestry placed him in the minor nobility, but his father was a lowly barber-surgeon. The family moved to Valladolid in 1551, back to Alcalá in 1553, then roamed southern Spain for years (with a brief sojourn in Seville in 1564). Miguel's schooling was naturally erratic and unconventional.[1] (In 1565 his elder sister Luisa, born 1546, became a Carmelite nun in Alcalá, where she was later prioress.) By 1566 Miguel was in Madrid, enjoying the favors of a literary patron; the following year marked his debut as a poet, with a sonnet celebrating the birth of an infanta (compare the ballad in "La gitanilla" on the birth of Philip IV).

The year 1569 found Cervantes (after a period in the army) in Italy, in the service of Cardinal Giulio Acquaviva, who had come to Spain as a papal legate. (It isn't clear whether Cervantes was fleeing from the law in Spain, wanted for a crime committed by a namesake.) By 1570 he was back in the Spanish army, journeying to many parts of Italy and imbibing the language and the advanced literary culture. One of the major events of his life was his participation in 1571 in the sea battle of Lepanto, off the Greek coast, in which Don Juan de Austria (nat-

1. His ostentatious, and sometimes misplaced, display of classical learning (not free from occasional errors) could have been derived later from writer's manuals or other reading.

ural son of Emperor Charles V), leading the coalition forces of Spain, Venice, and the papacy, roundly defeated a Turkish fleet. Cervantes was wounded by a harquebus shot in the chest, and lost the use of his left hand from another shot.

After six months' recuperation in Sicily, he fought in further battles in Greece and North Africa, and in 1575 was on his way back to Spain with powerful letters of recommendation when he and his brother Rodrigo were captured by Berber pirates and held for ransom in Algiers. The letters made his captors set his ransom extremely high, and he languished in Algiers for five years, though he made four attempts to escape (Rodrigo was ransomed in 1577). Finally, Trinitarian monks arranged for his ransom in 1580 just before he was to be transferred to inaccessible Constantinople. He was to quarry this part of his life in many of his writings, including plays, stories, and the famous Captive's Tale inserted into Part One of *Don Quijote*.

Back in Spain, his once promising military career (of which he remained extremely proud) cut off, he found much of the rest of his life (except for the moral rewards of authorship) an insipid anticlimax. In 1581 he went on a mission to Oran for Philip II. In 1582 he failed to obtain a post in the New World (almost surely lucrative), but he did enter the circle of Madrid court poets around that time, and wrote his famous play *El cerco de Numancia* (The Siege of Numantia), sometimes considered the best Spanish drama before Lope de Vega. In 1584 a daughter was born to him and his mistress, an actress (who died in 1598). In the same year, on a business trip to Esquivias (northwest of Aranjuez), he met a local landowner's daughter, eighteen years younger than he, whom he married two months later; this union was successful neither as a marriage of convenience nor as a love match, and he was to spend much time away from his wife.

Now Cervantes began a largely itinerant life working at piddling government jobs, though he also continued to write poems, plays, and novels; in 1585 he published the first part (never to be continued) of *La Galatea,* an artificial pastoral novel with verse passages, in the Italianate mode already current in Iberia. From 1587 to 1593, with his base in Seville, he was employed requisitioning provisions all over Andalusia for the Grand Armada (which attacked England in 1588) and other military ventures. Fiscal carelessness and other mishaps led to several imprisonments and at least one brief excommunication for seizing Church-owned grain. In 1594 he became a tax collector for Granada province, and subsequently deposited money with a defalcating banker. It was in jail in Seville in 1597 that he is said to have

conceived and planned *Don Quijote*.[2] In 1600, the year Rodrigo was killed in battle, Cervantes left Seville.

On and off between 1602 and 1605 Cervantes lived in Valladolid, where Philip III had moved the royal court. In that latter year, in which the first part of *Don Quijote* enjoyed a great success, he was jailed again when a nobleman was found murdered outside his house; the judicial inquiries revealed his low living standards and the unsavory behavior of some of his female relatives and wards. In 1606 he followed the court when it returned to Madrid. In 1609, a year in which three close relatives died, he joined a religious brotherhood. In 1610 he was unsuccessful in his bid to join the staff of the Conde de Lemos, who had been named Spanish viceroy of the Kingdom of Naples.

In 1613, when he joined the Franciscan Third Order, Cervantes published the *Novelas ejemplares*, three of which are included in this Dover volume (see separate discussion below). In 1614 he published his major poem, the 3,000-line *Viaje del Parnaso* (Trip to Parnassus), expressing his views on many contemporary writers. In 1615 he published not only the superb Second Part of *Don Quijote*, but also the *Ocho comedias, y ocho extremeses* (Eight Plays [in verse] and Eight Interludes [in prose]); the (farcical and satirical one-act, intermission-time) interludes, especially, are regarded as among his best work. Cervantes died of dropsy on April 22, 1616, just three days after dating the dedication to his last work (begun 1609), the romantic and fantastic adventure novel *Los trabajos de Persiles y Sigismunda* (The Travails of P. and S.), which his widow saw published posthumously the following year. In almost every literary genre he handled, Cervantes had been an experimenter, and had often displayed a decided anti-establishment attitude.

The *Novelas ejemplares*

There had been a long, but intermittent tradition of short prose narratives in Spain since early medieval times, a tradition revitalized in the sixteenth century: Juan de Timoneda's miscellany *Sobremesa y alivio de caminantes* (Travelers' Tablecloth and Comfort) appeared in 1563, and his *Patrañuelo* (Story Collection) in 1565; in 1575 there was

2. A dual-language *Selections from Don Quixote*, with the same editor and translator, is available from Dover Publications (ISBN 0-486-40666-0).

a new edition of Juan Manuel's great 1335 collection *El conde Lucanor* (Count Lucanor).[3] And many stories were inserted into long novels, as Cervantes himself did in Part One of *Don Quijote*. His wonderful set of twelve rather long stories, the *Novelas ejemplares* (Exemplary, or Model, Novellas), was first published in Madrid in 1613; printer, Juan de la Cuesta; bookseller, Francisco de Robles (the same team as for both parts of *Don Quijote*). The *privilegio* (official authorization to print) is dated August 1612; the dedication (to the above-mentioned Conde de Lemos, also dedicatee of *Don Quijote* II, *Ocho comedias,* and *Persiles*), July 14, 1613. The stories were probably written between 1600 and 1610, judging from internal evidence. *Novela,* which today means "novel," meant "story" at the time (a borrowing from Italian, and ultimately, perhaps, from Provençal).

In his proud Prologue, Cervantes claims to be the first to have *novelado* in Castilian (this has been taken to mean that he considered the earlier stories familiar to him as translations or adaptations). He also states that each of his stories can furnish some profitable *ejemplo* (most likely in the sense of "moral lesson," like the *exempla* [exhortatory anecdotes] in medieval sermons, though some scholars who fail to find any such lesson in some of the stories believe that he meant his tales were models of good writing, or even that he was only ribbing the reader). All the same, Cervantes adds, the stories are also for fun and relaxation, and they are clean because at his age he can't afford to forfeit his bliss in the afterlife (but there are strong double entendres even in innocent Preciosa's songs).

No two editors or commentators classify the stories in the same way (Italianate versus authentically Spanish, serious versus satirical, realistic versus more imaginative and even fantastic; with subcategories of realistic such as picaresque; etc., etc.). It's best, however, to consider each story individually (as we do below), because "the elements are so mixed in them" (to paraphrase Shakespeare—who died in the same year as Cervantes—in *Julius Caesar*). They don't appear in the complete volume in the sequence in which they seem to have been written, and there are various speculations as to the meaningfulness of their published sequence (see below). It has also been said that a set of stories without a narrative framework (such as the *Decameron* and *Heptameron* possess, for instance) was highly unusual at the time. Most of the *Novelas* are concerned with love and marriage; those in-

3. An English-language selection from *El conde Lucanor* is included in *Medieval Tales and Stories,* edited and translated by Stanley Appelbaum (Dover Publications; ISBN 0-486-41407-8).

cluded here, all very Spanish in flavor, are universally held to be the best, or among the best.

The Individual Stories

"La gitanilla." The first (and longest) story in the collection (chosen for that spot because of its scarcely troubled idyllic charm and its effervescent adventure?),[4] "The Gypsy Girl" has been called "one of the author's most beautiful and interesting" stories; and its heroine, "the most captivating and most successfully delineated of his female characters." It has been seen as one of the last-written items in the collection, because the document concerning Preciosa's birth places that event in 1595, and she is now fifteen—but that date could easily have been inserted at any time before publication.

The plot combines a multiple love story with realistic, picaresque elements; improbable, "romantic" events and states of mind (such as Preciosa's innocence in the midst of crime, and her *savoir vivre,* incredible for her age and situation) intermesh with carefully observed Gypsy folkways (though these, too, are glorified vis-à-vis contemporary opinions of Gypsies, and even Cervantes's own in "El coloquio de los perros"). Yet the author's obvious belief that heredity does more than environment to mold the personality borders on racism, as his three "purely Spanish" protagonists display their natural leadership qualities: they are not only brighter than their Gypsy companions, but even excel them at physical sports.[5]

"La gitanilla" contains a number of mediocre poems (though one of the ballad-meter ones has been called the author's best of that type) which show that Cervantes at least kept trying, although he was no match in verse for the many good, or even truly great, poets of his own day, let alone the best of earlier times.

There are many folkloric, traditional, and literary sources for various parts of the story. La Carducha's ruse to retain Andrés is, of course, related to the false accusation of Benjamin in Genesis. The figure of Preciosa has been compared with that of a female entertainer in the *Libro de Apolonio* (ca. 1240, but based on Greco-Roman

4. One commentator sees it as a story about freedom (the Gypsy life, and the strong individual who flouts social conventions), contrasting with the second story in the volume, "El amante liberal" (The Generous Lover), a story of captivity among Muslims.
5. The revelation at the end spares the hero the ignominy of marrying a Gypsy, just as the Anglo heroes of some later westerns would be similarly saved from marrying squaws or halfbreeds.

sources) and with Marina, the innocent in the brothel in Shakespeare's *Pericles*. The self-sacrificing rivals Andrés and Clemente have been said to go back to various characters in medieval Spanish literature and in Cervantes's other works. For instance, "El coloquio de los perros" contains a reference to a page who joined the Gypsies for love of a woman, and the play *Pedro de Urdemalas* (one of the *Ocho comedias*) concerns an analogous situation, even including a felicitously unmasked identity at the end.

Conversely, "La gitanilla" has had remarkable literary and musical descendants, especially in the Romantic era, when Cervantes was worshipped. The first performance of the German play *Preciosa*, an adaptation of Cervantes's story by Pius Alexander Wolff, an eminent actor who had been Goethe's associate in uplifting the theater in Weimar, took place in 1821; the songs and other incidental music by Carl Maria von Weber helped keep the play on the German boards throughout the nineteenth century. In 1835, surely not by accident, the Duque de Rivas gave the name of Preciosilla to the Gypsy girl in his epoch-making play *Don Álvaro; o la fuerza del sino* (Don Álvaro; or, The Power of Fate); she is Preziosilla, the principal mezzo-soprano, in the great operatic adaptation of that play, Verdi's *La forza del destino* (1862; libretto by Francesco Maria Piave). The ballerina assoluta Fanny Elssler achieved international fame in 1839 in *La Gypsy* (composers: Benoit, Thomas, and Marliani; librettist: Vernoy de Saint-Georges; choreographer: Mazilier), directly inspired by "La gitanilla." This ballet was in turn converted into the 1843 opera *The Bohemian Girl* by Michael William Balfe (libretto: Alfred Bunn), in which the heroine, kidnapped by Gypsies in childhood, dreams memorably that she "dwelt in marble halls." Other Romantic-era Gypsy-girl stories and stage works which, though their plots are quite different, have an analogous inspiration are the play *Don César de Bazan* (by Dennery and Dumanoir, 1844), its English-language operatic adaptation *Maritana* by Vincent Wallace (1845; libretto by Edward Fitzball), and even Mérimée's "Carmen" (1845–1852) and Bizet's opera—not to mention the unforgettable figure of the Gypsy street dancer Esmeralda in Hugo's *Notre-Dame de Paris* (1828–1831).

"Rinconete y Cortadillo." This, the third of the *Novelas*, probably written in 1601 or shortly thereafter,[6] emulates the new phenomenon

6. It is mentioned in Part One of *Don Quijote* (1605), and a variant version is extant in a manuscript dated to before 1609. The Castalia edition of the *Novelas* (see below) includes this variant, as well as two versions of another story that is generally considered spurious (many works were wrongly attributed to Cervantes in the past).

of the picaresque novel (the numerous adventures of rogues, penniless drifters, and criminals), which had been inaugurated by Part One of Mateo Alemán's *Guzmán de Alfarache* in 1599 (45 years after the anonymous proto-picaresque *Lazarillo de Tormes*).[7] "Rinconete y Cortadillo" has been called "one of the major works of Cervantes's maturity." For those who find an intentional sequence of stories in the 1613 *Novelas* volume, a sequence concerned with relative states of freedom, "Rinconete" reveals the actual limits to what might be imagined as a rogue's total freedom. Of course, Cervantes had every opportunity, including jail time there, to study the thriving underworld of Seville and its corrupt authorities. The first act of his play *El rufián dichoso* (The Holy Thug), another of the *Ocho comedias*, portrays a similar milieu.

The names of the two eponymous heroes have some meaning. *Rincón* means "corner," and one earlier translator has rendered the character's name as "Sharper." The name Cortado ("cut," past participle) reflects the word plays in the story on cutting out cloth and cutting purses; he is also the younger boy, and presumably shorter of stature. (Other meaningful names of characters are mentioned in footnotes.) Oddly, the boys eventually all but drop out of what has begun as a record of their vicissitudes. Once they arrive at the lair of Monipodio, the Peachum of this *Beggar's Opera* (he also makes a cameo appearance in "El coloquio de los perros"), the story, though still rich (almost too much so) in incidents, becomes an essentially static *cuadro de costumbres* (tableau of folkways), a sort of "day in the life of crooks in Seville." The prevalence of dialogue, and the lowlife atmosphere, have led some commentators to relate this work to the theatrical interlude genre which Cervantes handled with such mastery.

The very last sentence of the story contains two features that should be noted: (1) A sequel is promised (Cervantes made other such promises in *La Galatea* and "El coloquio de los perros"; this kind of promise has been seen as merely a literary convention of the time). (2) The author assures us that his tale will serve as an *ejemplo* (like the medieval *exempla*): a guide to good conduct. This strengthens the case for that particular meaning of *ejemplar* in the title of the collection.

"El coloquio de los perros." This story, the last (and second longest) in the collection (and thus seen by some critics as its summing up, if not its very raison d'être), has been called the volume's

7. *Lazarillo de Tormes* is available as a dual-language book, translated and edited by Stanley Appelbaum, from Dover Publications—ISBN 0-486-41431-0.

"chief work" and its "most lively and complex, from an ideological as well as an esthetic viewpoint." Since Cervantes refers in it to Lope de Vega's pastoral novel *Arcadia,* it couldn't have been written before 1599, and it must also precede the expulsion of the Moriscos from Spain in 1609; the only datable incident in the story refers to the years 1589–1590.

The full title of the story reads: "Novela y coloquio que pasó entre Cipión y Berganza, perros del hospital de la Resurrección, que está en la ciudad de Valladolid, fuera de la Puerta del Campo, a quien comúnmente llaman los perros de Mahudes" (Story and dialogue that took place between Scipio and Berganza, dogs of the Hospital of the Resurrection outside the Puerta del Campo in the city of Valladolid, dogs generally known as belonging to Mahudes [the charitable hospital keeper]).

Is it a separate story? Yes, if you believe Cervantes's indication that there are twelve in the collection. No, if you consider it an integral part of another story in which it is quasi-embedded, "El casamiento engañoso" (The Deceptive Marriage).

"El casamiento engañoso" is about an army officer taking a sweat cure for syphilis in the hospital at Valladolid; he had been infected by his wife, as he narrates to a friend. While he was once dining with another officer, a woman entered whom he quickly fell in love with and married in haste. She was a wonderful cook and housekeeper, and he was blissful for a few days, though she was also mysterious. A visitress arrived one day, and his wife persuaded him to move to another house for a week because, as a harmless deception on her fiancé, a nobleman, that woman wished to pass their house off temporarily as hers. It turned out that she *was* the real owner of the house, not his wife. Meanwhile, his wife had disappeared, as had his belongings and a male "cousin" of hers, his only consolation being that she was fooled, too, because his gear had little value. He began to lose his hair, and he discovered his illness. In the hospital, there were two dogs guarding the place and carrying lanterns for alms-seekers. He has written down what they said one night behind his bed. (Here, the all-but self-standing "Coloquio" comes in, his record of the dogs' dialogue [there's just a fleeting reference to him in their dialogue]). After the "Coloquio," the "Casamiento" ends swiftly: the officer's friend believes he made up the whole thing, but he has enjoyed it and he urges him to write the other dog's story as well.

The dialoguing dogs are amazed at their new-found power of speech, but *not* at their apparent lifelong ability to understand all human utterances, no matter how abstruse, and to reflect on them ju-

diciously. They also possess a highly sensitive conscience, which sometimes makes them refrain from eating (nothing could be more undoglike than that!). They are concerned with making their stories morally profitable to their audience (again, the "exemplary" approach). Berganza, the only one to narrate his life, is a typical *pícaro* with many consecutive masters in the lower or criminal classes. Scipio, who keeps on promising to tell his own life, interjects philosophical thoughts, keeps Berganza from digressing too widely (this has been seen as a satire on the lengthy, wide-ranging *Guzmán de Alfarache*), and gives pointers on the correct way to tell stories (these self-referential tenets on the art of writing have sent some critics into ecstasies; they laud the "Coloquio" as a "meta-story" combining author, text, reader, and critic in one package). A series of episodic tableaux, full of loopholes and leaving many strings hanging which it might seem an author's duty to tie up, "El coloquio," like "Rinconete," tends to peter out, and stops short rather than ends.

Connections, some very tenuous, have been made with Cervantes's life. He spent childhood years in Valladolid, and some of the narrative may reflect his youthful fancies about the place. His praise of the Jesuit grammar school in Seville (its teachers are just about the only people Berganza meets who aren't distasteful to him) has misled many into a firm belief that he studied there. As for Montilla (south of Córdoba), he was there around 1592, and could have heard about La Camacha's trial for witchcraft, which took place there in the mid-1550s. Cervantes is unusually negative in this story, denigrating even the Gypsies, for whom he finds good words in "La gitanilla," and the Moriscos (baptized Moors allowed to reside in Spain until 1609), whose expulsion he sympathizes with in Part Two of *Don Quijote* (their crime in his eyes in "Coloquio" is that they work hard and save money!).

Many sources have been cited for the story. "As for the talking animals, Cervantes himself refers to Apuleius's *Golden Ass,* and he might also have mentioned Lucian, another writer of the second century A.D. The dialogue form could have been influenced by Lucian, and by the famous dialogues published in 1530 by Alfonso de Valdés.

The Nature of This Edition

The *Novelas ejemplares* are difficult reading today. Not only is the language old, full of words that have become obsolete or have undergone semantic change; Cervantes also devilishly uses every resource

of Baroque Spanish: word plays, ellipses, rambling and disjointed syntax, partially quoted proverbs, slang and thieves' jargon, technical terminology of contemporary institutions (army, law, government), words garbled by uneducated speakers, and what have you. Even experts disagree on many details. This Dover translation, as complete and literal as possible (because of the pedagogical aims of dual-language editions), attempts to match a lot of the pyrotechnics of the original, but this is sometimes impossible, and occasionally footnotes are the only ways of indicating, "Laugh, it's a joke." This translation leans heavily (and, even so, there are still a few conjectures) on the extensive annotation (it, in turn, a summary of generations of scholarship) in three Spanish-only editions: (1) that of Antonio Rey Hazas and Florencio Sevilla Arroyo (four stories only), Colección Austral, Espasa Calpe, Madrid, 1997; (2) that of Juan Bautista Avalle-Arce, Clásicos Castalia, Madrid, 1982 (3 vols.); and (3) that of Harry Sieber, Letras Hispánicas, Cátedra, Madrid, 1980 (2 vols.).[8] One previous English translation (from the 1960s), by a popular Hispanist, was also consulted; this Dover translator gratefully acknowledges receiving many useful tips (and confirmations of conjectures) from that version, as well as a degree of consolation, because even there, there were a (very) few indubitable flubs and bad guesses, not to mention a slight amount of shortening and paraphrasing that a dual-language edition couldn't countenance.

In accordance with current editorial practice, the Spanish text is here discreetly modernized in spelling and punctuation. Some of Cervantes's internal inconsistencies (he always wrote like a god who never rereads his copy) have been pointed out indulgently in footnotes.

8. Serious readers are referred to those annotations for lengthy historical and other explanations of many terms, which it was out of the question to expatiate on here.

Contents

La gitanilla

Parece que los gitanos y gitanas solamente nacieron en el mundo para ser ladrones: nacen de padres ladrones, críanse con ladrones, estudian para ladrones y, finalmente, salen con ser ladrones corrientes y molientes a todo ruedo; y la gana del hurtar y el hurtar son en ellos como acidentes inseparables, que no se quitan sino con la muerte.

Una, pues, desta nación, gitana vieja, que podía ser jubilada en la ciencia de Caco, crió una muchacha en nombre de nieta suya, a quien puso nombre Preciosa, y a quien enseñó todas sus gitanerías y modos de embelecos y trazas de hurtar. Salió la tal Preciosa la más única bailadora que se hallaba en todo el gitanismo, y la más hermosa y discreta que pudiera hallarse, no entre los gitanos, sino entre cuantas hermosas y discretas pudiera pregonar la fama. Ni los soles, ni los aires, ni todas las inclemencias del cielo, a quien más que otras gentes están sujetos los gitanos, pudieron deslustrar su rostro ni curtir las manos; y lo que es más, que la crianza tosca en que se criaba no descubría en ella sino ser nacida de mayores prendas que de gitana, porque era en estremo cortés y bien razonada. Y, con todo esto, era algo desenvuelta, pero no de modo que descubriese algún género de deshonestidad; antes, con ser aguda, era tan honesta, que en su presencia no osaba alguna gitana, vieja ni moza, cantar cantares lascivos ni decir palabras no buenas. Y, finalmente, la abuela conoció el tesoro que en la nieta tenía; y así, determinó el águila vieja sacar a volar su aguilucho y enseñarle a vivir por sus uñas.

Salió Preciosa rica de villancicos, de coplas, seguidillas y zarabandas, y de otros versos, especialmente de romances, que los cantaba con especial donaire. Porque su taimada abuela echó de ver que tales juguetes y gracias, en los pocos años y en la mucha hermosura de su nieta, habían de ser felicísimos atractivos e incentivos para acrecentar su caudal; y así, se los procuró y buscó por todas las vías que pudo, y no faltó poeta que se los diese: que también hay poetas que se acomodan con gitanos, y les venden sus obras, como los hay para ciegos,

The Gypsy Girl

It would seem that Gypsy men and women were only born into the world to be thieves: they are born to parents who are thieves, they grow up among thieves, they study to be thieves, and finally succeed in being thoroughgoing thieves on every occasion; and the desire for stealing, and the act of stealing, are like inalienable traits in them, not extinguished except by death.

Well, then, one of this race, an old Gypsy woman, who was probably a past master at the art of Cacus,[1] raised up a girl who she claimed was her granddaughter, and to whom she gave the name of Preciosa; to her she taught all her Gypsy ways, methods of deceit, and ploys for stealing. This Preciosa became the most wonderful dancer to be found in all Gypsydom, and the most beautiful and clever girl to be found not only among the Gypsies, but among all the beautiful and clever girls blazoned by fame. Neither the sunshine, nor the wind, nor any inclemency of the weather, to which the Gypsies are exposed more than other peoples, were able to tarnish her face or tan her hands; and, what's more, her rough upbringing only revealed that she had been born with greater gifts than a Gypsy girl, because she was extremely polite and well spoken. Together with all this, she was somewhat free and easy, but not in such a way as to manifest any sort of indecency; on the contrary, though sharp-witted, she was so modest that in her presence no Gypsy woman, old or young, dared to sing off-color songs or utter improper words. And finally her grandmother realized what a treasure she possessed in her granddaughter, so the old eagle resolved to let her eaglet fly and to teach her how to live by her talons.

Preciosa turned out to be rich in carols, songs, seguidillas, sarabands, and other verses, especially ballads, which she sang with particular charm: because her crafty grandmother came to see that such trifles and witty recitations, given her granddaughter's youth and great beauty, would surely be most felicitous attractions and incentives to increase her wealth. So she sought and searched for them every way she could, and many a poet gave them to her, because there are also poets who get along with Gypsies and sell them their works, just as there are poets for blind beg-

1. An arch-thief of Greco-Roman myth.

que les fingen milagros y van a la parte de la ganancia. De todo hay en el mundo, y esto de la hambre tal vez hace arrojar los ingenios a cosas que no están en el mapa.

Crióse Preciosa en diversas partes de Castilla, y, a los quince años de su edad, su abuela putativa la volvió a la Corte y a su antiguo rancho, que es adonde ordinariamente le tienen los gitanos, en los campos de Santa Bárbara, pensando en la Corte vender su mercadería, donde todo se compra y todo se vende. Y la primera entrada que hizo Preciosa en Madrid fue un día de Santa Ana, patrona y abogada de la villa, con una danza en que iban ocho gitanas, cuatro ancianas y cuatro muchachas, y un gitano, gran bailarín, que las guiaba. Y, aunque todas iban limpias y bien aderezadas, el aseo de Preciosa era tal, que poco a poco fue enamorando los ojos de cuantos la miraban. De entre el son del tamborín y castañetas y fuga del baile salió un rumor que encarecía la belleza y donaire de la gitanilla, y corrían los muchachos a verla y los hombres a mirarla. Pero cuando la oyeron cantar, por ser la danza cantada, ¡allí fue ello! Allí sí que cobró aliento la fama de la gitanilla, y de común consentimiento de los diputados de la fiesta, desde luego le señalaron el premio y joya de la mejor danza; y cuando llegaron a hacerla en la iglesia de Santa María, delante de la imagen de Santa Ana, después de haber bailado todas, tomó Preciosa unas sonajas, al son de las cuales, dando en redondo largas y ligerísimas vueltas, cantó el romance siguiente:

—Árbol preciosísimo
que tardó en dar fruto
años que pudieron
cubrirle de luto,
y hacer los deseos
del consorte puros,
contra su esperanza
no muy bien seguros;
de cuyo tardarse
nació aquel disgusto
que lanzó del templo
al varón más justo;
santa tierra estéril
que al cabo produjo
toda la abundancia
que sustenta el mundo;
casa de moneda

gars who make up miracles for them and share in their proceeds. There's a little of everything in the world, and the pinch of hunger sometimes makes gifted people venture on most unusual pursuits.

Preciosa grew up in various parts of Castile; when she was fifteen, her reputed grandmother brought her back to the capital and her former camp on Saint Barbara's Fields, where the Gypsies generally reside; she intended to sell her merchandise in the capital, where everything is bought and sold. And Preciosa's first entry into Madrid was on the feast of Saint Anne,[2] patroness and advocate of the city, performing a dance in which eight Gypsy women took part, four old ones and four girls, and a Gypsy man, a fine dancer, who directed them. And though they were all clean and well dressed, Preciosa's finery was such that she gradually enamored the eyes of every onlooker. From amid the din of the tabor and castanets and the height of the dance, emerged a buzz of voices praising the Gypsy girl's beauty and charm, and the boys ran over to see her, and the men to look at her. But when they heard her sing, because it was a dance with song, that was the limit! Yes, that's where the Gypsy girl's renown took wing, and by the general consensus of the organizers of the celebration she was immediately given the reward and prize for the best dance; and when they came to perform it in Saint Mary's church in front of the image of Saint Anne, after all the women had danced Preciosa took a tambourine, to the jingling of which, as she made long, very light turns all around, she sang the following ballad:

—Most precious tree
that delayed in bearing fruit
for years which were able
to cover her with mourning,
and in fulfilling the pure
desires of her husband,
very insecure desires
in contrast to what he had hoped;
from which delay
arose that displeasure
which drove from the temple
that most just of men;
a barren holy ground
that finally produced
all the abundance
that sustains the world;
a mint

2. July 26.

do se forjó el cuño
que dio a Dios la forma
que como hombre tuvo;
madre de una hija
en quien quiso y pudo
mostrar Dios grandezas
sobre humano curso.
Por vos y por ella
sois, Ana, el refugio
do van por remedio
nuestros infortunios.
En cierta manera,
tenéis, no lo dudo,
sobre el nieto, imperio
pïadoso y justo.
A ser comunera
del alcázar sumo,
fueran mil parientes
con vos de consuno.
¡Qué hija, y qué nieto,
y qué yerno! Al punto,
a ser causa justa,
cantárades triunfos.
Pero vos, humilde,
fuistes el estudio
donde vuestra hija
hizo humildes cursos;
y agora a su lado,
a Dios el más junto,
gozáis de la alteza
que apenas barrunto.

El cantar de Preciosa fue para admirar a cuantos la escuchaban. Unos decían: «¡Dios te bendiga la muchacha!» Otros: «¡Lástima es que esta mozuela sea gitana! En verdad, en verdad, que merecía ser hija de un gran señor». Otros había más groseros, que decían: «¡Dejen crecer a la rapaza, que ella hará de las suyas! ¡A fe que se va añudando en ella gentil red barredera para pescar corazones!» Otro, más humano, más basto y más modorro, viéndola andar tan ligera en el baile, le dijo: «¡A ello, hija, a ello! ¡Andad, amores, y pisad el polvito atán menudito!» Y ella respondió, sin dejar el baile: «¡Y pisarélo yo atán menudó!»

Acabáronse las vísperas y la fiesta de Santa Ana, y quedó Preciosa algo cansada, pero tan celebrada de hermosa, de aguda y de discreta

where the die was forged
which gave God the shape
he assumed as a man;
mother of a daughter
in whom God wished and was able
to show greatness
beyond human nature.
Through yourself and through her
you, Anne, are the refuge
to which our misfortunes
resort for a remedy.
In a certain manner,
I don't doubt it, you possess
a pious and just
control over your Grandson.
As a partaker
in the loftiest palace,
a thousand relatives
were together with you.
What a daughter, and what a Grandson,
and what a son-in-law! Immediately,
the occasion being a just one,
you must have sung triumphantly.
But you, humble one,
were the school
where your daughter
learned humble lessons;
and now at her side,
right next to God,
you enjoy the loftiness
which I barely glimpse.

Preciosa's song caused amazement in every listener. Some said: "God bless you, girl!" Others: "It's a pity this little lass is a Gypsy! Truly, truly she deserves to be the daughter of a great lord." There were other, more vulgar men, who said: "Let the kid grow up and she'll play some tricks! Honestly, a fine trawl for fishing up hearts is being woven in her!" Another man, more humane, more rustic, and more sluggish, seeing her dance so lightfootedly, called to her: "Go to it, girl, go to it! Go on, love, and tread the dust into fine powder!" To which she picked up the song quotation, while continuing to dance: "And I'll tread it into fine powder!"

The eve and feast of Saint Anne came to an end, leaving Preciosa somewhat tired, but so renowned for her beauty, wit, cleverness, and skill as a dancer that knots of people discussed her throughout the capital. Two

y de bailadora, que a corrillos se hablaba della en toda la Corte. De allí a quince días, volvió a Madrid con otras tres muchachas, con sonajas y con un baile nuevo, todas apercebidas de romances y de cantarcillos alegres, pero todos honestos; que no consentía Preciosa que las que fuesen en su compañía cantasen cantares descompuestos, ni ella los cantó jamás, y muchos miraron en ello y la tuvieron en mucho.

Nunca se apartaba della la gitana vieja, hecha su Argos, temerosa no se la despabilasen y traspusiesen; llamábala nieta, y ella la tenía por abuela. Pusiéronse a bailar a la sombra en la calle de Toledo, y de los que las venían siguiendo se hizo luego un gran corro; y, en tanto que bailaban, la vieja pedía limosna a los circunstantes, y llovían en ella ochavos y cuartos como piedras a tablado; que también la hermosura tiene fuerza de despertar la caridad dormida.

Acabado el baile, dijo Preciosa:

—Si me dan cuatro cuartos, les cantaré un romance yo sola, lindísimo en estremo, que trata de cuando la Reina nuestra señora Margarita salió a misa de parida en Valladolid y fue a San Llorente; dígoles que es famoso, y compuesto por un poeta de los del número, como capitán del batallón.

Apenas hubo dicho esto, cuando casi todos los que en la rueda estaban dijeron a voces:

—¡Cántale, Preciosa, y ves aquí mis cuatro cuartos!

Y así granizaron sobre ella cuartos, que la vieja no se daba manos a cogerlos. Hecho, pues, su agosto y su vendimia, repicó Preciosa sus sonajas y, al tono correntío y loquesco, cantó el siguiente romance:

—Salió a misa de parida
la mayor reina de Europa,
en el valor y en el nombre
rica y admirable joya.
Como los ojos se lleva,
se lleva las almas todas
de cuantos miran y admiran
su devoción y su pompa.
Y, para mostrar que es parte
del cielo en la tierra toda,
a un lado lleva el sol de Austria,

weeks later, she returned to central Madrid with three other girls, a tambourine, and a new dance; they were all equipped with ballads and songs that were merry, but all of them decent; because Preciosa wouldn't allow the women who accompanied her to sing licentious songs, nor did she ever do so, and many people observed this and esteemed her for it.

The old Gypsy woman, who had become her Argus, never left her side, in fear lest she be abducted and hidden away; she called her her granddaughter, and the girl considered her to be her grandmother. The dancers began to perform on the Calle de Toledo, and at once those who had been following them made a large circle around them; while they were dancing, the old woman asked the bystanders for alms and was showered with ochavos and cuartos,[3] which fell as profusely as stones thrown at a mark in a competition; because beauty, too, has the power to awaken sleeping charity.

After the dance, Preciosa said:

"If you give me four cuartos, I'll sing you a solo ballad, an extremely pretty one, about the occasion when our queen Margaret attended a mass for newly delivered mothers in Valladolid at Saint Lawrence's;[4] I assure you, it's worthwhile, written by a poet as respectable as an army roster clerk or a battalion captain."

As soon as she had finished speaking, almost everyone in the circle exclaimed loudly:

"Sing it, Preciosa, here are my four cuartos!"

And so, cuartos hailed down on her, and the old woman had all she could do to pick them up. Well, then, her grain harvest and grape harvest over, Preciosa struck her tambourine and, in merry, madcap tones, sang the following ballad:

—Off to new mothers' mass
went the greatest queen in Europe,
in her value and in her name, meaning "pearl,"
a rich and wonderful jewel.
Just as she attracts the eyes,
she attracts all the souls
of those who behold and wonder at
her devoutness and her pomp.
And, to show that she is part
of heaven throughout the earth,
on one side she has the sun of Austria;

3. Copper coins, the ochavo being worth two maravedis; and the cuarto, four.
4. Margaret of Austria, wife of Philip III, attended this mass on May 31, 1605, after giving birth to the future Philip IV.

al otro, la tierna Aurora.
A sus espaldas le sigue
un Lucero que a deshora
salió la noche del día
que el cielo y la tierra lloran.
Y si en el cielo hay estrellas
que lucientes carros forman,
en otros carros su cielo
vivas estrellas adornan.
Aquí el anciano Saturno
la barba pule y remoza,
y, aunque es tardo, va ligero;
que el placer cura la gota.
El dios parlero va en lenguas
lisonjeras y amorosas,
y Cupido en cifras varias,
que rubíes y perlas bordan.
Allí va el furioso Marte
en la persona curiosa
de más de un gallardo joven,
que de su sombra se asombra.
Junto a la casa del Sol
va Júpiter; que no hay cosa
difícil a la privanza
fundada en prudentes obras.
Va la Luna en las mejillas
de una y otra humana diosa;
Venus casta, en la belleza
de las que este cielo forman.
Pequeñuelos Ganimedes
cruzan, van, vuelven y tornan
por el cinto tachonado
de esta esfera milagrosa.
Y, para que todo admire
y todo asombre, no hay cosa
que de liberal no pase
hasta el estremo de pródiga.
Milán con sus ricas telas
allí va en vista curiosa;
las Indias con sus diamantes,
y Arabia con sus aromas.

on her other side, the gentle dawn.[5]
Behind her follows
a morning star who unexpectedly
shone forth on the night of the day
which heaven and earth lament.
And if in the sky there are stars
which form shining carriages,
in other carriages bright stars
adorn their own sky.
Here ancient Saturn
smoothes and freshens his beard,
and, though slow of step, walks briskly,
for pleasure heals gout.
Apollo, the loquacious god, is present
in flattering, loving tongues,
and Cupid in various emblems
embroidered with rubies and pearls.
There goes furious Mars,
whose person excites
more than one gallant youth
who stands in awe of his shadow.
Next to the house of the sun
goes Jupiter; for there is nothing
difficult to the position of confidant
based on prudent deeds.
The moon is present in the cheeks
of many a human goddess;
chaste Venus, in the beauty
of the women who comprise this sky.
Tiny Ganymede-pages
crisscross back and forth
along the spangled girdle
of this miraculous sphere.
And, so that all may be amazed
and all stand in awe, there is nothing
which does not exceed generosity,
to the point of prodigality.
Milan with its rich fabrics
is present, forming an unusual sight;
the Indies with their diamonds,
and Arabia with its perfumes.

---

5. The sun is Philip III. The dawn is their daughter. Later on, the morning star is the new prince; Saturn is the archbishop; Mars is the captain of the guard; Jupiter is the king's privy councillor. The mournful day is Good Friday.

Con los mal intencionados
va la envidia mordedora,
y la bondad en los pechos
de la lealtad española.
La alegría universal,
huyendo de la congoja,
calles y plazas discurre,
descompuesta y casi loca.
A mil mudas bendiciones
abre el silencio la boca,
y repiten los muchachos
lo que los hombres entonan.
Cual dice: «Fecunda vid,
crece, sube, abraza y toca
el olmo felice tuyo
que mil siglos te haga sombra
para gloria de ti misma,
para bien de España y honra,
para arrimo de la Iglesia,
para asombro de Mahoma».
Otra lengua clama y dice:
«Vivas, ¡oh blanca paloma!,
que nos has de dar por crías
águilas de dos coronas,
para ahuyentar de los aires
las de rapiña furiosas;
para cubrir con sus alas
a las virtudes medrosas».
Otra, más discreta y grave,
más aguda y más curiosa
dice, vertiendo alegría
por los ojos y la boca:
«Esta perla que nos diste,
nácar de Austria, única y sola,
¡qué de máquinas que rompe!,
¡qué de disignios que corta!,
¡qué de esperanzas que infunde!,
¡qué de deseos mal logra!,
¡qué de temores aumenta!,
¡qué de preñados aborta!»
En esto, se llegó al templo
del Fénix santo que en Roma
fue abrasado y quedó vivo
en la fama y en la gloria.

Along with the ill-intentioned
goes biting envy,
while kindness fills the bosom
of loyal Spaniards.
Universal merriment,
shunning sorrow,
fills streets and squares,
in nearly mad disorder.
To a thousand unspoken blessings
silence opens its lips,
and the boys repeat
what the men intone.
One man says: "Fertile vine,
grow, rise, embrace and touch
your happy elm,
and may he shade you for a thousand centuries
for your own glory,
for the good and honor of Spain,
for the support of the Church,
for the awe of Mohammed!"
Another tongue calls and says:
"Long may you live, O white dove,
you who shall give us as fledglings
eagles bearing two crowns,
to frighten from the sky
the rabid eagles of prey,
and to cover with their wings
the timorous virtues!"
Another tongue, more prudent and grave,
keener and more comely,
says, pouring forth joy
from eyes and lips:
"This pearl you have given us,
shell of Austria, this unique, singular pearl,
how many machinations it destroys,
how many evil plans it cuts short,
how many hopes it inspires,
how many evil wishes it thwarts,
how many fears it increases,
how many embryos it aborts!"
Meanwhile, they have reached the temple
of the saintly phoenix who in Rome
was burned but remained alive
in renown and glory.

A la imagen de la vida,
a la del cielo señora,
a la que por ser humilde
las estrellas pisa agora,
a la madre y Virgen junto,
a la hija y a la esposa
de Dios, hincada de hinojos,
Margarita así razona:
«Lo que me has dado te doy,
mano siempre dadivosa;
que a do falta el favor tuyo,
siempre la miseria sobra.
Las primicias de mis frutos
te ofrezco, Virgen hermosa:
tales cuales son las mira,
recibe, ampara y mejora.
A su padre te encomiendo,
que, humano Atlante, se encorva
al peso de tantos reinos
y de climas tan remotas.
Sé que el corazón del rey
en las manos de Dios mora,
y sé que puedes con Dios
cuanto quieres piadosa».
Acabada esta oración,
otra semejante entonan
himnos y voces que muestran
que está en el suelo la gloria.
Acabados los oficios
con reales ceremonias,
volvió a su punto este cielo
y esfera maravillosa.

Apenas acabó Preciosa su romance, cuando del ilustre auditorio y grave senado que la oía, de muchas se formó una voz sola que dijo:

—¡Torna a cantar, Preciosica, que no faltarán cuartos como tierra!

Más de docientas personas estaban mirando el baile y escuchando el canto de las gitanas, y en la fuga dél acertó a pasar por allí uno de los tinientes de la villa, y, viendo tanta gente junta, preguntó qué era; y fuele respondido que estaban escuchando a la gitanilla hermosa, que cantaba. Llegóse el tiniente, que era curioso, y escuchó un rato, y, por no ir contra su gravedad, no escuchó el romance hasta la fin; y, habiéndole parecido por todo estremo bien la gitanilla, mandó a un paje suyo dijese a la gitana vieja que al anochecer fuese a su casa con las gi-

To the image of life,
that of the Queen of Heaven,
who because she was humble
now treads upon the stars,
to the mother who is also a virgin,
to the daughter and bride
of God, kneeling down,
Margaret speaks as follows:
"What you have given me I give to you,
ever-generous hand,
for where your favor is lacking
misery always abounds.
The first portion of my fruit
I offer to you, beautiful Virgin:
such as it is, behold it,
receive it, protect it, improve it.
I commend to you his father,
who, a human Atlas, bows down
beneath the weight of so many realms
and distant climes.
I know that the king's heart
rests in the hands of God,
and I know that God is open
to anything you wish, pious one."
After that prayer,
a similar one is intoned
by hymning voices which show
that glory is on the earth.
When the service
and royal ceremony was over,
this heaven and marvelous sphere
returned to its proper place.

As soon as Preciosa had finished her ballad, from the many voices of the illustrious listeners and grave senators who had heard her a single voice was formed, saying:

"Sing again, Preciosica, for there will be no lack of cuartos in great plenty!"

Over two hundred people were watching the Gypsy women's dance and listening to their singing. At the height of the performance one of the high constables of the city happened to pass by and, seeing so many people assembled, asked what was going on. He was told that they were listening to the beautiful Gypsy girl, who was singing. The constable came up, being curious, and listened for a while, but, so as not to impair his

tanillas, que quería que las oyese doña Clara, su mujer. Hízolo así el paje, y la vieja dijo que sí iría.

Acabaron el baile y el canto, y mudaron lugar; y en esto llegó un paje muy bien aderezado a Preciosa, y, dándole un papel doblado, le dijo:

—Preciosica, canta el romance que aquí va, porque es muy bueno, y yo te daré otros de cuando en cuando, con que cobres fama de la mejor romancera del mundo.

—Eso aprenderé yo de muy buena gana —respondió Preciosa—; y mire, señor, que no me deje de dar los romances que dice, con tal condición que sean honestos; y si quisiere que se los pague, concertémonos por docenas, y docena cantada y docena pagada; porque pensar que le tengo de pagar adelantado es pensar lo imposible.

—Para papel, siquiera, que me dé la señora Preciosica —dijo el paje—, estaré contento; y más, que el romance que no saliere bueno y honesto, no ha de entrar en cuenta.

—A la mía quede el escogerlos —respondió Preciosa.

Y con esto, se fueron la calle adelante, y desde una reja llamaron unos caballeros a las gitanas. Asomóse Preciosa a la reja, que era baja, y vio en una sala muy bien aderezada y muy fresca muchos caballeros que, unos paseándose y otros jugando a diversos juegos, se entretenían.

—¿Quiérenme dar barato, ceñores? —dijo Preciosa (que, como gitana, hablaba ceceoso, y esto es artificio en ellas, que no natureleza).

A la voz de Preciosa y a su rostro, dejaron los que jugaban el juego y el paseo los paseantes; y los unos y los otros acudieron a la reja por verla, que ya tenían noticia della, y dijeron:

—Entren, entren las gitanillas, que aquí les daremos barato.

—Caro sería ello —respondió Preciosa— si nos pellizcacen.

—No, a fe de caballeros —respondió uno—; bien puedes entrar, niña, segura, que nadie te tocará a la vira de tu zapato; no, por el hábito que traigo en el pecho.

Y púsose la mano sobre uno de Calatrava.

—Si tú quieres entrar, Preciosa —dijo una de las tres gitanillas que iban con ella—, entra en hora buena; que yo no pienso entrar adonde hay tantos hombres.

—Mira, Cristina —respondió Preciosa—: de lo que te has de guardar es de un hombre solo y a solas, y no de tantos juntos; porque antes el ser muchos quita el miedo y el recelo de ser ofendidas.

gravity, he didn't hear the ballad out to its end; having found the Gypsy girl extremely good, he sent one of his pages to bid the old Gypsy come to his house at nightfall with the girls, because he wanted his wife Doña Clara to hear them. The page did so, and the old woman said she'd come.

They finished their song and dance, and moved elsewhere; at that time, a very well dressed page came to Preciosa and, handing her a folded note, said:

"Preciosica, sing the ballad written here, because it's very good, and I'll give you others from time to time, so you can gain the reputation of the world's best ballad singer."

"I'll be very glad to learn it," Preciosa replied, "and look, sir, don't fail to give me the ballads you mention, as long as they're decent; and if you want me to pay you for them, let's make a deal by the dozen: a dozen sung and a dozen paid for. Because to think I must pay you in advance is to think the impossible."

"Even an I.O.U. that Miss Preciosica gives me," said the page, "will satisfy me; besides, if any ballad doesn't turn out to be good and decent, it won't be charged for on the account."

"Let it be *my* account to choose them," replied Preciosa.

And, with that, they proceeded up the street, and some gentlemen called to the Gypsy women from a barred window. Preciosa went up to the window, which was low, and beheld in a very well adorned, very cool parlor a number of gentlemen whiling away their time, some walking up and down, others playing various games of chance.

"Do you wish to give me a tip from your winnings, theñores?" asked Preciosa (being a Gypsy girl, she lisped; this is a mannerism of theirs, not an effect of nature).

At Preciosa's voice and the sight of her face, the gamblers left their game, and the strollers their stroll, and both groups came to the window to see her, for they had already heard of her, and they said:

"Come in, come in, Gypsy girls, and we'll give you a share in our winnings."

"It would cost us dear," replied Preciosa, "if you were to pinch us."

"No, on our honor as gentlemen," one of them replied. "You can set your mind at ease, my girl, because no one here will touch even the welt of your shoe; no, by this order I wear on my chest."

And he put his hand to the badge of the Order of Calatrava.

"If you want to go in, Preciosa," said one of the three Gypsy girls who were with her, "go right ahead, but I don't intend to enter a place with so many men."

"Look, Cristina," replied Preciosa, "what you have to guard against is one man alone, and not this many together; because, on the contrary, the presence of many relieves us of the fear and suspicion of being affronted.

Advierte, Cristinica, y está cierta de una cosa: que la mujer que se determina a ser honrada, entre un ejército de soldados lo puede ser. Verdad es que es bueno huir de las ocasiones, pero han de ser de las secretas y no de las públicas.

—Entremos, Preciosa —dijo Cristina—, que tú sabes más que un sabio.

Animólas la gitana vieja, y entraron; y apenas hubo entrado Preciosa, cuando el caballero del hábito vio el papel que traía en el seno, y llegándose a ella se le tomó, y dijo Preciosa:

—¡Y no me le tome, señor, que es un romance que me acaban de dar ahora, que aún no le he leído!

—Y ¿sabes tú leer, hija? —dijo uno.

—Y escribir —respondió la vieja—; que a mi nieta hela criado yo como si fuera hija de un letrado.

Abrió el caballero el papel y vio que venía dentro dél un escudo de oro, y dijo:

—En verdad, Preciosa, que trae esta carta el porte dentro; toma este escudo que en el romance viene.

—¡Basta! —dijo Preciosa—, que me ha tratado de pobre el poeta, pues cierto que es más milagro darme a mí un poeta un escudo que yo recebirle; si con esta añadidura han de venir sus romances, traslade todo el *Romancero general* y envíemelos uno a uno, que yo les tentaré el pulso, y si vinieren duros, seré yo blanda en recebillos.

Admirados quedaron los que oían a la gitanica, así de su discreción como del donaire con que hablaba.

—Lea, señor —dijo ella—, y lea alto: veremos si es tan discreto ese poeta como es liberal.

Y el caballero leyó así:

—Gitanica, que de hermosa
te pueden dar parabienes:
por lo que de piedra tienes
te llama el mundo Preciosa.

Desta verdad me asegura
esto, como en ti verás;
que no se apartan jamás
la esquiveza y la hermosura.

Si como en valor subido
vas creciendo en arrogancia,
no le arriendo la ganancia

Learn this, Cristinica, and be assured of one thing: that a woman resolved on being honorable can be so amid an army of soldiers. It's true that it's a good idea to avoid risks, but they need to be private ones, not public ones."

"Let's go in, Preciosa," said Cristina, "because you know more than a wise man."

The old Gypsy woman encouraged them, and they went in; no sooner had Preciosa entered than the knight with the order caught sight of the paper she had in her bodice; coming up to her, he took it, and Preciosa said:

"Don't take it away from me, sir, it's a ballad I've just been given and I haven't read it yet!"

"So you know how to read, my girl?" one man asked.

"And write," the old woman replied; "because I brought up my granddaughter as if she were a lawyer's daughter."

The knight unfolded the paper and, finding that it had a gold escudo wrapped in it, he said:

"Truly, Preciosa, this letter has its postage inside it; take this escudo that was in the ballad."

"Enough!" said Preciosa. "The poet has treated me like a pauper, because it's surely a greater miracle for a poet to give me an escudo than for me to receive it; if his ballads are to come with this supplement, let him copy out the whole printed ballad collection[6] and send them to me one by one; I'll feel them, and if they feel hard, I'll receive them softly."

Those who heard the Gypsy girl were amazed both by her wisdom and by her witty manner of speaking.

"Read it, sir," she said, "and read it aloud; we'll see whether this poet is as clever as he is generous."

And the knight read as follows:

—Gypsy girl, for your beauty
you are to be congratulated;
because of that in you which is like a stone
the world calls you "precious."

I am assured of that verity
by this, which you'll find in yourself:
there is never a separation between
disdainfulness and beauty.

If, to match your high worth,
you increase your haughtiness,
I surely don't envy

6. The *Romancero general*, a compilation of earlier ballad collections, was published in Madrid in 1600.

a la edad en que has nacido;
 que un basilisco se cría
en ti, que mate mirando,
y un imperio que, aunque blando,
nos parezca tiranía.
 Entre pobres y aduares,
¿cómo nació tal belleza?
O ¿cómo crió tal pieza
el humilde Manzanares?
 Por esto será famoso
al par del Tajo dorado
y por Preciosa preciado
más que el Ganges caudaloso.
 Dices la buenaventura,
y dasla mala contino;
que no van por un camino
tu intención y tu hermosura.
 Porque en el peligro fuerte
de mirarte o contemplarte
tu intención va a desculparte,
y tu hermosura a dar muerte.
 Dicen que son hechiceras
todas las de tu nación,
pero tus hechizos son
de más fuerzas y más veras;
 pues por llevar los despojos
de todos cuantos te ven,
haces, ¡oh niña!, que estén
tus hechizos en tus ojos.
 En sus fuerzas te adelantas,
pues bailando nos admiras,
y nos matas si nos miras,
y nos encantas si cantas.
 De cien mil modos hechizas:
hables, calles, cantes, mires;
o te acerques, o retires,
el fuego de amor atizas.
 Sobre el más esento pecho
tienes mando y señorío,
de lo que es testigo el mío,
de tu imperio satisfecho.
 Preciosa joya de amor,
esto humildemente escribe

this era into which you were born;
  for a basilisk is being reared
in you which will kill with its eyes,
and a domination which, though mild,
will seem to us like tyranny.
  How did such beauty arise
amid poverty and Gypsy camps?
And how did the humble Manzanares[7]
create such a specimen?
  For this it will be as famous
as the gold-laden Tagus
and prized for Preciosa
more than the copious Ganges.
  You tell fortunes,
and you predict bad things constantly,
since your intentions and your beauty
don't go hand in hand.
  Because, in the great danger
of beholding or contemplating you,
your intentions lead one to forgive you,
but your beauty leads to death.
  All the women of your race
are said to be sorceresses,
but your sorcery is
stronger and truer;
  since, to carry off the spoils
of every man who sees you,
my girl, you make
your sorcery reside in your eyes.
  You excel in its powers,
since you amaze us when you dance,
kill us if you look at us,
and enchant us with your chanting.
  You bewitch us in a hundred thousand ways:
whether you speak, fall silent, sing, or gaze;
whether you approach or withdraw,
you stir up the fire of love.
  Over the most unconcerned heart
you wield command and mastery;
to this, mine bears witness,
content to be your subject.
  Precious jewel of love,
this is humbly written

7. Madrid's river.

el que por ti muere y vive,
pobre, aunque humilde amador.

—En «pobre» acaba el último verso —dijo a esta sazón Preciosa—: ¡mala señal! Nunca los enamorados han de decir que son pobres, porque a los principios, a mi parecer, la pobreza es muy enemiga del amor.

—¿Quién te enseña eso, rapaza? —dijo uno.

—¿Quién me lo ha de enseñar? —respondió Preciosa—. ¿No tengo yo mi alma en mi cuerpo? ¿No tengo ya quince años? Y no soy manca, ni renca, ni estropeada del entendimiento. Los ingenios de las gitanas van por otro norte que los de las demás gentes: siempre se adelantan a sus años; no hay gitano necio, ni gitana lerda; que, como el sustentar su vida consiste en ser agudos, astutos y embusteros, despabilan el ingenio a cada paso y no dejan que críe moho en ninguna manera. ¿Veen estas muchachas, mis compañeras, que están callando y parecen bobas? Pues éntrenles el dedo en la boca y tiéntenlas las cordales, y verán lo que verán. No hay muchacha de doce que no sepa lo que de veinte y cinco, porque tienen por maestros y preceptores al diablo y al uso, que les enseña en una hora lo que habían de aprender en un año.

Con esto que la gitanilla decía, tenía suspensos a los oyentes, y los que jugaban le dieron barato, y aun los que no jugaban. Cogió la hucha de la vieja treinta reales, y más rica y más alegre que una Pascua de Flores, antecogió sus corderas y fuese en casa del señor teniente, quedando que otro día volvería con su manada a dar contento aquellos tan liberales señores.

Ya tenía aviso la señora doña Clara, mujer del señor teniente, cómo habían de ir a su casa las gitanillas, y estábalas esperando como el agua de mayo ella y sus doncellas y dueñas, con las de otra señora vecina suya, que todas se juntaron para ver a Preciosa. Y apenas hubieron entrado las gitanas, cuando entre las demás resplandeció Preciosa como la luz de una antorcha entre otras luces menores. Y así, corrieron todas a ella: unas la abrazaban, otras la miraban, éstas la bendecían, aquéllas la alababan. Doña Clara decía:

—¡Éste sí que se puede decir cabello de oro! ¡Éstos sí que son ojos de esmeraldas!

La señora su vecina la desmenuzaba toda, y hacía pepitoria de todos

by one who dies and lives for you,
a poor man, but a humble lover.

"The last line has the word 'poor,'" Preciosa then said, "a bad sign! Lovers should never say that they're poor, because at the outset, it seems to me, poverty is quite an enemy to love."

"Who taught you that, youngster?" one man asked.

"Who had to teach it to me?" replied Preciosa. "Don't I have a soul in my body? Am I not already fifteen? And I'm not one-handed, lame in the hip, or crippled in my intelligence. The minds of Gypsy girls follow a different direction from those of other people: they're always smart for their age; no Gypsy man is a fool, no Gypsy woman is dull-witted; because, since their staying alive depends on their being alert, shrewd, and deceitful, they sharpen their wits at every turn and don't let mold accumulate at all. Do you see these girls, my companions, who are keeping silent and who look like fools? Well, put your finger in their mouth and feel their wisdom teeth, and you'll see what you see. There's no Gypsy girl of twelve who doesn't know what a twenty-five-year-old knows, because they have for teachers and instructors the devil and experience, which teaches them in one hour what would otherwise take them a year to learn."

This speech of the Gypsy girl's astonished her listeners, and the gamblers gave her a tip, and even the men who weren't gambling. The old woman's purse collected thirty reales,[8] and, richer and jollier than an Easter Sunday, she assembled her lambs and departed for the constable's house, it being agreed that some other day she'd return with her flock to delight those very generous gentlemen.

Doña Clara, the constable's wife, had already been informed that the Gypsy girls were to come to her house, and she was awaiting them with eager anticipation[9] with her maids and lady companions, as well as those of another lady, a neighbor; all had assembled to see Preciosa. As soon as the Gypsies entered, Preciosa shone forth among all the rest like the light of a torch among other, fainter lights. And so, all the women rushed up to her: some embraced her, others looked at her, one group blessed her, another group praised her. Doña Clara said:

"Yes, this can really be called golden hair. These really are emerald eyes!"

The neighbor lady scrutinized her all over, making a jumble of all her

8. One real was worth 34 maravedis. 9. Literally: "as if they were springtime showers."

sus miembros y coyunturas. Y, llegando a alabar un pequeño hoyo que Preciosa tenía en la barba, dijo:

—¡Ay, qué hoyo! En este hoyo han de tropezar cuantos ojos le miraren.

Oyó esto un escudero de brazo de la señora doña Clara, que allí estaba, de luenga barba y largos años, y dijo:

—¿Ése llama vuesa merced hoyo, señora mía? Pues yo sé poco de hoyos, o ése no es hoyo, sino sepultura de deseos vivos. ¡Por Dios, tan linda es la gitanilla que hecha de plata o de alcorza no podría ser mejor! ¿Sabes decir la buenaventura, niña?

—De tres o cuatro maneras —respondió Preciosa.

—¿Y eso más? —dijo doña Clara—. Por vida del tiniente, mi señor, que me la has de decir, niña de oro, y niña de plata, y niña de perlas, y niña de carbuncos, y niña del cielo, que es lo más que puedo decir.

—Denle, denle la palma de la mano a la niña, y con qué haga la cruz —dijo la vieja—, y verán qué de cosas les dice; que sabe más que un doctor de melecina.

Echó mano a la faldriquera la señora tenienta, y halló que no tenía blanca. Pidió un cuarto a sus criadas, y ninguna le tuvo, ni la señora vecina tampoco. Lo cual visto por Preciosa, dijo:

—Todas las cruces, en cuanto cruces, son buenas; pero las de plata o de oro son mejores; y el señalar la cruz en la palma de la mano con moneda de cobre, sepan vuesas mercedes que menoscaba la buenaventura, a lo menos la mía; y así, tengo afición a hacer la cruz primera con algún escudo de oro, o con algún real de a ocho, o, por lo menos, de a cuatro, que soy como los sacristanes: que cuando hay buena ofrenda, se regocijan.

—Donaire tienes, niña, por tu vida —dijo la señora vecina.

Y, volviéndose al escudero, le dijo:

—Vos, señor Contreras, ¿tendréis a mano algún real de a cuatro? Dádmele, que, en viniendo el doctor, mi marido, os le volveré.

—Sí tengo —respondió Contreras—, pero téngole empeñado en veinte y dos maravedís que cené anoche. Dénmelos, que yo iré por él en volandas.

—No tenemos entre todas un cuarto —dijo doña Clara—, ¿y pedís veinte y dos maravedís? Andad, Contreras, que siempre fuistes impertinente.

Una doncella de las presentes, viendo la esterilidad de la casa, dijo a Preciosa:

—Niña, ¿hará algo al caso que se haga la cruz con un dedal de plata?

limbs and joints. Finally, praising a little dimple that Preciosa had in her chin, she said:

"Oh, what a dimple! It's a pit into which every eye that views it must tumble."

This was heard by a footman of Doña Clara's who was present, an elderly man with a long beard, and he said:

"Do you call that a pit, your ladyship? Well, either I don't know much about pits, or that isn't a pit but a grave for ardent desires. By God, the Gypsy girl is so pretty that she couldn't be more so if she were made of silver or cake icing! Do you know how to tell fortunes, my child?"

"In three or four ways," Preciosa replied.

"That, too?" said Doña Clara. "On the life of my husband the constable, you must tell mine, golden girl, silver girl, pearl girl, garnet girl, heavenly girl, which is the most I can say."

"Show her, show the girl the palm of your hand, and something to cross *her* palm with," the old woman said, "and you'll see how many things she tells you; because she knows more than a doctor of medicine."

The constable's wife put her hand in her pocket and discovered that she didn't have a half-maravedi. She asked her servants for a cuarto, but no one had one, not even the neighbor. Seeing this, Preciosa said:

"Every crossing of a palm is good, insofar as it's a cross, but those made with silver or gold are better; I'll have your ladyships know that to cross a palm with a copper coin makes the reading worse, at least mine; and so, I'm fond of making the first cross with some golden escudo, or some silver coin, an eight-real one or at least a four-real one, because I'm like the sacristans: when there's a good offering, they're happy."

"You're witty, my girl, on your life!" said the neighbor.

And, turning to the footman, she said:

"You, Señor Contreras, would you have any four-real piece handy? Give it to me, and when my husband the doctor arrives, I'll return it to you."

"I do have one," Contreras replied, "but I left it as security for the twenty-two maravedis my supper cost last night. Give me that amount, and I'll fetch the silver coin in a flash."

"We don't have a cuarto between us," said Doña Clara, "and you're asking for twenty-two maravedis? Get away with you, Contreras, you've always been a trifler."

One of the maids in attendance, seeing how barren the household was, said to Preciosa:

"My girl, will it help at all to cross your palm with a silver thimble?"

—Antes —respondió Preciosa—, se hacen las cruces mejores del mundo con dedales de plata, como sean muchos.

—Uno tengo yo —replicó la doncella—; si éste basta, hele aquí, con condición que también se me ha de decir a mí la buenaventura.

—¿Por un dedal tantas buenasventuras? —dijo la gitana vieja—. Nieta, acaba presto, que se hace noche.

Tomó Preciosa el dedal y la mano de la señora tenienta, y dijo:

—Hermosita, hermosita,
la de las manos de plata,
más te quiere tu marido
que el rey de las Alpujarras.
Eres paloma sin hiel,
pero a veces eres brava
como leona de Orán,
o como tigre de Ocaña.
Pero en un tras, en un tris,
el enojo se te pasa,
y quedas como alfinique,
o como cordera mansa.
Riñes mucho y comes poco:
algo celosita andas;
que es juguetón el tiniente,
y quiere arrimar la vara.
Cuando doncella, te quiso
uno de una buena cara;
que mal hayan los terceros,
que los gustos desbaratan.
Si a dicha tú fueras monja,
hoy tu convento mandaras,
porque tienes de abadesa
más de cuatrocientas rayas.
No te lo quiero decir . . . ;
pero poco importa, vaya:
enviudarás, y otra vez,
y otras dos, serás casada.
No llores, señora mía;
que no siempre las gitanas
decimos el *Evangelio*;
no llores, señora, acaba.
Como te mueras primero
que el señor tiniente, basta
para remediar el daño
de la viudez que amenaza.

"In fact," Preciosa replied, "the best crosses in the world are made with silver thimbles, provided there are a lot of them."

"I have one," the maid retorted. "If that's enough, here it is, on the condition that you tell *my* fortune, too."

"So many readings for one thimble?" said the old Gypsy woman. "Granddaughter, finish quickly, because night is falling."

Preciosa took the thimble and the hand of the constable's wife, and said:

—Lovely lady, lovely lady,
lady with hands of silver,
your husband loves you more
than the king of Alpujarra.
You are a dove devoid of gall,
but at times you are as wild
as a lioness of Oran,
or a Hyrcanian tigress.
But in the twinkling of an eye
your anger passes
and you become like sugar candy,
or like a meek lamb.
You quarrel a lot and eat little:
you have a somewhat jealous nature,
because the constable is amorous
and likes to "ease his baton."
When you were young, you were loved
by a man with a good face;
the devil take all meddlers,
because they disrupt romances.
If by chance you were a nun,
by now you'd be head of your convent,
because over four hundred lines
indicate you're abbess material.
I don't want to tell you this . . .
but what does it matter? Out with it:
you'll be widowed and once more,
and twice more, you'll get married.
Don't cry, my lady,
because Gypsy women don't always
utter the gospel truth;
don't cry, lady, stop.
If you die before
the constable does, that will be enough
to undo the damage
of the widowhood that threatens you.

Has de heredar, y muy presto,
hacienda en mucha abundancia;
tendrás un hijo canónigo,
la iglesia no se señala;
de Toledo no es posible.
Una hija rubia y blanca
tendrás, que si es religiosa,
también vendrá a ser perlada.
Si tu esposo no se muere
dentro de cuatro semanas,
veráslе corregidor
de Burgos o Salamanca.
Un lunar tienes, ¡qué lindo!
¡Ay Jesús, qué luna clara!
¡Qué sol, que allá en los antípodas
escuros valles aclara!
Más de dos ciegos por verle
dieran más de cuatro blancas.
¡Agora sí es la risica!
¡Ay, que bien haya esa gracia!
Guárdate de las caídas,
principalmente de espaldas,
que suelen ser peligrosas
en las principales damas.
Cosas hay más que decirte;
si para el viernes me aguardas,
las oirás, que son de gusto,
y algunas hay de desgracias.

Acabó su buenaventura Preciosa, y con ella encendió el deseo de todas las circunstantes en querer saber la suya; y así se lo rogaron todas, pero ella las remitió para el viernes venidero, prometiéndole que tendrían reales de plata para hacer las cruces.

En esto vino el señor tiniente, a quien contaron maravillas de la gitanilla; él las hizo bailar un poco, y confirmó por verdaderas y bien dadas las alabanzas que a Preciosa habían dado; y, poniendo la mano en la faldriquera, hizo señal de querer darle algo, y, habiéndola espulgado, y sacudido, y rascado muchas veces, al cabo sacó la mano vacía y dijo:

—¡Por Dios, que no tengo blanca! Dadle vos, doña Clara, un real a Preciosica, que yo os le daré después.

—¡Bueno es eso, señor, por cierto! ¡Sí, ahí está el real de manifiesto! No hemos tenido entre todas nosotras un cuarto para hacer la señal de la cruz, ¿y quiere que tengamos un real?

You're going to inherit, and very soon,
very abundant property;
you'll have a son who's a prebendary,
but I can't see of what cathedral;
it can't be of Toledo.
You'll have a blonde, white-skinned
daughter who, if she becomes a nun,
will also come to be an abbess.
If your husband doesn't die
within four weeks,
you'll see him civil governor
of Burgos or Salamanca.
You have a mole, how pretty!
Oh, Lord, what a bright moon!
What a sun, illuminating dark valleys
down in the antipodes!
To see it, more than two blind men
would give more than two maravedis.
Now here comes that sweet smile!
Oh, a blessing on that charming thing!
Watch out for falls,
especially on your back,
because they're generally dangerous
for prominent ladies.
There are more things to tell you;
if you wait for me till Friday
you'll hear them with pleasure,
though a few portend disaster.

Preciosa finished her palm reading, with which she kindled a desire in every bystander to have her own fortune told; and so, they all requested it, but she put them off until the coming Friday and they promised her they'd have silver reales to cross her palm with.

Just then the constable arrived, and the women lauded the Gypsy girl highly to him; he made them dance a little, and declared that the praises they had given Preciosa were true and justified; putting his hand in his pocket, he indicated that he wanted to give her something, but after examining it closely, shaking it, and scraping it several times, he finally withdrew his hand empty, saying:

"By God, I don't have a half-maravedi! You, Doña Clara, give a real to Preciosica, and I'll give you one later."

"That's a good one, sir, for sure! Yes, there's the real for all to see! Among all of us we didn't have a cuarto to cross her palm with, and you expect us to have a real?"

—Pues dadle alguna valoncica vuestra, o alguna cosita; que otro día nos volverá a ver Preciosa, y la regalaremos mejor.

A lo cual dijo doña Clara:

—Pues, porque otra vez venga, no quiero dar nada ahora a Preciosa.

—Antes, si no me dan nada —dijo Preciosa—, nunca más volveré acá. Mas sí volveré, a servir a tan principales señores, pero trairé tragado que no me han de dar nada, y ahorraréme la fatiga del esperallo. Coheche vuesa merced, señor tiniente; coheche y tendrá dineros, y no haga usos nuevos, que morirá de hambre. Mire, señora: por ahí he oído decir (y, aunque moza, entiendo que no son buenos dichos) que de los oficios se ha de sacar dineros para pagar las condenaciones de las residencias y para pretender otros cargos.

—Así lo dicen y lo hacen los desalmados —replicó el teniente—, pero el juez que da buena residencia no tendrá que pagar condenación alguna, y el haber usado bien su oficio será el valedor para que le den otro.

—Habla vuesa merced muy a lo santo, señor teniente —respondió Preciosa—; ándese a eso y cortarémosle de los harapos para reliquias.

—Mucho sabes, Preciosa —dijo el tiniente—. Calla, que yo daré traza que sus Majestades te vean, porque eres pieza de reyes.

—Querránme para truhana —respondió Preciosa—, y yo no lo sabré ser, y todo irá perdido. Si me quisiesen para discreta, aún llevarme hían, pero en algunos palacios más medran los truhanes que los discretos. Yo me hallo bien con ser gitana y pobre, y corra la suerte por donde el cielo quisiere.

–Ea, niña— dijo la gitana vieja—, no hables más, que has hablado mucho, y sabes más de lo que yo te he enseñado. No te asotiles tanto, que te despuntarás; habla de aquello que tus años permiten, y no te metas en altanerías, que no hay ninguna que no amenace caída.

—¡El diablo tienen estas gitanas en el cuerpo! —dijo a esta sazón el tiniente.

Despidiéronse las gitanas, y, al irse, dijo la doncella del dedal:

—Preciosa, dime la buenaventura, o vuélveme mi dedal, que no me queda con qué hacer labor.

–Señora doncella —respondió Preciosa—, haga cuenta que se la he

"Then give her some Vandyke collar of yours, or some little trifle; for Preciosa will come to see us again another day, and we'll give her a better present."

To which Doña Clara replied:

"Well, to make sure she comes again, I won't give anything to Preciosa now."

"Oh, no," said Preciosa, "if you don't give me anything, I'll never come back here. Yet, I *will* come back, to serve such prominent people, but I'll resign myself to the fact that they won't give me anything, and I'll be spared the bother of expecting it. Take bribes, my lord constable; take bribes and you'll make money; don't start new customs, or you'll starve to death. Look, madam: around here I've heard say (and, though young, I realize that these sayings are improper) that one must make money out of one's official position in order to pay the auditors' fines and to apply for other posts."

"That's what impious people say and do," retorted the constable, "but a judge who gives a good account of his administration won't have to pay any fine, and making good use of one's office will be the guarantee for receiving another one."

"Your lordship speaks very piously, constable," replied Preciosa. "Keep it up, and we'll be snipping strips off your clothes for relics."

"You're very wise, Preciosa," said the constable. "Be still, for I'll see to it that Their Majesties see you, because you're fit for a king."[10]

"They'll want me as a jester," Preciosa replied, "and I won't know how to be one, and all will go for nought. If they wanted me as a clever person, they'd still take me, but in some palaces jesters thrive better than wise man. I'm satisfied being a Gypsy girl and poor, and let my luck run wherever heaven wishes."

"Come girl," said the old Gypsy woman, "don't talk any more, because you've talked a lot, and you know more than I taught you. Don't try to be so sharp, or you'll blunt your point; speak about things suitable to your age, and don't aim for the heights, because each of them threatens a fall."

"These Gypsy women have the devil in them!" the constable said thereupon.

The Gypsy women took their leave and, as they were departing, the maid with the thimble said:

"Preciosa, tell my fortune, or give back my thimble, because I have no other one to sew with."

"Madam," replied Preciosa, "imagine that I *have* told it and get hold of

---

10. This prepares a pun, because *pieza de rey* meant both "something wonderful" and "a court jester."

dicho y provéase de otro dedal, o no haga vainillas hasta el viernes, que yo volveré y le diré más venturas y aventuras que las que tiene un libro de caballerías.

Fuéronse y juntáronse con las muchas labradoras que a la hora de las avemarías suelen salir de Madrid para volverse a sus aldeas; y entre otras vuelven muchas, con quien siempre se acompañaban las gitanas, y volvían seguras; porque la gitana vieja vivía en continuo temor no le salteasen a su Preciosa.

Sucedió, pues, que la mañana de un día que volvían a Madrid a coger la garrama con las demás gitanillas, en un valle pequeño que está obra de quinientos pasos antes que se llegue a la villa, vieron un mancebo gallardo y ricamente aderezado de camino. La espada y daga que traía eran, como decirse suele, una ascua de oro; sombrero con rico cintillo y con plumas de diversas colores adornado. Repararon las gitanas en viéndole, y pusiéronsele a mirar muy de espacio, admiradas de que a tales horas un tan hermoso mancebo estuviese en tal lugar, a pie y solo.

Él se llegó a ellas, y, hablando con la gitana mayor, le dijo:

—Por vida vuestra, amiga, que me hagáis placer que vos y Preciosa me oyáis aquí aparte dos palabras, que serán de vuestro provecho.

—Como no nos desviemos mucho, ni nos tardemos mucho, sea en buen hora —respondió la vieja.

Y, llamando a Preciosa, se desviaron de las otras obra de veinte pasos; y así, en pie, como estaban, el mancebo les dijo:

—Yo vengo de manera rendido a la discreción y belleza de Preciosa, que después de haberme hecho mucha fuerza para escusar llegar a este punto, al cabo he quedado más rendido y más imposibilitado de escusallo. Yo, señoras mías (que siempre os he de dar este nombre, si el cielo mi pretensión favorece), soy caballero, como lo puede mostrar este hábito —y, apartando el herreruelo, descubrió en el pecho uno de los más calificados que hay en España—; soy hijo de Fulano —que por buenos respectos aquí no se declara su nombre—; estoy debajo de su tutela y amparo, soy hijo único, y el que espera un razonable mayorazgo. Mi padre está aquí en la Corte pretendiendo un cargo, y ya está consultado, y tiene casi ciertas esperanzas de salir con él. Y, con ser de la calidad y nobleza que os he referido, y de la que casi se os debe ya de ir trasluciendo, con todo eso, quisiera ser un gran señor para levantar a mi grandeza la humildad de Preciosa, haciéndola mi igual y mi señora. Yo no la pretendo para burlalla, ni en las veras del amor que la tengo puede caber género de burla alguna; sólo quiero servirla del modo que ella más gustare: su voluntad es la mía.

another thimble, or else do no hemstitching till Friday, when I'll be back and I'll tell you more fortunes and adventures than a book of chivalry contains."

They left and joined up with the numerous peasant women who usually leave Madrid at Angelus time to return to their villages; among them were many whom the Gypsy women always accompanied, so they would return in safety; because the old Gypsy woman lived in constant fear of her Preciosa being abducted.

Well, then, it so happened that, on the morning of one day when they were returning to Madrid to gather their spoils along with the other Gypsy girls, in a small valley located some five hundred paces before reaching town they saw an elegant young man richly dressed in multicolored clothing. The sword and dagger he wore were "a golden ember," as the saying goes; his hat had a rich band and was adorned with plumes of various colors. The Gypsy women halted on seeing him and began to observe him carefully, amazed that such a handsome youth should be in such a place at that hour, on foot and alone.

He came up to them and, addressing the eldest Gypsy woman, he said:

"On your life, my friend, give me the pleasure of having you and Preciosa listen to a word or two from me in private here; it will be to your advantage."

"As long as we don't go far off our path or aren't delayed too long, all right," the old woman replied.

She called to Preciosa, and the two of them turned aside some twenty paces from the others; and as they stood there, the young man said to them:

"I am here, so submissive to Preciosa's wisdom and beauty that, after doing myself great violence to avoid coming to this, I am finally left more submissive and more powerless to avoid it. I, my ladies (for I shall always call you that if heaven favors my request), am a knight, as this order can show." (Here, opening his wide, hoodless cape, he revealed on his breast one of the most famous ones that exist in Spain.) "I am the son of—." (He gave the name, but for good reasons it isn't stated here.) "I am under his guardianship and protection, I am an only child, and one who expects his due inheritance. My father is here in the capital applying for a post, he is already being considered for one and has almost a sure expectation of receiving it. And, though I am of the quality and nobility that I have informed you of, and of which you ought now nearly to have formed a clear notion, nevertheless I would like to be a grandee in order to raise to my high level the humble status of Preciosa, making her my equal and my lady. I am not seeking her in order to deceive her, nor is there any room in the sincerity of my love for her for any sort of deception; I merely wish to serve her in the way that most pleases her: her will is mine. For her,

Para con ella es de cera mi alma, donde podrá imprimir lo que quisiere; y para conservarlo y guardarlo no será como impreso en cera, sino como esculpido en mármoles, cuya dureza se opone a la duración de los tiempos. Si creéis esta verdad, no admitirá ningún desmayo mi esperanza; pero si no me creéis, siempre me tendrá temeroso vuestra duda. Mi nombre es éste —y díjosele—; el de mi padre ya os le he dicho. La casa donde vive es en tal calle, y tiene tales y tales señas; vecinos tiene de quien podréis informaros, y aun de los que no son vecinos también, que no es tan escura la calidad y el nombre de mi padre y el mío, que no le sepan en los patios de palacio, y aun en toda la Corte. Cien escudos traigo aquí en oro para daros en arra y señal de lo que pienso daros, porque no ha de negar la hacienda el que da el alma.

En tanto que el caballero esto decía, le estaba mirando Preciosa atentamente, y sin duda que no le debieron de parecer mal ni sus razones ni su talle; y, volviéndose a la vieja, le dijo:

—Perdóneme, abuela, de que me tomo licencia para responder a este tan enamorado señor.

—Responde lo que quisieres, nieta —respondió la vieja—, que yo sé que tienes discreción para todo.

Y Preciosa dijo:

—Yo, señor caballero, aunque soy gitana pobre y humildemente nacida, tengo un cierto espiritillo fantástico acá dentro, que a grandes cosas me lleva. A mí ni me mueven promesas, ni me desmoronan dádivas, ni me inclinan sumisiones, ni me espantan finezas enamoradas; y, aunque de quince años (que, según la cuenta de mi abuela, para este San Miguel los haré), soy ya vieja en los pensamientos y alcanzo más de aquello que mi edad promete, más por mi buen natural que por la esperiencia. Pero, con lo uno o con lo otro, sé que las pasiones amorosas en los recién enamorados son como ímpetus indiscretos que hacen salir a la voluntad de sus quicios; la cual, atropellando inconvenientes, desatinadamente se arroja tras su deseo, y, pensando dar con la gloria de sus ojos, da con el infierno de sus pesadumbres. Si alcanza lo que desea, mengua el deseo con la posesión de la cosa deseada, y quizá, abriéndose entonces los ojos del entendimiento, se vee ser bien que se aborrezca lo que antes se adoraba. Este temor engendra en mí un recato tal, que ningunas palabras creo y de muchas obras dudo. Una sola joya tengo, que la estimo en más que a la vida, que es la de mi entereza y virginidad, y no la tengo de vender a precio de prome-

my soul is like wax, on which she can imprint whatever she wishes; and to preserve and keep her wishes, it won't be like a wax impression, but like engraved marble, whose hardness resists the passage of time. If you believe this to be true, my hopes will admit no flagging, but if you don't believe me, your doubt will make me ever fearful. This is my name." (And he told it to them.) "I've already told you my father's. The house where he lives is on such-and-such Street, and looks like such-and-such; he has neighbors of whom you can make inquiries, and you can also ask people who aren't neighbors, because my father's rank and name, and mine, aren't so obscure that they aren't known in the palace courtyards, and even throughout the capital. I have here a hundred gold escudos to give you as a token and sign of what I intend to give you, because a man who gives his soul won't withhold his property."

While the knight was saying this, Preciosa was studying him attentively, and without a doubt she couldn't have disapproved of either his words or his looks; addressing the old woman, she said:

"Forgive me, grandmother, if I take the liberty of replying to this most enamored gentleman."

"Make any reply you like, granddaughter," the old woman answered, "for I know you're wise enough for anything."

And Preciosa said:

"My lord knight, though I'm a poor and humbly born Gypsy, I have a certain fanciful spirit inside me that guides me to greatness. I am neither moved by promises, nor undermined by presents, nor swayed by submissiveness, nor awed by lovers' subtleties; and though only fifteen (for, according to my grandmother's reckoning, I'll be that age this Michaelmas),[11] I'm already old in thoughts and I think more deeply than expected from my age, more by my natural gifts than from experience. But, from one source or the other, I know that amorous passions in those who have just fallen in love are like imprudent urges that unhinge their willpower; their will, disregarding improprieties, foolishly dashes after their desire and, imagining that they are encountering the glory of their eyes, they encounter the hell of their sorrows. If they obtain what they desire, that desire diminishes with the possession of the thing desired, and perhaps, when the eyes of their understanding are then opened, they find it good to abhor what they formerly adored. The fear of this begets such caution in me that I don't believe any words and I doubt many actions. I possess one solitary jewel, which I esteem more highly than my life; it is the jewel of my intact virginity, and I'm not

11. September 29.

sas ni dádivas, porque, en fin, será vendida, y si puedo ser comprada, será de muy poca estima; ni me la han de llevar trazas ni embelecos: antes pienso irme con ella a la sepultura, y quizá al cielo, que ponerla en peligro que quimeras y fantasías soñadas la embistan o manoseen. Flor es la de la virginidad que, a ser posible, aun con la imaginación no había de dejar ofenderse. Cortada la rosa del rosal, ¡con qué brevedad y facilidad se marchita! Éste la toca, aquél la huele, el otro la deshoja, y, finalmente, entre las manos rústicas se deshace. Si vos, señor, por sola esta prenda venís, no la habéis de llevar sino atada con las ligaduras y lazos del matrimonio; que si la virginidad se ha de inclinar, ha de ser a este santo yugo, que entonces no sería perderla, sino emplearla en ferias que felices ganancias prometen. Si quisiéredes ser mi esposo, yo lo seré vuestra, pero han de preceder muchas condiciones y averiguaciones primero. Primero tengo de saber si sois el que decís; luego, hallando esta verdad, habéis de dejar la casa de vuestros padres y la habéis de trocar con nuestros ranchos; y, tomando el traje de gitano, habéis de cursar dos años en nuestras escuelas, en el cual tiempo me satisfaré yo de vuestra condición, y vos de la mía; al cabo del cual, si vos os contentáredes de mí, y yo de vos, me entregaré por vuestra esposa; pero hasta entonces tengo de ser vuestra hermana en el trato, y vuestra humilde en serviros. Y habéis de considerar que en el tiempo deste noviciado podría ser que cobrásedes la vista, que ahora debéis de tener perdida, o, por lo menos, turbada, y viésedes que os convenía huir de lo que ahora seguís con tanto ahínco. Y, cobrando la libertad perdida, con un buen arrepentimiento se perdona cualquier culpa. Si con estas condiciones queréis entrar a ser soldado de nuestra milicia, en vuestra mano está, pues, faltando alguna dellas, no habéis de tocar un dedo de la mía.

Pasmóse el mozo a las razones de Preciosa, y púsose como embelesado, mirando al suelo, dando muestras que consideraba lo que responder debía. Viendo lo cual Preciosa, tornó a decirle:

—No es este caso de tan poco momento, que en los que aquí nos ofrece el tiempo pueda ni deba resolverse. Volveos, señor, a la villa, y considerad de espacio lo que viéredes que más os convenga, y en este mismo lugar me podéis hablar todas las fiestas que quisiéredes, al ir o venir de Madrid.

A lo cual respondió el gentilhombre:

—Cuando el cielo me dispuso para quererte, Preciosa mía, determiné de hacer por ti cuanto tu voluntad acertase a pedirme, aunque nunca cupo en mi pensamiento que me habías de pedir lo que me pides; pero, pues es tu gusto que el mío al tuyo se ajuste y acomode,

going to sell it for promises or presents, because then after all it would be sold, and if I can be bought, it wouldn't be worth much; it won't be taken from me by schemes or deceptions: I intend to go to my grave with it, and maybe to heaven, rather than expose it to the risk of being fooled and mauled by dreamt-up chimeras and fantasies. The fine flower of any virginity is its refusal, if possible, to be insulted even in the imagination. Once the rose is cut from its bush, how quickly and easily it withers! One man touches it, another smells it, another tears off its petals, and finally it is crushed by rustic hands. Sir, if you have come for that jewel alone, you will only receive it tied with the cords and bonds of marriage; for if virginity is to submit, it must be to that sacred yoke; in that case, it wouldn't be lost, but employed in holidays that promise happy profits. If you'd like to be my spouse, I'll be yours, but many conditions and investigations must come first. First I must learn whether you are who you say you are; next, if I find this true, you must leave your parents' house and exchange it for our camps; assuming the garb of a Gypsy, you must study in our schools for two years, during which time I'll be satisfied as to your nature, and you as to mine; at the end of which, if you are contented with me, and I with you, I will submit to being your wife; but till then I must be treated like your sister and your humble servant. And you must consider that during the course of this novitiate you may possibly regain your eyesight, which now must be lost, or at least troubled, and you may see that it behooved you to shun what you now pursue so doggedly. And when lost freedom is regained, a good repentance makes up for any fault. If you want to enlist in our army on these terms, it lies in your hands, because if you fail to meet any of them, you'll never touch a finger of *my* hand."

The young man was astonished at Preciosa's words and seemed as if bewitched, staring at the ground and showing signs of deliberating on what reply he should make. Seeing this, Preciosa addressed him again:

"This isn't a matter of so little moment that, in the few moments now at our disposal, it can or ought to be resolved. Sir, return to town and consider at leisure what you find suits you best; you can talk to me on this spot on any feast day you wish, going to or coming from Madrid."

To which the nobleman replied:

"When heaven disposed that I should love you, my Preciosa, I resolved to do for you whatever you happened to wish to ask of me, though it never entered my mind that you would ask what you now do; but, since it is your pleasure that mine should adjust and adapt itself to yours, consider me a

cuéntame por gitano desde luego, y haz de mí todas las esperiencias que más quisieres; que siempre me has de hallar el mismo que ahora te significo. Mira cuándo quieres que mude el traje, que yo querría que fuese luego; que, con ocasión de ir a Flandes, engañaré a mis padres y sacaré dineros para gastar algunos días, y serán hasta ocho los que podré tardar en acomodar mi partida. A los que fueren conmigo, yo los sabré engañar de modo que salga con mi determinación. Lo que te pido es (si es que ya puedo tener atrevimiento de pedirte y suplicarte algo) que, si no es hoy, donde te puedes informar de mi calidad y de la de mis padres, que no vayas más a Madrid; porque no querría que algunas de las demasiadas ocasiones que allí pueden ofrecerse me saltease la buena ventura que tanto me cuesta.

—Eso no, señor galán —respondió Preciosa—: sepa que conmigo ha de andar siempre la libertad desenfadada, sin que la ahogue ni turbe la pesadumbre de los celos; y entienda que no la tomaré tan demasiada, que no se eche de ver desde bien lejos que llega mi honestidad a mi desenvoltura; y en el primero cargo en que quiero estaros es en el de la confianza que habéis de hacer de mí. Y mirad que los amantes que entran pidiendo celos, o son simples o confiados.

—Satanás tienes en tu pecho, muchacha —dijo a esta sazón la gitana vieja—: ¡mira que dices cosas que no las diría un colegial de Salamanca! Tú sabes de amor, tú sabes de celos, tú de confianzas: ¿cómo es esto?, que me tienes loca, y te estoy escuchando como a una persona espiritada, que habla latín sin saberlo.

—Calle, abuela —respondió Preciosa—, y sepa que todas las cosas que me oye son nonada, y son de burlas, para las muchas que de más veras me quedan en el pecho.

Todo cuanto Preciosa decía y toda la discreción que mostraba era añadir leña al fuego que ardía en el pecho del enamorado caballero. Finalmente, quedaron en que de allí a ocho días se verían en aquel mismo lugar, donde él vendría a dar cuenta del término en que sus negocios estaban, y ellas habrían tenido tiempo de informarse de la verdad que les había dicho. Sacó el mozo una bolsilla de brocado, donde dijo que iban cien escudos de oro, y dióselos a la vieja; pero no quería Preciosa que los tomase en ninguna manera, a quien la gitana dijo:

—Calla, niña, que la mejor señal que este señor ha dado de estar rendido es haber entregado las armas en señal de rendimiento; y el dar, en cualquiera ocasión que sea, siempre fue indicio de generoso pecho. Y acuérdate de aquel refrán que dice: «Al cielo rogando, y con el mazo dando». Y más, que no quiero yo que por mí pierdan las gitanas el nombre que por luengos siglos tienen adquerido de codiciosas

Gypsy from this very moment, and perform all the experiments on me that your heart desires; for you will always find me of the same mind I have just disclosed to you. Think about when you want me to change clothes; I'd like it to be right away, and on the pretext of going to fight in Flanders, I'll deceive my parents and get money for a few days' expenses; it won't take more than a week to arrange for my departure. I'll manage to deceive those who set out with me so that I achieve my resolution. What I ask of you is (if I may already be so bold as to request and beseech something of you) that, except for today, when you can inquire into my rank and that of my parents, you no longer go to Madrid, because I wouldn't want any of the all too numerous risks you may run there to rob me of the good fortune that is costing me so dear."

"I refuse, my suitor," Preciosa replied. "Know that I must always be accompanied by carefree liberty, which is not to be stifled or troubled by the heaviness of jealousy; but be assured that I won't take such great liberty that people can't see at a great distance that my chastity is as great as my sprightliness; the first thing I wish to impose on you is trust in me. Look: lovers who start out on a jealous footing are either foolish or conceited."

"You've got Satan in your heart, girl," the old Gypsy woman then said. "Just see: you're saying things that even a Salamanca student couldn't! You know about love, you know about jealousy, you know about trust: how? You drive me crazy, and I'm listening to you as to a possessed person who speaks Latin without knowing it."

"Quiet, grandmother," Preciosa replied. "Know that all the things you've heard me say are trifles and jokes compared to the many others, and truer ones, I have stored inside me."

Everything Preciosa said and all the wisdom she displayed added fuel to the fire burning in the enamored knight's heart. They finally decided that in a week's time they'd meet at the same place, where he'd come to render an account of the status of his doings, while the women would have had time to inquire into the truth of what he had told them. The young man drew out a brocade purse which he said contained a hundred gold escudos, and gave it to the old woman; but Preciosa absolutely forbade her to take it, whereupon the old Gypsy said:

"Quiet, girl! The best sign this gentleman has given of his submission is having handed over his arms in token of surrender; and, on any occasion whatsoever, a gift has always been an indication of a generous heart. And remember that proverb which says: 'God helps those who help themselves.' Besides, I don't want to be the cause of Gypsy women losing the reputation they've acquired for long centuries of being greedy and

y aprovechadas. ¿Cien escudos quieres tú que deseche, Preciosa, y de oro en oro, queu pueden andar cosidos en el alforza de una saya que no valga dos reales, y tenerlos allí como quien tiene un juro sobre las yerbas de Estremadura? Y si alguno de nuestros hijos, nietos o parientes cayere, por alguna desgracia, en manos de la justicia, ¿habrá favor tan bueno que llegue a la oreja del juez y del escribano como destos escudos, si llegan a sus bolsas? Tres veces por tres delitos diferentes me he visto casi puesta en el asno para ser azotada, y de la una me libró un jarro de plata, y de la otra una sarta de perlas, y de la otra cuarenta reales de a ocho que había trocado por cuartos, dando veinte reales más por el cambio. Mira, niña, que andamos en oficio muy peligroso y lleno de tropiezos y de ocasiones forzosas, y no hay defensas que más presto nos amparen y socorran como las armas invencibles del gran Filipo: no hay pasar adelante de su *Plus ultra*. Por un doblón de dos caras se nos muestra alegre la triste del procurador y de todos los ministros de la muerte, que son arpías de nosotras, las pobres gitanas, y más precian pelarnos y desollarnos a nosotras que a un salteador de caminos; jamás, por más rotas y desastradas que nos vean, nos tienen por pobres; que dicen que somos como los jubones de los gabachos de Belmonte: rotos y grasientos, y llenos de doblones.

—Por vida suya, abuela, que no diga más; que lleva término de alegar tantas leyes, en favor de quedarse con el dinero, que agote las de los emperadores; quédese con ellos, y buen provecho le hagan, y plega a Dios que los entierre en sepultura donde jamás tornen a ver la claridad del sol, ni haya necesidad que la vean. A estas nuestras compañeras será forzoso darles algo, que ha mucho que nos esperan, y ya deben de estar enfadadas.

—Así verán ellas —replicó la vieja —moneda déstas, como veen al Turco agora. Este buen señor verá si le ha quedado alguna moneda de plata, o cuartos, y los repartirá entre ellas, que con poco quedarán contentas.

—Sí traigo —dijo el galán.

Y sacó de la faldriquera tres reales de a ocho, que repartió entre las tres gitanillas, con que quedaron más alegres y más satisfechas que suele quedar un autor de comedias cuando, en competencia de otro, le suelen retular por las esquinas: «Víctor, Víctor».

En resolución, concertaron, como se ha dicho, la venida de allí a

opportunistic. You want me to turn down a hundred escudos, Preciosa, and in hard cash, which can be sewn into the tuck of a petticoat that isn't worth two reales, and can be kept there in the same way as somebody has perpetual grazing rights in Extremadura? And if any of our children, grandchildren, or relatives should fall into the hands of the law by some misfortune, will there be any inducement so strong in the ear of the judge or lawyer as these escudos, if they arrive in their purses? Three times, for three different crimes, I have found myself on the point of mounting the donkey to be flogged; once I was saved by a silver jug, another time by a string of pearls, and the third time by forty eight-real pieces that I got changed into cuartos, paying another twenty reales for the conversion. Look, girl, our calling is very dangerous and full of stumbling blocks and necessary risks, and there's no defense that protects and aids us more readily than the invincible arms of great Philip: you can't pass beyond the *Ne plus ultra*[12] motto in his coinage. For a doubloon bearing the two faces of Ferdinand and Isabella, a smile appears on the sad face of the attorney and all the minions of death, who are harpies to us poor Gypsy women and would rather fleece and flay *us* than a highway robber; no matter how tattered and torn they see us, they never believe we're poor; rather, they say we're like the jackets of Belmonte's Frenchmen: ripped and greasy, but full of doubloons."[13]

"On your life, grandmother, say no more; you sound as if you would cite so many laws in favor of keeping the money that you'd exhaust all the laws made by emperors; keep it, and much good may it do you, and may it please God that you bury it in a grave where it will never again see daylight, and that there will be no necessity that it should! We'll have to give our companions something, because they've been waiting for us a long time, and they must be annoyed."

"They'll see one of these coins," the old woman retorted, "just as readily as they see the Sultan of Turkey at this moment. This kind gentleman will see whether he still has some silver coin, or cuartos, and will distribute it to them, because they'll be satisfied with just a little."

"Yes, I have," said the suitor.

And he drew from his pocket three eight-real pieces, which he distributed among the three Gypsy girls, leaving them more happy and contented than the head of a theater company when, in a competition, his name is posted at street corners as the winner.

In a word, they decided, as we have said, to return in a week's time and

12. "Go no farther"; said to have been engraved on the Pillars of Hercules. 13. A certain Marquess of Belmonte was said to have grown rich by forcing new jackets on French migrant workers, keeping their money-stuffed ones.

ocho días, y que se había de llamar, cuando fuese gitano, Andrés Caballero; porque también había gitanos entre ellos deste apellido.

No tuvo atrevimiento Andrés (que así le llamaremos de aquí adelante) de abrazar a Preciosa; antes, enviándole con la vista el alma, sin ella, si así decirse puede, las dejó y se entró en Madrid; y ellas, contentísimas, hicieron lo mismo. Preciosa, algo aficionada, más con benevolencia que con amor, de la gallarda disposición de Andrés, ya deseaba informarse si era el que había dicho. Entró en Madrid, y, a pocas calles andadas, encontró con el paje poeta de las coplas y el escudo; y cuando él la vio, se llegó a ella, diciendo:

—Vengas en buen hora, Preciosa: ¿leíste por ventura las coplas que te di el otro día?

A lo que Preciosa respondió:

—Primero que le responda palabra, me ha de decir una verdad, por vida de lo que más quiere.

—Conjuro es ése —respondió el paje— que, aunque el decirla me costase la vida, no la negaré en ninguna manera.

—Pues la verdad que quiero que me diga —dijo Preciosa— es si por ventura es poeta.

—A serlo —replicó el paje—, forzosamente había de ser por ventura. Pero has de saber, Preciosa, que ese nombre de poeta muy pocos le merecen; y así, yo no lo soy, sino un aficionado a la poesía. Y para lo que he menester, no voy a pedir ni a buscar versos ajenos: los que te di son míos, y éstos que te doy agora también; mas no por esto soy poeta, ni Dios lo quiera.

—¿Tan malo es ser poeta? —replicó Preciosa.

—No es malo —dijo el paje—, pero el ser poeta a solas no lo tengo por muy bueno. Hase de usar de la poesía como de una joya preciosísima, cuyo dueño no la trae cada día, ni la muestra a todas gentes, ni a cada paso, sino cuando convenga y sea razón que la muestre. La poesía es una bellísima doncella, casta, honesta, discreta, aguda, retirada, y que se contiene en los límites de la discreción más alta. Es amiga de la soledad, las fuentes la entretienen, los prados la consuelan, los árboles la desenojan, las flores la alegran, y, finalmente, deleita y enseña a cuantos con ella comunican.

—Con todo eso —respondió Preciosa—, he oído decir que es pobrísima y que tiene algo de mendiga.

—Antes es al revés —dijo el paje—, porque no hay poeta que no sea rico, pues todos viven contentos con su estado: filosofía que la alcanzan pocos. Pero, ¿qué te ha movido, Preciosa, a hacer esta pregunta?

—Hame movido —respondió Preciosa— porque, como yo tengo a

that, when he became a Gypsy, the young man would be called Andrés Caballero, because there were Gypsies among them with that name.

Andrés (for so we shall call him from here on) wasn't bold enough to embrace Preciosa; instead, sending his soul after her as he watched her depart, without it, so to speak, he left them and entered Madrid; they, highly contented, did the same. Preciosa, somewhat taken with Andrés's elegant bearing (more out of friendly feelings than love) already wished to inquire into his identity. She entered Madrid and, after going down just a few streets, she met the poetic page of the escudo wrapped in a song; when he saw her, he came up to her and said:

"Welcome, Preciosa. Have you by any chance read the song I gave you the other day?"

To which Preciosa replied:

"Before I say one word in answer, you have to tell me something truly, on the life of the one you hold dearest."

"That's a request," the page replied, "that I won't refuse in any way, even if telling the truth should cost my life."

"Well, the truth I want you to tell me," said Preciosa, "is whether you are by chance a poet."

"If I were," the page replied, "it would *have* to be by chance. But I'll have you know, Preciosa, that very few deserve that name of poet; and so I'm not one, but a man fond of poetry. And for my needs I don't go requesting or seeking other people's verses: the ones I gave you are mine, and so are these which I give you now; but that doesn't make me a poet, God forbid!"

"Is it so bad to be a poet?" Preciosa replied.

"It isn't bad," said the page, "but I don't consider it very good to be only a poet. Poetry should be used like a very precious jewel, whose owner doesn't wear it every day or show it to everybody and at every turn, but only when it's fitting and justified to show it. Poetry is a very beautiful maiden, chaste, honorable, prudent, alert, withdrawn, who keeps within the bounds of the highest discretion. It is a friend of solitude; the fountains delight it, the meadows console it, the trees appease it, the flowers cheer it, and, lastly, it charms and instructs all those who communicate with it."

"Despite all that," Preciosa replied, "I've heard that it's very poor and has a touch of the beggar."

"No, just the opposite," said the page, "because there's no poet who isn't rich, since they all live satisfied with their lot: a philosophy attained by very few. But, Preciosa, what incited you to ask that question?"

Preciosa replied: "It was because, considering all or most poets to be

todos o los más poetas por pobres, causóme maravilla aquel escudo de oro que me distes entre vuestros versos envuelto; mas agora que sé que no sois poeta, sino aficionado de la poesía, podría ser que fuésedes rico, aunque lo dudo, a causa que por aquella parte que os toca de hacer coplas se ha de desaguar cuanta hacienda tuviéredes; que no hay poeta, según dicen, que sepa conservar la hacienda que tiene ni granjear la que no tiene.

—Pues yo no soy désos —replicó el paje—: versos hago, y no soy rico ni pobre; y sin sentirlo ni descontarlo, como hacen los ginoveses sus convites, bien puedo dar un escudo, y dos, a quien yo quisiere. Tomad, preciosa perla, este segundo papel y este escudo segundo que va en él, sin que os pongáis a pensar si soy poeta o no; sólo quiero que penséis y creáis que quien os da esto quisiera tener para daros las riquezas de Midas.

Y, en esto, le dio un papel; y, tentándole Preciosa, halló que dentro venía el escudo, y dijo:

—Este papel ha de vivir muchos años, porque trae dos almas consigo: una, la del escudo, y otra, la de los versos, que siempre vienen llenos de *almas* y *corazones*. Pero sepa el señor paje que no quiero tantas almas conmigo, y si no saca la una, no haya miedo que reciba la otra; por poeta le quiero, y no por dadivoso, y desta manera tendremos amistad que dure; pues más aína puede faltar un escudo, por fuerte que sea, que la hechura de un romance.

—Pues así es —replicó el paje— que quieres, Preciosa, que yo sea pobre por fuerza, no deseches el alma que en ese papel te envío, y vuélveme el escudo; que, como le toques con la mano, le tendré por reliquia mientras la vida me durare.

Sacó Preciosa el escudo del papel, y quedóse con el papel, y no le quiso leer en la calle. El paje se despidió, y se fue contentísimo, creyendo que ya Preciosa quedaba rendida, pues con tanta afabilidad le había hablado.

Y, como ella llevaba puesta la mira en buscar la casa del padre de Andrés, sin querer detenerse a bailar en ninguna parte, en poco espacio se puso en la calle do estaba, que ella muy bien sabía; y, habiendo andado hasta la mitad, alzó los ojos a unos balcones de hierro dorados, que le habían dado por señas, y vio en ella a un caballero de hasta edad de cincuenta años, con un hábito de cruz colorada en los pechos, de venerable gravedad y presencia; el cual, apenas también hubo visto la gitanilla, cuando dijo:

—Subid, niñas, que aquí os darán limosna.

A esta voz acudieron al balcón otros tres caballeros, y entre ellos

poor, I was surprised by that gold escudo you gave me wrapped in your poem; but now that I know that you aren't a poet, but only a man fond of poetry, you may very well be rich—though I doubt it, because the part of you that makes you write songs must make you squander all the property you own; for they say no poet is able to hold onto the property he has or to obtain what he hasn't got."

"Well, I'm not one of those," the page replied. "I write verses, and I'm neither rich nor poor; and without feeling the loss of it or charging for it, as the Genovese do with their banquets, I'm well able to give an escudo, or even two, two whomever I wish. Precious pearl, take this second sheet and the second escudo contained in it, without bothering to think about whether I'm a poet or not; I only want you to think and believe that the man who gives you this would like to have the riches of Midas to give them to you."

And therewith he handed her a paper; Preciosa, feeling it and finding there was an escudo in it, said:

"This paper will surely live many years, because it carries two souls with it: that of the coin and that of the verses, which are always full of 'souls' and 'hearts.' But know this, master page: I don't want so many souls with me, and if you don't remove one, have no fear of my accepting the other; I like you as a poet, not as a benefactor; that way, we'll have a lasting friendship; because one can more readily do without an escudo, however protective that 'shield' may be, than a newly created ballad."

The page replied: "Preciosa, seeing that you insist on my being poor, don't reject the soul I send you in that paper, but give me back the escudo; if you just touch it, I'll keep it as a relic as long as I live."

Preciosa took the escudo out of the paper, and was left with just the paper, which she didn't want to read on the street. The page took his leave, departing in high contentment, since he thought Preciosa had already surrendered, so affably had she spoken with him.

And since she had set her sights on looking for the home of Andrés's father, without wishing to stop and dance anywhere, before long she found herself on the street where it was located, which was very familiar to her. Having walked halfway down, she raised her eyes to some gilded iron balconies which had been described to her, and saw there a gentleman of about fifty with the badge of a red cross on his breast, a man of venerable gravity and presence; as soon as he caught sight of the Gypsy girl, he said:

"Come up, girls, you'll receive alms here."

The sound of his voice brought three other gentlemen to the balcony,

vino el enamorado Andrés, que, cuando vio a Preciosa, perdió la color y estuvo a punto de perder los sentidos: tanto fue el sobresalto que recibió con su vista. Subieron las gitanillas todas, sino la grande, que se quedó abajo para informarse de los criados de las verdades de Andrés.

Al entrar las gitanillas en la sala, estaba diciendo el caballero anciano a los demás:

—Ésta debe de ser, sin duda, la gitanilla hermosa que dicen que anda por Madrid.

—Ella es —replicó Andrés—, y sin duda es la más hermosa criatura que se ha visto.

—Así lo dicen —dijo Preciosa, que lo oyó todo en entrando—, pero en verdad que se deben de engañar en la mitad del justo precio. Bonita, bien creo que lo soy; pero tan hermosa como dicen, ni por pienso.

—¡Por vida de don Juanico, mi hijo —dijo el anciano—, que aún sois más hermosa de lo que dicen, linda gitana!

—Y ¿quién es don Juanico, su hijo? —preguntó Preciosa.

—Ese galán que está a vuestro lado —respondió el caballero.

—En verdad que pensé —dijo Preciosa— que juraba vuestra merced por algún niño de dos años: ¡mirad qué don Juanico y qué brinco! A mi verdad, que pudiera ya estar casado, y que, según tiene unas rayas en la frente, no pasarán tres años sin que lo esté, y muy a su gusto, si es que desde aquí allá no se le pierde o se le trueca.

—¡Basta! —dijo uno de los presentes—; ¿qué sabe la gitanilla de rayas?

En esto, las tres gitanillas que iban con Preciosa, todas tres se arrimaron a un rincón de la sala, y, cosiéndose las bocas unas con otras, se juntaron por no ser oídas. Dijo la Cristina:

—Muchachas, éste es el caballero que nos dio esta mañana los tres reales de a ocho.

—Así es la verdad —respondieron ellas—, pero no se lo mentemos, ni le digamos nada, si él no nos lo mienta; ¿qué sabemos si quiere encubrirse?

En tanto que esto entre las tres pasaba, respondió Preciosa a lo de las rayas:

—Lo que veo con los ojos, con el dedo lo adivino. Yo sé del señor don Juanico, sin rayas, que es algo enamoradizo, impetuoso y acelerado, y gran prometedor de cosas que parecen imposibles; y plega a Dios que no sea mentirosito, que sería lo peor de todo. Un viaje ha de hacer agora muy lejos de aquí, y uno piensa el bayo y otro el que le

one of whom was the enamored Andrés; when he saw Preciosa, he turned pale and was about to pass out, so great was the shock he received upon seeing her. All the Gypsy women went up, except the eldest, who remained downstairs to question the servants as to whether Andrés had told the truth.

When the Gypsy girls entered the parlor, the elderly gentleman was saying to the others:

"No doubt this must be the beautiful Gypsy girl who they say roams through Madrid."

"It is," said Andrés, "and no doubt she's the loveliest creature ever seen."

"So they say," said Preciosa, who had heard everything on entering, "but truly they must be fifty percent wrong. I do believe she's pretty, but as beautiful as they say, not a bit."

"On the life of my son Don Juanico," said the elderly man, "you're even more beautiful than they say, lovely Gypsy!"

"And who is your son Don Juanico?" Preciosa asked.

"This gentleman standing beside you," the knight replied.

"To tell the truth," Preciosa said, "I thought your lordship was swearing on the life of some two-year-old boy. Just look at this Don Juanico and this little trinket! As far as I can see, he might already be married and, according to some lines he has on his forehead, he will be before three years have passed, and very happily, unless between now and then he doesn't lose the opportunity or change his affections."

"Enough!" said one of those present. "What does this Gypsy girl know about lines?"

At that moment all three Gypsy girls accompanying Preciosa withdrew to a corner of the room and, placing their faces very close together, assembled there so as not to be heard. Cristina said:

"Girls, this is the knight who gave us the three eight-real pieces this morning."

"It's true," they replied, "but let's not mention it to him or say anything to him if he doesn't mention it to us. Who knows? He may want to keep it a secret."

While those three were conversing thus, Preciosa replied to the remark about the lines:

"What I see with my eyes, I divine with my finger. Without regard to lines, I know about Don Juanico that he's somewhat apt to fall in love, headstrong, and rash, and likes to make promises that seem impossible to keep; and may it please God that he isn't a little liar, which would be the worst thing of all. He is now to make a journey very far from here, and

ensilla; el hombre pone y Dios dispone; quizá pensará que va a Óñez y dará en Gamboa.

A esto respondió don Juan:

—En verdad, gitanica, que has acertado en muchas cosas de mi condición, pero en lo de ser mentiroso vas muy fuera de la verdad, porque me precio de decirla en todo acontecimiento. En lo del viaje largo has acertado, pues, sin duda, siendo Dios servido, dentro de cuatro o cinco días me partiré a Flandes, aunque tú me amenazas que he de torcer el camino, y no querría que en él me sucediese algún desmán que lo estorbase.

—Calle, señorito —respondió Preciosa—, y encomiéndese a Dios, que todo se hará bien; y sepa que yo no sé nada de lo que digo, y no es maravilla que, como hablo mucho y a bulto, acierte en alguna cosa, y yo querría acertar en persuadirte a que no te partieses, sino que sosegases el pecho y te estuvieses con tus padres, para darles buena vejez; porque no estoy bien con estas idas y venidas a Flandes, principalmente los mozos de tan tierna edad como la tuya. Déjate crecer un poco, para que puedas llevar los trabajos de la guerra; cuanto más que harta guerra tienes en tu casa: hartos combates amorosos te sobresaltan el pecho. Sosiega, sosiega, alborotadito, y mira lo que haces primero que te cases, y danos una limosnita por Dios y por quien tú eres; que en verdad que creo que ceres bien nacido. Y si a esto se junta el ser verdadero, yo cantaré la gala al vencimiento de haber acertado en cuanto te he dicho.

—Otra vez te he dicho, niña —respondió el don Juan que había de ser Andrés Caballero—, que en todo aciertas, sino en el temor que tienes que no debo de ser muy verdadero; que en esto te engañas, sin alguna duda. La palabra que yo doy en el campo, la cumpliré en la ciudad y adonde quiera, sin serme pedida, pues no se puede preciar de caballero quien toca en el vicio de mentiroso. Mi padre te dará limosna por Dios y por mí; que en verdad que esta mañana di cuanto tenía a unas damas, que a ser tan lisonjeras como hermosas, especialmente una dellas, no me arriendo la ganancia.

Oyendo esto Cristina, con el recato de la otra vez, dijo a las demás gitanas:

—¡Ay, niñas, que me maten si no lo dice por los tres reales de a ocho que nos dio esta mañana!

—No es así —respondió una de las dos—, porque dijo que eran

'the horse has one idea and the man who saddles it has another'; that is, 'man proposes and God disposes'; maybe he thinks he's going to one place and will wind up in another."[14]

To which Don Juan replied:

"Truly, little Gypsy, you have rightly guessed many aspects of my nature, but as to my being a liar, you're very far from the truth, since I pride myself on telling it on every occasion. As to the long journey, you're correct, since without a doubt, God willing, I'm leaving for Flanders in four or five days, although you threaten that I'll change course, and I wouldn't want any calamity to happen to me on the way to upset my plans."

"Be still, young master," replied Preciosa, "and commend yourself to God, for all will go well; and know that I know nothing of what I say, and it isn't surprising that, speaking a lot and in general terms, I'm sometimes correct; I'd like to succeed in persuading you not to go, but instead to calm your spirits and stay with your parents and give them a happy old age; because I don't hold with these comings and goings to Flanders, especially for lads of such tender years as yours. Wait till you're a little older and can support the hardships of war; especially since you have enough war here at home: many a combat of love makes your heart leap. Calm down, calm down, little perturbed boy, and watch what you do before you marry, and give us some alms for the love of God and in accordance with your station, for in truth I believe you're well born. And if to that you add being truthful, I'll congratulate myself on my victory in guessing correctly as to all I've told you."

"Again I tell you, girl," replied Don Juan, who was to become Andrés Caballero, "that you're right on all counts, except for your fear that I'm probably not very truthful; there you're wrong, no doubt about it. The promise I make in the country I will keep in town or wherever, without being asked to, because no one can pride himself on being a gentleman who partakes of the vice of lying. My father will give you alms for God's sake and mine; for, in truth, this morning I gave all I had to some ladies, and if they're as cajoling as they are beautiful, especially one of them, I don't envy my position."

Hearing this, Cristina, as cautiously as before, said to the other Gypsy girls:

"Oh, girls, may I be killed if he isn't referring to the three eight-real pieces he gave us this morning!"

"He can't be," one of the other two replied, "because he said they were

---

14. The specific places in the Spanish text, Óñez and Gamboa, were two mutually hostile areas in the Basque country.

damas, y nosotras no lo somos; y, siendo él tan verdadero como dice, no había de mentir en esto.

—No es mentira de tanta consideración —respondió Cristina— la que se dice sin perjuicio de nadie, y en provecho y crédito del que la dice. Pero, con todo esto, veo que no nos dan nada, ni nos mandan bailar.

Subió en esto la gitana vieja y dijo:

—Nieta, acaba, que es tarde y hay mucho que hacer y más que decir.

—Y ¿qué hay, abuela? —preguntó Preciosa—. ¿Hay hijo o hija?

—Hijo, y muy lindo —respondió la vieja—. Ven, Preciosa, y oirás verdaderas maravillas.

—¡Plega a Dios que no muera de sobreparto! —dijo Preciosa.

—Todo se mirará muy bien —replicó la vieja—; cuanto más, que hasta aquí todo ha sido parto derecho, y el infante es como un oro.

—¿Ha parido alguna señora? —preguntó el padre de Andrés Caballero.

—Sí, señor —respondió la gitana—, pero ha sido el parto tan secreto, que no le sabe sino Preciosa y yo, y otra persona; y así, no podemos decir quién es.

—Ni aquí lo queremos saber —dijo uno de los presentes—, pero desdichada de aquella que en vuestras lenguas deposita su secreto y en vuestra ayuda pone su honra.

—No todas somos malas —respondió Preciosa—: quizá hay alguna entre nosotras que se precia de secreta y de verdadera, tanto cuanto el hombre más estirado que hay en esta sala; y vámonos, abuela, que aquí nos tienen en poco: pues en verdad que no somos ladronas ni rogamos a nadie.

—No os enojéis, Preciosa —dijo el padre—; que, a lo menos de vos, imagino que no se puede presumir cosa mala, que vuestro buen rostro os acredita y sale por fiador de vuestras buenas obras. Por vida de Preciosita, que bailéis un poco con vuestras compañeras: que aquí tengo un doblón de oro de a dos caras, que ninguna es como la vuestra, aunque son de dos reyes.

Apenas hubo oído esto la vieja, cuando dijo:

—Ea, niñas, haldas en cinta, y dad contento a estos señores.

Tomó las sonajas Preciosa, y dieron sus vueltas, hicieron y deshicieron todos sus lazos con tanto donaire y desenvoltura, que tras los pies se llevaban los ojos de cuantos las miraban, especialmente los de Andrés, que así se iban entre los pies de Preciosa, como si allí tuvieran el centro de su gloria. Pero turbósela la suerte de manera que

ladies, and we aren't; and, being as truthful as he says, he wouldn't lie about that."

Cristina replied: "A lie that is told to nobody's harm, but does credit to the man who tells it, isn't so momentous. But, despite all that, I see they aren't giving us anything or asking us to dance."

At that moment the old Gypsy woman came upstairs and said:

"Granddaughter, finish, for it's late and there's a lot to do, and even more to say."

"What is it, grandmother?" Preciosa asked. "Is it a boy or a girl?"

"A boy, and very pretty," the old woman replied. "Come, Preciosa, and you'll hear true wonders."

"May it please God that he doesn't die as soon as he's born!" said Preciosa.

"Everything will turn out very well," replied the old woman, "especially since up to now the entire delivery has been normal, and the infant is as good as gold."

"Has some lady given birth?" asked the father of Andrés Caballero.

"Yes, sir," the Gypsy answered, "but the birth has been so secret that only Preciosa and I, and one other person, know about it; so we can't tell you who it is."

"Nor does anyone here wish to know," said one of the men present, "but woe to the woman who confides her secret to your tongues and places her honor under your protection!"

"We aren't all bad," said Preciosa. "Perhaps there are some among us who pride themselves on keeping secrets and telling the truth just as much as the haughtiest man in this room; let's go, grandmother, because we're not highly regarded here: truly, we're not thieves and we don't beg of anyone."

"Don't get angry, Preciosa," the father said, "because of you at least I don't imagine anything bad can be suspected, for your kind face vouches for you and guarantees your good actions. On your life, Preciosita, dance a little with your companions, for I have here a gold doubloon with two faces, neither of which comes up to yours, though they belong to two monarchs."

As soon as the old woman heard that, she said:

"Come, girls, tuck up your skirts and satisfy these gentlemen."

Preciosa took the tambourine and they spun around, forming and dissolving all their twining figures with such charm and carefree spirit that their feet attracted the eyes of all who beheld them, especially those of Andrés, which followed Preciosa's feet as closely as if the focal point of their bliss were in that place. But fate so disturbed that bliss as to turn it

se la volvió en infierno; y fue el caso que en la fuga del baile se le cayó a Preciosa el papel que le había dado el paje, y, apenas hubo caído, cuando le alzó el que no tenía buen concepto de las gitanas, y, abriéndole al punto, dijo:

—¡Bueno; sonetico tenemos! Cese el baile, y escúchenle; que, según el primer verso, en verdad que no es nada necio.

Pesóle a Preciosa, por no saber lo que en él venía, y rogó que no le leyesen, y que se le volviesen; y todo el ahínco que en esto ponía eran espuelas que apremiaban el deseo de Andrés para oírle. Finalmente, el caballero le leyó en alta voz; y era éste:

—Cuando Preciosa el panderete toca
y hiere el dulce son los aires vanos,
perlas son que derrama con las manos;
flores son que despide de la boca.
Suspensa el alma, y la cordura loca,
queda a los dulces actos sobrehumanos,
que, de limpios, de honestos y de sanos,
su fama al cielo levantado toca.
Colgadas del menor de sus cabellos
mil almas lleva, y a sus plantas tiene
amor rendidas una y otra flecha.
Ciega y alumbra con sus soles bellos,
su imperio amor por ellos le mantiene,
y aún más grandezas de su ser sospecha.

—¡Por Dios —dijo el que leyó el soneto—, que tiene donaire el poeta que le escribió!

—No es poeta, señor, sino un paje muy galán y muy hombre de bien —dijo Preciosa.

(Mirad lo que habéis dicho, Preciosa, y lo que vais a decir; que ésas no son alabanzas del paje, sino lanzas que traspasan el corazón de Andrés, que las escucha. ¿Queréislo ver, niña? Pues volved los ojos y veréisle desmayado encima de la silla, con un trasudor de muerte; no penséis, doncella, que os ama tan de burlas Andrés que no le hieran y sobresalten el menor de vuestros descuidos. Llegaos a él en hora buena, y decilde algunas palabras al oído, que vayan derechas al corazón y le vuelvan de su desmayo. ¡No, sino andaos a traer sonetos cada día en vuestra alabanza y veréis cuál os le ponen!)

Todo esto pasó así como se ha dicho: que Andrés, en oyendo el soneto, mil celosas imaginaciones le sobresaltaron. No se desmayó, pero perdió la color de manera que, viéndole su padre, le dijo:

—¿Qué tienes, don Juan, que parece que te vas a desmayar, según se te ha mudado el color?

into a hell: it so happened that at the height of the dance Preciosa dropped the paper that the page had given her, and the moment it fell it was picked up by the man who had a low opinion of Gypsy women. Unfolding it at once, he said:

"Fine! Here we have a little sonnet! Let the dance stop, and everybody listen, because, to go by the first line, it's really nothing silly."

Preciosa was vexed because she didn't know what it said; she begged them not to read it but to give it back to her; yet all her urging in this regard merely spurred Andrés's desire to hear it. Finally, the gentleman read it aloud; it went as follows:

—When Preciosa strikes the tambourine
and the sweet sound smites the empty air,
those are pearls which her hands scatter,
those are flowers which her lips emit.
Our soul remains rapt, and our wisdom mad,
at those sweet superhuman actions,
which are so pure, chaste, and wholesome
that her renown is raised to the skies.
Tied to the least of her hairs
she carries a thousand souls along, and at her feet
Love surrenders both his golden and his leaden arrow.
She blinds and dazzles with her lovely suns;
Love maintains her dominion for her with their aid,
and suspects even further grandeurs in her nature.

"My God!" said the man who read the sonnet. "How elegant the poet is who wrote it!"

"He isn't a poet, sir, but a very gallant page and a very respectable man," said Preciosa.

(Think about what you've said, Preciosa, and what you're about to say: those aren't praises of the page, but lances that pierce Andrés's heart as he hears them. Do you want to see this, girl? Then turn your eyes and you'll behold him swooning on his chair, with a deathly perspiration; don't think, maiden, that Andrés's love for you is so deceitful that he isn't wounded and smitten by the least of your heedless remarks. Go over to him at once and speak a few words in his ear that will go right to his heart and bring him out of his faint. No, but go on every day carrying around sonnets in your praise, and you'll see what a state they'll put him in!)

All this happened just as described: hearing the sonnet, Andrés was assailed by a thousand jealous imaginings. He didn't actually faint, but he became so pale that his father, seeing him, asked:

"What's wrong, Don Juan? You look as if you're going to faint, the way your color changed!"

—Espérense —dijo a esta sazón Preciosa—; déjenmele decir unas ciertas palabras al oído y verán como no se desmaya.

Y, llegándose a él, le dijo, casi sin mover los labios:

—¡Gentil ánimo para gitano! ¿Cómo podréis, Andrés, sufrir el tormento de toca, pues no podéis llevar el de un papel?

Y, haciéndole media docena de cruces sobre el corazón, se apartó dél; y entonces Andrés respiró un poco, y dio a entender que las palabras de Preciosa le habían aprovechado.

Finalmente, el doblón de dos caras se le dieron a Preciosa, y ella dijo a sus compañeras que le trocaría y repartiría con ellas hidalgamente. El padre de Andrés le dijo que le dejase por escrito las palabras que había dicho a don Juan, que las quería saber en todo caso. Ella dijo que las diría de muy buena gana, y que entendiesen que, aunque parecían cosa de burla, tenían gracia especial para preservar el mal del corazón y los váguidos de cabeza, y que las palabras eran:

«Cabecita, cabecita,
tente en ti, no te resbales,
y apareja dos puntales
de la paciencia bendita.
Solicita
la bonita
confiancita;
no te inclines
a pensamientos ruines;
verás cosas
que toquen en milagrosas,
Dios delante
y San Cristóbal gigante».

—Con la mitad destas palabras que le digan, y con seis cruces que le hagan sobre el corazón a la persona que tuviere váguidos de cabeza —dijo Preciosa—, quedará como una manzana.

Cuando la gitana vieja oyó el ensalmo y el embuste, quedó pasmada; y más lo quedó Andrés, que vio que todo era invencion de su agudo ingenio. Quedáronse con el soneto, porque no quiso pedirle Preciosa, por no dar otro tártago a Andrés; que ya sabía ella, sin ser enseñada, lo que era dar sustos y martelos, y sobresaltos celosos a los rendidos amantes.

Despidiéronse las gitanas, y, al irse, dijo Preciosa a don Juan:

—Mire, señor, cualquiera día desta semana es próspero para partidas, y ninguno es aciago; apresure el irse lo más presto que pudiere,

"Wait," Preciosa then said, "let me say certain words in his ear, and you'll see that he won't faint."

Going over to him, she said, almost without moving her lips:

"What courage for a Gypsy! Andrés, how will you undergo the water torture during interrogations if you can't stand being tortured by a sheet of paper?"

And, tracing a half-dozen crosses on his chest, she moved away from him; then Andrés breathed a little more easily and indicated that Preciosa's words had done him good.

Finally, the doubloon with two faces was given to Preciosa, and she told her companions she'd change it and share it with them nobly. Andrés's father asked her to write down the words she had spoken to Don Juan, for he wished to know them at all events. She said she'd gladly recite them; the gentlemen were to understand that, though they sounded humorous, they had a special power to prevent heartaches and dizziness. The words were:

Little head, little head,
contain yourself, don't slip away,
and prepare two props
of blessed patience.
Seek for
comforting
trustfulness;
don't be inclined
toward evil thoughts;
you'll see things
that are almost miraculous,
with God to guide you,
and Saint Christopher the giant.

"If you say half these words to a person who gets dizzy, and if you make six crosses over his heart," Preciosa said, "he'll be fit as a fiddle."

When the old Gypsy woman heard that fake charm, she was astonished; and Andrés even more so, seeing that it was all an invention of her sharp wits. The gentlemen kept the sonnet, because Preciosa didn't want to ask for it, to avoid vexing Andrés again; for she already knew, without being taught, what it meant to give frights and torments and fits of jealousy to submissive lovers.

The Gypsy women took leave and, as they were going, Preciosa said to Don Juan:

"Look, sir, any day this week is propitious for departures, and none is inauspicious; hasten your going as much as you can, for an easygoing, free, and very pleasant life awaits you, if you're willing to adapt to it."

que le aguarda una vida ancha, libre y muy gustosa, si quiere acomodarse a ella.

—No es tan libre la del soldado, a mi parecer —respondió don Juan—, que no tenga más de sujeción que de libertad; pero, con todo esto, haré como viere.

—Más veréis de lo que pensáis —respondió Preciosa—, y Dios os lleve y traiga con bien, como vuestra buena presencia merece.

Con estas últimas palabras quedó contento Andrés, y las gitanas se fueron contentísimas.

Trocaron el doblón, repartiéronle entre todas igualmente, aunque la vieja guardiana llevaba siempre parte y media de lo que se juntaba, así por la mayoridad, como por ser ella el aguja por quien se guiaban en el maremagno de sus bailes, donaires, y aun de sus embustes.

Llegóse, en fin, el día que Andrés Caballero se apareció una mañana en el primer lugar de su aparecimiento, sobre una mula de alquiler, sin criado alguno. Halló en él a Preciosa y a su abuela, de las cuales conocido, le recibieron con mucho gusto. Él les dijo que le guiasen al rancho antes que entrase el día y con él se descubriesen las señas que llevaba, si acaso le buscasen. Ellas, que, como advertidas, vinieron solas, dieron la vuelta, y de allí a poco rato llegaron a sus barracas.

Entró Andrés en la una, que era la mayor del rancho, y luego acudieron a verle diez o doce gitanos, todos mozos y todos gallardos y bien hechos, a quien ya la vieja había dado cuenta del nuevo compañero que les había de venir, sin tener necesidad de encomendarles el secreto; que, como ya se ha dicho, ellos le guardan con sagacidad y puntualidad nunca vista. Echaron luego ojo a la mula, y dijo uno dellos:

—Ésta se podrá vender el jueves en Toledo.

—Eso no —dijo Andrés—, porque no hay mula de alquiler que no sea conocida de todos los mozos de mulas que trajinan por España.

—Por Dios, señor Andrés —dijo uno de los gitanos—, que, aunque la mula tuviera más señales que las que han de preceder al día tremendo, aquí la transformáramos de manera que no la conociera la madre que la parió ni el dueño que la ha criado.

—Con todo eso —respondió Andrés—, por esta vez se ha de seguir y tomar el parecer mío. A esta mula se ha de dar muerte, y ha de ser enterrada donde aun los huesos no parezcan.

—¡Pecado grande! —dijo otro gitano—: ¿a una inocente se ha de quitar la vida? No diga tal el buen Andrés, sino haga una cosa: mírela bien agora, de manera que se le queden estampadas todas sus señales en la memoria, y déjenmela llevar a mí; y si de aquí a dos horas la conociere, que me lardeen como a un negro fugitivo.

"A soldier's life isn't so free, in my opinion," Don Juan replied, "that it doesn't involve more subjection than freedom; but nevertheless I'll do as I see fit."

"You'll see more than you think," Preciosa replied, "and may God guide you and maintain you well, as your goodly presence deserves."

With these last words Andrés remained contented, and the Gypsy women departed highly so.

They exchanged the doubloon and shared the amount among themselves equally, though their old guardian always took a share and a half of what they collected, not only because she was the eldest, but also because she was the compass that guided them on the ocean of their dancing, graciousness, and even their cozening.

The day finally arrived on which Andrés Caballero showed up in the morning in the spot where he had first appeared, now riding a hired she-mule, and without any servant. On that spot he found Preciosa and her grandmother, who, on recognizing him, greeted him warmly. He asked them to lead him to their camp before full daylight, when he might be discovered by his appearance if he were by chance being sought. Having prudently come alone, the women turned back and soon reached their huts.

Andrés entered one, the biggest in the camp, and immediately ten or twelve Gypsy men came over to see him, all young, dashing, and well built; the old woman had already informed them of the new comrade who would arrive, having no need to enjoin secrecy on them, because, as I have said, they maintain it with an unheard-of sagacity and exactness. Then they cast their eyes on the mule, and one of them said:

"That can be sold in Toledo on Thursday."

"No," said Andrés, "because every hired-out mule is familiar to every muleteer who roams through Spain."

"By God, señor Andrés," said one of the Gypsies, "even if the mule had more signs and distinguishing features than those which are to precede Judgment Day, we'll transform her here so that the mother who bore her, or the owner who raised her, wouldn't recognize her."

"All the same," Andrés replied, "this time my judgment must be accepted and followed. This mule must be killed, and buried where even her bones won't show up."

"A real sin!" said another Gypsy. "To take the life of an innocent creature? Don't say that, good Andrés, but do just this: take a good look at her now, so that her entire appearance is engraved in your memory, and let *me* take her away; and if, two hours from now, you recognize her, let me be tortured with hot melted fat like a runaway African slave!"

—En ninguna manera consentiré —dijo Andrés— que la mula no muera, aunque más me aseguren su transformación. Yo temo ser descubierto si a ella no la cubre la tierra. Y, si se hace por el provecho que de venderla puede seguirse, no vengo tan desnudo a esta cofradía, que no pueda pagar de entrada más de lo que valen cuatro mulas.

—Pues así lo quiere el señor Andrés Caballero —dijo otro gitano—, muera la sin culpa; y Dios sabe si me pesa, así por su mocedad, pues aún no ha cerrado (cosa no usada entre mulas de alguiler), como porque debe ser andariega, pues no tiene costras en las ijadas, ni llagas de la espuela.

Dilatóse su muerte hasta la noche, y en lo que quedaba de aquel día se hicieron las ceremonias de la entrada de Andrés a ser gitano, que fueron: desembarazaron luego un rancho de los mejores del aduar, y adornáronle de ramos y juncia; y, sentándose Andrés sobre un medio alcornoque, pusiéronle en las manos un martillo y unas tenazas, y, al son de dos guitarras que dos gitanos tañían, le hicieron dar dos cabriolas; luego le desnudaron un brazo, y con una cinta de seda nueva y un garrote le dieron dos vueltas blandamente.

A todo se halló presente Preciosa y otras muchas gitanas, viejas y mozas; que las unas con maravilla, otras con amor, le miraban; tal era la gallarda disposición de Andrés, que hasta los gitanos le quedaron aficionadísimos.

Hechas, pues, las referidas ceremonias, un gitano viejo tomó por la mano a Preciosa, y, puesto delante de Andrés, dijo:

—Esta muchacha, que es la flor y la nata de toda la hermosura de las gitanas que sabemos que viven en España, te la entregamos, ya por esposa o ya por amiga, que en esto puedes hacer lo que fuere más de tu gusto, porque la libre y ancha vida nuestra no está sujeta a melindres ni a muchas ceremonias. Mírala bien, y mira si te agrada, o si vees en ella alguna cosa que te descontente; y si la vees, escoge entre las doncellas que aquí están la que más te contentare; que la que escogieres te daremos; pero has de saber que una vez escogida, no la has de dejar por otra, ni te has de empachar ni entremeter, ni con las casadas ni con las doncellas. Nosotros guardamos inviolablemente la ley de la amistad: ninguno solicita la prenda del otro; libres vivimos de la amarga pestilencia de los celos. Entre nosotros, aunque hay muchos incestos, no hay ningún adulterio; y, cuando le hay en la mujer propia, o alguna bellaquería en la amiga, no vamos a la justicia a pedir castigo: nosotros somos los jueces y los verdugos de nuestras esposas o amigas; con la misma facilidad las matamos, y las enterramos por las montañas y desiertos, como si fueran animales nocivos; no hay pariente que las

"I absolutely refuse," said Andrés, "to let the mule live, no matter how different you assure me she'll look. I'm afraid of being discovered if the earth doesn't cover her. And, if you're doing this for the profit that may come from selling her, I haven't come to this brotherhood so bare that I can't pay an admittance fee worth more than four mules."

"Since Señor Andrés Caballero wishes it so," said another Gypsy, "let the blameless one die, though God knows how it grieves me, not only because of her youth, seeing that she's under seven (an unusual thing for hired mules), but also because she must be a good traveler, seeing that she has no scabs on her flanks or spur sores."

Her death was delayed until nightfall, and in the remaining daylight hours they performed the ceremonies of Andrés's initiation as a Gypsy, which were as follows: First they cleared out one of the best dwellings in the camp and adorned it with branches and reeds. Seating Andrés on the stump of a cork oak, they placed in his hands a hammer and a pair of tongs, and, to the music of two guitars played by two Gypsies, they made him cut two capers; then they bared one of his arms and gently encircled it twice with a ribbon of new silk stiffened by a stick.

Preciosa and many other Gypsy women, old and young, attended all these rites, some looking on with surprise, others lovingly; such was Andrés's gallant nature that even the male Gypsies became extremely attached to him.

Well, when the above-mentioned ceremonies were over, an old Gypsy man took Preciosa by the hand and, taking his stand in front of Andrés, said:

"This girl, who is the fine flower of all the beauty of the Gypsy women we know to be living in Spain, we hand over to you, either as a wife or as a mistress, for in this matter you may do what you like best, because our free, untrammeled life is not subject to priggishness or much ceremony. Take a good look at her and see whether she pleases you or you see anything in her to put you off; if you do reject her, choose the girl that pleases you best among the others here; for we shall give you the one you choose; but you must know that, once she is chosen, you may not leave her for another, nor must you dally or toy with either married women or maidens. We maintain inviolate the law of friendship: no one tries to take another man's jewel; we live free of the bitter plague of jealousy. Among us, though there are many cases of incest, there is no adultery; and when it occurs in one's own wife, or one's mistress cheats on him, we don't go to law to seek redress: we are the judges and the executioners of our wives or mistresses; we kill them, burying them on mountains or in the wilderness, as readily as if

vengue, ni padres que nos pidan su muerte. Con este temor y miedo ellas procuran ser castas, y nosotros, como ya he dicho, vivimos seguros. Pocas cosas tenemos que no sean comunes a todos, excepto la mujer o la amiga, que queremos que cada una sea del que le cupo en suerte. Entre nosotros así hace divorcio la vejez como la muerte: el que quisiere puede dejar la mujer vieja, como él sea mozo, y escoger otra que corresponda al gusto de sus años. Con estas y con otras leyes y estatutos nos conservamos y vivimos alegres; somos señores de los campos, de los sembrados, de las selvas, de los montes, de las fuentes y de los ríos. Los montes nos ofrecen leña de balde; los árboles, frutas; las viñas, uvas; las huertas, hortaliza; las fuentes, agua; los ríos, peces, y los vedados, caza; sombra, las peñas; aire fresco, las quiebras; y casas, las cuevas. Para nosotros las inclemencias del cielo son oreos, refrigerio las nieves, baños la lluvia, músicas los truenos y hachas los relámpagos. Para nosotros son los duros terreros colchones de blandas plumas: el cuero curtido de nuestros cuerpos nos sirve de arnés impenetrable que nos defiende; a nuestra ligereza no la impiden grillos, ni la detienen barrancos, ni la contrastan paredes; a nuestro ánimo no le tuercen cordeles, ni le menoscaban garruchas, ni le ahogan tocas, ni le doman potros. Del *sí* al *no* no hacemos diferencia cuando nos conviene: siempre nos preciamos más de mártires que de confesores. Para nosotros se crían las bestias de carga en los campos, y se cortan las faldriqueras en las ciudades. No hay águila, ni ninguna otra ave de rapiña, que más presto se abalance a la presa que se le ofrece, que nosotros nos abalanzamos a las ocasiones que algún interés nos señalen; y, finalmente, tenemos muchas habilidades que felice fin nos prometen; porque en la cárcel cantamos, en el potro callamos, de día trabajamos y de noche hurtamos; o, por mejor decir, avisamos que nadie viva descuidado de mirar dónde pone su hacienda. No nos fatiga el temor de perder la honra, ni nos desvela la ambición de acrecentarla; ni sustentamos bandos, ni madrugamos a dar memoriales, ni acompañar magnates ni a solicitar favores. Por dorados techos y suntuosos palacios estimamos estas barracas y movibles ranchos; por cuadros y países de Flandes, los que nos da la naturaleza en esos levantados riscos y nevadas peñas, tendidos prados y espesos bosques que a cada paso a los ojos se nos muestran. Somos astrólogos rústicos, porque, como casi siempre dormimos al cielo descubierto, a todas horas sabemos las que son del día y las que son de la noche; vemos cómo arrincona y barre la aurora las estrellas del cielo, y cómo ella sale con su compañera el alba, alegrando el aire, enfriando el agua y humedeciendo la tierra; y luego, tras ellas, el sol, dorando cumbres

they were harmful animals; no relative avenges them, no parents ask us to account for their death. With this fear and threat they strive to be chaste, and we, as I've said, live in peace. We possess few things that aren't common property, except wives and mistresses; we want each of *them* to belong to the man to whose lot she fell. Among us, both old age and death create a divorce: if a man likes, he can abandon an old wife, as long as he himself is young, and can choose another who suits the taste of his age. With these and other laws and statutes we maintain ourselves and live a happy life; we are masters of the open fields, the tilled land, the woods, the forests, the springs, and the rivers. The forests offer us free firewood; the trees, fruit; the vines, grapes; the gardens, produce; the springs, water; the rivers, fish; and the preserves, game; we obtain shade from the rocks, fresh air from their fissures, and houses from their caves. For us, the inclemencies of the weather are breezes; the snows, coolness; the rain, a bath; the thunder, music; and the lightning, torches. For us, hard terrains are mattresses with soft feathers; the tanned skin on our bodies serves as an impenetrable armor to protect us; our swiftness is not impeded by fetters, detained by ravines, or resisted by walls; our spirit is not twisted by ropes, diminished by strappados, drowned by water tortures, or cowed by the rack. We make no difference between yes and no when it suits us: we always pride ourselves on being martyrs rather than confessors. For us the beasts of burden are raised in the country and purses are cut in towns. No eagle or other bird of prey swoops down more swiftly onto an offered quarry than we hurl ourselves at the opportunities that betoken some gain; and, lastly, we have many skills that promise us a happy ending; because we sing in prison, we're silent on the rack, we work by day, and we steal by night; or, to be more exact, we take care that no one is careless about where he puts his property. We aren't vexed by the fear of losing our honor, or kept awake by the ambition to augment it; we don't support factions, we don't get up early to submit petitions, accompany magnates, or seek favors. Like gilded roofs and sumptuous palaces to us are these huts and movable camps; like Flemish paintings and landscapes, those provided to us by nature in these lofty crags and snowy peaks, extensive meadows and dense woods, which we see before us with every step we take. We are rustic astronomers because, almost always sleeping outdoors, we always know what time of day or night it is; we see how Daybreak corrals the stars and sweeps them from the sky, and how she issues forth with her companion the Dawn, brightening the air, cooling the water, and moistening the earth; and then, after them, the sun, 'gilding summits' (as some

(como dijo el otro poeta) y rizando montes: ni tememos quedar helados por su ausencia cuando nos hiere a soslayo con sus rayos, ni quedar abrasados cuando con ellos particularmente nos toca; un mismo rostro hacemos al sol que al yelo, a la esterilidad que a la abundancia. En conclusión, somos gente que vivimos por nuestra industria y pico, y sin entremeternos con el antiguo refrán: «Iglesia, o mar, o casa real»; tenemos lo que queremos, pues nos contentamos con lo que tenemos. Todo esto os he dicho, generoso mancebo, porque no ignoréis la vida a que habéis venido y el trato que habéis de profesar, el cual os he pintado aquí en borrón; que otras muchas e infinitas cosas iréis descubriendo en él con el tiempo, no menos dignas de consideración que las que habéis oído.

Calló, en diciendo esto el elocuente y viejo gitano, y el novicio dijo que se holgaba mucho de haber sabido tan loables estatutos, y que él pensaba hacer profesión en aquella orden tan puesta en razón y en políticos fundamentos; y que sólo le pesaba no haber venido más presto en conocimiento de tan alegre vida, y que desde aquel punto renunciaba la profesión de caballero y la vanagloria de su ilustre linaje, y lo ponía todo debajo del yugo, o, por mejor decir, debajo de las leyes con que ellos vivían, pues con tan alta recompensa le satisfacían el deseo de servirlos, entregándole a la divina Preciosa, por quien él dejaría coronas e imperios, y sólo los desearía para servirla.

A lo cual respondió Preciosa:

—Puesto que estos señores legisladores han hallado por sus leyes que soy tuya, y que por tuya te me han entregado, yo he hallado por la ley de mi voluntad, que es la más fuerte de todas, que no quiero serlo si no es con las condiciones que antes que aquí vinieses entre los dos concertamos. Dos años has de vivir en nuestra compañía primero que de la mía goces, porque tú no te arrepientas por ligero, ni yo quede engañada por presurosa. Condiciones rompen leyes; las que te he puesto sabes: si las quisieres guardar, podrá ser que sea tuya y tú seas mío; y donde no, aún no es muerta la mula, tus vestidos están enteros, y de tus dineros no te falta un ardite; la ausencia que has hecho no ha sido aún de un día; que de lo que dél falta te puedes servir y dar lugar que consideres lo que más te conviene. Estos señores bien pueden entregarte mi cuerpo; pero no mi alma, que es libre y nació libre, y ha de ser libre en tanto que yo quisiere. Si te quedas, te estimaré en mucho; si te vuelves, no te tendré en menos; porque, a mi parecer, los ímpetus amorosos corren a rienda suelta, hasta que encuentran con la razón o con el desengaño; y no querría yo que fueses tú para conmigo como es el cazador, que, en alcanzado la liebre que

poet said) 'and curling the forests'; nor do we fear being chilled by its absence when its beams strike us at a slant, or being burned when it beats down on us directly; we put on the same face for both sun and frost, barrenness and abundance. In conclusion, we're folk who live by our wits and our gift of gab, and without meddling with that old proverb 'Church, sea, or royal palace if you wish to prosper,' we have what we want because we're satisfied with what we have. I've told you all this, noble youth, so that you don't remain ignorant of the life you've come to and the ways you must profess, which I've given you a rough sketch of here; for you'll continue to discover an infinity of other things about them in time which are no less worthy of consideration than those you've heard."

With those words the eloquent old Gypsy fell silent, and the novice said that he was greatly pleased to have learned such praiseworthy statutes; that he intended to take vows in that order, which was based so soundly on reason and civic principles; and that his only regret was not having come sooner to know such a merry life. From that moment on, he said, he renounced the calling of knighthood and the vainglory of his illustrious lineage, placing everything under the yoke or, rather, under the laws they lived by, because they were contenting his desire to serve them with such a lofty reward, giving him the divine Preciosa, for whom he'd leave crowns and empires, which he'd only desire in order to serve her.

To which Preciosa replied:

"Although these legislators have found in their laws that I am yours, and have handed me over to you as your property, I have found in the law of my own wishes, which is the strongest of all, that I don't want to be yours except on the terms we both agreed upon before you came here. You must live in our company for two years before you enjoy mine, so that you don't regret having been thoughtless and I am not fooled by being hasty. Special agreements abrogate laws; you know those I've imposed upon you: if you want to abide by them, I may become yours, and you mine; if not, your mule isn't dead yet, your clothes are intact, and not a cent of your money is missing; you haven't been absent even a day so far; you can make use of the rest of the day to take time to think over what suits you best. These gentlemen may very well hand over my body to you, but not my soul, which is free and was born free, and will remain free as long as I wish. If you stay, I'll esteem you highly; if you go back, I won't think less of you; because, as I see it, the urgings of love gallop with a free rein until they come up against reason or disappointment; and I wouldn't like you to be to me like a hunter who, overtaking the hare he's pursuing, catches it, then lets it go, to chase another one that's running away. There

sigue, la coge y la deja por correr tras otra que le huye. Ojos hay engañados que a la primera vista tan bien les parece el oropel como el oro, pero a poco rato bien conocen la diferencia que hay de lo fino a lo falso. Ésta mi hermosura que tú dices que tengo, que la estimas sobre el sol y la encareces sobre el oro, ¿qué sé yo si de cerca te parecerá sombra, y tocada, cairás en que es de alquimia? Dos años te doy de tiempo para que tantees y ponderes lo que será bien que escojas o será justo que deseches; que la prenda que una vez comprada nadie se puede deshacer della, sino con la muerte, bien es que haya tiempo, y mucho, para miralla y remiralla, y ver en ella las faltas o las virtudes que tiene; que yo no me rijo por la bárbara e insolente licencia que estos mis parientes se han tomado de dejar las mujeres, o castigarlas, cuando se les antoja; y, como yo no pienso hacer cosa que llame al castigo, no quiero tomar compañía que por su gusto me deseche.

—Tienes razón, ¡oh Preciosa! —dijo a este punto Andrés—; y así, si quieres que asegure tus temores y menoscabe tus sospechas, jurándote que no saldré un punto de las órdenes que me pusieres, mira qué juramento quieres que haga, o qué otra seguridad puedo darte, que a todo me hallarás dispuesto.

—Los juramentos y promesas que hace el cautivo porque le den libertad, pocas veces se cumplen con ella —dijo Preciosa—; y así son, según pienso, los del amante: que, por conseguir su deseo, prometerá las alas de Mercurio y los rayos de Júpiter, como me prometió a mí un cierto poeta, y juraba por la laguna Estigia. No quiero juramentos, señor Andrés, ni quiero promesas; sólo quiero remitirlo todo a la esperiencia deste noviciado, y a mí se me quedará el cargo de guardarme, cuando vos le tuviéredes de ofenderme.

—Sea ansí —respondió Andrés—. Sola una cosa pido a estos señores y compañeros míos, y es que no me fuercen a que hurte ninguna cosa por tiempo de un mes siquiera; porque me parece que no he de acertar a ser ladrón si antes no preceden muchas liciones.

—Calla, hijo —dijo el gitano viejo—, que aquí te industriaremos de manera que salgas un águila en el oficio; y cuando le sepas, has de gustar dél de modo que te comas las manos tras él. ¡Ya es cosa de burla salir vacío por la mañana y volver cargado a la noche al rancho!

—De azotes he visto yo volver a algunos desos vacíos –dijo Andrés.

—No se toman truchas, etcétera —replicó el viejo—: todas las cosas desta vida están sujetas a diversos peligros, y las acciones del ladrón al de las galeras, azotes y horca; pero no porque corra un navío tormenta, o se anega, han de dejar los otros de navegar. ¡Bueno sería que porque la guerra come los hombres y los caballos, dejase de haber

are deceived eyes which at first glance are as contented with tinsel as with gold, but before long they well know the difference between fine and false. This beauty you say I possess, esteeming it more highly than the sun and praising it beyond gold: how do I know whether, at close range, it won't seem like darkness to you, and, once assayed, you'll decide it's imitation? I give you two years' time to feel and weigh what you may rightly choose or properly reject; because a jewel which, once purchased, no one can get rid of, except at death, should be inspected and reinspected over a long period of time, to see its flaws or merits. I do not submit to the barbarous, insolent license which these relatives of mine have taken to abandon or punish wives whenever they feel like it; and, seeing that I don't intend to do anything that calls for punishment, I don't want to take on a companion who may spurn me at his pleasure."

"You're right, Preciosa!" Andrés then said. "And so, if you want me to calm your fears and lessen your doubts by swearing to you that I won't swerve an inch from any orders you give me, think about what oath you want me to swear, or what other security I can give you, for you'll find me ready for anything."

"The oaths and promises made by a captive to gain his freedom are seldom kept once he's free," said Preciosa, "and I believe it's the same with a lover; for, to obtain his desire, he'll promise the wings of Mercury and the lightning of Jupiter, just as a certain poet once made promises to me, swearing by the Stygian lake. I don't want oaths, master Andrés, nor do I want promises; I only want to leave everything to the experiment of this novitiate; I will take upon myself the responsibility of self-protection, whenever you decide to affront me."

"Be it so," replied Andrés. "I ask only one thing of you gentlemen, my new comrades: don't compel me to steal anything for at least a month, because I feel that I won't succeed as a thief without many lessons first."

"Quiet, son," said the old Gypsy man. "Here we'll instruct you so well that you'll turn out an ace at the job; and when you know it, you'll like it so much that you'll long to do it. It's really an amusing thing to set out empty-handed in the morning and come back to camp at night loaded down!"

"I've seen some of those empty-handed people come back loaded with lashes," said Andrés.

"You can't catch trout without getting your feet wet," the old man retorted. "All things in this life are subject to various dangers, and a thief's activity runs the risk of galleys, whippings, and the gallows. But men mustn't stop sailing because some ship runs into a storm, or goes under. It would be a fine thing if there were no more soldiers because war eats

soldados! Cuanto más, que el que es azotado por justicia, entre nosotros, es tener un hábito en las espaldas, que le parece mejor que si le trujese en los pechos, y de los buenos. El toque está en no acabar acoceando el aire en la flor de nuestra juventud y a los primeros delitos; que el mosqueo de las espaldas, ni el apalear el agua en las galeras, no lo estimamos en un cacao. Hijo Andrés, reposad ahora en el nido debajo de nuestras alas, que a su tiempo os sacaremos a volar, y en parte donde no volváis sin presa; y lo dicho dicho: que os habéis de lamer los dedos tras cada hurto.

—Pues, para recompensar —dijo Andrés— lo que yo podía hurtar en este tiempo que se me da de venia, quiero repartir docientos escudos de oro entre todos los del rancho.

Apenas hubo dicho esto, cuando arremetieron a él muchos gitanos; y, levantándole en los brazos y sobre los hombros, le cantaban el «¡Víctor, víctor!, y el "¡Grande Andrés!"», añadiendo: «¡Y viva, viva Preciosa, amada prenda suya!» Las gitanas hicieron lo mismo con Preciosa, no sin envidia de Cristina y de otras gitanillas que se hallaron presentes: que la envidia tan bien se aloja en los aduares de los bárbaros y en las chozas de pastores como en palacios de príncipes, y esto de ver medrar al vecino que me parece que no tiene más méritos que yo, fatiga.

Hecho esto, comieron lautamente; repartióse el dinero prometido con equidad y justicia; renováronse las alabanzas de Andrés, subieron al cielo la hermosura de Preciosa. Llegó la noche, acocotaron la mula y enterráronla de modo que quedó seguro Andrés de ser por ella descubierto; y también enterraron con ella sus alhajas, como fueron silla y freno y cinchas, a uso de los indios, que sepultan con ellos sus más ricas preseas.

De todo lo que había visto y oído y de los ingenios de los gitanos quedó admirado Andrés, y con propósito de seguir y conseguir su empresa, sin entremeterse nada en sus costumbres; o, a lo menos, escusarlo por todas las vías que pudiese, pensando exentarse de la jurisdición de obedecellos en las cosas injustas que le mandasen, a costa de su dinero.

Otro día les rogó Andrés que mudasen de sitio y se alejasen de Madrid, porque temía ser conocido si allí estaba. Ellos dijeron que ya tenían determinado irse a los montes de Toledo, y desde allí correr y garramar toda la tierra circunvecina. Levantaron, pues, el rancho y diéronle a Andrés una pollina en que fuese, pero él no la quiso, sino irse a pie, sirviendo de lacayo a Preciosa, que sobre otra iba: ella contentísima de ver cómo triunfaba de su gallardo escudero, y él ni más ni menos, de ver junto a sí a la que había hecho señora de su albedrío.

up men and horses! Especially since, among us, to be publicly flogged is to have a badge on your back which you like better than one worn on the breast: one of the best. The trick is not to end up kicking the air in the prime of our youth and for our earliest crimes; because we consider being lashed on the back, or churning up water in the galleys, as nothing at all. Andrés, my boy, repose for now in the nest beneath our wings, for when the time is right we'll set you flying, and in places where you won't return without a prey; and I stick by what I said: after every theft you'll lick your fingers with pleasure."

"Well, to make up for what I might have stolen during this period of grace," said Andrés, "I want to hand out two hundred gold escudos among everyone in camp."

As soon as he said this, many Gypsy men rushed him and, raising him in their arms and onto their shoulders, they chanted "The winner" and "Great Andrés," adding "And long live Preciosa, his beloved sweetheart!" The women did the same to Preciosa, not without arousing the envy of Cristina and other Gypsy girls who were present; for envy dwells in barbarian camps and shepherds' hovels just as it does in princely palaces, and it's vexing to see a neighbor prospering whom you don't consider more deserving than yourself.

After this, they ate a splendid meal; the promised money was doled out equitably and fairly; Andrés's praises were sung again, and Preciosa's beauty was lauded to the skies. Night fell and the mule was killed with a blow to the back of the head and buried so deep that Andrés felt safe from being discovered on its account; with it they buried its trappings, such as saddle, bridle, and girths, just as Indians bury their richest jewels along with the dead.

Andrés was amazed at all he had seen and heard and at the cleverness of the Gypsies; he was resolved to pursue his enterprise and succeed in it, without taking any part in their ways, or at least avoiding this in every way he could, intending to exempt himself from the bondage of obeying any unjust orders they might give him by paying them off with his money.

The next day, Andrés asked them to break camp and move far away from Madrid, because he was afraid of being recognized if he stayed there. They said they had already decided to go to the hills around Toledo and, from that vantage point, raid and plunder the surrounding territory. So they broke camp and gave Andrés a young she-ass to ride on; he refused it, preferring to walk, acting as a servant to Preciosa, who rode another young donkey; she was highly pleased to see how she lorded it over her gallant squire, and he felt the same, having beside him the girl whom he had made mistress over his free will.

¡Oh poderosa fuerza deste que llaman dulce dios de la amargura (título que le ha dado la ociosidad y el descuido nuestro), y con qué veras nos avasallas, y cuán sin respecto nos tratas! Caballero es Andrés, y mozo de muy buen entendimiento, criado casi toda su vida en la Corte y con el regalo de sus ricos padres; y desde ayer acá ha hecho tal mudanza, que engañó a sus criados y a sus amigos, defraudó las esperanzas que sus padres en él tenían; dejó el camino de Flandes, donde había de ejercitar el valor de su persona y acrecentar la honra de su linaje, y se vino a postrarse a los pies de una muchacha, y a ser su lacayo; que, puesto que hermosísima, en fin, era gitana: privilegio de la hermosura, que trae al redopelo y por la melena a sus pies a la voluntad más esenta.

De allí a cuatro días llegaron a una aldea dos leguas de Toledo, donde asentaron su aduar, dando primero algunas prendas de plata al alcalde del pueblo, en fianzas de que en él ni en todo su término no hartarían ninguna cosa. Hecho esto, todas las gitanas viejas, y algunas mozas, y los gitanos, se esparcieron por todos los lugares, o, a lo menos, apartados por cuatro y cinco leguas de aquel donde habían asentado su real. Fue con ellos Andrés a tomar la primera lición de ladrón; pero, aunque le dieron muchas en aquella salida, ninguna se le asentó; antes, correspondiendo a su buena sangre, con cada hurto que sus maestros hacían se le arrancaba a él el alma; y tal vez hubo que pagó de su dinero los hurtos que sus compañeros habían hecho, conmovido de las lágrimas de sus dueños; de lo cual los gitanos se desesperaban, diciéndole que era contravenir a sus estatutos y ordenanzas, que prohibían la entrada a la caridad en sus pechos, la cual, en teniéndola, habían de dejar de ser ladrones, cosa que no les estaba bien en ninguna manera.

Viendo, pues, esto Andrés, dijo que él quería hurtar por sí solo, sin ir en compañía de nadie; porque para huir del peligro tenía ligereza, y para cometelle no le faltaba el ánimo; así que, el premio o el castigo de lo que hurtase quería que fuese suyo.

Procuraron los gitanos disuadirle deste propósito, diciéndole que le podrían suceder ocasiones donde fuese necesaria la compañía, así para acometer como para defenderse, y que una persona sola no podía hacer grandes presas. Pero, por más que dijeron, Andrés quiso ser ladrón solo y señero, con intención de apartarse de la cuadrilla y comprar por su dinero alguna cosa que pudiese decir que la había hurtado, y deste modo cargar lo que menos pudiese sobre su conciencia.

Usando, pues, desta industria, en menos de un mes trujo más provecho a la compañía que trujeron cuatro de los más estirados ladrones della; de que no poco se holgaba Preciosa, viendo a su tierno

Oh, what a mighty power is that of the being who is called "sweet god of bitterness" (a title given him by our idleness and carelessness); how truly you make us your vassals, and how disrespectfully you treat us! Andrés is a knight, a lad of very high intelligence, reared almost all his life in the capital amid the comfort provided by his rich parents; and since yesterday he has changed so much that he has deceived his servants and friends and cheated the hopes his parents had of him; has abandoned the road to Flanders, where he was to display his personal valor and augment the honor of his lineage; and has come to prostrate himself at a girl's feet and be her servant; for, most beautiful as she was, she was after all a Gypsy—a privilege of beauty, which violently reduces to submissiveness the most impartial will.

Four days later, they reached a village two leagues from Toledo, where they set up camp, first giving some silver objects to the mayor, as an assurance that they wouldn't steal anything in the village or all its limits. Afterward, all the old Gypsy women, and some of the young ones, and the Gypsy men scattered through every hamlet, or at least the ones four or five leagues distant from the one where they had camped. Andrés went with them to take his first lesson in theft; but, even though they gave him many lessons during that excursion, none stuck with him; on the contrary, in accordance with his noble blood, his soul was pained by every theft his teachers committed; and there were times when he paid with his own money the value of his comrades' thefts, touched by the tears of the property owners. The Gypsies fretted over this, telling him that he was contravening their statutes and ordinances, which forbade the entrance of charity into their hearts; if they acquired charitable feelings, they would have to stop stealing, which in no way suited them.

So Andrés, seeing this, said that he wanted to steal on his own, with no one for company, because he was fast enough to escape danger, and brave enough to face it; so that he wanted the reward or punishment for his thefts to be his alone.

The Gypsies tried to talk him out of that resolve, saying that he could run into risky situations in which their company was needed, for both offense and defense, and that one individual couldn't gain much booty. But, no matter what they said, Andrés insisted on being a lone-wolf thief, intending to get away from the gang and to buy with his money things he could say he had stolen, thus loading the least possible burden on his conscience.

So, using this stratagem, in less than a month he brought more profit to the group than any four of its most notorious thieves; Preciosa was highly pleased at this, seeing her tender lover such a fine, capable thief.

amante tan lindo y tan despejado ladrón. Pero, con todo eso, estaba temerosa de alguna desgracia; que no quisiera ella verle en afrenta por todo el tesoro de Venecia, obligada a tenerle aquella buena voluntad por los muchos servicios y regalos que su Andrés le hacía.

Poco más de un mes se estuvieron en los términos de Toledo, donde hicieron su agosto, aunque era por el mes de setiembre, y desde allí se entraron en Estremadura, por ser tierra rica y caliente. Pasaba Andrés con Preciosa honestos, discretos y enamorados coloquios, y ella poco a poco se iba enamorando de la discreción y buen trato de su amante; y él, del mismo modo, si pudiera crecer su amor, fuera creciendo: tal era la honestidad, discreción y belleza de su Preciosa. A doquiera que llegaban, él se llevaba el precio y las apuestas de corredor y de saltar más que ninguno; jugaba a los bolos y a la pelota estremadamente; tiraba la barra con mucha fuerza y singular destreza. Finalmente, en poco tiempo voló su fama por toda Estremadura, y no había lugar donde no se hablase de la gallarda disposición del gitano Andrés Caballero y de sus gracias y habilidades; y al par desta fama corría la de la hermosura de la gitanilla, y no había villa, lugar ni aldea donde no los llamasen para regocijar las fiestas votivas suyas, o para otros particulares regocijos. Desta manera, iba el aduar rico, próspero y contento, y los amantes gozosos con sólo mirarse.

Sucedió, pues, que, teniendo el aduar entre unas encinas, algo apartado del camino real, oyeron una noche, casi a la mitad della, ladrar sus perros con mucho ahínco y más de lo que acostumbraban; salieron algunos gitanos, y con ellos Andrés, a ver a quién ladraban, y vieron que se defendía dellos un hombre vestido de blanco, a quien tenían dos perros asido de una pierna; llegaron y quitáronle, y uno de los gitanos le dijo:

—¿Quién diablos os trujo por aquí, hombre, a tales horas y tan fuera de camino? ¿Venís a hurtar por ventura? Porque en verdad que habéis llegado a buen puerto.

—No vengo a hurtar —respondió el mordido—, ni sé si vengo o no fuera de camino, aunque bien veo que vengo descaminado. Pero decidme, señores, ¿está por aquí alguna venta o lugar donde pueda recogerme esta noche y curarme de las heridas que vuestros perros me han hecho?

—No hay lugar ni venta donde podamos encaminaros —respondió Andrés—; mas, para curar vuestras heridas y alojaros esta noche, no os faltará comodidad en nuestros ranchos. Veníos con nosotros, que, aunque somos gitanos, no lo parecemos en la caridad.

Nevertheless, she was afraid of some misfortune, because she didn't want to see him endure infamy, not for all the treasures of Venice. She was obliged to bear her Andrés that good will for all the services he did her, and the gifts he gave her.

They remained in the Toledo area for a little over a month, making their "August harvest" there, even though it was September; from there they entered Extremadura, because it was a wealthy and warm region. Andrés and Preciosa had honorable, prudent, and loving conversations, and she gradually fell in love with her suitor's wisdom and fine behavior; likewise, if it was possible to love her more, he did, such were his Preciosa's chastity, wisdom, and beauty. Wherever they traveled, he won more prizes and wagers for running and jumping than anyone else; he played ninepins and pelota extremely well; he hurled the iron bar with great strength and unusual skill. Finally, before very long his renown spread throughout Extremadura, and in every hamlet people spoke about the gallant nature of the Gypsy Andrés Caballero, and of his grace and talents; similarly, the renown of the Gypsy girl's beauty spread, and there was no town, hamlet, or village where they weren't summoned to brighten up the votive feasts, or for other special festivities. In this way the Gypsy camp became rich, prosperous, and contented, and the lovers were in bliss at the mere sight of each other.

Well, it came about that, while encamped among some holm oaks, somewhat aside from the highway, about midnight one night they heard their dogs barking very fiercely and more loudly than usual; a few Gypsies went out, Andrés among them, to see whom they were barking at, and saw a man dressed in white defending himself from them; two dogs had gripped him by a leg. They came and released him, and one of the Gypsies asked:

"What the hell are you doing here, fellow, at this hour and so far from the road? Have you come to steal by any chance? Because, in truth, you've come to the right place."

"I'm not here to steal," the bitten man replied, "and I don't know whether I'm far from the road or not, though I see clearly I've gone astray. But tell me, gentlemen, is there any inn or hamlet around here where I can lodge tonight and tend to the wounds your dogs have given me?"

"There's no hamlet or inn to which we can direct you," Andrés replied, "but, as for tending to your wounds and lodging you tonight, you won't lack hospitality in our camp. Come with us, for, though we're Gypsies, we don't resemble them when it comes to charity."

—Dios la use con vosotros —respondió el hombre—; y llevadme donde quisiéredes, que el dolor desta pierna me fatiga mucho.

Llegóse a él Andrés y otro gitano caritativo (que aun entre los demonios hay unos peores que otros, y entre muchos malos hombres suele haber algún bueno), y entre los dos le llevaron. Hacía la noche clara con la luna, de manera que pudieron ver que el hombre era mozo de gentil rostro y talle; venía vestido todo de lienzo blanco, y atravesada por las espaldas y ceñida a los pechos una como camisa o talega de lienzo. Llegaron a la barraca o toldo de Andrés, y con presteza encendieron lumbre y luz, y acudió luego la abuela de Preciosa a curar el herido, de quien ya le habían dado cuenta. Tomó algunos pelos de los perros, friólos en aceite, y, lavando primero con vino dos mordeduras que tenía en la pierna izquierda, le puso los pelos con el aceite en ellas y encima un poco de romero verde mascado; lióselo muy bien con paños limpios y santiguóle las heridas y díjole:

—Dormid, amigo, que, con el ayuda de Dios, no será nada.

En tanto que curaban al herido, estaba Preciosa delante, y estúvole mirando ahincadamente, y lo mismo hacía él a ella, de modo que Andrés echó de ver en la atención con que el mozo la miraba; pero echólo a que la mucha hermosura de Preciosa se llevaba tras sí los ojos. En resolución, después de curado el mozo, le dejaron solo sobre un lecho hecho de heno seco, y por entonces no quisieron preguntarle nada de su camino ni de otra cosa.

Apenas se apartaron dél, cuando Preciosa llamó a Andrés aparte y le dijo:

—¿Acuérdaste, Andrés, de un papel que se me cayó en tu casa cuando bailaba con mis compañeras, que, según creo, te dio un mal rato?

—Sí acuerdo —respondió Andrés—, y era un soneto en tu alabanza, y no malo.

—Pues has de saber, Andrés —replicó Preciosa—, que el que hizo aquel soneto es ese mozo mordido que dejamos en la choza; y en ninguna manera me engaño, porque me habló en Madrid dos o tres veces, y aun me dio un romance muy bueno. Allí andaba, a mi parecer, como paje; mas no de los ordinarios, sino de los favorecidos de algún príncipe; y en verdad te digo, Andrés, que el mozo es discreto, y bien razonado, y sobremanera honesto, y no sé qué pueda imaginar desta su venida y en tal traje.

—¿Qué puedes imaginar, Preciosa? —respondió Andrés—. Ninguna otra cosa sino que la misma fuerza que a mí me ha hecho gitano le ha hecho a él parecer molinero y venir a buscarte. ¡Ah,

"May God have charity with you!" the man replied. "Take me wherever you want, because the pain in this leg is very troublesome to me."

Andrés went up to him with another charitable Gypsy (for even among devils some are worse than others, and among a number of evil men there is usually some good one), and the two of them lifted him up. It was a clear, moonlight night, so that they could see the man was young, with a pleasant face and appearance; he was dressed all in white cloth, and slung over his back and tied across his chest he wore a sort of shirt or cloth sack. They reached Andrés's hut or tent, and quickly lit a fire and a lamp; then Preciosa's grandmother came to tend the wounded man, of whom she had already been informed. She took a few hairs of the dogs, fried them in oil, and, first washing with wine two bites he had in his left leg, she placed the hairs and oil on them, with a little chewed-up green rosemary on top; she bound the wound up carefully with clean bandages, spoke a few prayers over them, and said to the man:

"Sleep, friend, for, with God's help, it won't be serious."

While they were tending the wounded man, Preciosa stood in front of him, staring at him intently, as he did at her, so that Andrés noticed the attention with which the young man was gazing at her; but he attributed this to Preciosa's great beauty, which drew all eyes. In a word, after the young man had been tended to, they left him alone on a bed of dry hay, and for the moment refrained from asking him any questions about his destination or anything else.

As soon as they moved away from him, Preciosa called Andrés aside and said:

"Andrés, do you remember a piece of paper which I dropped in your house while dancing with my companions, and which, as I believe, affected you badly?"

"Yes, I remember," Andrés replied. "It was a sonnet in your praise, and not a bad one."

"Then I want you to know, Andrés," Preciosa replied, "that the writer of that sonnet is the young man who was bitten, and whom we left in the hovel; I can't possibly be wrong, because he spoke to me in Madrid two or three times, and even gave me a very good ballad. There, as I believe, he was dressed as a page, but not one of the ordinary ones: one of those favored by some great nobleman. And I tell you truly, Andrés, that the fellow is clever, well spoken, and exceedingly honorable, and I don't know what to think about his arrival here in that getup."

"What *can* you think, Preciosa?" Andrés replied. "Only that the same force which turned me into a Gypsy has made him dress like a miller and come looking for you. Oh, Preciosa, Preciosa, how clear it's becoming that

Preciosa, Preciosa, y cómo se va descubriendo que te quieres preciar de tener más de un rendido! Y si esto es así, acábame a mí primero y luego matarás a este otro, y no quieras sacrificarnos juntos en las aras de tu engaño, por no decir de tu belleza.

—¡Válame Dios —respondió Preciosa—, Andrés, y cuán delicado andas, y cuán de un sotil cabello tienes colgadas tus esperanzas y mi crédito, pues con tanta facilidad te ha penetrado el alma la dura espada de los celos! Dime, Andrés: si en esto hubiera artificio o engaño alguno, ¿no supiera yo callar y encubrir quién era este mozo? ¿Soy tan necia, por ventura, que te había de dar ocasión de poner en duda mi bondad y buen término? Calla, Andrés, por tu vida, y mañana procura sacar del pecho deste tu asombro adónde va, o a lo que viene. Podría ser que estuviese engañada tu sospecha, como yo no lo estoy de que sea el que he dicho. Y, para más satisfación tuya, pues ya he llegado a términos de satisfacerte, de cualquiera manera y con cualquiera intención que ese mozo venga, despídele luego y haz que se vaya, pues todos los de nuestra parcialidad te obedecen, y no habrá ninguno que contra tu voluntad le quiera dar acogida en su rancho; y, cuando esto así no suceda, yo te doy mi palabra de no salir del mío, ni dejarme ver de sus ojos, ni de todos aquellos que tú quisieres que no me vean. Mira, Andrés, no me pesa a mí de verte celoso, pero pesarme ha mucho si te veo indiscreto.

—Como no me veas loco, Preciosa —respondió Andrés—, cualquiera otra demonstración será poca o ninguna para dar a entender adónde llega y cuánto fatiga la amarga y dura presunción de los celos. Pero, con todo eso, yo haré lo que me mandas, y sabré, si es que es posible, qué es lo que este señor paje poeta quiere, dónde va, o qué es lo que busca; que podría ser que por algún hilo que sin cuidado muestre, sacase yo todo el ovillo con que temo viene a enredarme.

—Nunca los celos, a lo que imagino —dijo Preciosa—, dejan el entendimiento libre para que pueda juzgar las cosas como ellas son. Siempre miran los celosos con antojos de allende, que hacen las cosas pequeñas, grandes; los enanos, gigantes, y las sospechas, verdades. Por vida tuya y por la mía, Andrés, que procedas en esto, y en todo lo que tocare a nuestros conciertos, cuerda y discretamente; que si así lo hicieres, sé que me has de conceder la palma de honesta y recatada, y de verdadera en todo estremo.

Con esto se despidió de Andrés, y él se quedó esperando el día para tomar la confesión al herido, llena de turbación el alma y de mil contrarias imaginaciones. No podía creer sino que aquel paje había venido allí atraído de la hermosura de Preciosa; porque piensa el ladrón que todos son de su condición. Por otra parte, la satisfación que

you want to pride yourself on having more than one submissive lover! If that's the case, finish me off first and then kill this other man; don't try to sacrifice us together on the altar of your deceit, not to say: of your beauty."

"God help me, Andrés!" Preciosa replied. "How touchy you are, and on what a slender hair you hang your hopes and my reputation, if the hard sword of jealousy has so easily pierced your soul! Tell me, Andrés: if I were being at all artful or deceitful in this, couldn't I have kept still and concealed that boy's identity? Am I by chance so stupid as to give you occasion to cast doubts on my kindness and good nature? Quiet, Andrés, on your life, and tomorrow try to worm out of this bugaboo of yours where he's going, or what he's come for. Maybe your suspicions are mistaken, though *I'm* not as to his being who I said. And, for your greater satisfaction, since I've already made it my goal to satisfy you—whatever way and for whatever purpose this boy has come, send him packing right away and make him go, since everyone in our group obeys you, and no one will want to receive him in his hut against your will; and if that doesn't happen, I promise you not to step outside of *mine,* or let him catch a glimpse of me, or let anyone else do so whom you don't want to see me. Look, Andrés, I'm not sorry to see you jealous, but I'd be very sorry to see you foolish."

"As long as you don't see me crazy, Preciosa," Andrés replied. "Any other proof would be negligible or null to make you understand the extent and the vexation of the bitter and hard suspicions of a jealous man. Nevertheless, I'll do what you command, and, if it all possible, I'll find out what this young page and poet wants, where he's going, or what he's after; maybe one thread that he reveals unwittingly will unravel the whole skein in which I'm afraid he has come to entangle me."

"As far as I can see," said Preciosa, "jealousy never leaves the mind clear enough to be able to judge things as they are. Jealous men always see things through magnifying lenses, which make little things big, turning dwarfs into giants and suspicions into truths. On your life and mine, Andrés, proceed in this matter, and in everything relating to our agreement, sanely and prudently; if you do, I know that you will give me the palm for chastity and modesty, and extreme truthfulness."

Therewith she took leave of Andrés, and he remained awaiting the daylight in order to hear the wounded man's confession, his soul filled with turmoil and a thousand contradictory imaginings. He could believe only that the page had come there drawn by Preciosa's beauty; because a thief thinks everyone is of the same nature as himself. On the other hand, the satisfaction that Preciosa had given him seemed to be so strong that it

Preciosa le había dado le parecía ser de tanta fuerza, que le obligaba a vivir seguro y a dejar en las manos de su bondad toda su ventura.

Llegóse el día, visitó al mordido; preguntóle cómo se llamaba y adónde iba, y cómo caminaba tan tarde y tan fuera de camino; aunque primero le preguntó cómo estaba, y si se sentía sin dolor de las mordeduras. A lo cual respondió el mozo que se hallaba mejor a sin dolor alguno, y de manera que podía ponerse en camino. A lo de decir su nombre y adónde iba, no dijo otra cosa sino que se llamaba Alonso Hurtado, y que iba a Nuestra Señora de la Peña de Francia a un cierto negocio, y que por llegar con brevedad caminaba de noche, y que la pasada había perdido el camino, y acaso había dado con aquel aduar; donde los perros que le guardaban le habían puesto del modo que había visto.

No le pareció a Andrés legítima esta declaración, sino muy bastarda, y de nuevo volvieron a hacerle cosquillas en el alma sus sospechas; y así, le dijo:

—Hermano, si yo fuera juez y vos hubiérades caído debajo de mi jurisdición por algún delito, el cual pidiera que se os hicieran las preguntas que yo os he hecho, la respuesta que me habéis dado obligara a que os apretara los cordeles. Yo no quiero saber quién sois, cómo os llamáis o adónde vais; pero adviértoos que, si os conviene mentir en este vuestro viaje, mintáis con más apariencia de verdad. Decís que vais a la Peña de Francia, y dejáisla a la mano derecha, más atrás deste lugar donde estamos bien treinta leguas; camináis de noche por llegar presto, y vais fuera de camino por entre bosques y encinares que no tienen sendas apenas, cuanto más caminos. Amigo, levantaos y aprended a mentir, y andad en hora buena. Pero, por este buen aviso que os doy, ¿no me diréis una verdad? (Que sí diréis, pues tan mal sabéis mentir). Decidme: ¿sois por ventura uno que yo he visto muchas veces en la Corte, entre paje y caballero, que tenía fama de ser gran poeta; uno que hizo un romance y un soneto a una gitanilla que los días pasados andaba en Madrid, que era tenida por singular en la belleza? Decídmelo, que yo os prometo por la fe de caballero gitano de guardaros el secreto que vos viéredes que os conviene. Mirad que negarme la verdad, de que no sois el que yo digo, no llevaría camino, porque este rostro que yo veo aquí es el que vi en Madrid. Sin duda alguna que la gran fama de vuestro entendimiento me hizo muchas veces que os mirase como a hombre raro e insigne, y así se me quedó en la memoria vuestra figura, que os he venido a conocer por ella, aun puesto en el diferente traje en que estáis agora del en que yo os vi entonces. No os turbéis; animaos, y no penséis que habéis llegado a un pueblo de

obliged him to live in peace and leave all his fortunes in the hands of her goodness.

Day arrived and he visited the man who had been bitten; he asked him his name and destination, and why he was walking so late and so far from the road, though first he asked him how he was feeling, and whether the bites were no longer hurting him. To which the young man replied that he was feeling better and suffering no pain, so that he could set out again. As for his name and destination, all he said was that he was called Alonso Hurtado, and that he was going on certain business to Our Lady of the Crag of France;[15] to get there quickly, he had been walking at night; the night before, he had strayed from the road and had happened to find that camp, where the dogs guarding it had caused the injuries Andrés had seen.

Andrés didn't find this statement legitimate, but very much of a bastard, and his suspicions began to irritate his soul again, so that he said:

"Brother, if I were a judge and you had come before my bench for some crime that required me to ask you the questions I just have, the answer you've given me would oblige me to stretch you on the rack. I don't want to know who you are, what you're called, or where you're heading; but I advise you, if it suits you to lie about this journey of yours, to tell lies that sound more like the truth. You say you're going to the Crag of France, but you've left it behind on your right, a good thirty leagues behind the place we're in; you were walking at night to gain time, but you left the road and walked among woods and oak groves that barely have paths, let alone roads. Friend, get up and learn how to lie, and leave at once. But, in exchange for this good advice I'm giving you, won't you tell me one true thing? (You surely will, because you're such a bad liar.) Tell me: are you by chance a man I've often seen in the capital, something between a page and a gentleman, who had the renown of being a great poet, a man who wrote a ballad and a sonnet to a Gypsy girl who was lately in Madrid and was considered outstandingly beautiful? Tell me this, and I promise you on the word of a gentleman Gypsy to keep any secret you find convenient. Look, to deny the truth, saying you're not the man I mean, won't wash, because the face I see here is the one I saw in Madrid. No doubt, your great reputation for intelligence made me gaze at you often as at a rare, illustrious man, and your face remained so fixed in my memory that I've recognized you by it, though you're now wearing clothes different from those I saw you in then. Don't get upset; take heart, and imagine not that you've fallen into a den of thieves, but into a place

15. A Dominican monastery southwest of Salamanca.

ladrones, sino a un asilo que os sabrá guardar y defender de todo el mundo. Mirad, yo imagino una cosa, y si es ansí como la imagino, vos habéis topado con vuestra buena suerte en haber encontrado conmigo. Lo que imagino es que, enamorado de Preciosa, aquella hermosa gitanica a quien hicisteis los versos, habéis venido a buscarla, por lo que yo no os tendré en menos, sino en mucho más; que, aunque gitano, la esperiencia me ha mostrado adónde se estiende la poderosa fuerza de amor, y las transformaciones que hace hacer a los que coge debajo de su jurisdición y mando. Si esto es así, como creo que sin duda lo es, aquí está la gitanica.

—Sí, aquí está, que yo la vi anoche —dijo el mordido; razón con que Andrés quedó como difunto, pareciéndole que había salido al cabo con la confirmación de sus sospechas—. Anoche la vi —tornó a referir el mozo—, pero no me atreví a decirle quién era, porque no me convenía.

—Desa manera —dijo Andrés—, vos sois el poeta que yo he dicho.

—Sí soy —replicó el mancebo—; que no lo puedo ni lo quiero negar. Quizá podía ser que donde he pensado perderme hubiese venido a ganarme, si es que hay fidelidad en las selvas y buen acogimiento en los montes.

—Hayle, sin duda —respondió Andrés—, y entre nosotros, los gitanos, el mayor secreto del mundo. Con esta confianza podéis, señor, descubrirme vuestro pecho, que hallaréis en el mío lo que veréis, sin doblez alguno. La gitanilla es parienta mía, y está sujeta a lo que quisiere hacer della; si la quisiéredes por esposa, yo y todos sus parientes gustaremos dello; y si por amiga, no usaremos de ningún melindre, con tal que tengáis dineros, porque la codicia por jamás sale de nuestros ranchos.

—Dineros traigo —respondió el mozo—: en estas mangas de camisa que traigo ceñida por el cuerpo vienen cuatrocientos escudos de oro.

Éste fue otro susto mortal que recibió Andrés, viendo que el traer tanto dinero no era sino para conquistar o comprar su prenda; y, con lengua ya turbada, dijo:

—Buena cantidad es ésa; no hay sino descubriros, y manos a labor, que la muchacha, que no es nada boba, verá cuán bien le está ser vuestra.

—¡Ay amigo! —dijo a esta sazón el mozo—, quiero que sepáis que la fuerza que me ha hecho mudar de traje no es la de amor, que vos decís, ni de desear a Preciosa, que hermosas tiene Madrid que pueden y saben robar los corazones y rendir las almas tan bien y mejor que las más hermosas gitanas, puesto que confieso que la hermosura de vuestra parienta a todas las que yo he visto se aventaja. Quien me tiene en este traje, a pie y mordido de perros, no es amor, sino desgracia mía.

of asylum that can save and protect you from the whole world. Look, I see one thing, and if it's as I see it, you have encountered your good luck in coming across me. What I see is that, in love with Preciosa, that beautiful Gypsy girl to whom you wrote poems, you have come looking for her; for that, I'll think none the less of you; in fact, all the more; for, though I'm a Gypsy, experience has taught me how extensive the mighty force of love is, and the metamorphoses it causes those to undergo who are caught beneath its rule and command. If this is true, as I believe it surely is, the Gypsy girl is here."

"Yes, she's here, because I saw her last night," said the bitten man; hearing this, Andrés became like a dead man, believing that he had definitely confirmed his suspicions. "I saw her last night," the young man repeated, "but I didn't dare tell her who I was, because it didn't suit my purposes."

"So that you're the poet I mentioned," said Andrés.

"Yes, I am," the lad replied. "I can't deny it and I don't want to. It may be that where I thought I was getting lost I've found safety for myself, if there's fidelity in forests and hospitality on hills."

"No doubt there is," Andrés replied, "and among us Gypsies there's the greatest secrecy in the world. Having this trust, sir, you may open your heart to me; in mine you'll find just what you see, without any duplicity. The Gypsy girl is a relative of mine, and is obliged to do what I demand of her; if you should want her for your wife, I and all her other relatives will be very happy; if you want her for a mistress, we won't be at all finicky, as long as you've got money, because greed never departs from our encampments."

"I've got money with me," the youth replied. "In these shirtsleeves I have tied around my body there are four hundred gold escudos."

This gave Andrés another mortal fright; he saw that the carrying of so much money could only be for the purpose of conquering or buying his sweetheart; with a tongue already thick, he said:

"That's a large amount; all you have to do is reveal yourself and set to work, because the girl, who's no fool, will see how good it is for her to belong to you."

"Ah, my friend!" the youth then said. "I'd like you to know that the power which made me change clothes isn't the power of love, as you say, or of desire for Preciosa, because Madrid has beautiful women able to steal hearts and make souls surrender just as well as, if not better than, the most beautiful Gypsies, although I confess that the beauty of your kinswoman exceeds all I've seen. What brings me to wear this garb, to go on foot, and to be bitten by dogs, is not love but my misfortune."

Con estas razones que el mozo iba diciendo, iba Andrés cobrando los espíritus perdidos, pareciéndole que se encaminaban a otro paradero del que él se imaginaba; y deseoso de salir de aquella confusión, volvió a reforzarle la seguridad con que podía descubrirse; y así, él prosiguió diciendo:

—«Yo estaba en Madrid en casa de un título, a quien servía no como a señor, sino como a pariente. Éste tenía un hijo, único heredero suyo, el cual, así por el parentesco como por ser ambos de una edad y de una condición misma, me trataba con familiaridad y amistad grande. Sucedió que este caballero se enamoró de una doncella principal, a quien él escogiera de bonísima gana para su esposa, si no tuviera la voluntad sujeta, como buen hijo, a la de sus padres, que aspiraban a casarle más altamente; pero, con todo eso, la servía a hurto de todos los ojos que pudieran, con las lenguas, sacar a la plaza sus deseos; solos los míos eran testigos de sus intentos. Y una noche, que debía de haber escogido la desgracia para el caso que ahora os diré, pasando los dos por la puerta y calle desta señora, vimos arrimados a ella dos hombres, al parecer, de buen talle. Quiso reconocerlos mi pariente, y apenas se encaminó hacia ellos, cuando echaron con mucha ligereza mano a las espadas y a dos broqueles, y se vinieron a nosotros, que hicimos lo mismo, y con iguales armas nos acometimos. Duró poco la pendencia, porque no duró mucho la vida de los dos contrarios, que, de dos estocadas que guiaron los celos de mi pariente y la defensa que yo le hacía, las perdieron (caso estraño y pocas veces visto). Triunfando, pues, de lo que no quisiéramos, volvimos a casa, y, secretamente, tomando todos los dineros que podimos, nos fuimos a San Jerónimo, esperando el día, que descubriese lo sucedido y las presunciones que se tenían de los matadores. Supimos que de nosotros no había indicio alguno, y aconsejáronnos los prudentes religiosos que nos volviésemos a casa, y que no diésemos ni despertásemos con nuestra ausencia alguna sospecha contra nosotros. Y, ya que estábamos determinados de seguir su parecer, nos avisaron que los señores alcaldes de Corte habían preso en su casa a los padres de la doncella y a la misma doncella, y que entre otros criados a quien tomaron la confesión, una criada de la señora dijo cómo mi pariente paseaba a su señora de noche y de día; y que con este indicio habían acudido a buscarnos, y no hallándonos, sino muchas señales de nuestra fuga, se confirmó en toda la Corte ser nosotros los matadores de aquellos dos caballeros, que lo eran, y muy principales. Finalmente, con parecer del conde mi pariente, y del de los religiosos, después de quince días que estuvimos escondidos en el monasterio, mi camarada, en hábito de fraile, con otro fraile se fue la vuelta de Aragón, con intención de pasarse a Italia, y

Hearing these latest words of the youth, Andrés regained his lost courage, as it seemed to him they were tending toward an end different from the one he had imagined; and, eager to escape from that confusion, he once more assured him how safe it was for him to reveal the truth; so the youth continued:

"I was in Madrid in the home of a nobleman whom I served not as my master, but as my kinsman. He had a son, his sole heir, who, since we were related and both of the same age and nature, treated me with great familiarity and friendship. This gentleman happened to fall in love with a girl from a prominent family, whom he would most gladly have chosen as his wife had his wishes not been constrained, like the good son he was, by those of his parents, who aspired to a loftier marriage for him; nevertheless, he continued to woo her out of sight of all eyes which, along with tongues, might disclose his desires; only mine were witnesses of his intentions. And one night, which misfortune must have chosen for the event I shall soon narrate, as the two of us passed by this lady's street door, we saw leaning against it two men, seemingly of good appearance. My kinsman wanted to see who they were, but as soon as he walked toward them, they very swiftly laid hand to their swords and two bucklers, and approached us. We did the same, and assaulted them with equal arms. The fight didn't last long, because the lives of our two opponents didn't last long: with two thrusts guided by my kinsman's jealousy and my defense of him, they lost them (a strange, very rare event). So, then, triumphing over something we hadn't wanted, we returned home and, secretly taking all the money we could, we fled to asylum in Saint Jerome's, waiting for daylight to reveal what had happened and any suspicions as to who the killers might be. We knew that nothing pointed to us, and the prudent monks advised us to return home, neither giving nor arousing by our absence any suspicion against us. But, when already determined to follow their advice, we were informed that the chief magistrates of the capital had arrested in their home the girl's parents and the girl herself, and that among other servants whose statements they were taking, one of the lady's maids described how my kinsman used to court her lady night and day; on this notice, they had come looking for us; when they failed to find us, but found many signs of our escape, it was confirmed all over the capital that we were the killers of those two gentlemen, for so they were, and very highly placed. Finally, on the advice of my relative the count, and of the monks, after hiding in the monastery for two weeks, my comrade, in a friar's habit, left in the direction of Aragon with another friar, intending to cross over to Italy, and from there to

desde allí a Flandes, hasta ver en qué paraba el caso. Yo quise dividir y apartar nuestra fortuna, y que no corriese nuestra suerte por una misma derrota; seguí otro camino diferente del suyo, y, en hábito de mozo de fraile, a pie, salí con un religioso, que me dejó en Talavera; desde allí aquí he venido solo y fuera de camino, hasta que anoche llegué a este encinal, donde me ha sucedido lo que habéis visto. Y si pregunté por el camino de la Peña de Francia, fue por responder algo a lo que se me preguntaba; que en verdad que no sé dónde cae la Peña de Francia, puesto que sé que está más arriba de Salamanca.»

—Así es verdad —respondió Andrés—, y ya la dejáis a mano derecha, casi veinte leguas de aquí; porque veáis cuán derecho camino llevábades si allá fuérades.

—El que yo pensaba llevar —replicó el mozo— no es sino a Sevilla; que allí tengo un caballero ginovés, grande amigo del conde mi pariente, que suele enviar a Génova gran cantidad de plata, y llevo disignio que me acomode con los que la suelen llevar, como uno dellos; y con esta estratagema seguramente podré pasar hasta Cartagena, y de allí a Italia, porque han de venir dos galeras muy presto a embarcar esta plata. Ésta es, buen amigo, mi historia: mirad si puedo decir que nace más de desgracia pura que de amores aguados. Pero si estos señores gitanos quisiesen llevarme en su compañía hasta Sevilla, si es que van allá, yo se lo pagaría muy bien; que me doy a entender que en su compañía iría más seguro, y no con el temor que llevo.

—Sí llevarán —respondió Andrés—; y si no fuéredes en nuestro aduar, porque hasta ahora no sé si va al Andalucía, iréis en otro que creo que habemos de topar dentro de dos días, y con darles algo de lo que lleváis, facilitaréis con ellos otros imposibles mayores.

Dejóle Andrés, y vino a dar cuenta a los demás gitanos de lo que el mozo le había contado y de lo que pretendía, con el ofrecimiento que hacía de la buena paga y recompensa. Todos fueron de parecer que se quedase en el aduar. Sólo Preciosa tuvo el contrario, y la abuela dijo que ella no podía ir a Sevilla, ni a sus contornos, a causa que los años pasados había hecho una burla en Sevilla a un gorrero llamado Triguillos, muy conocido en ella, al cual le había hecho meter en una tinaja de agua hasta el cuello, desnudo en carnes, y en la cabeza puesta una corona de ciprés, esperando el filo de la media noche para salir de la tinaja a cavar y sacar un gran tesoro que ella le había hecho creer que estaba en cierta parte de su casa. Dijo que, como oyó el buen gorrero tocar a maitines, por no perder la coyuntura, se dio tanta priesa

Flanders, until he could see how things turned out. I decided to separate and divide our fortunes, so that our fate wouldn't depend on a single route; I took another road different from his and, dressed as a friar's servant, on foot, I set out with a monk, who left me at Talavera; from there to here I've come alone and off the road, until last night I reached this oak grove where you saw what happened to me. And if I asked for the way to the Crag of France, it was only to make some reply to what I was asked, because I truly don't know where the Crag of France is, except that it's farther up than Salamanca."

"That's true," Andrés replied, "and you've already left it behind on your right, nearly twenty leagues from here;[16] so that you can see what a direct road you were following if you were going there."

"The only road I intended to take," the youth replied, "is the one to Seville; there I know a Genovese gentleman, a great friend of my relative the count, who is accustomed to send a great quantity of silver to Genoa; my plan is to take a place with the people who usually transport it, as one of them; by that stratagem I will surely be able to get to Cartagena, and from there to Italy, because two galleys are to come very soon to take on that silver. That, good friend, is my story: see if I can't say that it arises more from pure misfortune than from diluted, unrequited love! But if these good Gypsies were willing to take me along with them to Seville, if they're going there, I'd pay them very handsomely for it; because I realize I'd be safer in their company, and not as fearful as I now am."

"They *will* take you," Andrés replied, "and if it isn't in our group, because up to now I don't know if it's going to Andalusia, you'll go with another which I think we'll meet up with in two days; if you give them some of what you have with you, you'll overcome even greater difficulties with them."

Andrés left him and went to inform the other Gypsies of what the youth had told him and what he wanted to do, along with his offer of good payment and reward. They all thought he should stay in their camp. Only Preciosa was of the opposite opinion, and her grandmother told her she couldn't go to Seville or its environs because years earlier she had played a trick on a sponger named Triguillos, very well known there; she had made him enter a huge earthenware jar, up to his neck in water, stripped naked, with a cypress wreath on his head, awaiting the stroke of midnight before emerging from the jar to dig up and raise a great treasure she had made him believe was buried in a certain part of his house. She said that, when this fine sponger heard the matins bell, he made such haste in getting out of the jar, so as not to miss the proper moment, that he and it fell

16. A page or two earlier, it was "a good thirty leagues."

a salir de la tinaja, que dio con ella y con él en el suelo, y con el golpe y con los cascos se magulló las carnes, derramóse el agua y él quedó nadando en ella, y dando voces que se anegaba. Acudieron su mujer y sus vecinos con luces, y halláronle haciendo efectos de nadador, soplando y arrastrando la barriga por el suelo, y meneando brazos y piernas con mucha priesa, y diciendo a grandes voces: «¡Socorro, señores, que me ahogo!»; tal le tenía el miedo, que verdaderamente pensó que se ahogaba. Abrazáronse con él, sacáronle de aquel peligro, volvió en sí, contó la burla de la gitana, y, con todo eso, cavó en la parte señalada más de un estado en hondo, a pesar de todos cuantos le decían que era embuste mío; y si no se lo estorbara un vecino suyo, que tocaba ya en los cimientos de su casa, él diera con entrambas en el suelo, si le dejaran cavar todo cuanto él quisiera. Súpose este cuento por toda la ciudad, y hasta los muchachos le señalaban con el dedo y contaban su credulidad y mi embuste.

Esto contó la gitana vieja, y esto dio por escusa para no ir a Sevilla. Los gitanos, que ya sabían de Andrés Caballero que el mozo traía dineros en cantidad, con facilidad le acogieron en su compañía y se ofrecieron de guardarle y encubrirle todo el tiempo que él quisiese, y determinaron de torcer el camino a mano izquierda y entrarse en la Mancha y en el reino de Murcia.

Llamaron al mozo y diéronle cuenta de lo que pensaban hacer por él; él se lo agradeció y dio cien escudos de oro para que los repartiesen entre todos. Con esta dádiva quedaron más blandos que unas martas; sólo a Preciosa no contentó mucho la quedada de don Sancho, que así dijo el mozo que se llamaba; pero los gitanos se le mudaron en el de Clemente, y así le llamaron desde allí adelante. También quedó un poco torcido Andrés, y no bien satisfecho de haberse quedado Clemente, por parecerle que con poco fundamento había dejado sus primeros designios. Mas Clemente, como si le leyera la intención, entre otras cosas le dijo que se holgaba de ir al reino de Murcia, por estar cerca de Cartagena, adonde si viniesen galeras, como él pensaba que habían de venir, pudiese con facilidad pasar a Italia. Finalmente, por traelle más ante los ojos y mirar sus acciones y escudriñar sus pensamientos, quiso Andrés que fuese Clemente su camarada, y Clemente tuvo esta amistad por gran favor que se le hacía. Andaban siempre juntos, gastaban largo, llovían escudos, corrían, saltaban, bailaban y tiraban la barra mejor que ninguno de los gitanos, y eran de las gitanas más que medianamente queridos, y de los gitanos en todo estremo respectados.

Dejaron, pues, a Estremadura y entráronse en la Mancha, y poco a poco fueron caminando al reino de Murcia. En todas las aldeas y lu-

to the floor, and the blow and the potsherds bruised his flesh; the water spilled and he remained swimming in it, shouting out that he was drowning. "His wife and neighbors came running with lights and found him going through a swimmer's motions, puffing and dragging his belly across the floor, making very swift arm and leg movements and crying loudly: 'Help, people, I'm drowning!' He was so frightened that he thought he really was. They seized him around his middle and rescued him from that danger; he recovered his senses and told them about the Gypsy's practical joke, but nevertheless dug a hole in the place indicated more than six feet deep, despite everyone who told him it was a trick of mine; and if he hadn't been prevented by a neighbor, when he had already reached the foundations of *his* house, he would have brought both houses crashing down if permitted to dig as much as he wanted. This story became known all over town, and even the little boys pointed to him and told about his gullibility and my trick."

This was narrated by the old Gypsy woman, who made it her pretext to avoid going to Seville. The Gypsies, who already knew from Andrés Caballero that the youth had a lot of money with him, readily welcomed him into their company and offered to guard and conceal him as long as he wished; they decided to deflect their route to the left and enter La Mancha and the kingdom of Murcia.

They summoned the youth and informed him of what they intended to do for him; he thanked them and gave them a hundred gold escudos to divide among them all. This gift made them as soft as marten fur; only Preciosa wasn't very contented with having Don Sancho remain (that's what the youth said his name was, but the Gypsies changed it to Clemente, and that's what they called him from then on). Andrés, too, was a little annoyed and not very satisfied to have Clemente stay, because it seemed to him that he had abandoned his first plan without a solid reason. But Clemente, as if reading his mind, told him among other things that he was glad to be going to the kingdom of Murcia because it was close to Cartagena, where, if galleys came, as he thought they would, he could easily cross over to Italy. Finally, to keep him in sight more, and to observe his actions and study his thoughts, Andrés insisted on Clemente being his chum, and Clemente considered this friendship as a great favor that was being done for him. They were always together, spending freely, showering escudos, running, jumping, dancing, and hurling the bar better than any of the Gypsies; and they were liked more than a little by the Gypsy women, and highly respected by the men.

So they left Extremadura and entered La Mancha, gradually proceeding toward the kingdom of Murcia. In all the villages and hamlets they

gares que pasaban había desafíos de pelota, de esgrima, de correr, de saltar, de tirar la barra y de otros ejercicios de fuerza, maña y ligereza, y de todos salían vencedores Andrés y Clemente, como de solo Andrés queda dicho. Y en todo este tiempo, que fueron más de mes y medio, nunca tuvo Clemente ocasión, ni él la procuró, de hablar a Preciosa, hasta que un día, estando juntos Andrés y ella, llegó él a la conversación, porque le llamaron, y Preciosa le dijo:

—Desde la vez primera que llegaste a nuestro aduar te conocí, Clemente, y se me vinieron a la memoria los versos que en Madrid me diste; pero no quise decir nada, por no saber con qué intención venías a nuestras estancias; y, cuando supe tu desgracia, me pesó en el alma, y se aseguró mi pecho, que estaba sobresaltado, pensando que como había don Juanes en el mundo, y que se mudaban en Andreses, así podía haber don Sanchos que se mudasen en otros nombres. Háblote desta manera porque Andrés me ha dicho que te ha dado cuenta de quién es y de la intención con que se ha vuelto gitano —y así era la verdad; que Andrés le había hecho sabidor de toda su historia, por poder comunicar con él sus pensamientos—. Y no pienses que te fue de poco provecho el conocerte, pues por mi respecto y por lo que yo de ti dije, se facilitó el acogerte y admitirte en nuestra compañía, donde plega a Dios te suceda todo el bien que acertares a desearte. Este buen deseo quiero que me pagues en que no afees a Andrés la bajeza de su intento, ni le pintes cuán mal le está perseverar en este estado; que, puesto que yo imagino que debajo de los candados de mi voluntad está la suya, todavía me pesaría de verle dar muestras, por mínimas que fuesen, de algún arrepentimiento.

A esto respondió Clemente:

—No pienses, Preciosa única, que don Juan con ligereza de ánimo me descubrió quién era: primero le conocí yo, y primero me descubrieron sus ojos sus intentos; primero le dije yo quién era, y primero le adiviné la prisión de su voluntad que tú señalas; y él, dándome el crédito que era razón que me diese, fió de mi secreto el suyo, y él es buen testigo si alabé su determinación y escogido empleo; que no soy, ¡oh Preciosa!, de tan corto ingenio que no alcance hasta dónde se estienden las fuerzas de la hermosura; y la tuya, por pasar de los límites de los mayores estremos de belleza, es disculpa bastante de mayores yerros, si es que deben llamarse yerros los que se hacen con tan forzosas causas. Agradézcote, señora, lo que en mi crédito dijiste, y yo pienso pagártelo en desear que estos enredos amorosos salgan a fines felices, y que tú goces de tu Andrés, y Andrés de su Preciosa, en conformidad y gusto de sus padres, porque de tan hermosa junta veamos en el mundo los más bellos renuevos que pueda formar la

passed through there were contests of pelota, fencing, running, jumping, hurling the bar, and other feats of strength, skill, and speed; from all of them Andrés and Clemente emerged as victors, as I said earlier about Andrés only. And in all this time, over a month and a half, Clemente never had, or sought, a chance to talk to Preciosa, until one day, when she and Andrés were together, he joined the conversation, because they called him over, and Preciosa said to him:

"As soon as you arrived in our camp I recognized you, Clemente, and I recalled the verses you gave me in Madrid; but I decided not to say anything, because I didn't know your purpose in coming to our settlement; and when I learned of your misfortune, I was truly sorry, and my heart, which had been alarmed, quieted down, thinking that, just as there were Don Juans in the world who changed into Andréses, there could also be Don Sanchos who changed into other names. I'm speaking to you this way because Andrés has told me that he has informed you of his identity and his purpose in becoming a Gypsy." (This was true: Andrés had let him know his whole story, in order to share his thoughts with him.) "And don't think that my recognizing you was of little use to you, since out of regard for me and because of what I said about you, it was easier to have you welcomed and admitted to our band, where I hope to God you will have all the good luck you may wish for yourself. I want you to repay me for this good will by not persuading Andrés that his aim is lowly or showing him how wrong he is to remain in this status; for, though I feel that his wishes are imprisoned by mine, I'd still be sorry to see him give signs, no matter how slight, of any regrets."

To which Clemente replied:

"Wonderful Preciosa, don't imagine that Don Juan revealed his identity to me thoughtlessly: before that, I knew him, and before that, his eyes revealed his intentions to me; before that, I told him who I was and before that, I divined the imprisonment of his will that you have mentioned; and, believing in me as it was right that he should, he entrusted his secret to my discretion, and he can readily testify that I praised his decision and chosen profession; for, Preciosa, I'm not so dull-witted as not to grasp how far the powers of beauty extend; and yours, because it surpasses the furthest extremes of beauty, is sufficient excuse for even greater errors, if those can be called errors which are made for such necessary reasons. Madam, I thank you for what you said in my behalf, and I intend to repay you for it by wishing that this romantic entanglement turns out happily, and that you enjoy your Andrés, and Andrés his Preciosa, with the consent and pleasure of his parents, so that from such a lovely pairing we may see in the world the most beautiful offspring that well-intentioned nature

bien intencionada naturaleza. Esto desearé yo, Preciosa, y esto le diré siempre a tu Andrés, y no cosa alguna que le divierta de sus bien colocados pensamientos.

Con tales afectos dijo las razones pasadas Clemente, que estuvo en duda Andrés si las había dicho como enamorado o como comedido; que la infernal enfermedad celosa es tan delicada, y de tal manera, que en los átomos del sol se pega, y de los que tocan a la cosa amada se fatiga el amante y se desespera. Pero, con todo esto, no tuvo celos confirmados, más fiado de la bondad de Preciosa que de la ventura suya, que siempre los enamorados se tienen por infelices en tanto que no alcanzan lo que desean. En fin, Andrés y Clemente eran camaradas y grandes amigos, asegurándolo todo la buena intención de Clemente y el recato y prudencia de Preciosa, que jamás dio ocasión a que Andrés tuviese della celos.

Tenía Clemente sus puntas de poeta, como lo mostró en los versos que dio a Preciosa, y Andrés se picaba un poco, y entrambos eran aficionados a la música. Sucedió, pues, que, estando el aduar alojado en un valle cuatro leguas de Murcia, una noche, por entretenerse, sentados los dos, Andrés al pie de un alcornoque, Clemente al de una encina, cada uno con una guitarra, convidados del silencio de la noche, comenzando Andrés y respondiendo Clemente, cantaron estos versos:

ANDRÉS

Mira, Clemente, el estrellado velo
con que esta noche fría
compite con el día,
de luces bellas adornando el cielo;
y en esta semejanza,
si tanto tu divino ingenio alcanza,
aquel rostro figura
donde asiste el estremo de hermosura.

CLEMENTE

Donde asiste el estremo de hermosura,
y adonde la preciosa
honestidad hermosa
con todo estremo de bondad se apura,
en un sujeto cabe,
que no hay humano ingenio que le alabe,
si no toca en divino,
en alto, en raro, en grave y peregrino.

can form. This I shall wish, Preciosa, and this I shall always say to your Andrés, not anything to make him swerve from his well-placed intentions."

Clemente spoke these words so emotionally that Andrés was in doubt as to whether he had spoken them as a lover or as an obliging person; for the hellish disease of jealousy is so captious, and of such a nature, that it concerns itself even with the specks of dust in a sunbeam, and the lover is vexed and worried by those which touch the woman he loves. Nevertheless, he wasn't seriously jealous, trusting more in Preciosa's goodness than in his own good luck, because lovers always consider themselves unhappy until they achieve their desires. Finally, Andrés and Clemente were chums and close friends, and everything was assured by Clemente's good intentions and the caution and prudence of Preciosa, who never gave Andrés occasion to be jealous where she was concerned.

Clemente had a touch of the poet, as he had demonstrated in the verses he had given Preciosa, and Andrés prided himself on this a little, too; both were fond of music. So it came about that, the camp being situated in a valley four leagues from Murcia, one night, for amusement, both seated, Andrés at the foot of a cork oak, Clemente at the foot of a holm oak, each holding a guitar, allured by the silence of the night, they sang these verses, Andrés beginning and Clemente giving the response:

ANDRÉS

Behold, Clemente, the starry veil
with which this cold night
competes with the day,
adorning the sky with lovely lamps;
and in this simile,
if your divine mind reaches so far,
picture that face
in which the extreme of beauty resides.

CLEMENTE

In which the extreme of beauty resides,
and where precious,
beautiful chastity
reaches its limits,
confined in a single person
beyond the praise of all human skill,
unless it touches on the divine,
the lofty, the rare, the grave, and the unusual.

Andrés

En alto, en raro, en grave y peregrino
estilo nunca usado,
al cielo levantado,
por dulce al mundo y sin igual camino,
tu nombre, ¡oh gitanilla!,
causando asombro, espanto y maravilla,
la fama yo quisiera
que le llevara hasta la octava esfera.

Clemente

Que le llevara hasta la octava esfera
fuera decente y justo,
dando a los cielos gusto,
cuando el son de su nombre allá se oyera,
y en la tierra causara,
por donde el dulce nombre resonara,
música en los oídos,
paz en las almas, gloria en los sentidos.

Andrés

Paz en las almas, gloria en los sentidos
se siente cuando canta
la sirena, que encanta
y adormece a los más apercebidos;
y tal es mi Preciosa,
que es lo menos que tiene ser hermosa:
dulce regalo mío,
corona del donaire, honor del brío.

Clemente

Corona del donaire, honor del brío
eres, bella gitana,
frescor de la mañana,
céfiro blando en el ardiente estío;
rayo con que Amor ciego
convierte el pecho más de nieve en fuego;
fuerza que ansí la hace,
que blandamente mata y satisface.

Señales iban dando de no acabar tan presto el libre y el cautivo, si no sonara a sus espaldas la voz de Preciosa, que las suyas había escuchado. Suspendiólos el oírla, y, sin moverse, prestándola maravillosa atención, la escucharon. Ella (o no sé si de improviso, o si en algún tiempo los versos que cantaba le compusieron), con estremada gracia, como si para responderles fueran hechos, cantó los siguientes:

ANDRÉS

In a lofty, rare, grave, and unusual
mode of speech never used before,
I'll raise to the skies
(so sweet it is to the world) on a novel path
your name, O Gypsy girl,
causing awe, amazement, and marvel,
and I'd like fame
to carry it up to the eighth sphere of fixed stars.

CLEMENTE

To carry it up to the eighth sphere
would be reasonable and proper,
giving pleasure to the heavens
when the sound of her name is heard there;
and on earth it would create,
wherever the sweet name resounded,
music in people's ears,
peace in their souls, glory in their senses.

ANDRÉS

Peace in their souls, glory in their senses,
is felt when that siren
sings who enchants
and lulls to sleep the best-forearmed men;
and such is my Preciosa,
for her beauty is the least of her possessions:
my sweet delight,
crown of grace, honor of mettle.

CLEMENTE

Crown of grace, honor of mettle,
are you, lovely Gypsy,
coolness of morning,
soft zephyr in blazing summer;
lightning bolt with which blind Love
turns the most snow-laden breast into fire;
a power that makes her such
that she softly kills and satisfies.

The free man and the captive gave signs that they wouldn't have ended so soon, had not the voice of Preciosa, who had been listening to theirs, sounded behind them. Hearing her, they stopped short and, immobile, giving her extreme attention, they listened to her. She (I don't know whether she was improvising or the verses she sang had been written for her at some time), with extreme grace, sang the following lines, which seemed intentionally composed as a response to the men's strophes:

—En esta empresa amorosa,
donde el amor entretengo,
por mayor ventura tengo
ser honesta que hermosa.
La que es más humilde planta,
si la subida endereza,
por gracia o naturaleza
a los cielos se levanta.
En este mi bajo cobre,
siendo honestidad su esmalte,
no hay buen deseo que falte
ni riqueza que no sobre.
No me causa alguna pena
no quererme o no estimarme;
que yo pienso fabricarme
mi suerte y ventura buena.
Haga yo lo que en mí es,
que a ser buena me encamine,
y haga el cielo y determine
lo que quisiere después.
Quiero ver si la belleza
tiene tal prerrogativa,
que me encumbre tan arriba,
que aspire a mayor alteza.
Si las almas son iguales,
podrá la de un labrador
igualarse por valor
con las que son imperiales.
De la mía lo que siento
me sube al grado mayor,
porque majestad y amor
no tienen un mismo asiento.

Aquí dio fin Preciosa a su canto, y Andrés y Clemente se levantaron a recebilla. Pasaron entre los tres discretas razones, y Preciosa descubrió en las suyas su discreción, su honestidad y su agudeza, de tal manera que en Clemente halló disculpa la intención de Andrés, que aún hasta entonces no la había hallado, juzgando más a mocedad que a cordura su arrojada determinación.

Aquella mañana se levantó el aduar y se fueron a alojar en un lugar de la jurisdición de Murcia, tres leguas de la ciudad, donde le sucedió a Andrés una desgracia que le puso en punto de perder la vida. Y fue que, después de haber dado en aquel lugar algunos vasos y prendas de plata en fianzas, como tenían de costumbre, Preciosa y su abuela y

—In this romantic enterprise,
in which I foster love,
I consider it greater good fortune
to be chaste than to be beautiful.
The humblest plant,
if it ascends straightly,
by grace or nature
rises to the skies.
In this my lowly copper,
its enamel being chastity,
no good desire is lacking,
no wealth is not abundant.
I'm not caused any grief
by not being loved or esteemed,
because I intend to manufacture
my own luck and good fortune.
Let me do what's in me to do,
let me set out to be good,
then let heaven decide to do
what it likes afterward.
I want to see whether beauty
has so great a prerogative
that it carries me so high up
that I aspire to greater heights.
If all souls are equal,
that of a peasant may
equal in value
those belonging to emperors.
That which I feel in mine
raises me to the highest degree,
because majesty and love
don't have the same stability.

Here Preciosa brought her song to an end, and Andrés and Clemente arose to welcome her. The three had a clever conversation, and in her words Preciosa so fully revealed her wisdom, chastity, and wit that Andrés's decision found forgiveness from Clemente, which it had not found till then, the page having considered his friend's impulsive resolve to be more puerile than sane.

That morning they broke camp and went to lodge in a hamlet within the jurisdiction of Murcia, three leagues from that city, where a misfortune befell Andrés which brought him close to losing his life. It was as follows. After depositing some silver vessels and objects in that hamlet as security, as was their custom, Preciosa and her grandmother and Cristina,

Cristina, con otras dos gitanillas y los dos, Clemente y Andrés, se alojaron en un mesón de una viuda rica, la cual tenía una hija de edad de diez y siete o diez y ocho años, algo más desenvuelta que hermosa; y, por más señas, se llamaba Juana Carducha. Ésta, habiendo visto bailar a las gitanas y gitanos, la tomó el diablo, y se enamoró de Andrés tan fuertemente que propuso de decírselo y tomarle por marido, si él quisiese, aunque a todos sus parientes les pesase; y así, buscó coyuntura para decírselo, y hallóla en un corral donde Andrés había entrado a requerir dos pollinos. Llegóse a él, y con priesa, por no ser vista, le dijo:

—Andrés —que ya sabía su nombre—, yo soy doncella y rica; que mi madre no tiene otro hijo sino a mí, y este mesón es suyo; y amén desto tiene muchos majuelos y otros dos pares de casas. Hasme parecido bien: si me quieres por esposa, a ti está; respóndeme presto, y si eres discreto, quédate y verás qué vida nos damos.

Admirado quedó Andrés de la resolución de la Carducha, y con la presteza que ella pedía le respondió:

—Señora doncella, yo estoy apalabrado para casarme, y los gitanos no nos casamos sino con gitanas; guárdela Dios por la merced que me quería hacer, de quien yo no soy digno.

No estuvo en dos dedos de caerse muerta la Carducha con la aceda respuesta de Andrés, a quien replicara si no viera que entraban en el corral otras gitanas. Salióse corrida y asendereada, y de buena gana se vengara si pudiera. Andrés, como discreto, determinó de poner tierra en medio y desviarse de aquella ocasión que el diablo le ofrecía; que bien leyó en los ojos de la Carducha que sin los lazos matrimoniales se le entregara a toda su voluntad, y no quiso verse pie a pie y solo en aquella estacada; y así, pidió a todos los gitanos que aquella noche se partiesen de aquel lugar. Ellos, que siempre le obedecían, lo pusieron luego por obra, y, cobrando sus fianzas aquella tarde, se fueron.

La Carducha, que vio que en irse Andrés se le iba la mitad de su alma, y que no le quedaba tiempo para solicitar el cumplimiento de sus deseos, ordenó de hacer quedar a Andrés por fuerza, ya que de grado no podía. Y así, con la industria, sagacidad y secreto que su mal intento le enseñó, puso entre las alhajas de Andrés, que ella conoció por suyas, unos ricos corales y dos patenas de plata, con otros brincos suyos; y, apenas habían salido del mesón, cuando dio voces, diciendo que aquellos gitanos le llevaban robadas sus joyas, a cuyas voces acudió la justicia y toda la gente del pueblo.

Los gitanos hicieron alto, y todos juraban que ninguna cosa lleva-

with two other Gypsy girls and the two men Clemente and Andrés, took rooms in the inn of a rich widow, who had a daughter of seventeen or eighteen, somewhat more pert than good-looking; to be specific, her name was Juana Carducha. After she saw the Gypsy men and women dance, the devil got into her, and she fell so deeply in love with Andrés that she determined to tell him so and take him as her husband, if he wished, even if all her relatives objected; so she sought an opportunity to tell him, and found him in a livestock yard which Andrés had entered to acquire two young donkeys. Going up to him hurriedly, to avoid being seen, she said:

"Andrés" (she already knew his name), "I'm a maiden and rich; my mother has no other child but me, and this inn is hers; besides that, she owns many vineyards and two other houses. I like your looks: if you want me as a wife, it's up to you; answer me quickly, and if you're wise, stay here and you'll see what a fine life we'll have."

Andrés was amazed at Carducha's resolve, and as quickly as she requested he replied:

"Miss, I'm engaged to be married and we Gypsies marry only Gypsy women; may God keep you for the favor you wished to do me, which I don't deserve!"

The Carducha girl was within an ace of dropping dead at Andrés's chilly reply, to which she would have retorted had she not seen other Gypsy women entering the yard. She left, ashamed and vexed, and would have liked to take revenge if she could. Like a wise man, Andrés decided to make tracks and avoid that opportunity the devil was offering him; for he had read clearly in the Carducha girl's eyes that even without the bonds of matrimony she'd surrender to him most willingly, and he didn't want to find himself facing the enemy alone on that dangerous ground; so he asked all the Gypsies to leave that hamlet that night. They, who always obeyed him, undertook this at once and, reclaiming their deposits that afternoon, departed.

The Carducha girl, feeling that Andrés's departure was robbing her of half her soul, and seeing that she didn't have enough time to request the fulfillment of her desires, contrived to make Andrés remain by force, since she couldn't make him stay willingly. So, with the wiliness, shrewdness, and secrecy which her evil intentions taught her, she placed among Andrés's belongings, which she recognized as being his, some expensive bits of coral and two silver religious medallions, with some other trinkets of hers; and, as soon as they had left the inn, she cried out, saying that those Gypsies had stolen her jewelry; the police and everyone in the hamlet came running at that outcry.

The Gypsies halted, and all swore that they had nothing stolen with

ban hurtada, y que ellos harían patentes todos los sacos y repuestos de su aduar. Desto se congojó mucho la gitana vieja, temiendo que en aquel escrutinio no se manifestasen los dijes de la Preciosa y los vestidos de Andrés, que ella con gran cuidado y recato guardaba; pero la buena de la Carducha lo remedió con mucha brevedad todo, porque al segundo envoltorio que miraron dijo que preguntasen cuál era el de aquel gitano gran bailador, que ella le había visto entrar en su aposento dos veces, y que podría ser que aquél las llevase. Entendió Andrés que por él lo decía y, riéndose, dijo:

—Señora doncella, ésta es mi recámara y éste es mi pollino; si vos halláredes en ella ni en él lo que os falta, yo os lo pagaré con las setenas, fuera de sujetarme al castigo que la ley da a los ladrones.

Acudieron luego los ministros de la justicia a desvalijar el pollino, y a pocas vueltas dieron con el hurto, de que quedó tan espantado Andrés y tan absorto, que no pareció sino estatua, sin voz, de piedra dura.

—¿No sospeché yo bien? —dijo a esta sazón la Carducha—. ¡Mirad con qué buena cara se encubre un ladrón tan grande!

El alcalde, que estaba presente, comenzó a decir mil injurias a Andrés y a todos los gitanos, llamándolos de públicos ladrones y salteadores de caminos. A todo callaba Andrés, suspenso e imaginativo, y no acababa de caer en la traición de la Carducha. En esto, se llegó a él un soldado bizarro, sobrino del alcalde, diciendo:

—¿No veis cuál se ha quedado el gitanico podrido de hurtar? Apostaré yo que hace melindres y que niega el hurto, con habérsele cogido en las manos; que bien haya quien no os echa en galeras a todos. ¡Mirad si estuviera mejor este bellaco en ellas, sirviendo a su Majestad, que no andarse bailando de lugar en lugar y hurtando de venta en monte! A fe de soldado, que estoy por darle una bofetada que le derribe a mis pies.

Y, diciendo esto, sin más ni más, alzó la mano y le dio un bofetón tal, que le hizo volver de su embelesamiento, y le hizo acordar que no era Andrés Caballero, sino don Juan, y caballero; y, arremetiendo al soldado con mucha presteza y más cólera, le arrancó su misma espada de la vaina y se la envainó en el cuerpo, dando con él muerto en tierra.

Aquí fue el gritar del pueblo, aquí el amohinarse el tío alcalde, aquí el desmayarse Preciosa y el turbarse Andrés de verla desmayada; aquí el acudir todos a las armas y dar tras el homicida. Creció la confusión, creció la grita, y, por acudir Andrés al desmayo de Preciosa, dejó de acudir a su defensa; y quiso la suerte que Clemente no se hallase al desastrado suceso, que con los bagajes había ya salido del pueblo.

them, and that they'd open all the sacks and bundles in their horde. This greatly distressed the old Gypsy woman, who feared that that investigation might uncover Preciosa's baby trinkets and Andrés's clothes, which she was keeping with great care and caution; but the good Carducha girl very quickly took care of that problem: at the second bundle they inspected, she asked them which was the one belonging to that Gypsy who was such a good dancer, because she had seen him enter her room twice and he might be the one who stole the objects. Andrés understood that he was the one she meant, and he said with a smile:

"Miss, this is my baggage and this is my donkey; if you find in either one of them what you've lost, I'll repay you seven times the amount, besides subjecting myself to the punishment that the law deals out to thieves."

At once the minions of the law ran over to disburden the donkey, and after a very little rummaging they found the stolen items, at which Andrés became so alarmed and distraught that he resembled a mute statue of hard stone.

"Weren't my suspicions correct?" the Carducha girl then said. "See what a nice face masks such a big crook!"

The mayor, who was present, started to heap a thousand insults on Andrés and all the Gypsies, calling them common thieves and highway robbers. To all this Andrés made no reply; astonished and lost in wonder, he had not yet caught on to the Carducha girl's treachery. Meanwhile, a too high-spirited soldier, nephew of the mayor, came up to him, saying:

"Can't you see what a state he's in, this rotten little Gypsy thief? I'll bet he fusses around and denies the theft, even though caught red-handed; all of you should be sent to the galleys! Consider whether this crook wouldn't be better there, serving His Majesty, rather than going around from hamlet to hamlet dancing and stealing wherever he can! On my honor as a soldier, I'm going to give him a slap that will knock him down at my feet!"

And saying this, with no further ado, he raised his hand and gave him such a smack that he aroused him from his stupor and made him remember that he wasn't Andrés Caballero but Don Juan, and a knight; assailing the soldier very quickly and even more angrily, he pulled the man's sword from its sheath and buried it in his body, leaving him dead on the ground.

Thereupon the people shouted, the mayor and uncle of the soldier became enraged, Preciosa fainted, and Andrés got upset at seeing her faint; thereupon everyone seized weapons and noisily pursued the murderer. The confusion increased, the shouting got louder, and Andrés, because he was attending to Preciosa's faint, failed to attend to his own defense; as luck would have it, Clemente wasn't present at the disastrous event because he

Finalmente, tantos cargaron sobre Andrés, que le prendieron y le aherrojaron con dos muy gruesas cadenas. Bien quisiera el alcalde ahorcarle luego, si estuviera en su mano, pero hubo de remitirle a Murcia, por ser de su jurisdición. No le llevaron hasta otro día, y en el que allí estuvo, pasó Andrés muchos martirios y vituperios que el indignado alcalde y sus ministros y todos los del luga le hicieron. Prendió el alcalde todos los más gitanos y gitanas que pudo, porque los más huyeron, y entre ellos Clemente, que temió ser cogido y descubierto.

Finalmente, con la sumaria del caso y con una gran cáfila de gitanos, entraron el alcalde y sus ministros con otra mucha gente armada en Murcia, entre los cuales iba Preciosa, y el pobre Andrés, ceñido de cadenas, sobre un macho y con esposas y piedeamigo. Salió toda Murcia a ver los presos, que ya se tenía noticia de la muerte del soldado. Pero la hermosura de Preciosa aquel día fue tanta, que ninguno la miraba que no la bendecía, y llegó la nueva de su belleza a los oídos de la señora corregidora, que por curiosidad de verla hizo que el corregidor, su marido, mandase que aquella gitanica no entrase en la cárcel, y todos los demás sí. Y a Andrés le pusieron en un estrecho calabozo, cuya escuridad, y la falta de la luz de Preciosa, le trataron de manera que bien pensó no salir de allí sino para la sepultura. Llevaron a Preciosa con su abuela a que la corregidora la viese, y, así como la vio, dijo:

—Con razón la alaban de hermosa.

Y, llegándola a sí, la abrazó tiernamente, y no se hartaba de mirarla, y preguntó a su abuela que qué edad tendría aquella niña.

—Quince años —respondió la gitana—, dos meses más a menos.

—Esos tuviera agora la desdichada de mi Costanza. ¡Ay, amigas, que esta niña me ha renovado mi desventura! —dijo la corregidora.

Tomó en esto Preciosa las manos de la corregidora, y, besándoselas muchas veces, se las bañaba con lágrimas y le decía:

—Señora mía, el gitano que está preso no tiene culpa, porque fue provocado: llamáronle ladrón, y no lo es; diéronle un bofetón en su rostro, que es tal, que en él se descubre la bondad de su ánimo. Por Dios y por quien vos sois, señora, que le hagáis guardar su justicia, y que el señor corregidor no se dé priesa a ejecutar en él el castigo con que las leyes le amenazan; y si algún agrado os ha dado mi hermosura, entretenedla con entretener el preso, porque en el fin de su vida está

had already left town with the baggage train. Finally, so many people assaulted Andrés that he was captured and loaded down with two very heavy chains. The mayor would have liked nothing better than to hang him right away, if it were up to him, but he had to send him on to Murcia, because crimes in his hamlet had to be tried there. He wasn't taken away until the next day; during the day that he remained there, Andrés suffered many inflictions and insults at the hands of the furious mayor, his minions, and everyone in the hamlet. The mayor arrested as many of the other Gypsy men and women as he could; most of them escaped, including Clemente, who was afraid of being caught and unmasked.

Finally, with the written indictment and a great multitude of Gypsies, the mayor, his minions, and many other armed people entered Murcia; among them were Preciosa and poor Andrés, who was wrapped in chains, riding a mule, and wearing handcuffs and a head restraint.[17] All Murcia turned out to see the prisoners, for news of the soldier's death had already arrived. But Preciosa's beauty that day was such that she was blessed by every beholder, and the news of her beauty came to the ears of the civil governor's wife, who, out of curiosity to see her, bade her husband the governor give orders that that Gypsy girl was not to be jailed, though all the others were. Andrés was placed in a narrow cell, whose darkness, and the lack of Preciosa's radiance, affected him so badly that he didn't expect to leave it except to be buried. Preciosa and her grandmother were taken for the governor's wife to see; as soon as that lady did see the girl, she said:

"You are rightly praised for your beauty."

And, going up to her, she embraced her warmly, and couldn't look at her enough. She asked the girl's grandmother how old she might be.

"Fifteen," replied the Gypsy, "give or take two months."

"That's how old my unhappy Costanza would have been now. Ah, friends, how this girl has renewed my grief!" said the governor's wife.

Then Preciosa took the hands of the governor's wife and, kissing them many times, bathed them with tears and said:

"My lady, the Gypsy prisoner is innocent, because he was provoked: he was called a thief, and he isn't; he was slapped in that face of his which is so fine that it reveals the goodness of his mind. For the sake of God and for your own worth, madam, make him receive a fair trial and don't let the governor be too hasty to punish him as the laws threaten; if my beauty has given you any pleasure, keep it alive by keeping the prisoner alive, because the end of his life would be the end of mine. He is to be my hus-

17. A forked piece of iron confining the chin, so that the criminal can't lower his head and hide his face.

el de la mía. Él ha de ser mi esposo, y justos y honestos impedimentos han estorbado que aun hasta ahora no nos habemos dado las manos. Si dineros fueren menester para alcanzar perdón de la parte, todo nuestro aduar se venderá en pública almoneda, y se dará aún más de lo que pidieren. Señora mía, si sabéis qué es amor, y algún tiempo le tuvistes, y ahora le tenéis a vuestro esposo, doleos de mí, que amo tierna y honestamente al mío.

En todo el tiempo que esto decía, nunca la dejó las manos, ni apartó los ojos de mirarla atentísimamente, derramando amargas y piadosas lágrimas en mucha abundancia. Asimismo, la corregidora la tenía a ella asida de las suyas, mirándola ni más ni menos, con no menor ahínco y con no más pocas lágrimas. Estando en esto, entró el corregidor, y, hallando a su mujer y a Preciosa tan llorosas y tan encadenadas, quedó suspenso, así de su llanto como de la hermosura. Preguntó la causa de aquel sentimiento, y la respuesta que dio Preciosa fue soltar las manos de la corregidora y asirse de los pies del corregidor, diciéndole:

—¡Señor, misericordia, misericordia! ¡Si mi esposo muere, yo soy muerta! Él no tiene culpa; pero si la tiene, déseme a mí la pena, y si esto no puede ser, a lo menos entreténgase el pleito en tanto que se procuran y buscan los medios posibles para su remedio; que podrá ser que al que no pecó de melicia le enviase el cielo la salud de gracia.

Con nueva suspensión quedó el corregidor de oír las discretas razones de la gitanilla, y que ya, si no fuera por no dar indicios de flaqueza, le acompañara en sus lágrimas.

En tanto que esto pasaba, estaba la gitana vieja considerando grandes, muchas y diversas cosas; y, al cabo de toda esta suspensión y imaginación, dijo:

—Espérenme vuesas mercedes, señores míos, un poco, que yo haré que estos llantos se conviertan en risa, aunque a mí me cueste la vida.

Y así, con ligero paso, se salió de donde estaba, dejando a los presentes confusos con lo que dicho había. En tanto, pues, que ella volvía, nunca dejó Preciosa las lágrimas ni los ruegos de que se entretuviese la causa de su esposo, con intención de avisar a su padre que viniese a entender en ella. Volvió la gitana con un pequeño cofre debajo del brazo, y dijo al corregidor que con su mujer y ella se entrasen en un aposento, que tenía grandes cosas que decirles en secreto. El corregidor, creyendo que algunos hurtos de los gitanos quería descubrirle, por tenerle propicio en el pleito del preso, al momento se retiró con ella y con su mujer en su recámara, adonde la gitana, hincándose de rodillas ante los dos, les dijo:

band, and only proper and honorable obstacles have prevented us from taking the vows up to now. If money should be needed to gain a pardon from the prosecutor, we Gypsies will sell all our possessions by public auction, and we'll give even more than what's asked. My lady, if you know what love is, and have ever felt it, and feel it now for your husband, pity me, for I love mine tenderly and honorably."

All the time she was saying this, she never let go of the lady's hands or ceased staring at her most attentively, while shedding bitter, pious tears in great abundance. Likewise, the governor's wife grasped her with *her* hands, gazing at her in the same way, just as fixedly and with no fewer tears. At this point, the governor came in and, finding his wife and Preciosa so tearful and clinging, he was amazed both at their tears and at the girl's beauty. He asked the reason for that emotion, and Preciosa's reply was to release his wife's hands and take hold of the governor's feet, saying:

"Sir, mercy, mercy! If my husband dies, I'll die, too! He's innocent, but if he's guilty, let me be the one punished and, if that's impossible, at least let the trial be postponed while we seek and search for every means possible to remedy matters; because possibly heaven will send the salvation of grace to the man who didn't sin through malice."

The governor was amazed once more on hearing the Gypsy girl's wise words; by now, except that he didn't want to show signs of weakness, he would have joined her in her tears.

While this was going on, the old Gypsy woman was pondering many different weighty matters; after all this period of amazement and bewilderment, she said:

"Wait for me a little, your lordship and ladyship; for I shall make this weeping turn into laughter, even it if costs my life."

And so, with swift steps, she left the spot she had occupied, leaving all present confused by her words. So, the whole time preceding her return, Preciosa never stopped crying or begging for her husband's case to be postponed, intending to inform his father and tell him to come and intercede. The Gypsy woman came back with a small coffer under her arm, and asked the governor to go into another room with her and his wife, because she had important things to tell them in private. The governor, thinking she wanted to disclose some of the Gypsies' thefts to him, to gain his favor at the prisoner's trial, withdrew at once with her and his wife into his dressing room, where the Gypsy woman, kneeling down before the couple, said:

—Si las buenas nuevas que os quiero dar, señores, no merecieren alcanzar en albricias el perdón de un gran pecado mío, aquí estoy para recebir el castigo que quisiéredes darme; pero antes que le confiese quiero que me digáis, señores, primero, si conocéis estas joyas.

Y, descubriendo un cofrecico donde venían las de Preciosa, se le puso en las manos al corregidor, y, en abriéndole, vio aquellos dijes pueriles; pero no cayó en lo que podían significar. Mirólos también la corregidora, pero tampoco dio en la cuenta; sólo dijo:

—Éstos son adornos de alguna pequeña criatura.

—Así es la verdad —dijo la gitana—; y de qué criatura sean lo dice ese escrito que está en ese papel doblado.

Abrióle con priesa el corregidor y leyó que decía:

> Llamábase la niña doña Constanza de Azevedo y de Meneses; su madre, doña Guiomar de Meneses, y su padre, don Fernando de Azevedo, caballero del hábito de Calatrava. Desparecíla día de la Ascensión del Señor, a las ocho de la mañana, del año de mil y quinientos y noventa y cinco. Traía la niña puestos estos brincos que en este cofre están guardados.

Apenas hubo oído la corregidora las razones del papel, cuando reconoció los brincos, se los puso a la boca, y, dándoles infinitos besos, se cayó desmayada. Acudió el corregidor a ella, antes que a preguntar a la gitana por su hija, y, habiendo vuelto en sí, dijo:

—Mujer buena, antes ángel que gitana, ¿adónde está el dueño, digo la criatura cuyos eran estos dijes?

—¿Adónde, señora? —respondió la gitana—. En vuestra casa la tenéis: aquella gitanica que os sacó las lágrimas de los ojos es su dueño, y es sin duda alguna vuestra hija; que yo la hurté en Madrid de vuestra casa el día y hora que ese papel dice.

Oyendo esto la turbada señora, soltó los chapines, y desalada y corriendo salió a la sala adonde había dejado a Preciosa, y hallóla rodeada de sus doncellas y criadas, todavía llorando. Arremetió a ella, y, sin decirle nada, con gran priesa le desabrochó el pecho y miró si tenía debajo de la teta izquierda una señal pequeña, a modo de lunar blanco, con que había nacido, y hallóle ya grande, que con el tiempo se había dilatado. Luego, con la misma celeridad, la descalzó, y descubrió un pie de nieve y de marfil, hecho a torno, y vio en él lo que buscaba, que era que los dos dedos últimos del pie derecho se trababan el uno con el otro por medio con un poquito de carne, la cual, cuando niña, nunca se la habían querido cortar por no darle pesadumbre. El pecho, los dedos, los brincos, el día señalado del hurto, la confesión de

"If the good news I wish to give you, my lord and lady, doesn't deserve to receive as a reward pardon for a great sin of mine, I am here to receive any punishment you want to give me; but before I confess it, I want you to tell me first whether you recognize these jewels."

And, disclosing a small coffer containing those of Preciosa, she placed it in the governor's hands; opening it, he saw those baby trinkets, but he didn't realize their significance. The governor's wife looked at them, too, but she didn't recognize them, either. All she said was:

"These are adornments for some tiny baby."

"That's true," said the Gypsy woman, "and the writing on this folded paper tells what baby they belonged to."

The governor unfolded it quickly and read the following:

> The child was called Doña Costanza de Azevedo y de Meneses; her mother, Doña Guiomar de Meneses; and her father, Don Fernando de Azevedo, knight of the Order of Calatrava. I kidnapped her on Ascension Day, at eight in the morning, in the year fifteen ninety-five. The child was wearing the trinkets that are kept in this coffer.

As soon as the governor's wife heard the words on the paper, she recognized the trinkets, put them to her lips, and, giving them an infinity of kisses, fainted away. The governor ran up to her before asking the Gypsy woman about their daughter; when his wife came to, she said:

"Good woman, angel rather than Gypsy, where is their owner, I mean the baby whose trinkets these were?"

"Where, my lady?" the Gypsy woman replied. "You have her in your house: that Gypsy girl who elicited the tears from your eyes is their owner, and beyond any doubt your daughter; for I kidnapped her from your house in Madrid the day and hour stated on that paper."

Hearing this, the lady, in turmoil, removed her chopines and, running anxiously, went out into the room where she had left Preciosa; she found her still crying, surrounded by her maids and servantwomen. She dashed over to her and, without a word, very hastily unfastened her bodice to see whether she had a small mark she had been born with, like a white mole, below her left breast. She found it, now large, for it had grown with the years. Then, with the same speed, she took off her shoe, revealing a foot of snow and ivory, beautifully shaped, and found on it what she was looking for: the two last toes on her right foot were joined together by a small membrane which they had never wanted to cut when she was a baby, to avoid making her suffer. The breast, the toes, the trinkets, the day of the abduction, the Gypsy's confession, and the happy jolt

la gitana y el sobresalto y alegría que habían recebido sus padres cuando la vieron, con toda verdad confirmaron en el alma de la corregidora ser Preciosa su hija. Y así, cogiéndola en sus brazos, se volvió con ella adonde el corregidor y la gitana estaban.

Iba Preciosa confusa, que no sabía a qué efeto se habían hecho con ella aquellas diligencias; y más, viéndose llevar en brazos de la corregidora, y que le daba de un beso hasta ciento. Llegó, en fin, con la preciosa carga doña Guiomar a la presencia de su marido, y, trasladándola de sus brazos a los del corregidor, le dijo:

—Recebid, señor, a vuestra hija Costanza, que ésta es sin duda; no lo dudéis, señor, en ningún modo, que la señal de los dedos juntos y la del pecho he visto; y más, que a mí me lo está diciendo el alma desde el instante que mis ojos la vieron.

—No lo dudo —respondió el corregidor, teniendo en sus brazos a Preciosa—, que los mismos efetos han pasado por la mía que por la vuestra; y más, que tantas puntualidades juntas, ¿cómo podían suceder, si non fuera por milagro?

Toda la gente de casa andaba absorta, preguntando unos a otros qué sería aquello, y todos daban bien lejos del blanco; que, ¿quién había de imaginar que la gitanilla era hija de sus señores? El corregidor dijo a su mujer y a su hija, y a la gitana vieja, que aquel caso estuviese secreto hasta que él le descubriese; y asimismo dijo a la vieja que él la perdonaba el agravio que le había hecho en hurtarle el alma, pues la recompensa de habérsela vuelto mayores albricias recebía; y que sólo le pesaba de que, sabiendo ella la calidad de Preciosa, la hubiese desposado con un gitano, y más con un ladrón y homicida.

—¡Ay! —dijo a esto Preciosa—, señor mío, que ni es gitano ni ladrón, puesto que es matador; pero fuelo del que le quitó la honra, y no pudo hacer menos de mostrar quién era y matarle.

—¿Cómo que no es gitano, hija mía? —dijo doña Guiomar.

Entonces la gitana vieja contó brevemente la historia de Andrés Caballero, y que era hijo de don Francisco de Cárcamo, caballero del hábito de Santiago, y que se llamaba don Juan de Cárcamo; asimismo del mismo hábito, cuyos vestidos ella tenía, cuando los mudó en los de gitano. Contó también el concierto que entre Preciosa y don Juan estaba hecho, de aguardar dos años de aprobación para desposarse o no. Puso en su punto la honestidad de entrambos y la agradable condición de don Juan.

Tanto se admiraron desto como del hallazgo de su hija, y mandó el corregidor a la gitana que fuese por los vestidos de don Juan. Ella lo hizo ansí, y volvió con otro gitano que los trujo.

her parents had felt on seeing her, fully confirmed in the soul of the governor's wife the truth of Preciosa's being her daughter. And so, taking her in her arms, she went back with her to where she had left her husband and the Gypsy woman.

Preciosa was confused, not knowing for what purpose she had been examined so; and even more so, finding herself borne away in the embrace of the governor's wife, who was showering kisses on her. Doña Guiomar finally came with her precious burden into her husband's presence and, transferring her from her arms to the governor's, said to him:

"Sir, receive your daughter Costanza, for it is she beyond a doubt; don't doubt it, sir, in any way, because I have seen the sign of the joined toes and that of her breast; besides, my soul has been telling me so since I first laid eyes on her."

"I don't doubt it," the governor said, holding Preciosa in his arms, "because the same things occurred in my soul as in yours; besides, how could there be so many coincidences together without a miracle?"

The entire household was dumbfounded, each person asking the other what was going on, but they were all wide of the mark; for who could imagine that the Gypsy girl was the daughter of their employers? The governor asked his wife and daughter and the old Gypsy to keep the matter a secret until he divulged it; likewise, he told the old woman that he forgave her the offense she had done him by stealing his soul, since the act of returning her to him deserved even a greater reward, and that he was only grieved that, knowing Preciosa's rank, she had engaged her to a Gypsy, and a thief and murderer, to boot.

"Ah," Preciosa replied to that, "my lord, he is neither a Gypsy nor a thief, though he is a killer; but the man he killed had sullied his honor, and he could do no less than show who he was and kill him."

"What do you mean by saying he isn't a Gypsy, daughter?" asked Doña Guiomar.

Then the old Gypsy woman briefly narrated the history of Andrés Caballero, saying that he was the son of Don Francisco de Cárcamo, knight of the Order of Santiago, and was really called Don Juan de Cárcamo; he was of the same order, and she had been keeping his clothes ever since he had exchanged them for a Gypsy's. She also told of the agreement that had been made between Preciosa and Don Juan, to wait two years on approval before marrying or not. She emphasized the chastity of the couple and Don Juan's pleasant nature.

They were as amazed at this as at the discovery of their daughter, and the governor sent the Gypsy woman to fetch Don Juan's clothes. She went, and returned with a Gypsy man who was carrying them.

En tanto que ella iba y volvía, hicieron sus padres a Preciosa cien mil preguntas, a quien respondió con tanta discreción y gracia que, aunque no la hubieran reconocido por hija, los enamorara. Preguntáronla si tenía alguna afición a don Juan. Respondió que no más de aquella que le obligaba a ser agradecida a quien se había querido humillar a ser gitano por ella; pero que ya no se estendería a más el agradecimiento de aquello que sus señores padres quisiesen.

—Calla, hija Preciosa —dijo su padre—, que este nombre de Preciosa quiero que se te quede, en memoria de tu pérdida y de tu hallazgo; que yo, como tu padre, tomo a cargo el ponerte en estado que no desdiga de quién eres.

Suspiró oyendo esto Preciosa, y su madre (como era discreta, entendió que suspiraba de enamorada de don Juan) dijo a su marido:

—Señor, siendo tan principal don Juan de Cárcamo como lo es, y queriendo tanto a nuestra hija, no nos estaría mal dársela por esposa.

Y él resondió:

—Aun hoy la habemos hallado, ¿y ya queréis que la perdamos? Gocémosla algún tiempo; que, en casándola, no será nuestra, sino de su marido.

—Razón tenéis, señor —respondió ella—, pero dad orden de sacar a don Juan, que debe de estar en algún calabozo.

—Sí estará —dijo Preciosa—; que a un ladrón, matador y, sobre todo, gitano, no le habrán dado mejor estancia.

—Yo quiero ir a verle, como que le voy a tomar la confesión —respondió el corregidor—, y de nuevo os encargo, señora, que nadie sepa esta historia hasta que yo lo quiera.

Y, abrazando a Preciosa, fue luego a la cárcel y entró en el calabozo donde don Juan estaba, y no quiso que nadie entrase con él. Hallóle con entrambos pies en un cepo y con las esposas a las manos, y que aún no le habían quitado el piedeamigo. Era la estancia escura, pero hizo que por arriba abriesen una lumbrera, por donde entraba luz, aunque muy escasa; y, así como le vio, le dijo:

—¿Cómo está la buena pieza? ¡Que así tuviera yo atraillados cuantos gitanos hay en España, para acabar con ellos en un día, como Nerón quisiera con Roma, sin dar más de un golpe! Sabed, ladrón puntoso, que yo soy el corregidor desta ciudad, y vengo a saber, de mí a vos, si es verdad que es vuestra esposa una gitanilla que viene con vosotros.

Oyendo esto Andrés, imaginó que el corregidor se debía de haber

While the old woman was going to and fro, Preciosa's parents asked her a thousand questions, to which she replied with such wisdom and grace that, even if they hadn't acknowledged her as their daughter, they would have fallen in love with her. They asked her whether she had any affection for Don Juan. She replied: not more than that which obliged her to be grateful to a man who had wanted to humble himself and be a Gypsy for her sake; but now her gratitude for that wouldn't go beyond what her parents wished.

"Be still, my daughter Preciosa," said her father, "because I want you to keep this name of Preciosa, in memory of our losing you and finding you; for I, as your father, take it upon myself to place you in a position fully corresponding to your birth."

Hearing this, Preciosa sighed, and her mother (who, being clever, understood that she sighed because she loved Don Juan) said to her husband:

"Sir, Don Juan de Cárcamo being as nobly born as he is, and loving our daughter so much, it wouldn't be wrong for us to give him her hand."

And he replied:

"We've just found her today, and you want us to lose her already? Let's enjoy her company for a while; for when she marries she'll belong not to us but to her husband."

"You're right, sir," she replied, "but give orders to release Don Juan, who must be in some cell."

"Yes, he must," said Preciosa, "for they surely haven't given better quarters to a thief, a murderer, and, above all, a Gypsy."

"I want to go see him, as if to hear his confession," the governor said, "and once more, madam, I enjoin upon you that no one is to hear this story until I so wish."

And, embracing Preciosa, he went straight to the jail and entered Don Juan's cell, not allowing anyone else to come in with him. He found him with both feet in the stocks and the cuffs on his hands; the head restraint had not yet been removed. The space was dark, but he ordered a skylight to be opened up above, which let in light, though not much. As soon as he saw him, he said:

"How is my fine fellow? I wish I had every Gypsy in Spain enchained like this, to get rid of them in one day, just as Nero[18] wanted to kill all Romans at a single blow! Know this, proud thief: I am the civil governor of this city, and I've come to find out, directly from you, whether it's true that a Gypsy girl who travels with your horde is your bride."

Hearing this, Andrés imagined that the governor must have fallen in

18. Really, Caligula. No annotation I have seen comments on this error.

enamorado de Preciosa; que los celos son de cuerpos sutiles y se entran por otros cuerpos sin romperlos, apartarlos ni dividirlos; pero, con todo esto, respondió:

—Si ella ha dicho que yo soy su esposo, es mucha verdad; y si ha dicho que no lo soy, también ha dicho verdad, porque no es posible que Preciosa diga mentira.

—¿Tan verdadera es? —respondió el corregidor—. No es poco serlo, para ser gitana. Ahora bien, mancebo, ella ha dicho que es vuestra esposa, pero que nunca os ha dado la mano. Ha sabido que, según es vuestra culpa, habéis de morir por ella; y hame pedido que antes de vuestra muerte la despose con vos, porque se quiere honrar con quedar viuda de un tan gran ladrón como vos.

—Pues hágalo vuesa merced, señor corregidor, como ella lo suplica; que, como yo me despose con ella, iré contento a la otra vida, como parta désta con nombre de ser suyo.

—¡Mucho la debéis de querer! —dijo el corregidor.

—Tanto —respondió el preso—, que, a poderlo decir, no fuera nada. En efeto, señor corregidor, mi causa se concluya: yo maté al que me quiso quitar la honra; yo adoro a esa gitana, moriré contento si muero en su gracia, y sé que no nos ha de faltar la de Dios, pues entrambos habremos guardado honestamente y con puntualidad lo que nos prometimos.

—Pues esta noche enviaré por vos —dijo el corregidor—, y en mi casa os desposaréis con Preciosica, y mañana a mediodía estaréis en la horca, con lo que yo habré cumplido con lo que pide la justicia y con el deseo de entrambos.

Agradecióselo Andrés, y el corregidor volvió a su casa y dio cuenta a su mujer de lo que con don Juan había pasado, y de otras cosas que pensaba hacer.

En el tiempo que él faltó dio cuenta Preciosa a su madre de todo el discurso de su vida, y de cómo siempre había creído ser gitana y ser nieta de aquella vieja; pero que siempre se había estimado en mucho más de lo que de ser gitana se esperaba. Preguntóle su madre que le dijese la verdad: si quería bien a don Juan de Cárcamo. Ella, con vergüenza y con los ojos en el suelo, le dijo que por haberse considerado gitana, y que mejoraba su suerte con casarse con un caballero de hábito y tan principal como don Juan de Cárcamo, y por haber visto por experiencia su buena condición y honesto trato, alguna vez le había mirado con ojos aficionados; pero que, en resolución, ya había dicho que no tenía otra voluntad de aquella que ellos quisiesen.

Llegóse la noche, y, siendo casi las diez, sacaron a Andrés de la cár-

love with Preciosa; for jealousy is made of subtle particles which enter other bodies without tearing, dividing, or separating them. Nevertheless, he replied:

"If she said I'm her husband, it's quite true; if she said I'm not, she also told the truth, because it's impossible for Preciosa to tell a lie."

"She's that truthful?" the governor replied. "That's quite something for a Gypsy woman. Now, then, young man, she said that she's engaged to you but that she never married you. She has learned that your crime is such that you must die for it, and she has asked me to marry her to you before your death, because she wishes the honor of being the widow of such a great thief."

"Then let your worship do as she implores, governor; for, as long as I marry her, I'll go gladly to the next world, if I leave this one with the renown of being hers."

"You must love her very much!" said the governor.

"So much," the prisoner replied, "that it goes far beyond words can say. In fact, governor, let my case be concluded: I killed the man who wanted to take away my honor; I worship that Gypsy, I'll die contented if I die in her good graces, and I know that we won't lack God's, since we both shall have kept our mutual promise honorably and with exactness."

"Then, tonight I'll send for you," the governor said, "and in my house you will marry Preciosica, and at noon tomorrow you'll be on the gallows, whereby I shall have fulfilled the demands of the law and the desires of you two."

Andrés thanked him, and the governor returned home and told his wife about his talk with Don Juan and about other things he intended to do.

While he was out, Preciosa had told her mother the whole story of her life: how she had always thought she was a Gypsy and that old woman's granddaughter, but had always regarded herself much more highly than was to be expected of a Gypsy. Her mother asked her to tell her the truth as to whether she loved Don Juan de Cárcamo. Modestly, her eyes cast down, she said that, believing herself a Gypsy, whose lot would be bettered by marrying a knight and great nobleman like Don Juan de Cárcamo, and having experienced his good nature and honorable ways, she had sometimes looked on him with affectionate eyes; but that, in a word, she had already said that she had no wishes other than her parents'.

Night came and, when it was nearly ten, Andrés was taken from the

cel, sin las esposas y el piedeamigo, pero no sin una gran cadena que desde los pies todo el cuerpo le ceñía. Llegó dese modo, sin ser visto de nadie, sino de los que le traían, en casa del corregidor, y con silencio y recato le entraron en un aposento, donde le dejaron solo. De allí a un rato entró un clérigo y le dijo que se confesase, porque había de morir otro día. A lo cual respondió Andrés:

—De muy buena gana me confesaré, pero ¿cómo no me desposan primero? Y si me han de desposar, por cierto que es muy malo el tálamo que me espera.

Doña Guiomar, que todo esto sabía, dijo a su marido que eran demasiados los sustos que a don Juan daba; que los moderase, porque podría ser perdiese la vida con ellos. Parecióle buen consejo al corregidor, y así entró a llamar al que le confesaba, y díjole que primero habían de desposar al gitano con Preciosa, la gitana, y que después se confesaría, y que se encomendase a Dios de todo corazón, que muchas veces suele llover sus misericordias en el tiempo que están más secas las esperanzas.

En efeto, Andrés salió a una sala donde estaban solamente doña Guiomar, el corregidor, Preciosa y otros dos criados de casa. Pero, cuando Preciosa vio a don Juan ceñido y aherrojado con tan gran cadena, descolorido el rostro y los ojos con muestra de haber llorado, se le cubrió el corazón y se arrimó al brazo de su madre, que junto a ella estaba, la cual, abrazándola consigo, le dijo:

—Vuelve en ti, niña, que todo lo que vees ha de redundar en tu gusto y provecho.

Ella, que estaba ignorante de aquello, no sabía cómo consolarse, y la gitana vieja estaba turbada, y los circunstantes, colgados del fin de aquel caso.

El corregidor dijo:

—Señor tiniente cura, este gitano y esta gitana son los que vuesa merced ha de desposar.

—Eso no podré yo hacer si no preceden primero las circunstancias que para tal caso se requieren. ¿Dónde se han hecho las amonestaciones? ¿Adónde está la licencia de mi superior, para que con ella se haga el desposorio?

—Inadvertencia ha sido mía —respondió el corregidor—, pero yo haré que el vicario la dé.

—Pues hasta que la vea —respondió el tiniente cura—, estos señores perdonen.

jail, without the handcuffs and the head restraint, but not without a large chain wrapped around his whole body from his feet up. In this fashion he arrived, observed by no one but those who brought him, at the governor's house; silently and cautiously they brought him to a room where they left him alone. After a while a priest came in and asked him to make confession, for he was to die the following day. To which Andrés replied:

"I'll make confession very gladly, but why don't they marry me first? And if they're going to marry me, the bridal chamber that awaits me is certainly a very bad one."

Doña Guiomar, who knew of all this, told her husband that he was giving Don Juan too much of a scare; he should moderate it, because the youth might die of it. The governor found this to be good advice, so he went in to call the priest who was confessing him, telling him that they had first to marry the Gypsy to the Gypsy girl Preciosa, and that he'd make confession afterward; the prisoner should commend himself to God with all his heart, because God is frequently accustomed to shower his mercies just when hopes have most withered.

In fact, Andrés came into a parlor where the only ones present were Doña Guiomar, the governor, Preciosa, and two household servants. But when Preciosa saw Don Juan encircled and fettered with such a large chain, his face pale and his eyes showing signs of weeping, her heart grew overcast and she leaned on the arm of her mother, who was beside her. Her mother, embracing her closely, said:

"Get hold of yourself, girl, for all you see will turn out for your pleasure and profit."

She, unaware of what was going on, couldn't console herself, and the old Gypsy woman[19] was upset, as were the bystanders, anxious to see how this situation would end.

The governor said:

"Curate, it's this Gypsy man and Gypsy woman that your worship is to marry."

"I can't do it unless the formalities necessary to the occasion are first complied with. Where were the banns posted? Where is the license from my superior allowing me to perform the wedding?"

"It was carelessness on my part," replied the governor, "but I'll see to it that the vicar gives it to you."

"Well, till I see it," the curate replied, "these people must forgive me."

19. Who has not been listed among "the only ones present."

Y, sin replicar más palabra, porque no sucediese algún escándalo, se salió de casa y los dejó a todos confusos.

—El padre ha hecho muy bien —dijo a esta sazón el corregidor—, y podría ser fuese providencia del cielo ésta, para que el suplicio de Andrés se dilate; porque, en efeto, él se ha de desposar con Preciosa y han de preceder primero las amonestaciones, donde se dará tiempo al tiempo, que suele dar dulce salida a muchas amargas dificultades; y, con todo esto, quería saber de Andrés, si la suerte encaminase sus sucesos de manera que sin estos sustos y sobresaltos se hallase esposo de Preciosa, si se tendría por dichoso, ya siendo Andrés Caballero, o ya don Juan de Cárcamo.

Así como oyó Andrés nombrarse por su nombre, dijo:

—Pues Preciosa no ha querido contenerse en los límites del silencio y ha descubierto quién soy, aunque esa buena dicha me hallara hecho monarca del mundo, la tuviera en tanto, que pusiera término a mis deseos, sin osar desear otro bien sino el del cielo.

—Pues, por ese buen ánimo que habéis mostrado, señor don Juan de Cárcamo, a su tiempo haré que Preciosa sea vuestra legítima consorte, y agora os la doy y entrego en esperanza por la más rica joya de mi casa, y de mi vida; y de mi alma; y estimadla en lo que decís, porque en ella os doy a doña Costanza de Meneses, mi única hija, la cual, si os iguala en el amor, no os desdice nada en el linaje.

Atónito quedó Andrés viendo el amor que le mostraban, y en breves razones doña Guiomar contó la pérdida de su hija y su hallazgo, con las certísimas señas que la gitana vieja había dado de su hurto; con que acabó don Juan de quedar atónito y suspenso, pero alegre sobre todo encarecimiento. Abrazó a sus suegros, llamóles padres y señores suyos, besó las manos a Preciosa, que con lágrimas le pedía las suyas.

Rompióse el secreto, salió la nueva del caso con la salida de los criados que habían estado presentes; el cual sabido por el alcalde, tío del muerto, vio tomados los caminos de su venganza, pues no había de tener lugar el rigor de la justicia para ejecutarla en el yerno del corregidor.

Vistióse don Juan los vestidos de camino que allí había traído la gitana; volviéronse las prisiones y cadenas de hierro en libertad y cadenas de oro; la tristeza de los gitanos presos, en alegría, pues otro día los dieron en fiado. Recibió el tío del muerto la promesa de dos mil ducados, que le hicieron porque bajase de la querella y perdonase a don Juan, el cual, no olvidándose de su camarada Clemente, le hizo buscar; pero no le hallaron ni supieron dél, hasta que desde allí a

And without pronouncing another word, to avoid any uproar, he left the house, and left them all in confusion.

"The priest was perfectly right," the governor then said, "and perhaps this delay is heaven-sent, to postpone Andrés's execution; because, in fact, he must first be betrothed to Preciosa, and before that the banns must be posted, which will allow us to wait, and time generally gives a welcome resolution to many bitter difficulties; besides, I wanted to learn from Andrés, if fate dealt with him so he could be Preciosa's husband without these scares and alarms, whether he'd consider himself fortunate, either as Andrés Caballero or as Don Juan de Cárcamo."

As soon as Andrés heard his real name mentioned, he said:

"Since Preciosa didn't choose to be confined to secrecy and has revealed my identity—even though good fortune were to make me ruler of the world, I'd esteem her so highly that I'd renounce my other desires, without daring to desire any further blessing other than that of heaven."

"Well, because of this good spirit you have manifested, Don Juan de Cárcamo, I'll bring it about in time that Preciosa becomes your legitimate wife, and now I give and entrust her to you, in expectation, as the richest jewel in my home, and my life, and my soul; esteem her as highly as you said, because in her I am giving you Doña Costanza de Meneses, my only daughter, who, if she matches you in love, is no whit lower than you in rank."

Andrés was amazed at the love they showed him, and briefly Doña Guiomar recounted the loss of her daughter and her rediscovery, with the trustworthy signs of her abduction that the old Gypsy woman had given; at this, Don Juan reached the height of his astonishment and amazement, but was happier than words can tell. He embraced his in-laws, called them his parents and masters, and kissed the hands of Preciosa, who tearfully asked him for his.

The secret was divulged, and the news of the event spread abroad as the servants who had been present left the room; when this was learned by the mayor who was the dead man's uncle, he saw that the road to his revenge had been closed, since the rigor of the law wouldn't extend to punishing the governor's son-in-law.

Don Juan put on the multicolored clothes that the Gypsy woman had brought there; the fetters and iron chains changed into freedom and golden chains; and the sadness of the imprisoned Gypsies, into merriment, because they were bailed out on the following day. The victim's uncle was promised two thousand ducats, offered to him to withdraw his complaint and pardon Don Juan, who, not forgetting his chum Clemente, had him looked for; but they didn't find him or hear about him until, four

cuatro días tuvo nuevas ciertas que se había embarcado en una de dos galeras de Génova que estaban en el puerto de Cartagena, y ya se habían partido.

Dijo el corregidor a don Juan que tenía por nueva cierta que su padre, don Francisco de Cárcamo, estaba proveído por corregidor de aquella ciudad, y que sería bien esperalle, para que con su beneplácito y consentimiento se hiciesen las bodas. Don Juan dijo que no saldría de lo que él ordenase, pero que, ante todas cosas, se había de desposar con Preciosa. Concedió licencia el arzobispo para que con sola una amonestación se hiciese. Hizo fiestas la ciudad, por ser muy bienquisto el corregidor, con luminarias, toros y cañas el día del desposorio; quedóse la gitana vieja en casa, que no se quiso apartar de su nieta Preciosa.

Llegaron las nuevas a la Corte del caso y casamiento de la gitanilla; supo don Francisco de Cárcamo ser su hijo el gitano y ser la Preciosa la gitanilla que él había visto, cuya hermosura disculpó con él la liviandad de su hijo, que ya le tenía por perdido, por saber que no había ido a Flandes; y más, porque vio cuán bien le estaba el casarse con hija de tan gran caballero y tan rico como era don Fernando de Azevedo. Dio priesa a su partida, por llegar presto a ver a sus hijos, y dentro de veinte días ya estaba en Murcia, con cuya llegada se renovaron los gustos, se hicieron las bodas, se contaron las vidas, y los poetas de la ciudad, que hay algunos, y muy buenos, tomaron a cargo celebrar el estraño caso, juntamente con la sin igual belleza de la gitanilla. Y de tal manera escribió el famoso licenciado Pozo, que en sus versos durará la fama de la Preciosa mientras los siglos duraren.

Olvidábaseme de decir cómo la enamorada mesonera descubrió a la justicia no ser verdad lo del hurto de Andrés el gitano, y confesó su amor y su culpa, a quien no respondió pena alguna, porque en la alegría del hallazgo de los desposados se enterró lal venganza y resucitó la clemencia.

days later, Don Juan received trustworthy news that he had embarked on one of two Genovese galleys that were in port at Cartagena, and he had already sailed.

The governor told Don Juan that he knew for a certainty that his father, Don Francisco de Cárcamo, had been appointed as governor of that city, and that it would be wise to await him, so that the wedding could take place with his blessing and consent. Don Juan said that he would obey his orders implicitly, but that, before anything else, he had to be formally betrothed to Preciosa. The archbishop gave permission for this to be done after only one posting of the banns. The city prepared a festival, because the governor was very well liked, ,with illuminations, bullfights, and jousts on the day of the betrothal; the old Gypsy woman remained in the household, for she didn't want to part from her granddaughter Preciosa.

News of the event and the Gypsy girl's coming marriage reached the capital; Don Francisco de Cárcamo learned that his son was the Gypsy and Preciosa was the Gypsy girl he had seen; in his eyes her beauty excused the flightiness of his son, whom he had already considered lost on learning that he hadn't gone to Flanders; all the more so, because he saw how advantageous it was for him to marry the daughter of a nobleman as great and as wealthy as Don Fernando de Azevedo. He hastened his departure, in order to see his children soon, and in twenty days he was already in Murcia; his arrival renewed their pleasures, the wedding was held, their stories were told, and the poets of the city (for there are some, and very good ones) made it their task to celebrate the strange event, as well as the Gypsy girl's matchless beauty. And the noteworthy graduate Pozo wrote so well that in his lines the fame of Preciosa will last as long as time.

I almost forgot to tell how the lovelorn innkeeper's daughter revealed to the law that Andrés the Gypsy hadn't really stolen anything; she confessed her love and her crime, which met with no penalty, because, in the joy of the discovery of the newlyweds, revenge was buried and clemency revived.

Rinconete y Cortadillo

En la venta del Molinillo, que está puesta en los fines de los famosos campos de Alcudia, como vamos de Castilla a la Andalucía, un día de los calurosos del verano, se hallaron en ella acaso dos muchachos de hasta edad de catorce a quince años: el uno ni el otro no pasaban de diez y siete; ambos de buena gracia, pero muy descosidos, rotos y maltratados; capa, no la tenían; los calzones eran de lienzo y las medias de carne. Bien es verdad que lo enmendaban los zapatos, porque los del uno eran alpargates, tan traídos como llevados, y los del otro picados y sin suelas, de manera que más le servían de cormas que de zapatos. Traía el uno montera verde de cazador, el otro un sombrero sin toquilla, bajo de copa y ancho de falda. A la espalda, y ceñida por los pechos, traía el uno una camisa de color de camuza, encerrada y recogida toda en una manga; el otro venía escueto y sin alforjas, puesto que en el seno se le parecía un gran bulto, que, a lo que después pareció, era un cuello de los que llaman valones, almidonado con grasa, y tan deshilado de roto, que todo parecía hilachas. Venían en él envueltos y guardados unos naipes de figura ovada, porque de ejercitarlos se les habían gastado las puntas, y porque durasen más se las cercenaron y los dejaron de aquel talle. Estaban los dos quemados del sol, las uñas caireladas y las manos no muy limpias; el uno tenía una media espada, y el otro un cuchillo de cachas amarillas, que los suelen llamar vaqueros.

Saliéronse los dos a sestear en un portal, o cobertizo, que delante de la venta se hace; y, sentándose frontero el uno del otro, el que parecía de más edad dijo al más pequeño:

—¿De qué tierra es vuesa merced, señor gentilhombre, y para adónde bueno camina?

—Mi tierra, señor caballero —respondió el preguntado—, no la sé, ni para dónde camino, tampoco.

—Pues en verdad —dijo el mayor— que no parece vuesa merced

Rinconete and Cortadillo

At the Inn of the Little Windmill,[1] which is situated on the edge of the well-known valley of Alcudia, coming from Castile to Andalusia, there chanced, one hot summer day, to be two boys of fourteen or fifteen (neither of them was over seventeen), both nice-looking but very tattered, torn, and battered; cape, they had none; their breeches were of cloth, their stockings of their own skin. To be sure, this lack was compensated for by the presence of shoes, because one wore hemp sandals, which were worn to a frazzle, and the other had soleless, "openwork" shoes, which were more like a hobble to him than like footgear. One wore a green huntsman's cap, the other a hat without a band, low of crown and broad of brim. One had across his back and tied over his chest a pale yellow shirt, all stuffed and tucked up into a baggy sleeve; the other was free of carrying-bags, though a large bulky object could be seen under his shirt-front, which appeared later to be one of those collars called Vandykes, stiff with grease and so threadbare that it seemed to be in shreds. Wrapped and kept safe in it were some playing cards that were oval in shape because long use had destroyed their corners and, to make them last longer, they had been clipped and left in that shape. Both boys were sunburnt, and had long, dark fingernails and not very clean hands; one wore half a sword, the other a knife with a yellow handle, of the type called cowherd's knives.

The two wandered out to take their siesta in an entranceway or shed in front of the inn; sitting down opposite each other, the older-looking one said to the younger one:

"From what homeland does your worship come, my good gentleman, and where are you headed?"

"My land, gentle knight," replied his interlocutor, "I know not, nor whither I'm bound."

"Since, truly," said the older boy, "your worship doesn't seem to have

1. South of Ciudad Real, halfway between Toledo and Córdoba.

del cielo, y que éste no es lugar para hacer su asiento en él; que por fuerza se ha de pasar adelante.

—Así es —respondió el mediano—, pero yo he dicho verdad en lo que he dicho, porque mi tierra no es mía, pues no tengo en ella más de un padre que no me tiene por hijo y una madrastra que me trata como alnado; el camino que llevo es a la ventura, y allí le daría fin donde hallase quien me diese lo necesario para pasar esta miserable vida.

—Y ¿sabe vuesa merced algún oficio? —preguntó el grande.

Y el menor respondió:

—No sé otro sino que corro como una liebre, y salto como un gamo y corto de tijera muy delicadamente.

—Todo eso es muy bueno, útil y provechoso —dijo el grande—, porque habrá sacristán que le dé a vuesa merced la ofrenda de Todos Santos, porque para el Jueves Santo le corte florones de papel para el monumento.

—No es mi corte desa manera —respondió el menor—, sino que mi padre, por la misericordia del cielo, es sastre y calcetero, y me enseñó a cortar antiparas, que, como vuesa merced bien sabe, son medias calzas con avampiés, que por su propio nombre se suelen llamar polainas; y córtolas tan bien, que en verdad que me podría examinar de maestro, sino que la corta suerte me tiene arrinconado.

—Todo eso y más acontece por los buenos —respondió el grande—, y siempre he oído decir que las buenas habilidades son las más perdidas, pero aún edad tiene vuesa merced para enmendar su ventura. Mas, si yo no me engaño y el ojo no me miente, otras gracias tiene vuesa merced secretas, y no las quiere manifestar.

—Sí tengo —respondió el pequeño—, pero no son para en público, como vuesa merced ha muy bien apuntado.

A lo cual replicó el grande:

—Pues yo le sé decir que soy uno de los más secretos mozos que en gran parte se puedan hallar; y, para obligar a vuesa merced que descubra su pecho y descanse conmigo, le quiero obligar con descubrirle el mío primero; porque imagino que no sin misterio nos ha juntado aquí la suerte, y pienso que habemos de ser, déste hasta el último día de nuestra vida, verdaderos amigos. «Yo, señor hidalgo, soy natural de la Fuenfrida, lugar conocido y famoso por los ilustres pasajeros que por él de contino pasan; mi nombre es Pedro del Rincón; mi padre es persona de calidad, porque es ministro de la Santa Cruzada: quiero

dropped from heaven, and this is no place to settle in, you must necessarily travel on."

"Correct," replied the younger, "but what I said is true, because my homeland isn't mine, since all I have there is a father who disowns me and a stepmother who treats me like a stepchild; I'm headed for wherever my luck takes me, and I'll stop wandering when I find someone to give me the means to live this miserable life."

"And does your worship know any trade?" the bigger boy asked.

And the younger one replied:

"The only one I know is running like a hare, leaping like a fallow deer, and using a pair of scissors very neatly."

"All of that is very fine, useful, and profitable," said the big boy, "because some sacristan will surely give your worship the offering of All Saints' Day[2] if you cut out paper flowers for him to adorn the sepulchre on Holy Thursday."

"My cutting isn't of that type," the younger boy replied; "it's that my father, through heaven's mercy, is a tailor and hosier, and he taught me how to cut out leggings, which, as your worship is well aware, are half-stockings with foot-pieces, and are properly called gaiters; and I cut them out so well, that I could really get a license as a master hosier, except that my cut-up luck has me pinned in a corner."

"Such things and worse happen for the best," the big boy replied, "and I've always heard that good skills are the most wasted; but your worship is still young enough to repair your fortunes. Yet, if I'm not mistaken and my eyes don't deceive me, your worship has other hidden talents, which you don't wish to reveal."

"Yes, I do," the younger boy replied, "but they're not for the public ear, as your worship has so well indicated."

To which the big boy replied:

"Well, I can tell you that I'm one of the most discreet fellows you can find for miles around; and to make your worship open your heart and relax with me, I shall oblige you by opening mine first; because it seems to me that fate hasn't brought us together here without some secret purpose, and I think that we are to be true friends, from today till the last day of our life. I, your lordship, am a native of Fuenfría, a spot well known and famous for the illustrious travelers who constantly pass through it.[3] My name is Pedro del Rincón; my father is a person of quality, because he's an official of the Holy Crusade: I mean, he sells papal indulgences to fi-

2. Bread and wine. 3. Royals had to take that mountain pass near Segovia to reach certain palaces.

decir que es bulero, o buldero, como los llama el vulgo. Algunos días le acompañé en el oficio, y le aprendí de manera, que no daría ventaja en echar las bulas al que más presumiese en ello. Pero, habiéndome un día aficionado más al dinero de las bulas que a las mismas bulas, me abracé con un talego y di conmigo y con él en Madrid, donde con las comodidades que allí de ordinario se ofrecen, en pocos días saqué las entrañas al talego y le dejé con más dobleces que pañizuelo de desposado. Vino el que tenía a cargo el dinero tras mí, prendiéronme, tuve poco favor, aunque, viendo aquellos señores mi poca edad, se contentaron con que me arrimasen al aldabilla y me mosqueasen las espaldas por un rato, y con que saliese desterrado por cuatro años de la Corte. Tuve paciencia, encogí los hombros, sufrí la tanda y mosqueo, y salí a cumplir mi destierro, con tanta priesa, que no tuve lugar de buscar cabalgaduras. Tomé de mis alhajas las que pude y las que me parecieron más necesarias, y entre ellas saqué estos naipes —y a este tiempo descubrió los que se han dicho, que en el cuello traía—, con los cuales he ganado mi vida por los mesones y ventas que hay desde Madrid aquí, jugando a la veintiuna;» y, aunque vuesa merced los vee tan astrosos y maltratados, usan de una maravillosa virtud con quien los entiende, que no alzará que no quede un as debajo. Y si vuesa merced es versado en este juego, verá cuánta ventaja lleva el que sabe que tiene cierto un as a la primera carta, que le puede servir de un punto y de once; que con esta ventaja, siendo la veintiuna envidada, el dinero se queda en casa. Fuera desto, aprendí de un cocinero de un cierto embajador ciertas tretas de quínolas y del parar, a quien también llaman el andaboba; que, así como vuesa merced se puede examinar en el corte de sus antiparas, así puedo yo ser maestro en la ciencia vilhanesca. Con esto voy seguro de no morir de hambre, porque, aunque llegue a un cortijo, hay quien quiera pasar tiempo jugando un rato. Y desto hemos de hacer luego la experiencia los dos: armemos la red, y veamos si cae algún pájaro destos arrieros que aquí hay; quiero decir que jugaremos los dos a la veintiuna, como si fuese de veras; que si alguno quisiere ser tercero, él será el primero que deje la pecunia.

—Sea en buen hora —dijo el otro—, y en merced muy grande tengo la que vuesa merced me ha hecho en darme cuenta de su vida, con que me ha obligado a que yo no le encubra la mía, que, diciéndola más breve, es ésta: «yo nací en el piadoso lugar puesto entre

nance the crusade; he's a *buldero,* as the lower class call them. For some days I accompanied him at his trade, and I learned it so well that I can outdo the man who prides himself the most on hawking indulgences. But one day, having taken a greater liking to the money from the indulgences than the indulgences themselves, I hugged a sackful to my heart and made off with it to Madrid, where, with the temptations usually offered there, I disemboweled the sack in a few days, leaving it more crumpled than a bridegroom's handkerchief. The man responsible for the money came after me, I was arrested and I didn't get off all that lightly, though when those gentlemen saw how young I was, they limited themselves to leaning me against the post in jail and flogging my back for a while, and exiling me from the capital for four years. I was patient, I shrugged my shoulders, I suffered the punishment and whipping, and I set out on my exile so quickly that I had no time to look for a mount. I took along all of my belongings that I could, the ones I thought most necessary, and among them I brought these cards." (And here he revealed the above-mentioned cards in the collar.) "With them I've earned my keep in every inn and tavern from Madrid to here, playing twenty-one. And though they're as filthy and mangled as your worship sees, they have marvelous powers for the man who understands them: he won't cut the deck without uncovering an ace. And if your worship is familiar with cards, you'll see what an advantage accrues to the player whose first card is sure to be an ace, because he can count it as one point or eleven; with that advantage, when you go for twenty-one, the money stays at home. Besides that, I learned from a certain ambassador's cook certain tricks in four-hand flush and in the card-matching game, which is also called 'the sucker's game.' And, just as your worship cuts gaiters well enough to gain a license, I can be a master in the science of the pasteboards. Thereby I'm safe from starving to death, because, even if it's just a farmhouse I come to, there's someone who wants to pass the time playing a little cards. And the two of us shall experiment on this right away: let's spread the net and see whether some bird falls into it; that is, any of the muleteers staying here. I mean, we'll play twenty-one together as if it were a real game, and if someone else wants to take a *third* hand, he'll be the *first* to lose his money."[4]

"Fine with me," his companion said, "and I take it as a great favor that your worship recounted your life to me, whereby you've obliged me not to conceal my own, which, told as briefly as possible, is as follows. I was born in the pious hamlet located between Salamanca and Medina del

4. This last sentence contains complicated puns based on card-playing terminology; all this translation can do is preserve the joke on "third" and "first."

Salamanca y Medina del Campo; mi padre es sastre, enseñóme su oficio, y de corte de tisera, con mi buen ingenio, salté a cortar bolsas. Enfadóme la vida estrecha del aldea y el desamorado trato de mi madrastra. Dejé mi pueblo, vine a Toledo a ejercitar mi oficio, y en él he hecho maravillas; porque no pende relicario de toca ni hay faldriquera tan escondida que mis dedos no visiten ni mis tiseras no corten, aunque le estén guardando con ojos de Argos. Y, en cuatro meses que estuve en aquella ciudad, nunca fui cogido entre puertas, ni sobresaltado ni corrido de corchetes, ni soplado de ningún cañuto. Bien es verdad que habrá ocho días que una espía doble dio noticia de mi habilidad al Corregidor, el cual, aficionado a mis buenas partes, quisiera verme; mas yo, que, por ser humilde, no quiero tratar con personas tan graves, procuré de no verme con él, y así, salí de la ciudad con tanta priesa, que no tuve lugar de acomodarme de cabalgaduras ni blancas, ni de algún coche de retorno, o por lo menos de un carro».

—Eso se borre —dijo Rincón—; y, pues ya nos conocemos, no hay para qué aquesas grandezas ni altiveces: confesemos llanamente que no teníamos blanca, ni aun zapatos.

—Sea así —respondió Diego Cortado, que así dijo el menor que se llamaba—; y, pues nuestra amistad, como vuesa merced, señor Rincón, ha dicho, ha de ser perpetua, comencémosla con santas y loables ceremonias.

Y, levantándose, Diego Cortado abrazó a Rincón y Rincón a él tierna y estrechamente, y luego se pusieron los dos a jugar a la veintiuna con los ya referidos naipes, limpios de polvo y de paja, mas no de grasa y malicia; y, a pocas manos, alzaba tan bien por el as Cortado como Rincón, su maestro.

Salió en esto un arriero a refrescarse al portal, y pidió que quería hacer tercio. Acogiéronle de buena gana, y en menos de media hora le ganaron doce reales y veinte y dos maravedís, que fue darle doce lanzadas y veinte y dos mil pesadumbres. Y, creyendo el arriero que por ser muchachos no se lo defenderían, quiso quitalles el dinero; mas ellos, poniendo el uno mano a su media espada y el otro al de las cachas amarillas, le dieron tanto que hacer, que, a no salir sus compañeros, sin duda lo pasara mal.

A esta sazón, pasaron acaso por el camino una tropa de caminantes a caballo, que iban a sestear a la venta del Alcalde, que está media legua más adelante, los cuales, viendo la pendencia del arriero con los dos muchachos, los apaciguaron y les dijeron que si acaso iban a Sevilla, que se viniesen con ellos.

Campo; my father is a tailor, he taught me his trade, and by my wits I advanced from a cut-cloth to a cutpurse. I was fed up with the restricted village life and the loveless treatment I got from my stepmother. I left my hometown, and I went to Toledo to ply my trade; there I did wonders, because there's no reliquary on a wimple or pocket so well hidden that my fingers can't reach, or my scissors can't cut, even if they're guarded with Argus eyes. And in the four months I stayed in that city, I was never caught red-handed, or alarmed or chased by constables, or ratted on by any stoolie. It's true that about a week ago a double agent informed the city magistrate about my handiwork, and he, taking a liking to my talents, wanted to meet me; but, being a humble fellow, I don't like to rub elbows with such important people, and I tried to avoid the meeting; so I left town so fast that I had no time to fit myself out with a mount or with coin, or any return coach, or even a cart."

"Forget all that," said Rincón, "and now that we know each other, why keep up all this grand, highflown talk? Let's admit right out that we haven't a sou, or even shoes."

"All right," replied Diego Cortado, for that's what the younger boy said his name was, "and since our friendship, as your worship said, Señor Rincón, is to last forever, let's begin it with holy, praiseworthy ceremonies."

And, standing up, Diego Cortado hugged Rincón, and Rincón hugged him, warmly and tightly; then they both started playing twenty-one with the above-mentioned cards, cleaned of dust and straw but not of grease and cunning; and in a few hands Cortado cut to an ace as well as Rincón, his teacher.

At that moment a muleteer came outside to cool himself in the entranceway, and asked to take a hand. They welcomed him gladly, and in less than half an hour won off him twelve reales and twenty-two maravedis, which was like giving him twelve spears thrusts and twenty-two thousand sorrows. The muleteer, thinking that, because they were boys, they would put up no resistance, tried to take the money away from them; but they—one laying hand to his half-sword, and the other to his yellow-handled knife—gave him so much trouble that, if his companions hadn't come out, he would no doubt have had a bad time of it.

Just then a troop of men riding horses chanced to pass down the road, on their way to a siesta at the Inn of the Mayor, half a league further on. Seeing the fight between the muleteer and the two boys, they calmed them down and invited them to join them if they chanced to be heading for Seville.

—Allá vamos —dijo Rincón—, y serviremos a vuesas mercedes en todo cuanto nos mandaren.

Y, sin más detenerse, saltaron delante de las mulas y se fueron con ellos, dejando al arriero agraviado y enojado, y a la ventera admirada de la buena crianza de los pícaros, que les había estado oyendo su plática sin que ellos advirtiesen en ello. Y, cuando dijo al arriero que les había oído decir que los naipes que traían eran falsos, se pelaba las barbas, y quisiera ir a la venta tras ellos a cobrar su hacienda, porque decía que era grandísima afrenta, y caso de menos valer, que dos muchachos hubiesen engañado a un hombrazo tan grande como él. Sus compañeros le detuvieron y aconsejaron que no fuese, siquiera por no publicar su inhabilidad y simpleza. En fin, tales razones le dijeron, que, aunque no le consolaron, le obligaron a quedarse.

En esto, Cortado y Rincón se dieron tan buena maña en servir a los caminantes, que lo más del camino los llevaban a las ancas; y, aunque se les ofrecían algunas ocasiones de tentar las valijas de sus medios amos, no las admitieron, por no perder la ocasión tan buena del viaje de Sevilla, donde ellos tenían grande deseo de verse.

Con todo esto, a la entrada de la ciudad, que fue a la oración y por la puerta de la Aduana, a causa del registro y almojarifazgo que se paga, no se pudo contener Cortado de no cortar la valija o maleta que a las ancas traía un francés de la camarada; y así, con el de sus cachas le dio tan larga y profunda herida, que se parecían patentemente las entrañas, y sutilmente le sacó dos camisas buenas, un reloj de sol y un librillo de memoria, cosas que cuando las vieron no les dieron mucho gusto; y pensaron que, pues el francés llevaba a las ancas aquella maleta, no la había de haber ocupado con tan poco peso como era el que tenían aquellas preseas, y quisieran volver a darle otro tiento; pero no lo hicieron, imaginando que ya lo habrían echado menos y puesto en recaudo lo que quedaba.

Habíanse despedido antes que el salto hiciesen de los que hasta allí los habían sustentado, y otro día vendieron las camisas en el malbaratillo que se hace fuera de la puerta del Arenal, y dellas hicieron veinte reales. Hecho esto, se fueron a ver la ciudad, y admiróles la grandeza y sumptuosidad de su mayor iglesia, el gran concurso de gente del río, porque era en tiempo de cargazón de flota y había en él seis galeras, cuya vista les hizo suspirar, y aun temer el día que sus culpas les habían de traer a morar en ellas de por vida. Echaron de ver los muchos muchachos de la esportilla que por allí andaban; informáronse de uno dellos qué oficio era aquél, y si era de mucho trabajo, y de qué ganancia.

"We are," said Rincón, "and we'll serve your worships in any way you command."

Without any hesitation they leaped in front of the mules and departed with those men, leaving the muleteer affronted and angry, and the hostess of the inn amazed at the rascals' good breeding, because she had been listening to their conversation without their knowledge. And when she told the muleteer she had heard them say that their cards were marked, he was rabid and wanted to follow them to their inn to regain his money, because he said it was a terrible insult, which made him lose face, that two boys should have cheated a big, hulking man like him. His companions restrained him and advised him not to go, if only to avoid making public his lack of skill and his simplicity. Finally they spoke words to him which, though not consoling him, compelled him to stay put.

Meanwhile, Cortado and Rincón were so handy at serving the travelers that they were allowed to ride behind two of the men most of the way; and though several opportunities presented themselves to pilfer the bags of their temporary masters, they passed them up, so as not to lose such a good opportunity as a trip to Seville, where they greatly desired to be.

Nevertheless, when they entered the city, which was at nightfall at the Customs Gate, to be inspected and to pay duty on their goods, Cortado couldn't refrain from cutting open the bag or case which a Frenchman of the troop carried behind him; and so, with that knife of his he gave it such a broad and deep wound that its insides lay wide open. Deftly he drew out two good shirts, a sundial, and a memorandum book, things which didn't satisfy the boys much when they saw them. They thought that, if the Frenchman was carrying that case behind him, he couldn't have filled it with stuff amounting to as little as those treasures did, and they would have liked to give it another going-over, but they didn't, imagining that the men would have already discovered the loss and put the remainder in a safer place.

They had taken their leave before robbing the men who had sustained them till then, and the next day they sold the shirts in the flea market held outside the Puerta del Arenal, receiving twenty reales for them. After that, they went to see the city, marveling at the size and sumptuousness of its cathedral and the great crowds of people by the river, because it was the season for loading the fleet and there were six galleys on the river; the sight of them made them sigh and even fear the day when their crimes would bring them to spend their whole lives on them. They noticed the many boys with porter's baskets going to and fro there; they asked one of them what that job was like, whether it was hard work, and what it paid.

Un muchacho asturiano, que fue a quien le hicieron la pregunta, respondió que el oficio era descansado y de que no se pagaba alcabala, y que algunos días salía con cinco y con seis reales de ganancia, con que comía y bebía y triunfaba como cuerpo de rey, libre de buscar amo a quien dar fianzas y seguro de comer a la hora que quisiese, pues a todas lo hallaba en el más mínimo bodegón de toda la ciudad.

No les pareció mal a los dos amigos la relación del asturianillo, ni les descontentó el oficio, por parecerles que venía como de molde para poder usar el suyo con cubierta y seguridad, por la comodidad que ofrecía de entrar en todas las casas; y luego determinaron de comprar los instrumentos necesarios para usalle, pues lo podían usar sin examen. Y, preguntándole al asturiano qué habían de comprar, les respondió que sendos costales pequeños, limpios o nuevos, y cada uno tres espuertas de palma, dos grandes y una pequeña, en las cuales se repartía la carne, pescado y fruta, y en el costal, el pan; y él les guió donde lo vendían, y ellos, del dinero de la galima del francés, lo compraron todo, y dentro de dos horas pudieran estar graduados en el nuevo oficio, según les ensayaban las esportillas y asentaban los costales. Avisóles su adalid de los puestos donde habían de acudir: por las mañanas, a la Carnicería y a la plaza de San Salvador; los días de pescado, a la Pescadería y a la Costanilla; todas las tardes, al río; los jueves, a la Feria.

Toda esta lición tomaron bien de memoria, y otro día bien de mañana se plantaron en la plaza de San Salvador; y, apenas hubieron llegado, cuando los rodearon otros mozos del oficio, que, por lo flamante de los costales y espuertas, vieron ser nuevos en la plaza; hiciéronles mil preguntas, y a todas respondían con discreción y mesura. En esto, llegaron un medio estudiante y un soldado, y, convidados de la limpieza de las espuertas de los dos novatos, el que parecía estudiante llamó a Cortado, y el soldado a Rincón.

—En nombre sea de Dios —dijeron ambos.

—Para bien se comience el oficio —dijo Rincón—, que vuesa merced me estrena, señor mío.

A lo cual respondió el soldado:

—La estrena no será mala, porque estoy de ganancia y soy enamorado, y tengo de hacer hoy banquete a unas amigas de mi señora.

—Pues cargue vuesa merced a su gusto, que ánimo tengo y fuerzas para llevarme toda esta plaza, y aun si fuere menester que ayude a guisarlo, lo haré de muy buena voluntad.

Contentóse el soldado de la buena gracia del mozo, y díjole que si quería servir, que él le sacaría de aquel abatido oficio. A lo cual

A boy from Asturias, of whom they asked that information, replied that the work was easy and that you didn't pay tax on it; some days he made five or six reales profit, on which he ate, drank, and made as merry as a king, being free from seeking a master with whom he'd have to leave a security deposit, and sure of eating at any hour he wished, because at all hours he could find a meal at the lowest cookshop in the whole town.

The two friends thought well of the little Asturian boy's report, and weren't displeased at the job, which they thought suited them to a T, by allowing them to ply *their* trade in concealment and security and by opening the door of every house to them; at once they decided to buy the equipment necessary for working at it, since they needed no license to do so. And when they asked the Asturian what they needed to buy, he answered: a small sack, cleaned or new, for each, and for each three palm-leaf baskets, two large and one small, into which to place meat, fish, and fruit, respectively, the sack being for bread. He guided them to where all this was sold, and with the money raised from robbing the Frenchman they purchased it all, and in two hours might have been old hands at the new job, so well did the baskets and bags sit on them. Their chief informed them of the sites they had to frequent: in the morning, the main meat market and the Plaza de San Salvador; on fast days, the main fish market and the Costanilla; every afternoon, the river; Thursdays, the weekly market.

They carefully memorized this whole lesson, and the next day, early in the morning, they took up their stand in the Plaza de San Salvador; as soon as they arrived, they were surrounded by other boys of that calling, who, because their bags and baskets were so spic and span, saw that they were newcomers to the square; asked a thousand questions, they replied to each prudently and politely. At this point, there arrived an apparent student and a soldier, who were attracted by the cleanness of the two novices' baskets; the seeming student called over Cortado; and the soldier, Rincón.

"In the name of God!" they both said.

"May my job begin well!" said Rincón. "Your worship is my first customer, sir."

To which the soldier replied:

"Your beginning and your tip won't be bad, because I'm making a good living and I'm in love; today I want to give a party for some of my lady's girlfriends."

"Then load me down as much as you like, sir, because I have enough spirit and strength to carry away this whole square, and even if you needed me to help cook the food, I'd be very glad to."

The soldier was pleased at the lad's good attitude and said that if he wanted to be his servant, he'd take him out of that lowly calling. To which

respondió Rincón que, por ser aquel día el primero que le usaba, no le quería dejar tan presto, hasta ver, a lo menos, lo que tenía de malo y bueno; y, cuando no le contentase, él daba su palabra de servirle a él antes que a un canónigo.

Rióse el soldado, cargóle muy bien, mostróle la casa de su dama, para que la supiese de allí adelante y él no tuviese necesidad, cuando otra vez le enviase, de acompañarle. Rincón prometió fidelidad y buen trato. Diole el soldado tres cuartos, y en un vuelo volvió a la plaza, por no perder coyuntura; porque también desta diligencia les advirtió el asturiano, y de que cuando llevasen pescado menudo (conviene a saber: albures, o sardinas o acedías), bien podían tomar algunas y hacerles la salva, siquiera para el gasto de aquel día; pero que esto había de ser con toda sagacidad y advertimiento, porque no se perdiese el crédito, que era lo que más importaba en aquel ejercicio.

Por presto que volvió Rincón, ya halló en el mismo puesto a Cortado. Llegóse Cortado a Rincón, y preguntóle que cómo le había ido. Rincón abrió la mano y mostróle los tres cuartos. Cortado entró la suya en el seno y sacó una bolsilla, que mostraba haber sido de ámbar en los pasados tiempos; venía algo hinchada, y dijo:

—Con ésta me pagó su reverencia del estudiante, y con dos cuartos; mas tomadla vos, Rincón, por lo que puede suceder.

Y, habiéndosela ya dado secretamente, veis aquí do vuelve el estudiante trasudando y turbado de muerte; y, viendo a Cortado, le dijo si acaso había visto una bolsa de tales y tales señas, que, con quince escudos de oro en oro y con tres reales de a dos y tantos maravedís en cuartos y en ochavos, le faltaba, y que le dijese si la había tomado en el entretanto que con él había andado comprando. A lo cual, con estraño disimulo, sin alterarse ni mudarse en nada, respondió Cortado:

—Lo que yo sabré decir desa bolsa es que no debe de estar perdida, si ya no es que vuesa merced la puso a mal recaudo.

—¡Eso es ello, pecador de mí —respondió el estudiante—: que la debí de poner a mal recaudo, pues me la hurtaron!

—Lo mismo digo yo —dijo Cortado—; pero para todo hay remedio, si no es para la muerte, y el que vuesa merced podrá tomar es, lo primero y principal, tener paciencia; que de menos nos hizo Dios y un día viene tras otro día, y donde las dan las toman; y podría ser que, con el tiempo, el que llevó la bolsa se viniese a arrepentir y se la volviese a vuesa merced sahumada.

—El sahumerio le perdonaríamos —respondió el estudiante.

Y Cortado prosiguió diciendo:

—Cuanto más, que cartas de descomunión hay, paulinas, y buena

Rincón replied that, since it was the first day he was working at it, he didn't want to leave it so soon, at least not before seeing its good and bad points; if it didn't satisfy him, he gave his word that he'd rather serve *him* than a prebendary.

The soldier laughed, loaded him down heavily, and showed him his lady's house, so that he'd be familiar with it from then on and the soldier wouldn't need to escort him if he sent him there again. Rincón promised to be loyal and serviceable. The soldier gave him three cuartos, and in a trice he returned to the square, so as to let no opportunities slip by; because the Asturian boy had recommended that briskness to them as well, and had told them that, when they were carrying small fish, such as dace, sardines, or little flounders, they could take some for their own consumption, at least for their needs of that day; but this had to be done very shrewdly and cautiously, to avoid losing their reputation for honesty, which was what counted for most on that job.

Rincón returned very quickly but already found Cortado back on the same spot. Cortado came up to Rincón and asked him how he had made out. Rincón opened his hand and showed the three cuartos. Cortado thrust his inside his shirt and took out a purse which indicated it had been rubbed with ambergris in the past; it was rather bulky, and he said:

"This was my pay from his reverence the student, besides two cuartos; but you take it, Rincón, just in case."

After he had already given it to him secretly, behold, the student came back sweating and worried to death; seeing Cortado, he asked him whether he happened to see a purse of such and such a description, which he had lost; it contained fifteen solid-gold escudos, three two-real pieces, and a lot of money in cuartos and ochavos. He should tell him whether he had taken it while they were making purchases together. To which, with matchless dissimulation, his features showing not the least alteration, Cortado replied:

"All that I can say about that purse is that it's probably not lost, unless your worship put it in bad keeping."

"That's it, sinner that I am!" the student replied. "I must have put it in bad keeping, since it's been stolen!"

"That's what I say," Cortado said, "but there's a remedy for everything but death, and the remedy your worship can take is, first and foremost, to be patient; because you should never give up hope, and one day follows another, and give and take is fair play. And it may be that in time whoever took the purse will repent and return it to your worship in better condition."

"I'd forgo the better condition," the student replied.

And Cortado continued:

"Especially since there are edicts of excommunication, papal ones, and

diligencia, que es madre de la buena ventura; aunque, a la verdad, no quisiera yo ser el llevador de tal bolsa; porque, si es que vuesa merced tiene alguna orden sacra, parecerme hía a mí que había cometido algún grande incesto, o sacrilegio.

—Y ¡cómo que ha cometido sacrilegio! —dijo a esto el adolorido estudiante—; que, puesto que yo no soy sacerdote, sino sacristán de unas monjas, el dinero de la bolsa era del tercio de una capellanía, que me dio a cobrar un sacerdote amigo mío, y es dinero sagrado y bendito.

—Con su pan se lo coma —dijo Rincón a este punto—; no le arriendo la ganancia; día de juicio hay, donde todo saldrá en la colada, y entonces se verá quién fue Callejas y el atrevido que se atrevió a tomar, hurtar y menoscabar el tercio de la capellanía. Y ¿cuánto renta cada año? Dígame, señor sacristán, por su vida.

—¡Renta la puta que me parió! ¡Y estoy yo agora para decir lo que renta! —respondió el sacristán con algún tanto de demasiada cólera—. Decidme, hermanos, si sabéis algo; si no, quedad con Dios, que yo la quiero hacer pregonar.

—No me parece mal remedio ese —dijo Cortado—, pero advierta vuesa merced no se le olviden las señas de la bolsa, ni la cantidad puntualmente del dinero que va en ella; que si yerra en un ardite, no parecerá en días del mundo, y esto le doy por hado.

—No hay que temer deso —respondió el sacristán—, que lo tengo más en la memoria que el tocar de las campanas: no me erraré en un átomo.

Sacó, en esto, de la faldriquera un pañuelo randado para limpiarse el sudor, que llovía de su rostro como de alquitara; y, apenas le hubo visto Cortado, cuando le marcó por suyo. Y, habiéndose ido el sacristán, Cortado le siguió y le alcanzó en las Gradas, donde le llamó y le retiró a una parte; y allí le comenzó a decir tantos disparates, al modo de lo que llaman bernardinas, cerca del hurto y hallazgo de su bolsa, dándole buenas esperanzas, sin concluir jamás razón que comenzase, que el pobre sacristán estaba embelesado escuchándole. Y, como no acababa de entender lo que le decía, hacía que le replicase la razón dos y tres veces.

Estábale mirando Cortado a la cara atentamente y no quitaba los ojos de sus ojos. El sacristán le miraba de la misma manera, estando colgado de sus palabras. Este tan grande embelesamiento dio lugar a Cortado que concluyese su obra, y sutilmente le sacó el pañuelo de la faldriquera; y, despidiéndose dél, le dijo que a la tarde procurase de verle en aquel mismo lugar, porque él traía entre ojos que un muchacho de su mismo oficio y de su mismo tamaño, que era algo ladron-

careful diligence, which is the mother of good fortune; though, to tell the truth, I wouldn't want to be the man who stole that purse; because if your worship has taken any holy orders, it would seem to me that he had committed some great incest or sacrilege."

"And how he committed sacrilege!" the sorrowful student retorted. "Because, though I'm not a priest but only sacristan to some nuns, the money in the purse was that of four months' income from a chaplaincy, which a priest friend of mine asked me to collect, and it's sacred, blessed money."

"Make your bed and lie in it," Rincón then said. "I don't envy him; there's a judgment day, when everything comes out in the wash, and then we'll see who we were dealing with, and who the man was rash enough to take, steal, and diminish the income from the chaplaincy. And what's the yearly income? Tell me, sacristan, on your life."

"God damn the amount of income! Am I in the mood to tell you that?" the sacristan replied with somewhat excessive anger. "Tell me, brothers, if you know anything; if not, let me say good-bye, because I want to have the theft publicly announced."

"That sounds to me like a good measure to take," said Cortado, "but remember, sir: you mustn't omit the description of the purse or the exact amount of money in it; if you're off by one farthing, it will never, never show up, and this I can promise you."

"There's no fear of that," the sacristan replied, "because I remember it better than the peal of my church bells: I won't be off by a cent."

Then he drew from his pocket a lace-edged handkerchief to wipe his sweat, which was raining down his face as if from a still; as soon as Cortado saw it, he set his heart on it. After the sacristan left, Cortado followed him, catching up with him by the cathedral steps, where he called him and drew him aside; there he began spewing such nonsense, the kind called double talk, about the theft and recovery of his purse, holding out hopes to him, and never ending any argument he started, that the poor sacristan was dumbfounded listening to him. Since he couldn't manage to understand what he was saying, he kept making him repeat everything two or three times.

Cortado was looking him fixedly in the face, never taking his eyes off the other man's. The sacristan was looking at him in the same way, hanging on his every word. This great stupor allowed Cortado to finish his task; he deftly drew the handkerchief from his pocket; and, taking leave of him, he asked him to try to see him in that same spot in the afternoon, because he suspected that a boy of the same calling and same size, who was some-

cillo, le había tomado la bolsa, y que él se obligaba a saberlo, dentro de pocos o de muchos días.

Con esto se consoló algo el sacristán, y se despidió de Cortado, el cual se vino donde estaba Rincón, que todo lo había visto un poco apartado dél; y más abajo estaba otro mozo de la esportilla, que vio todo lo que había pasado y cómo Cortado daba el pañuelo a Rincón; y, llegándose a ellos, les dijo:

—Díganme, señores galanes: ¿voacedes son de mala entrada, o no?

—No entendemos esa razón, señor galán —respondió Rincón.

—¿Qué no entrevan, señores murcios? —respondió el otro.

—Ni somos de Teba ni de Murcia —dijo Cortado—. Si otra cosa quiere, dígala; si no, váyase con Dios.

—¿No lo entienden? —dijo el mozo—. Pues yo se lo daré a entender, y a beber, con una cuchara de plata; quiero decir, señores, si son vuesas mercedes ladrones. Mas no sé para qué les pregunto esto, pues sé ya que lo son; mas díganme: ¿cómo no han ido a la aduana del señor Monipodio?

—¿Págase en esta tierra almojarifazgo de ladrones, señor galán? —dijo Rincón.

—Si no se paga —respondió el mozo—, a lo menos regístranse ante el señor Monipodio, que es su padre, su maestro y su amparo; y así, les aconsejo que vengan conmigo a darle la obediencia, o si no, no se atrevan a hurtar sin su señal, que les costará caro.

—Yo pensé —dijo Cortado— que el hurtar era oficio libre, horro de pecho y alcabala; y que si se paga, es por junto, dando por fiadores a la garganta y a las espaldas. Pero, pues así es, y en cada tierra hay su uso, guardemos nosotros el désta, que, por ser la más principal del mundo, será el más acertado de todo él. Y así, puede vuesa merced guiarnos donde está ese caballero que dice, que ya yo tengo barruntos, según lo que he oído decir, que es muy calificado y generoso, y además hábil en el oficio.

—¡Y cómo que es calificado, hábil y suficiente! —respondió el mozo—. Eslo tanto, que en cuatro años que ha que tiene el cargo de ser nuestro mayor y padre no han padecido sino cuatro en el *finibusterrae*, y obra de treinta envesados y de sesenta y dos en gurapas.

—En verdad, señor —dijo Rincón—, que así entendemos esos nombres como volar.

thing of a thief, had taken his purse, and that he took it upon himself to make sure, in a few days or longer.

That consoled the sacristan a little, and he took leave of Cortado, who went up to where Rincón was standing; Rincón, at a little distance from him, had been watching the whole thing; further down was another boy porter, who had seen all that occurred and observed Cortado pass the handkerchief to Rincón. Coming up to them, he said:

"Tell me, gentlemen, are you in the racket or not?"

"We don't understand that word, sir," replied Rincón.

"You don't twig me, you *murcios*?"[5] the other replied.

"We're not from Thebes or Murcia," said Cortado. "If you want anything else, say so. If not, good-bye."

"You don't understand?" said the boy. "Well, then, I'll make you understand it, and give you a silver spoon to drink it with; what I meant, gentlemen, is: are your worships thieves? But I don't know why I'm asking, because I already know you are. Though, tell me: how come you haven't gone to Señor Monipodio's[6] customs house?"

"Is there a duty levied on thieves around here, sir?" Rincón asked.

"If you don't pay," the lad replied, "at least you have to register with Señor Monipodio, who is their father, teacher, and protector. So I advise you to come with me and put yourselves at his service; otherwise, don't dare to steal without his authorization, or you'll pay dearly for it."

"I thought," said Cortado, "that stealing was a free profession, exempt from taxes and duties; and that, if someone does pay, it's for keeps, with his neck or shoulders as guarantors. But since it's as you say, and every place has its own customs, let's abide by the ones here; since this city is the foremost in the world, its customs must be the best in the world. And so, your worship may lead us to the gentleman you named, who I already have an inkling, from what I've heard, is very noble and generous, as well as skillful at his job."

"I'll say he's noble, skillful, and competent!" the lad replied. "So much so that in the four years he's held the office of being our chief and father, only four of us have suffered punishment on the Finisterre, only about twenty have been tanned, and sixty-two shipped out."[7]

"Honestly, sir," said Rincón, "we understand those terms as much as we understand flying."

---

5. Thieves' jargon for "thieves." Hence, the pun that follows. 6. The name means "illegal combination or agreement." 7. Hanged, flogged, and sent to the galleys, respectively.

—Comencemos a andar, que yo los iré declarando por el camino —respondió el mozo—, con otros algunos, que así les conviene saberlos como el pan de la boca.

Y así, les fue diciendo y declarando otros nombres, de los que ellos llaman germanescos o de la germanía, en el discurso de su plática, que no fue corta, porque el camino era largo; en el cual dijo Rincón a su guía:

—¿Es vuesa merced, por ventura, ladrón?

—Sí —respondió él—, para servir a Dios y a las buenas gentes, aunque no de los muy cursados; que todavía estoy en el año del noviciado.

A lo cual respondió Cortado:

—Cosa nueva es para mí que haya ladrones en el mundo para servir a Dios y a la buena gente.

A lo cual respondió el mozo:

—Señor, yo no me meto en tologías; lo que sé es que cada uno en su oficio puede alabar a Dios, y más con la orden que tiene dada Monipodio a todos sus ahijados.

—Sin duda —dijo Rincón—, debe de ser buena y santa, pues hace que los ladrones sirvan a Dios.

—Es tan santa y buena —replicó el mozo—, que no sé yo si se podrá mejorar en nuestro arte. Él tiene ordenado que de lo que hurtáremos demos alguna cosa o limosna para el aceite de la lámpara de una imagen muy devota que está en esta ciudad, y en verdad que hemos visto grandes cosas por esta buena obra; porque los días pasados dieron tres ansias a un cuatrero que había murciado dos roznos, y con estar flaco y cuartanario, así las sufrió sin cantar como si fueran nada. Y esto atribuimos los del arte a su buena devoción, porque sus fuerzas no eran bastantes para sufrir el primer desconcierto del verdugo. Y, porque sé que me han de preguntar algunos vocablos de los que he dicho, quiero curarme en salud y decírselo antes que me lo pregunten. Sepan voacedes que *cuatrero* es ladrón de bestias; *ansia* es el tormento; *rosnos,* los asnos, hablando con perdón; *primer desconcierto* es las primeras vueltas de cordel que da el verdugo. Tenemos más: que rezamos nuestro rosario, repartido en toda la semana, y muchos de nosotros no hurtamos el día del viernes, ni tenemos conversación con mujer que se llame María el día del sábado.

—De perlas me parece todo eso —dijo Cortado—; pero dígame vuesa merced: ¿hácese otra restitución o otra penitencia más de la dicha?

—En eso de restituir no hay que hablar —respondió el mozo—, porque es cosa imposible, por las muchas partes en que se divide lo hurtado, llevando cada uno de los ministros y contrayentes la suya; y así, el primer hurtador no puede restituir nada; cuanto más, que no hay quien

"Let's start walking, and I'll explain them on the way," the lad replied, "along with some others, which it's as important for you to know as your daily bread."

And so, he kept telling them and explaining other terms in what's called thieves' jargon, in the course of his talk, which wasn't short, because the way was long; during which, Rincón asked their guide:

"Are you by any chance a thief, sir?"

"Yes," he replied, "so may it serve God and all good folk; but not one of the very experienced ones, because I'm still in my apprentice year."

To which Cortado replied:

"It's something new to me that there are thieves in the world to serve God and all good folk."

To which the lad replied:

"Sir, I don't meddle in 'thology'; all I know is that everyone in his own calling can praise God, especially with the set of orders Monipodio has given to all his godchildren."

"No doubt," said Rincón, "it must be good and holy, since it makes thieves serve God."

"It's so holy and good," the lad retorted, "that I don't know whether it could be bettered in our profession. He has ordered that we give something of what we steal as charity, to buy oil for the lamp of a very sacred image in this city; and truly we've seen great results from this good work, because recently they gave three tough times to a reiver who had pinched two mokes, and, even though he was weak and had quartan fever, he endured them without singing, as if they were nothing. And we in the trade attribute that to his great piety, because his strength wasn't even sufficient to endure the torturer's first turn. And, because I know you're going to ask me about certain terms I've used, I want to forestall you and explain them before you ask. I'll have you know that a 'reiver' is a stealer of livestock; a 'tough time' is torture on the rack; 'mokes' are donkeys, begging your pardon; and the 'first turn' is the first tightening of the ropes by the torturer. We do more: we recite our rosary, spreading it out over the week, and many of us don't steal on Fridays, and we don't have sex with any woman named María on Saturdays."

"All of that sounds marvelous to me," said Cortado, "but tell me, sir: do you make any restitution or do any other penance than what you mentioned?"

"That matter of restitution is out of the question," the lad replied; "it's impossible to do, because of the numerous shares the booty is divided into, each one of the participants and contracting parties getting one; and so, the original thief can't make any restitution, especially since no one or-

nos mande hacer esta diligencia, a causa que nunca nos confesamos; y si sacan cartas de excomunión, jamás llegan a nuestra noticia, porque jamás vamos a la iglesia al tiempo que se leen, si no es los días de jubileo, por la ganancia que nos ofrece el concurso de la mucha gente.

—Y ¿con sólo eso que hacen, dicen esos señores —dijo Cortadillo— que su vida es santa y buena?

—Pues ¿qué tiene de malo? —replicó el mozo—. ¿No es peor ser hereje o renegado, o matar a su padre y madre, o ser solomico?

—*Sodomita* querrá decir vuesa merced —respondió Rincón.

—Eso digo —dijo el mozo.

—Todo es malo —replicó Cortado—. Pero, pues nuestra suerte ha querido que entremos en esta cofradía, vuesa merced alargue el paso, que muero por verme con el señor Monipodio, de quien tantas virtudes se cuentan.

—Presto se les cumplirá su deseo —dijo el mozo—, que ya desde aquí se descubre su casa. Vuesas mercedes se queden a la puerta, que yo entraré a ver si está desocupado, porque éstas son las horas cuando él suele dar audiencia.

—En buena sea —dijo Rincón.

Y, adelantándose un poco el mozo, entró en una casa no muy buena, sino de muy mala apariencia, y los dos se quedaron esperando a la puerta. Él salió luego y los llamó, y ellos entraron, y su guía les mandó esperar en un pequeño patio ladrillado, y de puro limpio y aljimifrado parecía que vertía carmín de lo más fino. Al un lado estaba un banco de tres pies y al otro un cántaro desbocado con un jarrillo encima, no menos falto que el cántaro; a otra parte estaba una estera de enea, y en el medio un tiesto, que en Sevilla llaman maceta, de albahaca.

Miraban los mozos atentamente las alhajas de la casa, en tanto que bajaba el señor Monipodio; y, viendo que tardaba, se atrevió Rincón a entrar en una sala baja, de dos pequeñas que en el patio estaban, y vio en ella dos espadas de esgrima y dos broqueles de corcho, pendientes de cuatro clavos, y una arca grande sin tapa ni cosa que la cubriese, y otras tres esteras de enea tendidas por el suelo. En la pared frontera estaba pegada a la pared una imagen de Nuestra Señora, destas de mala estampa, y más abajo pendía una esportilla de palma, y, encajada en la pared, una almofía blanca, por do coligió Rincón que la esportilla servía de cepo para limosna, y la almofía de tener agua bendita, y así era la verdad.

Estando en esto, entraron en la casa dos mozos de hasta veinte años cada uno, vestidos de estudiantes; y de allí a poco, dos de la esportilla y un ciego; y, sin hablar palabra ninguno, se comenzaron a pasear por el

ders us to take that measure, because we never go to confession; and, if they issue edicts of excommunication, we never get to know about it, because we never go to church at the time they're read out, except on days of plenary indulgence, because of the profit presented by the crowds of people attending."

"And, doing only that," said Cortado, "your people say their life is holy and good?"

"Well, what's wrong in it?" the boy retorted. "Isn't it worse to be a heretic or apostate, or to kill your father and mother, or to be a solomic?"

"You surely mean 'sodomite,' sir," Rincón replied.

"That's what I said," the lad stated.

"It's all a bad business," Cortado retorted. "But since our fate has determined we should enter this brotherhood, step lively, sir, for I'm dying to meet Señor Monipodio, of whom so many virtues are recounted."

"Your desire will soon be granted," said the lad, "for his house is already visible from here. Wait at the door, gentlemen; I'll go in to see if he's free, because around this time he usually gives audience."

"May the time be right!" said Rincón.

And the lad, walking a little ahead of them, entered a house that wasn't very fine, but of a very bad aspect, while the two boys remained waiting at the door. He soon came out and called them, and they went in; their guide bade them wait in a little brick-paved patio, which was so clean and tidy it seemed to be oozing cochineal of the best quality. On one side was a three-footed bench and on the other a pitcher with a broken rim with a little jug on top of it that was no less defective than the pitcher; in another place there was a rush mat, and in the center a flowerpot (the word in Seville is *maceta*) with basil in it.

The young men observed the house furnishings carefully while waiting for Señor Monipodio to come down; noticing he was taking his time, Rincón ventured to go into a low-ceilinged room, one of two small ones entered from the patio; in it he saw two fencing foils and two cork bucklers hanging from four nails, a large chest without a lid or anything to cover it, and three more rush mats spread over the floor. Attached to the opposite wall was an image of Our Lady, a poorly printed one; lower down hung a little palm-leaf basket and, fixed into the wall, a white basin; so that Rincón gathered that the basket was used as a poor box and the basin to hold holy water, which was actually the case.

At this point, into the house came two young men, each about twenty, dressed as students, and soon after, two basket porters and a blind man; none of them uttering a word, they started to stroll in the patio. Before

patio. No tardó mucho, cuando entraron dos viejos de bayeta, con antojos que los hacían graves y dignos de ser respectados, con sendos rosarios de sonadoras cuentas en las manos. Tras ellos entró una vieja halduda, y, sin decir nada, se fue a la sala; y, habiendo tomado agua bendita, con grandísima devoción se puso de rodillas ante la imagen, y, a cabo de una buena pieza, habiendo primero besado tres veces el suelo y levantados los brazos y los ojos al cielo otras tantas, se levantó y echó su limosna en la esportilla, y se salió con los demás al patio. En resolución, en poco espacio se juntaron en el patio hasta catorce personas de diferentes trajes y oficios. Llegaron también de los postreros dos bravos y bizarros mozos, de bigotes largos, sombreros de grande falda, cuellos a la valona, medias de color, ligas de gran balumba, espadas de más de marca, sendos pistoletes cada uno en lugar de dagas, y sus broqueles pendientes de la pretina; los cuales, así como entraron, pusieron los ojos de través en Rincón y Cortado, a modo de que los estrañaban y no conocían. Y, llegándose a ellos, les preguntaron si eran de la cofradía. Rincón respondió que sí, y muy servidores de sus mercedes.

Llegóse en esto la sazón y punto en que bajó el señor Monipodio, tan esperado como bien visto de toda aquella virtuosa compañía. Parecía de edad de cuarenta y cinco a cuarenta y seis años, alto de cuerpo, moreno de rostro, cejijunto, barbinegro y muy espeso; los ojos, hundidos. Venía en camisa, y por la abertura de delante descubría un bosque: tanto era el vello que tenía en el pecho. Traía cubierta una capa de bayeta casi hasta los pies, en los cuales traía unos zapatos enchancletados, cubríanle las piernas unos zaragüelles de lienzo, anchos y largos hasta los tobillos; el sombrero era de los de la hampa, campanudo de copa y tendido de falda; atravesábale un tahalí por espalda y pechos a do colgaba una espada ancha y corta, y modo de las del perrillo; las manos eran cortas, pelosas, y los dedos gordos, y las uñas hembras y remachadas; las piernas no se le parecían, pero los pies eran descomunales de anchos y juanetudos. En efeto, él representaba el más rústico y disforme bárbaro del mundo. Bajó con él la guía de los dos, y, trabándoles de las manos, los presentó ante Monipodio, diciéndole:

Éstos son los dos buenos mancebos que a vuesa merced dije, mi sor Monipodio: vuesa merced los desamine y verá como son dignos de entrar en nuestra congregación.

—Eso haré yo de muy buena gana —respondió Monipodio.

Olvidábaseme de decir que, así como Monipodio bajó, al punto, todos los que aguardándole estaban le hicieron una profunda y larga

long, two old men dressed in baize came in, wearing spectacles that made them look serious and worthy of respect, each one had a rosary of rattling beads in his hands. After them came an old woman with long, wide petticoats, who, saying nothing, left for that side room; having taken holy water, she knelt before the image with extreme devoutness and, after a good while, having first kissed the floor three times and raised her arms and eyes to heaven the same number of times, she stood up, dropped her alms into the basket, and rejoined the others in the patio. In a word, in a short space of time some fourteen people with different costumes and trades assembled in the patio. Among the last to arrive were two young, mettlesome bravos with long mustaches, wide-brimmed hats, Vandyke collars, colored stockings, bulky garters, swords longer than the law allowed, each with a pistol instead of a dagger, and bucklers hanging from their belt; as soon as these two came in, they looked askance at Rincón and Cortado, as if surprised at seeing strangers there. Coming up to them, they asked them whether they were of the brotherhood. Rincón said they were, and the gentlemen's humble servants.

Finally the proper time arrived for Señor Monipodio to descend, as eagerly awaited as he was highly esteemed by all that virtuous company. He looked around forty-five or forty-six, tall, swarthy-faced, with eyebrows that met and a very thick black beard; his eyes were sunken. He was in his shirtsleeves, and through the front opening he revealed a forest, so hairy was his chest. He wore a baize cape that nearly reached his feet, on which he wore slipper-like shoes; his legs were covered by cloth breeches, wide and long, down to his ankles; his hat was of an underworld type, with a bell-shaped crown and a broad brim; he had a sword belt across his back and chest from which hung a broad, short sword of the make that has a little dog engraved on the blade.[8] His hands were short and hairy; his fingers, thick; and his nails, broad, short, and flattened; his legs didn't show, but his feet were unusually wide, with large toe knuckles. Indeed, he looked like the most coarse and misshapen barbarian in the world. With him there descended the guide of the two boys, who took them by the hand and introduced them to Monipodio, saying:

"These are the two fine fellows I told your worship about, Señor Monipodio; interrogate them and you'll find them worthy to enter our congregation."

"I'll do so gladly," Monipodio replied.

I nearly forgot to say that, at the very moment Monipodio came down, all those who had been awaiting him made a long, low bow to him, except

8. Made by Julián del Rey in Toledo in the fifteenth century.

reverencia, excepto los dos bravos, que, a medio magate, como entre ellos se dice, le quitaron los capelos, y luego volvieron a su paseo por una parte del patio, y por la otra se paseaba Monipodio, el cual preguntó a los nuevos el ejercicio, la patria y padres.

A lo cual Rincón respondió:

—El ejercicio ya está dicho, pues venimos ante vuesa merced; la patria no me parece de mucha importancia decilla, ni los padres tampoco, pues no se ha de hacer información para recebir algún hábito honroso.

A lo cual respondió Monipodio:

—Vos, hijo mío, estáis en lo cierto, y es cosa muy acertada encubrir eso que decís; porque si la suerte no corriere como debe, no es bien que quede asentado debajo de signo de escribano, ni en el libro de las entradas: «Fulano, hijo de Fulano, vecino de tal parte, tal día le ahorcaron, o le azotaron», o otra cosa semejante, que, por lo menos, suena mal a los buenos oídos; y así, torno a decir que es provechoso documento callar la patria, encubrir los padres y mudar los propios nombres; aunque para entre nosotros no ha de haber nada encubierto, y sólo ahora quiero saber los nombres de los dos.

Rincón dijo el suyo y Cortado también.

—Pues, de aquí adelante —respondió Monipodio—, quiero y es mi voluntad que vos, Rincón, os llaméis Rinconete, y vos, Cortado, Cortadillo, que son nombres que asientan como de molde a vuestra edad y a nuestras ordenanzas, debajo de las cuales cae tener necesidad de saber el nombre de los padres de nuestros cofrades, porque tenemos de costumbre de hacer decir cada año ciertas misas por las ánimas de nuestros difuntos y bienhechores, sacando el estupendo para la limosna de quien las dice de alguna parte de lo que se garbea; y estas tales misas, así dichas como pagadas, dicen que aprovechan a las tales ánimas por vía de naufragio, y caen debajo de nuestros bienhechores: el procurador que nos defiende, el guro que nos avisa, el verdugo que nos tiene lástima, el que, cuando alguno de nosotros va huyendo por la calle y detrás le van dando voces: «¡Al ladrón, al ladrón! ¡Deténganle, deténganle!», uno se pone en medio y se opone al raudal de los que le siguen, diciendo: «¡Déjenle al cuitado, que harta mala ventura lleva! ¡Allá se lo haya; castíguele su pecado!» Son también bienhechoras nuestras las socorridas, que de su sudor nos socorren, ansí en la trena como en las guras; y también lo son nuestros

the two bravos, who nonchalantly (as those people say) took off their hats to him, then continued to stroll across one part of the patio while Monipodio strolled across the other. He asked the newcomers about their calling, their birthplace, and their parents.

To which Rincón replied:

"Our calling is obvious, since we've come to see your worship; I don't consider it very important to tell you my birthplace, or my parents either, because this isn't a case of an official inquiry for awarding some badge of honor."

To which Monipodio replied:

"You're right, son, and it's very correct to conceal those things; because if your luck runs out on you, it isn't good to be registered by some lawyer's clerk or in some record book as "So-and-so, son of so-and-so, resident of somewhere, hanged or whipped on such-and-such a day," or anything else like that, which, at the very least, sounds bad to proper ears; and so I repeat that it's useful advice to keep mum about your birthplace, hide your parents' names, and change your own; though among us nothing need be concealed, and for now all I want to know is the name of both of you."

Rincón told his, and Cortado did the same.

"Well, from here on," Monipodio replied, "I wish and it is my desire that you, Rincón, be called Rinconete, and you, Cortado, Cortadillo, which are names which fit like a glove your age and our statutes, which make it necessary for us to know the names of our members' parents, because it's our custom to have certain masses read each year for the souls of our deceased and our benefactors, taking the 'stupend' to pay the priest from some part of our haul; and it's said that these masses, both read and paid for, are of use to those souls in purgatory by way of 'suffering,'[9] And counted in the number of our benefactors are the lawyer who defends us; the cop who advises us; the executioner who pities us; the man who, when one of us is escaping down the street, followed by people yelling 'Stop thief, stop thief,' blocks the way of the mob chasing him and says 'Let the poor guy go, he's got enough bad luck; it's his affair, let the burden of his sin be his punishment!' Other benefactresses to us are the whores who help us out, at the cost of their sweat, both in stir and in the galleys; and so are our fathers and mothers who bring us into the world, and the lawyer who, when well disposed, finds that no misdeed is a crime and no crime merits a severe penalty. For all those I've men-

9. The Spanish has *naufragio* ("shipwreck"—which Rinconete will joke about) instead of *sufragio* ("suffrage," i.e., prayers for souls in purgatory).

padres y madres, que nos echan al mundo, y el escribano, que si anda de buena, no hay delito que sea culpa ni culpa a quien se dé mucha pena; y, por todos estos que he dicho, hace nuestra hermandad cada año su adversario con la mayor popa y soledad que podemos.

—Por cierto —dijo Rinconete, ya confirmado con este nombre—, que es obra digna del altísimo y profundísimo ingenio que hemos oído decir que vuesa merced, señor Monipodio, tiene. Pero nuestros padres aún gozan de la vida; si en ella les alcanzáremos, daremos luego noticia a esta felicísima y abogada confraternidad, para que por sus almas se les haga ese naufragio o tormenta, o ese adversario que vuesa merced dice, con la solenidad y pompa acostumbrada; si ya no es que se hace mejor con popa y soledad, como también apuntó vuesa merced en sus razones.

—Así se hará, o no quedará de mí pedazo —replicó Monipodio.

Y, llamando a la guía, le dijo:

—Ven acá, Ganchuelo: ¿están puestas las postas?

—Sí —dijo la guía, que Ganchuelo era su nombre—: tres centinelas quedan avizorando, y no hay que temer que nos cojan de sobresalto.

—Volviendo, pues, a nuestro propósito —dijo Monipodio—, querría saber, hijos, lo que sabéis, para daros el oficio y ejercicio conforme a vuestra inclinación y habilidad.

—Yo —respondió Rinconete— sé un poquito de floreo de Vilhán; entiéndeseme el retén; tengo buena vista para el humillo; juego bien de la sola, de las cuatro y de las ocho; no se me va por pies el raspadillo, verrugueta y el colmillo; éntrome por la boca de lobo como por mi casa, y atreveríame a hacer un tercio de chanza mejor que un tercio de Nápoles, y a dar un astillazo al más pintado mejor que dos reales prestados.

—Principios son —dijo Monipodio—, pero todas ésas son flores de cantueso viejas, y tan usadas, que no hay principiante que no las sepa, y sólo sirven para alguno que sea tan blanco que se deje matar de media noche abajo; pero andará el tiempo y vernos hemos: que, asentando sobre ese fundamento media docena de liciones, yo espero en Dios que habéis de salir oficial famoso, y aun quizá maestro.

—Todo será para servir a vuesa merced y a los señores cofrades —respondió Rinconete.

—Y vos, Cortadillo, ¿qué sabéis? —preguntó Monipodio.

tioned our brotherhood celebrates their yearly 'adversary' with the greatest 'poop and circumcise' we can manage."

"Surely," said Rinconete, already confirmed with that name, "it's a deed worthy of the most lofty and profound intelligence that we've heard your worship possesses, Señor Monipodio. But our parents are still living; if we outlive them, then we'll notify this most felicitous and learned brotherhood, so that that 'suffering' shipwreck, or storm, or that 'adversary' celebration, may be made for their souls with all due pomp and circumstance; unless it's better performed with 'poop and circumcise,' as your worship also remarked in your speech."

"And so it shall, or there won't be a piece left of me," Monipodio replied.

And calling the boys' guide, he said:

"Come here, Ganchuelo:[10] are the guards on duty?"

"Yes," said the guide, for Ganchuelo was his name, "three sentinels are watching, and we need not fear being taken by surprise."

"Then, getting back to our subject," said Monipodio, "I'd like to hear what you can do, boys, so I can give you tasks and assignments suited to your likings and skills."

"I," replied Rinconete, "know a little bit about card sharping; I understand hiding cards up my sleeve; I have a good eye for marking cards with smoke; I know how to win tricks without a partner, how to plant cards in the deck, and 'play the eight'; I'm a good hand at marking cards by scraping, making bumps on them, and polishing sections of them; I'm right at home at pretending to lose at first, and I'd venture to act like a shill right there with the best of them,[11] or to palm off bad cards on the greatest expert just as nicely as you please."

"That's a beginning," said Monipodio, "but all those are old, trivial ruses, so common that every beginner knows them, and they're only good against someone so green that he lets himself be fleeced unmercifully; but time will tell and we'll see; because, building on that foundation with a half-dozen lessons, I expect you, with God's help, to turn out a famous practitioner, and maybe even a master."

"I'll do all I can to serve your worship and my esteemed fellow members," replied Rinconete.

"And you, Cortadillo, what can you do?" asked Monipodio.

---

10. The name contains the word *gancho* ("hook"), implying stealing. 11. Literally, "better than a Naples regiment," with a pun on *tercio* ("third party, shill") and *tercio* ("infantry regiment").

—Yo —respondió Cortadillo— sé la treta que dicen mete dos y saca cinco, y sé dar tiento a una faldriquera con mucha puntualidad y destreza.

—¿Sabéis más? —dijo Monipodio.

—No, por mis grandes pecados —respondió Cortadillo.

—No os aflijáis, hijo —replicó Monipodio—, que a puerto y a escuela habéis llegado donde ni os anegaréis ni dejaréis de salir muy bien aprovechado en todo aquello que más os conviniere. Y en esto del ánimo, ¿cómo os va, hijos?

—¿Cómo nos ha de ir —respondió Rinconete— sino muy bien? Ánimo tenemos para acometer cualquiera empresa de las que tocaren a nuestro arte y ejercicio.

—Está bien —replicó Monipodio—, pero querría yo que también le tuviésedes para sufrir, si fuese menester, media docena de ansias sin desplegar los labios y sin decir esta boca es mía.

—Ya sabemos aquí —dijo Cortadillo—, señor Monipodio, qué quiere decir ansias, y para todo tenemos ánimo; porque no somos tan ignorantes que no se nos alcance que lo que dice la lengua paga la gorja; y harta merced le hace el cielo al hombre atrevido, por no darle otro título, que le deja en su lengua su vida o su muerte, ¡como si tuviese más letras un *no* que un *sí!*

—¡Alto, no es menester más! —dijo a esta sazón Monipodio—. Digo que sola esa razón me convence, me obliga, me persuade y me fuerza a que desde luego asentéis por cofrades mayores y que se os sobrelleve el año del noviciado.

—Yo soy dese parecer —dijo uno de los bravos.

Y a una voz lo confirmaron todos los presentes, que toda la plática habían estado escuchando, y pidieron a Monipodio que desde luego les concediese y permitiese gozar de las inmunidades de su cofradía, porque su presencia agradable y su buena plática lo merecía todo. Él respondió que, por dalles contento a todos, desde aquel punto se las concedía, y advirtiéndoles que las estimasen en mucho, porque eran no pagar media nata del primer hurto que hiciesen; no hacer oficios menores en todo aquel año, conviene a saber: no llevar recaudo de ningún hermano mayor a la cárcel, ni a la casa, de parte de sus contribuyentes; piar el turco puro; hacer banquete cuando, como y adonde quisieren, sin pedir licencia a su mayoral; entrar a la parte, desde luego, con lo que entrujasen los hermanos mayores, como uno dellos, y otras cosas que ellos tuvieron por merced señaladísima, y los demás, con palabras muy comedidas, las agradecieron mucho.

Estando en esto, entró un muchacho corriendo y desalentado, y dijo:

"I," Cortadillo replied, "know the trick called 'put in two fingers and pull out the prize,' and I can cut open a pocket very accurately and skillfully."

"Do you know any more?" asked Monipodio.

"No, great sinner that I am," replied Cortadillo.

"Don't fret, son," Monipodio replied, "for you've arrived in a port and school where you won't drown and won't fail to come out very well equipped with all you need most. As for courage, how do you stand, boys?"

"How should we," replied Rinconete, "except very well? We're brave enough to undertake any business involved in our profession and occupation."

"Good," Monipodio replied, "but I'd also like you to be brave enough to endure, if you should have to, a half-dozen 'tough times' without unbuttoning your lips or making a peep."

Cortadillo said: "Señor Monipodio, we already know what 'tough times' means, and we're brave enough for anything; because we're not so ignorant as not to grasp that what the tongue says, the neck pays for; and heaven does the bold man (not to call him anything else) a great favor by leaving his life or death to his own tongue—as if *no* had more letters than *sí!*"

"Stop! You need say no more!" Monipodio exclaimed. "I say that that speech alone convinces me, obliges me, persuades me, and compels me to accept you at once as elder members and to exempt you from the year of apprenticeship."

"I agree," said one of the bravos.

And this was ratified unanimously by all present, who had been listening to the whole conversation and now asked Monipodio to grant and allow them the privileges of their brotherhood at once, because their pleasant bearing and good words deserved it all. He replied that, to satisfy everyone, he granted it from that moment on, adjuring them to esteem this highly because these privileges were: not to hand over half of the first theft they committed; not to perform minor duties all that year, such as taking a collection for any elder member to jail, or to the brothel, by orders of the contributors thereto; to drink unmixed wine; to have a party where and when they liked without asking their supervisor's permission; to start sharing at once in the elder members' takings, as one of them; and other favors which they considered wonderful; and they and the others showed much gratitude for this in very polite words.

At this point, a boy came running in breathlessly, and said:

—El alguacil de los vagabundos viene encaminado a esta casa, pero no trae consigo gurullada.

—Nadie se alborote —dijo Monipodio—, que es amigo y nunca viene por nuestro daño. Sosiéguense, que yo le saldré a hablar.

Todos se sosegaron, que ya estaban algo sobresaltados, y Monipodio salió a la puerta, donde halló al alguacil, con el cual estuvo hablando un rato, y luego volvió a entrar Monipodio y preguntó:

—¿A quién le cupo hoy la plaza de San Salvador?

—A mí —dijo el de la guía.

—Pues ¿cómo —dijo Monipodio— no se me ha manifestado una bolsilla de ámbar que esta mañana en aquel paraje dio al traste con quince escudos de oro y dos reales de a dos y no sé cuántos cuartos?

—Verdad es —dijo la guía— que hoy faltó esa bolsa, pero yo no la he tomado, ni puedo imaginar quién la tomase.

—¡No hay levas conmigo! —replicó Monipodio—. ¡La bolsa ha de parecer, porque la pide el alguacil, que es amigo y nos hace mil placeres al año!

Tornó a jurar el mozo que no sabía della. Comenzóse a encolerizar Monipodio, de manera que parecía que fuego vivo lanzaba por los ojos, diciendo:

—¡Nadie se burle con quebrantar la más mínima cosa de nuestra orden, que le costará la vida! Manifiéstese la cica; y si se encubre por no pagar los derechos, yo le daré enteramente lo que le toca y pondré lo demás de mi casa; porque en todas maneras ha de ir contento el alguacil.

Tornó de nuevo a jurar el mozo y a maldecirse, diciendo que él no había tomado tal bolsa ni vístola de sus ojos; todo lo cual fue poner más fuego a la cólera de Monipodio, y dar ocasión a que toda la junta se alborotase, viendo que se rompían sus estatutos y buenas ordenanzas.

Viendo Rinconete, pues, tanta disensión y alboroto, parecióle que sería bien sosegalle y dar contento a su mayor, que reventaba de rabia; y, aconsejándose con su amigo Cortadillo, con parecer de entrambos, sacó la bolsa del sacristán y dijo:

—Cese toda cuestión, mis señores, que ésta es la bolsa, sin faltarle nada de lo que el alguacil manifiesta; que hoy mi camarada Cortadillo le dio alcance, con un pañuelo que al mismo dueño se le quitó por añadidura.

Luego sacó Cortadillo el pañizuelo y lo puso de manifiesto; viendo lo cual, Monipodio dijo:

—Cortadillo *el Bueno,* que con este título y renombre ha de quedar de aquí adelante, se quede con el pañuelo y a mi cuenta se quede la

"The constable responsible for vagabonds is heading for this house, but he has no bulls with him."

"No one get upset," said Monipodio, "because he's a friend and never comes to harm us. Calm down, 'cause I'm going out to talk to him."

They all calmed down, for they had been a little alarmed, and Monipodio went out the door, where he found the constable and chatted with him for a while, after which he came back in and asked:

"Who was assigned the Plaza de San Salvador today?"

"I was," said the boys' guide.

"Then, how come," Monipodio asked, "you didn't report to me a little perfumed purse that was pinched in that area this morning and contained fifteen gold escudos, two two-real pieces, and I don't know how many cuartos?"

"It's true," said the guide, "that that purse went missing today, but I didn't take it, and I can't imagine who could have."

"No fooling around with me!" Monipodio retorted. "The purse must show up, because the constable is asking for it; he's a friend, and does us a thousand favors every year!"

The lad swore again that he didn't know. Monipodio started to get angry, and live flames seemed to be shooting from his eyes as he said:

"Let no one get smart and break even the slightest law of our order, or it'll cost him his life! I want the purse to show up; if he's covering it up to avoid paying duty on it, I'll give him everything coming to him, and add some more from my own pocket; because, come what may, the constable must be satisfied."

The lad once again swore and cursed himself, saying he hadn't taken that purse or set eyes on it; all of which added more fuel to Monipodio's anger and made the whole assembly nervous, seeing their statutes and good ordinances being violated.

"Well, Rinconete, at the sight of so much dissension and turmoil, felt it would be good to calm it down and satisfy his chief, who was bursting with rage; conferring with his friend Cortadillo, and both agreeing, he took out the sacristan's purse and said:

"No more interrogations, gentlemen, for this is the purse, and it lacks none of what the constable reported. My buddy Cortadillo pinched it today, along with a handkerchief he relieved the same owner of as an encore."

Then Cortadillo took out the handkerchief and displayed it. Seeing it, Monipodio said:

"Cortadillo the good, for you are to have that title and renown henceforth, keep the handkerchief and let the gratification for this service be at

satisfación deste servicio; y la bolsa se ha de llevar el alguacil, que es de un sacristán pariente suyo, y conviene que se cumpla aquel refrán que dice: «No es mucho que a quien te da la gallina entera, tú des una pierna della». Más disimula este buen alguacil en un día que nosotros le podremos ni solemos dar en ciento.

De común consentimiento aprobaron todos la hidalguía de los dos modernos y la sentencia y parecer de su mayoral, el cual salió a dar la bolsa al alguacil; y Cortadillo se quedó confirmado con el renombre de *Bueno,* bien como si fuera don Alonso Pérez de Guzmán el Bueno, que arrojó el cuchillo por los muros de Tarifa para degollar a su único hijo.

Al volver, que volvió, Monipodio, entraron con él dos mozas, afeitados los rostros, llenos de color los labios y de albayalde los pechos, cubiertas con medios mantos de anascote, llenas de desenfado y desvergüenza: señales claras por donde, en viéndolas Rinconete y Cortadillo, conocieron que eran de la casa llana; y no se engañaron en nada. Y, así como entraron, se fueron con los brazos abiertos, la una a Chiquiznaque y la otra a Maniferro, que éstos eran los nombres de los dos bravos; y el de Maniferro era porque traía una mano de hierro, en lugar de otra que le habían cortado por justicia. Ellos las abrazaron con grande regocijo, y les preguntaron si traían algo con que mojar la canal maestra.

—Pues, ¿había de faltar, diestro mío? —respondió la una, que se llamaba la Gananciosa—. No tardará mucho a venir Silbatillo, tu trainel, con la canasta de colar atestada de lo que Dios ha sido servido.

Y así fue verdad, porque al instante entró un muchacho con una canasta de colar cubierta con una sábana.

Alegráronse todos con la entrada de Silbato, y al momento mandó sacar Monipodio una de las esteras de enea que estaban en el aposento, y tenderla en medio del patio. Y ordeño, asimismo, que todos se sentasen a la redonda; porque, en cortando la cólera, se trataría de lo que más conviniese. A esto, dijo la vieja que había rezado a la imagen:

—Hijo Monipodio, yo no estoy para fiestas, porque tengo un váguido de cabeza, dos días ha, que me trae loca; y más, que antes que sea mediodía tengo de ir a cumplir mis devociones y poner mis candelicas a Nuestra Señora de las Aguas y al Santo Crucifijo de Santo Agustín, que no lo dejaría de hacer si nevase y ventiscase. A lo que he

my cost; but the constable must take the purse, which belongs to a relative of his who's a sacristan, and we must abide by that proverb which says: 'If someone gives you a whole hen, it's not too much for you to give him one of its thighs.' That good constable shuts his eyes in one day to more than we could or do give him in a hundred."

With common consent, they all approved the noble action by the two novices, and the judgment and sentence of their leader, who went out to give the purse to the constable; and Cortadillo remained dubbed with the name of "the good," just as if he were Don Alonso Pérez de Guzmán the Good, who hurled the knife over the walls of Tarifa for cutting the throat of his only son.[12]

When Monipodio returned, two young women came in with him; their faces were made up, their lips were rouged and their bosoms smeared with ceruse, and they were draped in half-mantles of serge. They were full of devil-may-care shamelessness: clear tokens by which Rinconete and Cortadillo, seeing them, recognized them as being from the brothel; in which they were in no wise mistaken. As soon as they came in, they went over with open arms, one to Chiquiznaque and the other to Maniferro, which were the names of the two bravos; Maniferro got his because he had an iron hand to replace one that the law had cut off. The men embraced them with great joy, and asked them whether they had brought anything for wetting their whistle.

"And why shouldn't I, my swordsman?" replied one, who was called La Gananciosa.[13] Before long, little Silbato,[14] your messenger boy, will be here with the bleaching basket crammed with what God has seen fit to bestow on us."

And it was so, because a boy came in at once with a bleaching basket covered with a sheet.

All were cheered by Silbato's arrival, and at once Monipodio ordered them to take one of the mats that were in the room and to spread it out in the middle of the patio. Likewise, he ordered everyone to sit down around it, because while they had a snack they could discuss immediate business. Whereupon the old woman who had prayed to the image said:

"Monipodio, my son, I'm not up to a party, because I've had a dizzy spell for two days that's driving me crazy; besides, before noon I must go and make my devotions and light my candles for Our Lady of the Waters and the Holy Crucifix in Saint Augustine's, which I wouldn't omit to do if it were snowing and blowing a storm. What I came to tell you is that last

12. To avoid surrendering the city to the Moors, who were holding his captured son hostage (late thirteenth century). 13. "Moneymaker." 14. "Whistle."

venido es que anoche el Renegado y Centopiés llevaron a mi casa una canasta de colar, algo mayor que la presente, llena de ropa blanca; y en Dios y en mi ánima que venía con su cernada y todo, que los pobretes no debieron de tener lugar de quitalla, y venían sudando la gota tan gorda, que era una compasión verlos entrar ijadeando y corriendo agua de sus rostros, que parecían unos angelicos. Dijéronme que iban en seguimiento de un ganadero que había pesado ciertos carneros en la Carnicería, por ver si le podían dar un tiento en un grandísimo gato de reales que llevaba. No desembanastaron ni contaron la ropa, fiados en la entereza de mi conciencia; y así me cumpla Dios mis buenos deseos y nos libre a todos de poder de justicia, que no he tocado a la canasta, y que se está tan entera como cuando nació.

—Todo se le cree, señora madre —respondió Monipodio—, y estése así la canasta, que yo iré allá, a boca de sorna, y haré cala y cata de lo que tiene, y daré a cada uno lo que le tocare, bien y fielmente, como tengo de costumbre.

—Sea como vos lo ordenáredes, hijo —respondió la vieja—; y, porque se me hace tarde, dadme un traguillo, si tenéis, para consolar este estómago, que tan desmayado anda de contino.

—Y ¡qué tal lo beberéis, madre mía! —dijo a esta sazón la Escalanta, que así se llamaba la compañera de la Gananciosa.

Y, descubriendo la canasta, se manifestó una bota a modo de cuero, con hasta dos arrobas de vino, y un corcho que podría caber sosegadamente y sin apremio hasta una azumbre; y, llenándole la Escalanta, se le puso en las manos a la devotísima vieja, la cual, tomándole con ambas manos y habiéndole soplado un poco de espuma, dijo:

—Mucho echaste, hija Escalanta, pero Dios dará fuerzas para todo.

Y, aplicándosele a los labios, de un tirón, sin tomar aliento, lo trasegó del corcho al estómago, y acabó diciendo:

—De Guadalcanal es, y aun tiene un es no es de yeso el señorico. Dios te consuele, hija, que así me has consolado; sino que temo que me ha de hacer mal, porque no me he desayunado.

—No hará, madre —respondió Monipodio—, porque es trasañejo.

—Así lo espero yo en la Virgen —respondió la vieja.

Y añadió:

—Mirad, niñas, si tenéis acaso algún cuarto para comprar las candelicas de mi devoción, porque, con la priesa y gana que tenía de venir a traer las nuevas de la canasta, se me olvidó en casa la escarcela.

night the Renegade and the Centipede brought a bleaching basket to my house a little bigger than this one, full of linens; and, by God and my soul, it still had the ashes for the lye-making in it, because the poor fellows probably hadn't had the time to remove them, and they were sweating so profusely that it was a pity to see them come in panting, with water streaming down their faces, so that they resembled little angels. They told me they were going to follow a drover who had weighed some sheep at the main meat market, to see if they could poke a hole in a huge pouch of reales he was carrying. They didn't unload or count the linens, since they trusted my honesty and conscience; and so may God grant my good wishes and deliver us all from the hands of the law, I haven't touched the basket, which is as intact as the day it was born."

"I believe you completely, 'mother,'" replied Monipodio. "Leave the basket that way, and I'll go there at nightfall and count up what's in it, and give everyone his due share, properly and loyally, as I usually do."

"Let it be as you command, son," the old woman replied, "and, because I'm getting late, give me a little swig, if you've got one, to settle my stomach, which is constantly so upset."

"And what a drink you'll have, 'mother'!" said La Escalanta in reply (that was the name of La Gananciosa's companion).

And, the basket being uncovered, a sort of leather wineskin was revealed containing about eight gallons of wine, and a cork vessel that could contain about a half-gallon easily, without forcing; this La Escalanta filled and placed in the hands of the very devout old woman, who, taking it in both hands and blowing off a little froth, said:

"You've poured in a lot, Escalanta my girl, but God will make me strong enough for anything."

And, putting it to her lips, at one draft, without taking a breath, she decanted it from the cork vessel to her stomach, and said when she was done:

"It's from Guadalcanal,"[15] and still has a trace of gypsum in it, the little devil. My God comfort you, girl, as you've comforted me! Only, I'm afraid it will disagree with me, because I've had no breakfast."

"It won't, 'mother,'" Monipodio replied, "because it's over three years old."

"I hope so, by the Virgin," the old woman replied.

And she added.:

"Girls, look and see whether you possibly have some cuarto to buy the candles for my devotions, because I was so eager and in a rush to come and bring the news of the basket that I forgot my purse at home."

---

15. A famous wine-making spot in Seville province.

—Yo sí tengo, señora Pipota —(que éste era el nombre de la buena vieja) respondió la Gananciosa—; tome, ahí le doy dos cuartos: del uno le ruego que compre una para mí, y se la ponga al señor San Miguel; y si puede comprar dos, ponga la otra al señor San Blas, que son mis abogados. Quisiera que pusiera otra a la señora Santa Lucía, que, por lo de los ojos, también le tengo devoción, pero no tengo trocado; mas otro día habrá donde se cumpla con todos.

—Muy bien harás, hija, y mira no seas miserable; que es de mucha importancia llevar la persona las candelas delante de sí antes que se muera, y no aguardar a que las pongan los herederos o albaceas.

—Bien dice la madre Pipota —dijo la Escalanta.

Y, echando mano a la bolsa, le dio otro cuarto y le encargó que pusiese otras dos candelicas a los santos que a ella le pareciesen que eran de los más aprovechados y agradecidos. Con esto, se fue la Pipota, diciéndoles:

—Holgaos, hijos, ahora que tenéis tiempo; que vendrá la vejez y lloraréis en ella los ratos que perdistes en la mocedad, como yo los lloro; y encomendadme a Dios en vuestras oraciones, que yo voy a hacer lo mismo por mí y por vosotros, porque Él nos libre y conserve en nuestro trato peligroso, sin sobresaltos de justicia.

Y con esto, se fue.

Ida la vieja, se sentaron todos alrededor de la estera, y la Gananciosa tendió la sábana por manteles; y lo primero que sacó de la cesta fue un grande haz de rábanos y hasta dos docenas de naranjas y limones, y luego una cazuela grande llena de tajadas de bacallao frito. Manifestó luego medio queso de Flandes, y una olla de famosas aceitunas, y un plato de camarones, y gran cantidad de cangrejos, con su llamativo de alcaparrones ahogados en pimientos, y tres hogazas blanquísimas de Gandul. Serían los del almuerzo hasta catorce, y ninguno dellos dejó de sacar su cuchillo de cachas amarillas, si no fue Rinconete, que sacó su media espada. A los dos viejos de bayeta y a la guía tocó el escanciar con el corcho de colmena. Mas, apenas habían comenzado a dar asalto a las naranjas, cuando les dio a todos gran sobresalto los golpes que dieron a la puerta. Mandóles Monipodio que se sosegasen, y, entrando en la sala baja y descolgando un broquel, puesto mano a la espada, llegó a la puerta y con voz hueca y espantosa preguntó:

—¿Quién llama?

Respondieron de fuera:

—Yo soy, que no es nadie, señor Monipodio: Tagarete soy, centinela

"I do have some, Señora Pipota"[16] (for that was the good old woman's name), replied La Gananciosa; "here, take these two cuartos I'm giving you: please buy a candle for me with one of them, and light it for Saint Michael; and if you can buy two, light the other for Saint Blase; they're my patron saints. I'd like you to light another one for Saint Lucy, to whom I'm also devoted because she takes care of eyes, but I have no more change; there'll be another day when I can do it for all of them."

"You'll be doing a very good thing, daughter, and see that you aren't stingy; because it's very important for a person to provide the candles before he dies, and not wait for his heirs or executors to light them."

"Mother Pipota is right," said La Escalanta.

And, dipping into her purse, she gave her another cuarto and commissioned her to light two more candles for whatever saints she considered among the most beneficial and grateful. Then La Pipota departed, saying:

"Have fun, children, while you have time; for old age will come, and then you'll regret the good times you let slip by when you were young, just as I do; and commend me to God in your prayers, for I shall do the same for myself and for you, so that he may deliver us and keep us safe in our dangerous calling, without alarms from the law."

And therewith she left.

Once the old woman was gone, they all sat down around the mat, and La Gananciosa spread out the sheet as a tablecloth; the first thing she drew out of the basket was a big bunch of radishes and some two dozen oranges and lemons, then a large pan full of slices of fried cod. Then she revealed half of a Flemish cheese, and a jar of excellent olives, and a plate of shrimp, and a large number of crabs, with their condiment of capers smothered in peppers, and three very white loaves from Gandul.[17] There were some fourteen people lunching, none of whom failed to take out his yellow-handled knife, except Rinconete, who took out his half-sword. It was the duty of the two old men in baize and the guide to pour out wine with the section of a cork beehive. But no sooner had they begun to attack the oranges than they were all greatly alarmed by a knocking at the door. Monipodio ordered them to be calm; going into the low-ceilinged room and taking down a buckler and laying hand to his sword, he went to the door and asked in a hollow, frightening tone:

"Who's there?"

The reply from outside was:

"It's me, only me, Señor Monipodio: Tagarete, the sentinel for this

16. "Keg." 17. Another locality in Seville province.

desta mañana, y vengo a decir que vienen aquí Juliana la Cariharta, toda desgreñada y llorosa, que parece haberle sucedido algún desastre.

En esto llegó la que decía, sollozando, y, sintiéndola Monipodio, abrió la puerta, y mandó a Tagarete que se volviese a su posta y que de allí adelante avisase lo que viese con menos estruendo y ruido. Él dijo que así lo haría. Entró la Cariharta, que era una moza del jaez de las otras y del mismo oficio. Venía descabellada y la cara llena de tolondrones, y, así como entró en el patio, se cayó en el suelo desmayada. Acudieron a socorrerla la Gananciosa y la Escalanta, y, desabrochándola el pecho, la hallaron toda denegrida y como magullada. Echáronle agua en el rostro, y ella volvió en sí, diciendo a voces:

—¡La justicia de Dios y del Rey venga sobre aquel ladrón desuellacaras, sobre aquel cobarde bajamanero, sobre aquel pícaro lendroso, que le he quitado más veces de la horca que tiene pelos en las barbas! ¡Desdichada de mí! ¡Mirad por quién he perdido y gastado mi mocedad y la flor de mis años, sino por un bellaco desalmado, facinoroso e incorregible!

—Sosiégate, Cariharta —dijo a esta sazón Monipodio—, que aquí estoy yo que te haré justicia. Cuéntanos tu agravio, que más estarás tú en contarle que yo en hacerte vengada; dime si has habido algo con tu respecto; que si así es y quieres venganza, no has menester más que boquear.

—¿Qué respecto? —respondió Juliana—. Respectada me vea yo en los infiernos, si más lo fuere de aquel león con las ovejas y cordero con los hombres. ¿Con aquél había yo de comer más pan a manteles, ni yacer en uno? Primero me vea yo comida de adivas estas carnes, que me ha parado de la manera que ahora veréis.

Y, alzándose al instante las faldas hasta la rodilla, y aun un poco más, las descubrió llenas de cardenales.

—Desta manera —prosiguió— me ha parado aquel ingrato del Repolido, debiéndome más que a la madre que le parió. Y ¿por qué pensáis que lo ha hecho? ¡Montas, que le di yo ocasión para ello! No, por cierto, no lo hizo más sino porque, estando jugando y perdiendo, me envió a pedir con Cabrillas, su trainel, treinta reales, y no le envié más de veinte y cuatro, que el trabajo y afán con que yo los había ganado ruego yo a los cielos que vaya en descuento de mis pecados. Y, en pago desta cortesía y buena obra, creyendo él que yo le sisaba algo

morning. I've come to say that Juliana the Roundface is coming here all disheveled and weeping, and looking as if some disaster had befallen her."

Just then the woman he had described arrived, sobbing; Monipodio, hearing her, opened the door and ordered Tagarete to return to his post and, from then on, to report on what he saw with less racket and noise. He said he would. Roundface came in; she was a young girl of the same sort and the same calling as the others. Her hair was undone and her face was full of bruises; as soon as she reached the patio, she fell to the floor in a faint. La Gananciosa and La Escalanta ran over to help her and, undoing her bodice, they found her all black-and-blue, as if battered. They splashed water on her face and she came to, shouting:

"May the justice of God and the king fall on that shameless crook, that cowardly shoplifter, that lousy scoundrel whom I've saved from the gallows more times than he's got hairs in his beard![18] Unhappy woman that I am! Just see on whom I've spent and wasted my youth and the prime of my life: on a heartless, criminal, incorrigible wretch!"

"Calm down, Roundface," Monipodio then said, "for I'm here to see you get justice. Tell us how you were offended, and it'll take longer for you to tell it than for me to avenge you for it. Tell me whether you've had a run-in with your *respecto,* or fancy man.[19] If that's the case and you want revenge, all you have to do is spit it out."

"What respect?" replied Juliana. "May I see myself respected in hell, if I'm respected ever again by that fellow who's a lion to sheep and a lamb to men! Am I supposed to go on sharing meals with *him,* or sleep with him? I'd rather see my body eaten by jackals, this body that he's left in the state you now see!"

And, lifting her petticoats that moment to the knee, and even a little higher, she revealed that her skin was covered with bruises.

"That's how he left me," she continued, "that ingrate El Repolido, who owes more to me than to the mother who bore him. And why do you think he did it? Did I damn well give him a reason to? No, he surely did it only because, while he was gambling and losing, he sent his messenger boy Cabrillas to ask me for thirty reales, and I sent him only twenty-four, and I pray to heaven that the work and effort it cost me to earn them will make up for my sins! And, in repayment for that courtesy and charity, he, thinking that I was skimming a little off the sum he had fancifully reck-

---

18. One way a woman could do this was by agreeing to marry the offender; but, of course, she could also bribe the authorities, etc. 19. In Spanish (slang), *respe(c)to*: hence the puns in the next speech.

de la cuenta que él allá en su imaginación había hecho de lo que yo podía tener, esta mañana me sacó al campo, detrás de la Güerta del Rey, y allí, entre unos olivares, me desnudó, y con la petrina, sin escusar ni recoger los hierros, que en malos grillos y hierros le vea yo, me dio tantos azotes, que me dejó por muerta. De la cual verdadera historia son buenos testigos estos cardenales que miráis.

Aquí tornó a levantar las voces, aquí volvió a pedir justicia, y aquí se la prometió de nuevo Monipodio y todos los bravos que allí estaban. La Gananciosa tomó la mano a consolalla, diciéndole que ella diera de muy buena gana una de las mejores preseas que tenía porque le hubiera pasado otro tanto con su querido.

—Porque quiero —dijo— que sepas, hermana Cariharta, si no lo sabes, que a lo que se quiere bien se castiga; y cuando estos bellacones nos dan, y azotan y acocean, entonces nos adoran; si no, confiésame una verdad, por tu vida: después que te hubo Repolido castigado y brumado, ¿no te hizo alguna caricia?

—¿Cómo una? —respondió la llorosa—. Cien mil me hizo, y diera él un dedo de la mano porque me fuera con él a su posada; y aun me parece que casi se le saltaron las lágrimas de los ojos después de haberme molido.

—No hay dudar en eso —replicó la Gananciosa—. Y lloraría de pena de ver cuál te había puesto; que en estos tales hombres, y en tales casos, no han cometido la culpa cuando les viene el arrepentimiento; y tú verás, hermana, si no viene a buscarte antes que de aquí nos vamos, y a pedirte perdón de todo lo pasado, rindiéndosete como un cordero.

—En verdad —respondió Monipodio— que no ha de entrar por estas puertas el cobarde envesado, si primero no hace una manifiesta penitencia del cometido delito. ¿Las manos había él de ser osado ponerlas en el rostro de la Cariharta, ni en sus carnes, siendo persona que puede competir en limpieza y ganancia con la misma Gananciosa que está delante, que no lo puedo más encarecer?

—¡Ay! —dijo a esta sazón la Juliana—. No diga vuesa merced, señor Monipodio, mal de aquel maldito, que con cuán malo es, le quiero más que a las telas de mi corazón, y hanme vuelto el alma al cuerpo las razones que en su abono me ha dicho mi amiga la Gananciosa, y en verdad que estoy por ir a buscarle.

—Eso no harás tú por mi consejo —replicó la Gananciosa—, porque se estenderá y encanchará y hará tretas en ti como en cuerpo muerto. Sosiégate, hermana, que antes de mucho le verás venir tan arrepentido como he dicho; y si no viniere, escribirémosle un papel en coplas que le amargue.

oned up that I had, took me out to the country this morning, behind the King's Garden, and there, in an olive grove, he stripped me and with his belt, not removing or tucking away its iron trim (may I see him in evil fetters and irons!), he gave me so many blows that he left me for dead. And these bruises you see are honest witnesses to that true story."

Here she raised her voice again, here she demanded justice once more, and here Monipodio promised it to her again, as did all the bravos present. La Gananciosa took her hand to console her, saying that she'd gladly give one of the best jewels she owned if the same thing had happened to her with her lover.

"Because I want you to know, my sister Roundface, if you don't know it," she said, "that you always punish the one you love; and when those wretches hit us, whip us, and kick us, it's because they adore us; otherwise, admit one thing to me, on your life: after Repolido had punished and thrashed you, didn't he give you some caress?"

"Why just one?" the weeping woman replied. "He gave me a hundred thousand, and he'd have given a finger off his hand if I had gone to his rooms with him; and I even think there were almost tears in his eyes after he thrashed me."

"No doubt about it," replied La Gananciosa. "And he'd weep with pain to see the state he left you in; because such men, on such occasions, no sooner commit the wrong than repentance comes over them; and you'll see, sister, whether he doesn't come looking for you before we leave here, to ask your forgiveness for all that has passed, submitting to you like a lamb."

"Truly," replied Monipodio, "that whip-tanned coward won't enter these doors unless he first does public penance for the crime he committed. Is he to be so bold as to lay hands on Roundface's face, or her body, she being a person who can compete in cleanness and profitability with even La Gananciosa, who's standing here before us?—and I can't put it more strongly than that!"

"Ah!" Juliana then said. "Don't speak badly of that accursed man, Señor Monipodio, because, bad as he is, I love him more than my heartstrings, and the things my friend La Gananciosa has said in his behalf have restored my soul to my body, and I'm really about to go looking for him."

"If you take my advice, you won't," replied La Gananciosa, "because he'll puff himself up and become too courageous, and he'll thrust his sword into you as if into a dead body. Calm down, sister, because before long you'll see him arriving as repentant as I said; and if he doesn't come, we'll write him a letter in verse that will exasperate him."

—Eso sí —dijo la Cariharta—, que tengo mil cosas que escribirle.

—Yo seré el secretario cuando sea menester —dijo Monipodio—; y, aunque no soy nada poeta, todavía, si el hombre se arremanga, se atreverá a hacer dos millares de coplas en daca las pajas, y, cuando no salieren como deben, yo tengo un barbero amigo, gran poeta, que nos hinchirá las medidas a todas horas; y en la de agora acabemos lo que teníamos comenzado del almuerzo, que después todo se andará.

Fue contenta la Juliana de obedecer a su mayor; y así, todos volvieron a su *gaudeamus*, y en poco espacio vieron el fondo de la canasta y las heces del cuero. Los viejos bebieron *sine fine;* los mozos *adunia;* las señoras, los *quiries*. Los viejos pidieron licencia para irse. Diósela luego Monipodio, encargándoles viniesen a dar noticia con toda puntualidad de todo aquello que viesen ser útil y conveniente a la comunidad. Respondieron que ellos se lo tenían bien en cuidado y fuéronse.

Rinconete, que de suyo era curioso, pidiendo primero perdón y licencia, preguntó a Monipodio que de qué servían en la cofradía dos personajes tan canos, tan graves y apersonados. A lo cual respondió Monipodio que aquéllos, en su germanía y manera de hablar, se llamaban avispones, y que servían de andar de día por toda la ciudad avispando en qué casas se podía dar tiento de noche, y en seguir los que sacaban dinero de la Contratación o Casa de la Moneda, para ver dónde lo llevaban, y aun dónde lo ponían; y, en sabiéndolo, tanteaban la groseza del muro de la tal casa y diseñaban el lugar más conveniente para hacer los guzpátaros —que son agujeros— para facilitar la entrada. En resolución, dijo que era la gente de más o de tanto provecho que había en su hermandad, y que de todo aquello que por su industria se hurtaba llevaban el quinto, como Su Majestad de los tesoros; y que, con todo esto, eran hombres de mucha verdad, y muy honrados, y de buena vida y fama, temerosos de Dios y de sus conciencias, que cada día oían misa con estraña devoción.

—Y hay dellos tan comedidos, especialmente estos dos que de aquí se van agora, que se contentan con mucho menos de lo que por nuestros aranceles les toca. Otros dos que hay son palanquines, los cuales, como por momentos mudan casas, saben las entradas y salidas de todas las de la ciudad, y cuáles pueden ser de provecho y cuáles no.

—Todo me parece de perlas —dijo Rinconete—, y querría ser de algún provecho a tan famosa cofradía.

—Siempre favorece el cielo a los buenos deseos —dijo Monipodio.

Estando en esta plática, llamaron a la puerta; salió Monipodio a ver quién era, y, preguntándolo, respondieron:

"Yes, yes," said Roundface, "because I've got a thousand things to write him."

"I'll be the secretary if necessary," said Monipodio, "and, though I'm no poet, still, if a man rolls up his sleeves, he'll be bold enough to write two thousand stanzas in a trice; and, if they don't come out the way they should, I have a barber friend who's a great poet, and he'll fill up the gap at any hour; right now, let's finish the lunch we started; after that all will go well."

Juliana was pleased to obey her chief; and so they all returned to their beanfeast, and before long they could see the bottom of the basket and the dregs in the wineskin. The old men drank without an end; the young ones, aplenty; and the ladies, nine times, like the Kyries in the mass. The old men asked permission to leave. Monipodio granted it, ordering them to come and report exactly on anything they found useful and beneficial to the fellowship. They replied that this was always their great concern, and they departed.

Rinconete, curious by nature, first requesting leave to do so, asked Monipodio what good to the brotherhood were two characters so white-haired, grave, and corpulent. To which Monipodio replied that those men, in the members' jargon and way of speaking, were called 'casers,' and that their role was to walk all over town during the day seeking out houses that could be broken into at night, and to follow people who had drawn money out of the Chamber of Commerce or the Mint, to see where they were taking it, and even where they were putting it; when they found out, they would measure the thickness of that house's outer walls and mark the spot most suitable for making holes—that is, breaches—to make it easier to get in. In a word, he said they were the most useful, or equal to the most useful, people he had in his brotherhood, and that of everything stolen through their cunning they took a fifth, just as the king does from unearthed treasure; but that, all the same, they were very truthful men, very respectable, and of a good life and repute, God-fearing and with a sensitive conscience, hearing mass daily with extreme devoutness.

"And some of them are so obliging, especially those two who just left, that they're satisfied with much less than our regulations allow them. There are two others who are 'transport men': since they're constantly moving households, they know the entrances and exits of every house in town, and which ones can be of use to us or not."

All of that sounds grand to me," said Rinconete, "and I'd like to be of some service to such a famous brotherhood."

"Heaven always favors good desires," said Monipodio.

While they were conversing thus, there came a knock at the door; Monipodio went out to see who it was, and this reply was made to his question:

—Abra voacé, sor Monipodio, que el Repolido soy.

Oyó esta voz Cariharta y, alzando al cielo la suya, dijo:

—No le abra vuesa merced, señor Monipodio; no le abra a ese marinero de Tarpeya, a este tigre de Ocaña.

No dejó por esto Monipodio de abrir a Repolido; pero, viendo la Cariharta que le abría, se levantó corriendo y se entró en la sala de los broqueles, y, cerrando tras sí la puerta, desde dentro, a grandes voces decía:

—Quítenmele de delante a ese gesto de por demás, a ese verdugo de inocentes, asombrador de palomas duendas.

Maniferro y Chiquiznaque tenían a Repolido, que en todas maneras quería entrar donde la Cariharta estaba; pero, como no le dejaban, decía desde afuera:

—¡No haya más, enojada mía; por tu vida que te sosiegues, ansí te veas casada!

—¿Casada yo, malino? —respondió la Cariharta—. ¡Mirá en qué tecla toca! ¡Ya quisieras tú que lo fuera contigo, y antes lo sería yo con una sotomía de muerte que contigo!

—¡Ea, boba —replicó Repolido—, acabemos ya, que es tarde, y mire no se ensanche por verme hablar tan manso y venir tan rendido; porque, vive el Dador, si se me sube la cólera al campanario, que sea peor la recaída que la caída! Humíllese, y humillémonos todos, y no demos de comer al diablo.

—Y aun de cenar le daría yo —dijo la Cariharta—, porque te llevase donde nunca más mis ojos te viesen.

—¿No os digo yo? —dijo Repolido—. ¡Por Dios que voy oliendo, señora trinquete, que lo tengo de echar todo a doce, aunque nunca se venda!

A esto dijo Monipodio:

—En mi presencia no ha de haber demasías: la Cariharta saldrá, no por amenazas, sino por amor mío, y todo se hará bien; que las riñas entre los que bien se quieren son causa de mayor gusto cuando se hacen las paces. ¡Ah Juliana! ¡Ah niña! ¡Ah Cariharta mía! Sal acá fuera por mi amor, que yo haré que el Repolido te pida perdón de rodillas.

—Como él eso haga —dijo la Escalanta—, todas seremos en su favor y en rogar a Juliana salga acá fuera.

—Si esto ha de ir por vía de rendimiento que güela a menoscabo de

"Open up, Señor Monipodio, it's me, El Repolido."

Roundface heard his voice and, raising hers to the sky, said:

"Don't let him in, Señor Monipodio; don't let in that Tarpeian sailor, that Ocanian tiger!"[20]

All the same, Monipodio let Repolido in; when Roundface saw him doing that, she got up and ran into the room with the bucklers and, locking the door behind her, she shouted from inside:

"Get that ugly monster out of my sight, that torturer of innocents, that frightener of gentle doves!"

Maniferro and Chiquiznaque were restraining Repolido, who tried his best to get in where Roundface was; but, since they wouldn't release him, he called in from outside:

"Let it rest, don't be angry! On your life, calm down, so may you see yourself married!"

"I married, you villain?" Roundface answered. "Just see what he's harping on! I bet you'd like me to marry *you*, and I'd rather marry a 'skelton' than you!"

"Don't be silly," Repolido replied. "Let's stop fighting, because it's late. And take care not to get cocky because I'm talking so gently and being so submissive; because, as God lives, if the blood rises to my noggin, the relapse will be worse than the lapse! Be humble, and let's all be humble, and let's not quarrel bitterly!"

"I'd do my darnedest,"[21] Roundface said, "if the devil carried you away where I'd never lay eyes on you again."

"Didn't I say so?" said Repolido. "By God, I can smell it, missy whore: I've got to smash up everything!"[22]

At this, Monipodio said:

"No outrages are to be done in my presence: Roundface will come out, not by threats, but for love of me, and all will be well; because quarrels between people who love each other result in greater pleasure when they're made up. Ah, Juliana! Ah, girl! Ah, my Roundface! Come out for love of me, and I'll make El Repolido beg your forgiveness on his knees."

"If he does that," said La Escalanta, "all we women will plead in his behalf and ask Juliana to come out."

"If this must be done by way of a surrender that tends to make me lose

---

20. "Ocanian" (tiger) is a mistake for "Hyrcanian." The "sailor" (*marinero*) is a garbling of the words *Mira Nero* at the beginning of a traditional narrative ballad ("Nero looks down from the Tarpeian rock at burning Rome"). 21. Literally: "and let's not feed the devil." "I'd even give him supper." 22. Literally: "sell off everything by the dozen, even if no one ever buys it!"

la persona —dijo el Repolido—, no me rendiré a un ejército formado de esguízaros; mas si es por vía de que la Cariharta gusta dello, no digo yo hincarme de rodillas, pero un clavo me hincaré por la frente en su servicio.

Riyéronse desto Chiquiznaque y Maniferro, de lo cual se enojó tanto el Repolido, pensando que hacían burla dél, que dijo con muestras de infinita cólera:

—Cualquiera que se riere o se pensare reír de lo que la Cariharta, o contra mí, o yo contra ella hemos dicho o dijéremos, digo que miente y mentirá todas las veces que se riere, o lo pensare, como ya he dicho.

Miráronse Chiquiznaque y Maniferro de tan mal garbo y talle, que advirtió Monipodio que pararía en un gran mal si no lo remediaba; y así, poniéndose luego en medio dellos, dijo:

—No pase más adelante, caballeros; cesen aquí palabras mayores, y desháganse entre los dientes; y, pues las que se han dicho no llegan a la cintura, nadie las tome por sí.

—Bien seguros estamos —respondió Chiquiznaque— que no se dijeron ni dirán semejantes monitorios por nosotros; que, si se hubiera imaginado que se decían, en manos estaba el pandero que lo supiera bien tañer.

—También tenemos acá pandero, sor Chiquiznaque —replicó el Repolido—, y también, si fuere menester, sabremos tocar los cascabeles, y ya he dicho que el que se huelga, miente; y quien otra cosa pensare, sígame, que con un palmo de espada menos hará el hombre que sea lo dicho dicho.

Y, diciendo esto, se iba a salir por la puerta afuera. Estábalo escuchando la Cariharta, y cuando sintió que se iba enojado, salió diciendo:

—¡Ténganle no se vaya, que hará de las suyas! ¿No veen que va enojado, y es un Judas Macarelo en esto de la valentía? ¡Vuelve acá, valentón del mundo y de mis ojos!

Y, cerrando con él, le asió fuertemente de la capa, y, acudiendo también Monipodio, le detuvieron. Chiquiznaque y Maniferro no sabían si enojarse o si no, y estuviéronse quedos esperando lo que Repolido haría; el cual, viéndose rogar de la Cariharta y de Monipodio, volvió diciendo:

—Nunca los amigos han de dar enojo a los amigos, ni hacer burla de los amigos, y más cuando veen que se enojan los amigos.

—No hay aquí amigo —respondió Maniferro— que quiera enojar ni hacer burla de otro amigo; y, pues todos somos amigos, dense las manos los amigos.

A esto dijo Monipodio:

face," said El Repolido, "I won't surrender to a whole army of Swiss mercenaries; but if it's by a way that gives Roundface pleasure, I'll not only kneel down, I'll drive a nail through my forehead to serve her."

That made Chiquiznaque and Maniferro laugh, which got El Repolido so angry, thinking they were making fun of him, that he said with signs of infinite wrath:

"Whoever laughs or attempts to laugh at anything already said, or to be said, by Roundface against me or by me against her, I say he lies and will lie every time he laughs, or attempts to, as I said!"

Chiquiznaque and Maniferro exchanged such nasty, menacing looks that Monipodio realized this would end up very badly if he didn't intervene; so, immediately placing himself between them, he said:

"Let this stop here, gentlemen; let these rough words cease and melt in your teeth; and, since those already spoken don't call for swordplay, let nobody take them personally."

"We're quite sure," Chiquiznaque replied, "that such warnings weren't said, and won't be said, with us in mind; because if anyone had imagined that they were, the timbrel was in the hands of a man who knows how to beat it."

"We've got a timbrel here, too, Señor Chiquiznaque," retorted El Repolido, "and, if necessary, we'll also know how to play the bells; and I've already said that any man who's amused is a liar; and if anyone thinks differently, let him follow me, and a handbreadth of sword will convince him that I meant what I said."

And, saying this, he headed for the street door. Roundface had been listening to him, and when she heard him leaving in a rage, she came out, saying:

"Stop him from going, or he'll play his usual tricks! Don't you see he's leaving angry, and that he's a 'Judas Maccarellus' where boldness is concerned? Come back, hero of the world and of my heart!"

And, confronting him, she took firm hold of his cape; Monipodio came running, too, and they detained him. Chiquiznaque and Maniferro didn't know whether to get angry or not, and stood still waiting for what Repolido would do; he, finding himself implored by Roundface and Monipodio, came back, saying:

"Friends should never make each other angry, or make fun of each other, especially when they see their friends getting angry."

"There's no friend here," Maniferro replied, "who wants to anger or make fun of another friend; and since we're all friends, let friends shake hands."

To which Monipodio replied:

—Todos voacedes han hablado como buenos amigos, y como tales amigos se den las manos de amigos.

Diéronselas luego, y la Escalanta, quitándose un chapín, comenzó a tañer en él como en un pandero; la Gananciosa tomó una escoba de palma nueva, que allí se halló acaso, y, rascándola, hizo un son que, aunque ronco y áspero, se concertaba con el del chapín. Monipodio rompió un plato y hizo dos tejoletas, que, puestas entre los dedos y repicadas con gran ligereza, llevaba el contrapunto al chapín y a la escoba.

Espantáronse Rinconete y Cortadillo de la nueva invención de la escoba, porque hasta entonces nunca la habían visto. Conociólo Maniferro y díjoles:

—¿Admíranse de la escoba? Pues bien hacen, pues música más presta y más sin pesadumbre, ni más barata, no se ha inventado en el mundo; y en verdad que oí decir el otro día a un estudiante que ni el Negrofeo, que sacó a la Arauz del infierno; ni el Marión, que subió sobre el delfín y salió del mar como si viniera caballero sobre una mula de alquiler; ni el otro gran músico que hizo una ciudad que tenía cien puertas y otros tantos postigos, nunca inventaron mejor género de música, tan fácil de deprender, tan mañera de tocar, tan sin trastes, clavijas ni cuerdas, y tan sin necesidad de templarse; y aun voto a tal, que dicen que la inventó un galán desta ciudad, que se pica de ser un Héctor en la música.

—Eso creo yo muy bien —respondió Rinconete—, pero escuchemos lo que quieren cantar nuestros músicos, que parece que la Gananciosa ha escupido, señal de que quiere cantar.

Y así era la verdad, porque Monipodio le había rogado que cantase algunas seguidillas de las que se usaban; mas la que comenzó primero fue la Escalanta, y con voz sutil y quebradiza cantó lo siguiente:

Por un sevillano, rufo a lo valón,
tengo socarrado todo el corazón.

Siguió la Gananciosa cantando:

Por un morenico de color verde,
¿cuál es la fogosa que no se pierde?

Y luego Monipodio, dándose gran priesa al meneo de sus tejoletas, dijo:

Riñen dos amantes, hácese la paz:
si el enojo es grande, es el gusto más.

No quiso la Cariharta pasar su gusto en silencio, porque,

"All of you have spoken like good friends, and being such friends, they should shake hands like friends."

At once they shook hands, and La Escalanta, taking off one chopine, started to beat on it as if on a timbrel; La Gananciosa took a new palm-leaf broom that happened to be there and, strumming it, produced a sound which, though hoarse and harsh, harmonized with the sound of the chopine. Monipodio broke a dish, making two shards which, placed between his fingers and clicked very fast, supplied a counterpoint to the chopine and the broom.

Rinconete and Cortadillo were amazed at that novel use of the broom, which they had never seen before. Maniferro noticed this, and said:

"You admire the broom? Well, you're right, because livelier, more carefree, or cheaper music has never been invented in the world; in fact, I heard a student say the other day that neither 'Orphelus,' who led 'Eurycide' out of hell, nor 'Marion,' who rode a dolphin out of the ocean as if he were mounted on a hired mule, nor that other great musician[23] who built a city with a hundred main gates and a hundred postern gates, never invented a better sort of music, so easy to learn, so simple to play, without frets, pegs, or strings, and needing no tuning; and, by God, they say it was invented by a gallant of this city, who boasts of being a musical Hector."

"I can readily believe it," Rinconete replied, "but let's listen to what our musicians are going to sing, because it looks as if La Gananciosa has spat, a sign that she wants to sing."

And this was true, because Monipodio had asked her to sing a few of their customary seguidillas; but the first one to perform was la Escalanta, who in a thin, flexible voice sang as follows:

> For a man of Seville, redheaded as a Walloon,
> my heart is all scorched.

La Gananciosa followed, singing:

> For a swarthy man of youthful vigor
> what fiery woman doesn't ruin herself?

And then Monipodio, clicking his pieces of dish very fast, sang:

> Two lovers quarrel and make it up:
> if their anger is great, their pleasure is greater.

Roundface didn't want to keep silent about her pleasure and, taking an-

23. Respectively: Orpheus, Eurydice, Arion, and Amphion.

tomando otro chapín, se metió en danza, y acompañó a las demás diciendo:

> Detente, enojado, no me azotes más;
> que si bien lo miras, a tus carnes das.

—Cántese a lo llano —dijo a esta sazón Repolido—, y no se toquen estorias pasadas, que no hay para qué: lo pasado sea pasado, y tómese otra vereda, y basta.

Talle llevaban de no acabar tan presto el comenzado cántico, si no sintieran que llamaban a la puerta apriesa; y con ella salió Monipodio a ver quién era, y la centinela le dijo cómo al cabo de la calle había asomado el alcalde de la justicia, y que delante dél venían el Tordillo y el Cernícalo, corchetes neutrales. Oyéronlo los de dentro, y alborotáronse todos de manera que la Cariharta y la Escalanta se calzaron sus chapines al revés, dejó la escoba la Gananciosa, Monipodio sus tejoletas, y quedó en turbado silencio toda la música, enmudeció Chiquiznaque, pasmóse Repolido y suspendióse Maniferro; y todos, cuál por una y cuál por otra parte, desaparecieron, subiéndose a las azoteas y tejados, para escaparse y pasar por ellos a otra calle. Nunca ha disparado arcabuz a deshora, ni trueno repentino espantó así a banda de descuidadas palomas, como puso en alboroto y espanto a toda aquella recogida compañía y buena gente la nueva de la venida del alcalde de la justicia. Los dos novicios, Rinconete y Cortadillo, no sabían qué hacerse, y estuviéronse quedos, esperando ver en qué paraba aquella repentina borrasca, que no paró en más de volver la centinela a decir que el alcalde se había pasado de largo, sin dar muestra ni resabio de mala sospecha alguna.

Y, estando diciendo esto a Monipodio, llegó un caballero mozo a la puerta, vestido, como se suele decir, de barrio; Monipodio le entró consigo, y mandó llamar a Chiquiznaque, a Maniferro y al Repolido, y que de los demás no bajase alguno. Como se habían quedado en el patio, Rinconete y Cortadillo pudieron oír toda la plática que pasó Monipodio con el caballero recién venido, el cual dijo a Monipodio que por qué se había hecho tan mal lo que le había encomendado. Monipodio respondió que aún no sabía lo que se había hecho; pero que allí estaba el oficial a cuyo cargo estaba su negocio, y que él daría muy buena cuenta de sí.

Bajó en esto Chiquiznaque, y preguntóle Monipodio si había

other chopine, she started to dance and accompanied the other women, singing:

> Hold off, angry man, don't beat me any more;
> for if you think about it, it's your own flesh you're hitting.

"Sing without adornments," Repolido then said, "and don't mention stories from the past, because there's no reason to; let bygones be bygones, and take another path, and enough."

They looked as if they wouldn't finish all that soon the singsong they had begun, but they promptly heard knocking at the door; whereat Monipodio went out to see who it was, and the sentinel told him that the justice of the peace had appeared at the head of the street, preceded by Little Thrush[24] and Kestrel, impartial constables. Those inside heard this, and were all so alarmed that Roundface and La Escalanta put on their chopines backwards, La Gananciosa dropped the broom, and Monipodio his pieces of dish, and all the music fell into a troubled silence, Chiquiznaque was mute, Repolido was astonished, and Maniferro was amazed; all of them disappeared into different places, ascending to the terraces and roofs so they could escape into another street that way. Never did a harquebus going off unexpectedly, or sudden thunder, ever frighten a flock of carefree pigeons so badly as the news of the arrival of the justice of the peace alarmed and scared all of that secluded company of good folk. The two novices, Rinconete and Cortadillo, didn't know what to do with themselves and stood still, waiting to see how that sudden tempest would turn out; all that happened was that the sentinel came back to say that the justice had walked right by, without showing the least sign of any evil suspicions.

While he was telling Monipodio this, a young gentleman came to the door, dressed casually, as the expression goes; Monipodio let him in and sent for Chiquiznaque, Maniferro, and El Repolido; no one else was to come downstairs. Since they had remained in the patio, Rinconete and Cortadillo could hear the entire conversation between Monipodio and the gentleman who had just come; the latter asked Monipodio why he had executed his commission so badly. Monipodio replied that he still didn't know what had been done, but that the employee was present who had been assigned his business, and that he'd give a good accounting of himself.

At this point, Chiquiznaque came down, and Monipodio asked him

24. Or: "Grizzle."

cumplido con la obra que se le encomendó de la cuchillada de a catorce.

—¿Cuál? —respondió Chiquiznaque—. ¿Es la de aquel mercader de la Encrucijada?

—Ésa es —dijo el caballero.

—Pues lo que en eso pasa —respondió Chiquiznaque— es que yo le aguardé anoche a la puerta de su casa, y él vino antes de la oración; lleguéme cerca dél, marquéle el rostro con la vista, y vi que le tenía tan pequeño, que era imposible de toda imposibilidad caber en él cuchillada de catorce puntos; y, hallándome imposibilitado de poder cumplir lo prometido y de hacer lo que llevaba en mi destruición . . .

—*Instrucción* querrá vuesa merced decir —dijo el caballero—, que no *destruición*.

—Eso quise decir —respondió Chiquiznaque—. Digo que, viendo que en la estrecheza y poca cantidad de aquel rostro no cabían los puntos propuestos, porque no fuese mi ida en balde, di la cuchillada a un lacayo suyo, que a buen seguro que la pueden poner por mayor de marca.

—Más quisiera —dijo el caballero— que se la hubiera dado al amo una de a siete, que al criado la de a catorce. En efeto, conmigo no se ha cumplido como era razón, pero no importa; poca mella me harán los treinta ducados que dejé en señal. Beso a vuesas mercedes las manos.

Y, diciendo esto, se quitó el sombrero y volvió las espaldas para irse; pero Monipodio le asió de la capa de mezcla que traía puesta, diciéndole:

—Voacé se detenga y cumpla su palabra, pues nosotros hemos cumplido la nuestra con mucha honra y con mucha ventaja: veinte ducados faltan, y no ha de salir de aquí voacé sin darlos, o prendas que lo valgan.

—Pues ¿a esto llama vuesa merced cumplimiento de palabra —respondió el caballero—: dar la cuchillada al mozo, habiéndose de dar al amo?

—¡Qué bien está en la cuenta el señor! —dijo Chiquiznaque—. Bien parece que no se acuerda de aquel refrán que dice: «Quien bien quiere a Beltrán, bien quiere a su can».

—¿Pues en qué modo puede venir aquí a propósito ese refrán? —replicó el caballero.

—¿Pues no es lo mismo —prosiguió Chiquiznaque— decir: «Quien mal quiere a Beltrán, mal quiere a su can»? Y así, Beltrán es el mercader, voacé le quiere mal, su lacayo es su can; y dando al can se da a Beltrán, y la deuda queda líquida y trae aparejada ejecución; por eso no hay más sino pagar luego sin apercebimiento de remate.

—Eso juro yo bien —añadió Monipodio—, y de la boca me

whether he had accomplished the task he had been assigned, the one about the fourteen-stitch knife slash.

"Which one?" Chiquiznaque replied, "the one given to that merchant of the Crossroads?"

"Yes, that one," the gentleman said.

"Well, what happened there," Chiquiznaque replied, "is that I waited for him at his house door last evening, and he came before nightfall; I went up to him, sized up his face with my eyes, and saw it was so small that it was absolutely impossible for a fourteen-stitch slash to fit on it; finding myself unable to accomplish what was promised and to do what was in my destructions . . ."

"You mean, 'instructions,' sir," the gentleman said, "not 'destructions.'"

"That's what I meant," Chiquiznaque replied. "As I was saying, when I saw that the proposed stitches wouldn't fit on that narrow, small face, not wanting my trip to be for nothing, I gave the slash to one of his footmen, and I assure you it can count as a major one."

"I'd rather," the gentleman said, "you had given a seven-stitch one to the master than the fourteen-stitch one to the servant. In fact, you didn't carry out my commission properly, but it doesn't matter; the thirty ducats I left on deposit won't make much of a dent on me. I bid you gentlemen farewell."

And, saying this, he doffed his hat and turned away to leave; but Monipodio seized him by the cape of mixture material he was wearing, and said:

"Stop, sir, and keep your promise, since we have kept ours very honorably and very excellently: you still owe twenty ducats, and you won't leave here without paying them, or items of the equivalent value."

"Well, do you call this keeping your word, sir," the gentleman replied, "slashing the servant when it should have been his master?"

"How wrong you are, sir!" said Chiquiznaque. "You really seem not to remember that proverb which says: 'Love me, love my dog.'"

"Well, how can that proverb possibly apply here?" the gentleman retorted.

"Well, isn't it the same," Chiquiznaque continued, "as saying: 'Hate me, hate my dog'? And so, the 'me' is the merchant, you hate him, his footman is 'the dog'; hurting 'the dog' is the same as hurting 'me,' so your debt is still payable and can be duly called in; therefore, all that remains is to pay at once without a notice to settle up."

"I swear to all of that," Monipodio answered, "and Chiquiznaque, my

quitaste, Chiquiznaque amigo, todo cuanto aquí has dicho; y así, voacé, señor galán, no se meta en puntillos con sus servidores y amigos, sino tome mi consejo y pague luego lo trabajado; y si fuere servido que se le dé otra al amo, de la cantidad que pueda llevar su rostro, haga cuenta que ya se la están curando.

—Como eso sea —respondió el galán—, de muy entera voluntad y gana pagaré la una y la otra por entero.

—No dude en esto —dijo Monipodio— más que en ser cristiano; que Chiquiznaque se la dará pintiparada, de manera que parezca que allí se le nació.

—Pues con esa seguridad y promesa —respondió el caballero—, recíbase esta cadena en prendas de los veinte ducados atrasados y de cuarenta que ofrezco por la venidera cuchillada. Pesa mil reales, y podría ser que se quedase rematada, porque traigo entre ojos que serán menester otros catorce puntos antes de mucho.

Quitóse, en esto, una cadena de vueltas menudas del cuello y diósela a Monipodio, que al color y al peso bien vio que no era de alquimia. Monipodio la recibió con mucho contento y cortesía, porque era en estremo bien criado; la ejecución quedó a cargo de Chiquiznaque, que sólo tomó término de aquella noche. Fuese muy satisfecho el caballero, y luego Monipodio llamó a todos los ausentes y azorados. Bajaron todos, y, poniéndose Monipodio en medio dellos, sacó un libro de memoria que traía en la capilla de la capa y dióselo a Rinconete que leyese, porque él no sabía leer. Abrióle Rinconete, y en la primera hoja vio que decía:

MEMORIA DE LAS CUCHILLADAS
QUE SE HAN DE DAR ESTA SEMANA

La primera, al mercader de la encrucijada: vale cincuenta escudos. Están recebidos treinta a buena cuenta. Secutor, Chiquiznaque.

—No creo que hay otra, hijo —dijo Monipodio—; pasá adelante y mirá donde dice: MEMORIA DE PALOS.

Volvió la hoja Rinconete, y vio que en otra estaba escrito:

MEMORIA DE PALOS

Y más abajo decía:

Al bodegonero de la Alfalfa, doce palos de mayor cuantía a escudo cada uno. Están dados a buena cuenta ocho. El término, seis días. Secutor, Maniferro.

friend, in all that you said you took the words right out of my mouth. So you, my fine fellow, don't get standoffish with your servants and friends, but take my advice and pay right up for the work we did; if it's your wish that the master receive another slash, as big as his face can hold, just imagine that he's already receiving medical attention."

"Be that as it may," the gallant replied, "with a right good will I'll pay for both slashes entirely."

"Have no more doubt about it," said Monipodio, "than you doubt being a Christian; because Chiquiznaque will give him a slash pretty as a picture, so it looks as if he were born with it."

"Well, with that assurance and promise," the gentleman replied, "take this chain as a pledge for the twenty ducats' belated payment and for the forty I offer for the coming slash. It's worth a thousand reales, and maybe its value will get used up, because I suspect that other fourteen-stitchers will be wanted before long."

Saying this, he took from his neck a chain with small links and gave it to Monipodio, who saw clearly from its color and weight that it wasn't a fake. Monipodio took it with much gladness and courtesy, because he was extremely polite; the carrying out of the commission fell to Chiquiznaque, who said the job would be done that very night. The gentleman left very contented, and then Monipodio summoned all the frightened absentees. They all came down and Monipodio, standing in their midst, took out a memorandum book that was in the hood of his cape and handed it to Rinconete to read aloud, because he himself couldn't read. Rinconete opened it, and found written on the first leaf:

MEMO OF THE SLASHES
TO BE GIVEN THIS WEEK

The first, to the merchant of the Crossroads: payment, fifty escudos. Thirty received on deposit. To be carried out by: Chiquiznaque.

"I don't think there's another one, son," said Monipodio. "Keep going and look where it says: 'MEMO OF CUDGELING.'"

Rinconete turned the leaf, and saw written on another one:

MEMO OF CUDGELING

Further down it said:

To the cookshop owner at La Alfalfa, twelve of the hardest blows, @ one escudo apiece. Eight left on deposit. Deadline: six days. To be carried out by: Maniferro.

—Bien podía borrarse esa partida —dijo Maniferro—, porque esta noche traeré finiquito della.

—¿Hay más, hijo? —dijo Monipodio.

—Sí, otra —respondió Rinconete—, que dice así:

Al sastre corcovado que por mal nombre se llama el Silguero, seis palos de mayor cuantía, a pedimiento de la dama que dejó la gargantilla. Secutor, el Desmochado.

—Maravillado estoy —dijo Monipodio— cómo todavía está esa partida en ser. Sin duda alguna debe de estar mal dispuesto el Desmochado, pues son dos días pasados del término y no ha dado puntada en esta obra.

—Yo le topé ayer —dijo Maniferro—, y me dijo que por haber estado retirado por enfermo el corcovado no había cumplido con su débito.

—Eso creo yo bien —dijo Monipodio—, porque tengo por tan buen oficial al Desmochado, que, si no fuera por tan justo impedimento, ya él hubiera dado al cabo con mayores empresas. ¿Hay más, mocito?

—No señor —respondió Rinconete.

—Pues pasad adelante —dijo Monipodio—, y mirad donde dice: MEMORIAL DE AGRAVIOS COMUNES.

Pasó adelante Rinconete, y en otra hoja halló escrito:

MEMORIAL DE AGRAVIOS COMUNES.
CONVIENE A SABER: REDOMAZOS, UNTOS DE MIERA,
CLAVAZÓN DE SAMBENITOS Y CUERNOS, MATRACAS,
ESPANTOS, ALBOROTOS Y CUCHILLADAS FINGIDAS,
PUBLICACIÓN DE NIBELOS, ETC.

—¿Qué dice más abajo? —dijo Monipodio.

—Dice —dijo Rinconete—:

Unto de miera en la casa . . .

—No se lea la casa, que ya yo sé dónde es —respondió Monipodio—, y yo soy el *tuáutem* y esecutor desa niñería, y están dados a buena cuenta cuarto escudos, y el principal es ocho.

—Así es la verdad —dijo Rinconete—, que todo eso está aquí escrito; y aun más abajo dice:

Clavazón de cuernos.

—Tampoco se lea —dijo Monipodio— la casa, ni adónde; que basta que se les haga el agravio, sin que se diga en público; que es gran cargo de conciencia. A lo menos, más querría yo clavar cien cuernos y

"That entry can be crossed out," said Maniferro, "because I'll finish it off tonight."

"Is there any more, son?" asked Monipodio.

"Yes, another entry," Rinconete replied, "which reads:

To the humpbacked tailor nicknamed 'the Linnet,' six of the hardest blows, at the request of the lady who left the necklace. To be carried out by: 'The Mutilated.'"

"I'm surprised," said Monipodio, "that that item is still open. No doubt, the Mutilated must be indisposed, because the deadline passed two days ago, and he hasn't made a start on that job."

"I ran into him yesterday," Maniferro said, "and he told me that he hadn't accomplished his task because the hunchback was home, sick."

"I can well believe it," said Monipodio, "because I consider the Mutilated to be such a good employee that, if it weren't for such an understandable obstacle, by now he would have finished even bigger jobs. Anything else, son?"

"No, sir," Rinconete replied.

"Then keep going," said Monipodio, "up to where you find: MEMO OF COMMON MISCHIEFS."

Rinconete leafed through, and on another page he found written:

MEMO OF COMMON MISCHIEFS.
THAT IS: TOSSING FLASKS OF SMELLY LIQUID, SMEARING WITH JUNIPER OIL, NAILING UP NOTES OF INFAMY AND HORNS, SAYING THINGS TO SHAME PEOPLE, FRIGHTS, ALARMS, AND FALSE THREATS OF SLASHES, PUBLISHING SATIRICAL SLANDERS, ETC.

"What does it say under that?" asked Monipodio.

Rinconete replied: "It says:

A smearing with oil in the house of . . ."

"Don't read out the house; I know where it is," said Monipodio, "and I'm the one assigned to carry out that trifle, for which four escudos have been left on deposit, the total being eight."

"That's true," said Rinconete, "all of that is written here; and further down it says:

Nailing up horns."

"Don't read out that house, either," said Monipodio, "or where it is; it's enough that the insult is done them without announcing it publicly; for it's a great load on the conscience. At least, I'd rather nail up a hundred

otros tantos sambenitos, como se me pagase mi trabajo, que decillo sola una vez, aunque fuese a la madre que me parió.

—El esecutor desto es —dijo Rinconete— el Narigueta.

—Ya está eso hecho y pagado —dijo Monipodio—. Mirad si hay más, que si mal no me acuerdo, ha de haber ahí un espanto de veinte escudos; está dada la mitad, y el esecutor es la comunidad toda, y el término es todo el mes en que estamos; y cumpliráse al pie de la letra, sin que falte una tilde, y será una de las mejores cosas que hayan sucedido en esta ciudad de muchos tiempos a esta parte. Dadme el libro, mancebo, que yo sé que no hay más, y sé también que anda muy flaco el oficio; pero tras este tiempo vendrá otro y habrá que hacer más de lo que quisiéremos; que no se mueve la hoja sin la voluntad de Dios, y no hemos de hacer nosotros que se vengue nadie por fuerza; cuanto más, que cada uno en su causa suele ser valiente y no quiere pagar las hechuras de la obra que él se puede hacer por sus manos.

—Así es —dijo a esto el Repolido—. Pero mire vuesa merced, señor Monipodio, lo que nos ordena y manda, que se va haciendo tarde y va entrando el calor más que de paso.

—Lo que se ha de hacer —respondió Monipodio— es que todos se vayan a sus puestos, y nadie se mude hasta el domingo, que nos juntaremos en este mismo lugar y se repartirá todo lo que hubiere caído, sin agraviar a nadie. A Rinconete *el Bueno* y a Cortadillo se les da por distrito, hasta el domingo, desde la Torre del Oro, por defuera de la ciudad, hasta el postigo del Alcázar, donde se puede trabajar a sentadillas con sus flores; que yo he visto a otros, de menos habilidad que ellos, salir cada día con más de veinte reales en menudos, amén de la plata, con una baraja sola, y ésa con cuatro naipes menos. Este districto os enseñará Ganchoso; y, aunque os estendáis hasta San Sebastián y San Telmo, importa poco, puesto que es justicia mera mista que nadie se entre en pertenencia de nadie.

Besáronle la mano los dos por la merced que se les hacía, y ofreciéronse a hacer su oficio bien y fielmente, con toda diligencia y recato.

Sacó, en esto, Monipodio un papel doblado de la capilla de la capa, donde estaba la lista de los cofrades, y dijo a Rinconete que pusiese allí su nombre y el de Cortadillo; mas, porque no había tintero, le dio el papel para que lo llevase, y en el primer boticario los escribiese, poniendo: *Rinconete y Cortadillo, cofrades: noviciado, ninguno;*

horns and the same number of notes of infamy, as long as my work was paid for, than to announce it even once, though it were to the mother who bore me."

"The one to carry this out," said Rinconete, "is Little Nose."

"It's already done and paid for," said Monipodio. "See if there's any more, for if I remember correctly, there ought to be a scare at twenty escudos; half has been deposited, and the whole membership is to do it, and we've got the whole of this month to do it in; and it will be accomplished exactly as commissioned, dotting every I, and it will be one of the best things to happen in this city for a long, long time. Give me the book, boy, because I know there's no more; I also know that there hasn't been much work; but there will be better times, and we'll be booked for more than we want; for not a leaf stirs unless God wills, and we mustn't force anyone to take revenge; especially since everyone tends to be brave in his own cause, and people don't want to pay for work they can do with their own hands."

"Right," El Repolido said to this. "But, Señor Monipodio, sir, see to giving us your orders and commands, because it's getting late and it's getting hotter very quickly."

"What is to be done," Monipodio replied, "is for everyone to go to his post; no one should change posts until Sunday, when we'll meet in this same place and split up whatever we've taken in, with no injustice to anyone. To Rinconete the good and to Cortadillo I assign as their district, until Sunday, the area from the Golden Tower outside town up to the Alcázar postern, where they can work sitting down at their card sharping; because I've seen others, less skillful than they are, making over twenty reales in coppers, plus some silver, every day with a single deck—and a deck with four missing cards. Ganchoso[25] will show you that district; and even if you spread out up to San Sebastián and San Telmo, it hardly matters, although it's a strict law of ours that no one invade any one else's turf."

The two boys kissed his hand for the favor he was doing them, and promised to do their job well and faithfully, with all care and caution.

Then Monipodio took a folded sheet of paper from the hood of his cape, which contained the list of the members, and told Rinconete to add his name and Cortadillo's to it; but, because there was no inkwell, he gave him the paper to take away; he was to add their names at the next pharmacy, writing: "Rinconete and Cortadillo, members; apprentice period, none;

25. No doubt the "guide" earlier called Ganchuelo; no annotator I have seen remarks on this apparent slip.

Rinconete, floreo; Cortadillo, bajón»; y el día, mes y año, callando padres y patria.

Estando en esto, entró uno de los viejos avispones y dijo:

—Vengo a decir a vuesas mercedes cómo agora, agora, topé en Gradas a Lobillo el de Málaga, y díceme que viene mejorado en su arte de tal manera, que con naipe limpio quitará el dinero al mismo Satanás; y que por venir maltratado no viene luego a registrarse y a dar la sólita obediencia; pero que el domingo será aquí sin falta.

—Siempre se me asentó a mí —dijo Monipodio— que este Lobillo había de ser único en su arte, porque tiene las mejores y más acomodadas manos para ello que se pueden desear; que, para ser uno buen oficial en su oficio, tanto ha menester los buenos instrumentos con que le ejercita, como el ingenio con que le aprende.

—También topé —dijo el viejo— en una casa de posadas, en la calle de Tintores, al Judío, en hábito de clérigo, que se ha ido a posar allí por tener noticia que dos peruleros viven en la misma casa, y querría ver si pudiese trabar juego con ellos, aunque fuese de poca cantidad, que de allí podría venir a mucha. Dice también que el domingo no faltará de la junta y dará cuenta de su persona.

—Ese Judío también —dijo Monipodio— es gran sacre y tiene gran conocimiento. Días ha que no le he visto, y no lo hace bien. Pues a fe que si no se enmienda, que yo le deshaga la corona; que no tiene más órdenes el ladrón que las tiene el turco, ni sabe más latín que mi madre. ¿Hay más de nuevo?

—No —dijo el viejo—; a lo menos que yo sepa.

—Pues sea en buen hora —dijo Monipodio—. Voacedes tomen esta miseria —y repartió entre todos hasta cuarenta reales—, y el domingo no falte nadie, que no faltará nada de lo corrido.

Todos le volvieron las gracias. Tornáronse a abrazar Repolido y la Cariharta, la Escalanta con Maniferro y la Gananciosa con Chiquiznaque, concertando que aquella noche, después de haber alzado de obra en la casa, se viesen en la de la Pipota, donde también dijo que iría Monipodio, al registro de la canasta de colar, y que luego había de ir a cumplir y borrar la partida de la miera. Abrazó a Rinconete y a Cortadillo, y, echándolos su bendición, los despidió, encargándoles que no tuviesen jamás posada cierta ni de asiento, porque así convenía a la salud de todos. Acompañólos Ganchoso hasta enseñarles sus puestos, acordándoles que no faltasen el domingo, porque, a lo que creía y pensaba, Monipodio había de leer una lición de posición acerca de las cosas concernientes a su arte. Con esto, se fue, dejando a los dos compañeros admirados de lo que habían visto.

Rinconete, card sharp; Cortadillo, shoplifter," along with the day, month, and year; they didn't need to give their parents' names or their birthplace.

At this moment, one of the elderly "casers" came in and said:

"I've come to tell you gentlemen that just this minute I ran into Wolfcub from Málaga at the cathedral steps, and he told me that he's so improved at his trade that he can take even Satan's money with clean cards; because he's been manhandled, he hasn't come at once to sign in and promise you his usual obedience; but he'll be here Sunday without fail."

"I was always convinced," said Monipodio, "that Wolfcub would be paramount in his trade, because he has the best and aptest hands for it that anyone could wish; for, to be a good practitioner in your profession, you need the right tools to ply it with as much as you need the brains to learn it with."

"Also," the old man said, "in an apartment house on Dyers' Street, I ran into 'the Jew,' dressed as a priest; he's gone to live there because he found out that two men who got rich overseas are living in the same house, and he'd like to see whether he can get a game going with them, even for low stakes, because that could lead to a lot. He, too, says he won't miss Sunday's meeting, when he'll give an account of himself."

"This 'Jew,' too," said Monipodio, "is a real lynx and is very knowledgeable. I haven't seen him for days, and he's doing me wrong. Well, I swear that if he doesn't shape up, I'll ruin his tonsure, because that crook hasn't taken orders any more than a Turk has, and he knows no more Latin than my mother! Anything else new?"

"No," said the old man, "at least, not that I know of."

"Then, all right," said Monipodio. "All of you, take this pittance" (and he distributed a total of some forty reales among them all), "and everybody show up on Sunday, because none of the take will be missing."

Everybody thanked him. Repolido and Roundface embraced again, as did Escalanta and Maniferro, and La Gananciosa and Chiquiznaque. They arranged that that night, after finishing their work in the house, they'd meet at La Pipota's, where Monipodio said he'd go, too, to examine the bleaching basket, after which he had to go and finish the juniper-oil job so he could cross out that entry. He hugged Rinconete and Cortadillo and, blessing them, sent them out, ordering them never to have a fixed lodging or dwelling, because that was better for everyone's welfare. Ganchoso accompanied them until he showed them their posts, reminding them to be sure to show up on Sunday, because, as he thought and believed, Monipodio was going to give a masterly lesson on the things concerning their profession. Thereupon he departed, leaving the two comrades amazed at what they had seen.

Era Rinconete, aunque muchacho, de muy buen entendimiento, y tenía un buen natural; y, como había andado con su padre en el ejercicio de las bulas, sabía algo de buen lenguaje, y dábale gran risa pensar en los vocablos que había oído a Monipodio y a los demás de su compañía y bendita comunidad, y más cuando por decir *per modum sufragii* había dicho *per modo de naufragio*; y que sacaban el *estupendo,* por decir *estipendio,* de lo que se garbeaba; y cuando la Cariharta dijo que era Repolido como un *marinero de Tarpeya* y un tigre de *Ocaña,* por decir *Hircania,* con otras mil impertinencias (especialmente le cayó en gracia cuando dijo que el trabajo que había pasado en ganar los veinte y cuatro reales lo recibiese el cielo en descuento de sus pecados) a éstas y a otras peores semejantes; y, sobre todo, le admiraba la seguridad que tenían y la confianza de irse al cielo con no faltar a sus devociones, estando tan llenos de hurtos, y de homicidios y de ofensas a Dios. Y reíase de la otra buena vieja de la Pipota, que dejaba la canasta de colar hurtada, guardada en su casa y se iba a poner las candelillas de cera a las imágenes, y con ello pensaba irse al cielo calzada y vestida. No menos le suspendía la obediencia y respecto que todos tenían a Monipodio, siendo un hombre bárbaro, rústico y desalmado. Consideraba lo que había leído en su libro de memoria y los ejercicios en que todos se ocupaban. Finalmente, exageraba cuán descuidada justicia había en aquella tan famosa ciudad de Sevilla, pues casi al descubierto vivía en ella gente tan perniciosa y tan contraria a la misma naturaleza; y propuso en sí de aconsejar a su compañero no durasen mucho en aquella vida tan perdida y tan mala, tan inquieta, y tan libre y disoluta. Pero, con todo esto, llevado de sus pocos años y de su poca esperiencia, pasó con ella adelante algunos meses, en los cuales le sucedieron cosas que piden más luenga escritura; y así, se deja para otra ocasión contar su vida y milagros, con los de su maestro Monipodio, y otros sucesos de aquéllos de la infame academia, que todos serán de grande consideración y que podrán servir de ejemplo y aviso a los que las leyeren.

Rinconete, though still a boy, was very intelligent and had a good head; and, since he had gone around with his father selling indulgences, he knew something of correct speech, and he had a good laugh remembering the terms he had heard used by Monipodio and the rest of his company and blessed community, especially when, instead of *per modum suffragii,* he had said *per modo de naufragio,* and had said *estupendo* in place of *estipendio* when talking about their loot; or when Roundface said that Repolido was like a *marinero de Tarpeya* and a tiger from *Ocaña* instead of Hyrcania, with a thousand other impertinent mistakes (he found it particularly funny when she said she wished heaven to receive the work she had done to earn the twenty-four reales as a part payment for her sins), those and other similar or worse ones; above all, he was amazed at their certainty and confidence that they'd go to heaven by not neglecting their devotions, whereas they had committed so many thefts, murders, and offenses against God. And he laughed at that good old woman, La Pipota, who left the stolen bleaching basket safe at home while she went to light wax candles for the images, and thereby imagined she'd go to heaven with her clothes and shoes on. He was no less astonished at everyone's obedience to, and respect for, Monipodio, who was a barbarous, coarse, and heartless man. He pondered over what he had read in his memorandum book and the assignments they all carried out. Lastly, he wondered at the great carelessness of the law in that most famous city of Seville, since such pernicious and totally unnatural people lived there almost in plain sight; and he resolved to advise his comrade that neither of them should remain long in that life which was so profligate, so bad, so turbulent, so licentious, and so dissolute. Nevertheless, because of his youth and lack of experience, he kept it up for a few more months, during which things befell him which call for a longer narrative; and so, we reserve it for another occasion to recount his life and miracles, along with those of his teacher Monipodio, and other doings of the members of that infamous academy; all of this will be of great moment, and will be able to serve as a lesson and warning to those who read it.

El coloquio de los perros

CIPIÓN.—Berganza amigo, dejemos esta noche el Hospital en guarda de la confianza y retirémonos a esta soledad y entre estas esteras, donde podremos gozar sin ser sentidos desta no vista merced que el cielo en un mismo punto a los dos nos ha hecho.

BERGANZA.—Cipión hermano, óyote hablar y sé que te hablo, y no puedo creerlo, por parecerme que el hablar nosotros pasa de los términos de naturaleza.

CIPIÓN.—Así es la verdad, Berganza; y viene a ser mayor este milagro en que no solamente hablamos, sino en que hablamos con discurso, como si fuéramos capaces de razón, estando tan sin ella, que la diferencia que hay del animal bruto al hombre es ser el hombre animal racional, y el bruto, irracional.

BERGANZA.—Todo lo que dices, Cipión, entiendo, y el decirlo tú y entenderlo yo me causa nueva admiración y nueva maravilla. Bien es verdad que, en el discurso de mi vida, diversas y muchas veces he oído decir grandes prerrogativas nuestras: tanto, que parece que algunos han querido sentir que tenemos un natural distinto, tan vivo y tan agudo en muchas cosas, que da indicios y señales de faltar poco para mostrar que tenemos un no sé qué de entendimiento capaz de discurso.

CIPIÓN.—Lo que yo he oído alabar y encarecer es nuestra mucha memoria, el agradecimiento y gran fidelidad nuestra; tanto, que nos suelen pintar por símbolo de la amistad; y así, habrás visto (si has mirado en ello) que en las sepulturas de alabastro, donde suelen estar las figuras de los que allí están enterrados, cuando son marido y mujer, ponen entre los dos, a los pies, una figura de perro, en señal que se guardaron en la vida amistad y fidelidad inviolable.

BERGANZA.—Bien sé que ha habido perros tan agradecidos que se han arrojado con los cuerpos difuntos de sus amos en la misma sepultura. Otros han estado sobre las sepulturas donde estaban enterrados sus señores sin apartarse dellas, sin comer, hasta que se les acababa la

Dialogue of the Dogs

SCIPIO.—Berganza, my friend, let's trust the hospital to guard itself tonight, and let's withdraw to this secluded place and these mats, where we can enjoy, without being heard, this unique favor which heaven has granted us both simultaneously.

BERGANZA: Scipio, my brother, I hear you talk and I know I'm talking to you, yet I can't believe it, since it seems to me that for us to talk passes the bounds of nature.

SCIPIO: And it's true, Berganza; and this miracle is all the greater in that we're not only talking, but also speaking discursively, as if we were capable of reason, though we so lack it that the difference between a dumb animal and man is that man is a rational animal, and lower creatures, irrational.

BERGANZA: I understand all you're saying, Scipio, and your saying it and my understanding it causes me fresh amazement and fresh wonder. It's very true that, in the course of my life, I've heard many different times about great faculties we dogs possess: so much so, that it seems some have wished to feel that we have a natural instinct, so alert and so acute in many matters that it shows tokens and signs of coming only a little short of showing that we have a trace of intelligence that is capable of discourse.

SCIPIO: What *I've* heard praised and extolled is our very good memory, our gratitude and great fidelity; so much so, that we're generally depicted as the symbol of friendship; thus, you must have seen (if you paid attention to it) that on alabaster tombs, which generally include sculptures of those buried there, in the case of husbands and wives the artists place between the couple, at their feet, a sculptured dog, as a sign that, while they lived, they maintained inviolable friendship and fidelity.

BERGANZA: I'm well aware that there have been dogs so grateful that they've leaped into the very graves in which the dead bodies of their masters were being buried. Others have remained lying on their masters' graves, never moving away and refusing to eat until their life gave out. I

vida. Sé también que, después del elefante, el perro tiene el primer lugar de parecer que tiene entendimiento; luego, el caballo, y el último, la jimia.

CIPIÓN.—Ansí es, pero bien confesarás que ni has visto ni oído decir jamás que haya hablado ningún elefante, perro, caballo o mona; por donde me doy a entender que este nuestro hablar tan de improviso cae debajo del número de aquellas cosas que llaman portentos, las cuales, cuando se muestran y parecen, tiene averiguado la experiencia que alguna calamidad grande amenaza a las gentes.

BERGANZA.—Desa manera, no haré yo mucho en tener por señal portentosa lo que oí decir los días pasados a un estudiante, pasando por Alcalá de Henares.

CIPIÓN.—¿Qué le oíste decir?

BERGANZA.—Que de cinco mil estudiantes que cursaban aquel año en la Universidad, los dos mil oían Medicina.

CIPIÓN.—Pues, ¿qué vienes a inferir deso?

BERGANZA.—Infiero, o que estos dos mil médicos han de tener enfermos que curar (que sería harta plaga y mala ventura), o ellos se han de morir de hambre.

CIPIÓN.—Pero, sea lo que fuere, nosotros hablamos, sea portento o no; que lo que el cielo tiene ordenado que suceda, no hay diligencia ni sabiduría humana que lo pueda prevenir; y así, no hay para qué ponernos a disputar nosotros cómo o por qué hablamos; mejor será que este buen día, o buena noche, la metamos en nuestra casa; y, pues la tenemos tan buena en estas esteras y no sabemos cuánto durará esta nuestra ventura, sepamos aprovecharnos della y hablemos toda esta noche, sin dar lugar al sueño que nos impida este gusto, de mí por largos tiempos deseado.

BERGANZA.—Y aun de mí, que desde que tuve fuerzas para roer un hueso tuve deseo de hablar, para decir cosas que depositaba en la memoria; y allí, de antiguas y muchas, o se enmohecían o se me olvidaban. Empero, ahora, que tan sin pensarlo me veo enriquecido deste divino don de la habla, pienso gozarle y aprovecharme dél lo más que pudiere, dándome priesa a decir todo aquello que se me acordare, aunque sea atropellada y confusamente, porque no sé cuándo me volverán a pedir este bien, que por prestado tengo.

CIPIÓN.—Sea ésta la manera, Berganza amigo: que esta noche me cuentes tu vida y los trances por donde has venido al punto en que ahora te hallas, y si mañana en la noche estuviéremos con habla, yo te contaré la mía; porque mejor será gastar el tiempo en contar las propias que en procurar saber las ajenas vidas.

also know that, after the elephant, the dog comes first in seeming to possess intelligence; next, the horse; and last, the monkey.

SCIPIO: That's so, but you'll readily admit that you've never seen or heard of any elephant, dog, horse, or monkey speaking; hence, I take it that our extremely sudden ability to speak comes under the heading of those things called portents, which, when they manifest and show themselves, make the experienced certain that some great calamity is threatening people.

BERGANZA: In the same way, I wouldn't be going too far if I took as a portentous sign something I heard a student say recently while I was passing through Alcalá de Henares.

SCIPIO: What did you hear him say?

BERGANZA: That out of five thousand students matriculated in the university that year, two thousand were medical students.

SCIPIO: Well, what do you deduce from that?

BERGANZA: I deduce that, either those two thousand doctors will all have patients to treat (which would be a great plague and misfortune), or else they themselves will starve to death.

SCIPIO: But, be that as it may, we're speaking, portent or no portent; for that which heaven has ordained should happen can't be forestalled by any human precautions or wisdom; so there's no cause for us to start arguing about how or why we're speaking; it would be better to "make good use of this fine day," or fine night; and since we find it such a comfortable one on these mats, and we don't know how long this good luck of ours will last, let's wisely take advantage of it and talk all night long, without giving way to sleep, which would curtail this pleasure for us, a pleasure I've long wished for.

BERGANZA: So have I; ever since I've been strong enough to gnaw a bone I've wanted to speak, in order to relate things I was storing in my memory; there, they were getting so old and numerous that either they were getting moldy or I was forgetting them. But now, finding myself so unexpectedly endowed with this divine gift of speech, I intend to enjoy it and make as much use of it as I can, hastening to relate everything I remember, even if in a confused jumble, because I don't know when this blessing, which I have on loan, will be "called in" from me.

SCIPIO: Let this be the arrangement, Berganza, my friend: tonight you tell me your life and the stages by which you've reached the point you're now at, and if tomorrow night we can still speak, I'll tell you mine; because it will be better to spend the time telling our own lives than trying to find out about those of others.

BERGANZA.—Siempre, Cipión, te he tenido por discreto y por amigo; y ahora más que nunca, pues como amigo quieres decirme tus sucesos y saber los míos, y como discreto has repartido el tiempo donde podamos manifestallos. Pero advierte primero si nos oye alguno.

CIPIÓN.—Ninguno, a lo que creo, puesto que aquí cerca está un soldado tomando sudores; pero en esta sazón más estará para dormir que para ponerse a escuchar a nadie.

BERGANZA.—Pues si puedo hablar con ese seguro, escucha; y si te cansare lo que te fuere diciendo, o me reprehende o manda que calle.

CIPIÓN.—Habla hasta que amanezca, o hasta que seamos sentidos; que yo te escucharé de muy buena gana, sin impedirte sino cuando viere ser necesario.

BERGANZA.—«Paréceme que la primera vez que vi el sol fue en Sevilla y en su Matadero, que está fuera de la Puerta de la Carne; por donde imaginara (si no fuera por lo que después te diré) que mis padres debieron de ser alanos de aquellos que crían los ministros de aquella confusión, a quien llaman jiferos. El primero que conocí por amo fue uno llamado Nicolás el Romo, mozo robusto, doblado y colérico, como lo son todos aquellos que ejercitan la jifería. Este tal Nicolás me enseñaba a mí y a otros cachorros a que, en compañía de alanos viejos, arremetiésemos a los toros y les hiciésemos presa de las orejas. Con mucha facilidad salí un águila en esto.»

CIPIÓN.—No me maravillo, Berganza; que, como el hacer mal viene de natural cosecha, fácilmente se aprende el hacerle.

BERGANZA.—¿Qué te diría, Cipión hermano, de lo que vi en aquel Matadero y de las cosas exorbitantes que en él pasan? Primero, has de presuponer que todos cuantos en él trabajan, desde el menor hasta el mayor, es gente ancha de conciencia, desalmada, sin temer al Rey ni a su justicia; los más, amancebados; son aves de rapiña carniceras: mantiénense ellos y sus amigas de lo que hurtan. Todas las mañanas que son días de carne, antes que amanezca, están en el Matadero gran cantidad de mujercillas y muchachos, todos con talegas, que, viniendo vacías, vuelven llenas de pedazos de carne, y las criadas con criadillas y lomos medio enteros. No hay res alguna que se mate de quien no lleve esta gente diezmos y primicias de lo más sabroso y bien parado. Y, como en Sevilla no hay obligado de la carne, cada uno puede traer la que quisiere; y la que primero se mata, o es la mejor, o la de más baja postura, y con este concierto hay siempre mucha abundancia. Los dueños se encomiendan a esta buena gente que he dicho, no para que no les hurten (que esto es imposible), sino para que se moderen en las tajadas y socaliñas que hacen en las reses muertas, que las escamon-

BERGANZA: Scipio, I've always considered you a clever fellow and a friend; and now more than ever, since as a friend you want to tell me your adventures and hear mine, and as a clever fellow you've allotted the time in which we can reveal them. But first make sure no one's listening.

SCIPIO: No one, I think, though near here there's a soldier taking a sweating cure; but at this hour he's more likely to be sleeping than listening to anybody.

BERGANZA: Then if I can speak so privately, listen; and if you're wearied by what I tell you, either reprimand me or order me to keep still.

SCIPIO: Speak until daybreak, or until someone can overhear us; for I'll listen to you very gladly, interrupting you only when I consider it necessary.

BERGANZA: It seems to me that the first time I saw the sun was in Seville, at the municipal slaughterhouse, which is outside the Meat Gate; so that I'd imagine (except for something I'll tell you later) that my parents must have been two of the mastiffs reared by the workmen in that place of confusion, who are called slaughterers. The first one I knew to be my master was a fellow called Snub-nosed Nicolás, a strong, stocky, and bad-tempered man, like all those who practice that calling. This Nicolás taught me and other pups to attack the bulls, in the company of other mastiffs, and grip them by the ears. I very easily turned out to be a champion at that.

SCIPIO: I'm not surprised, Berganza: since evildoing comes naturally, it's easy to learn.

BERGANZA: What can I tell you, brother Scipio, of what I saw in that slaughterhouse and the excesses that take place there? First, you must assume that everyone working there, from the lowest employee to the highest, is of a very lax conscience, heartless, fearing neither the king nor his laws; most of them live in sin with women; they're bloodthirsty birds of prey, supporting themselves and their mistresses on what they steal. Every morning of days when meat eating is allowed, before dawn, the slaughterhouse is full of chippies and children, all carrying sacks that are empty on arrival but leave filled with pieces of meat, the servant girls carrying away bulls' testicles and half loins. No beast is killed from which those people don't receive tithes and firstfruits out of the tastiest and best cuts. And since Seville has no official meat supplier, anyone can bring in whatever he likes, and the first animal killed is either the best or the one the buyers make the lowest bid on; this arrangement insures that there's always great abundance. The owners put themselves in the hands of these fine people I've described, not to avoid being robbed (because that's impossible), but to make them more moderate in the fraudulent cuts they

dan y podan como si fuesen sauces o parras. Pero ninguna cosa me admiraba más ni me parecía peor que el ver que estos jiferos con la misma facilidad matan a un hombre que a una vaca; por quítame allá esa paja, a dos por tres meten un cuchillo de cachas amarillas por la barriga de una persona, como si acocotasen un toro. Por maravilla se pasa día sin pendencias, y sin heridas, y a veces sin muertes; todos se pican de valientes, y aun tienen sus puntas de rufianes; no hay ninguno que no tenga su ángel de guarda en la plaza de San Francisco, granjeado con lomos y lenguas de vaca. Finalmente, oí decir a un hombre discreto que tres cosas tenía el Rey por ganar en Sevilla: la calle de la Caza, la Costanilla y el Matadero.

CIPIÓN.—Si en contar las condiciones de los amos que has tenido y las faltas de sus oficios te has de estar, amigo Berganza, tanto como esta vez, menester será pedir al cielo nos conceda la habla siquiera por un año, y aun temo que, al paso que llevas, no llegarás a la mitad de tu historia. Y quiérote advertir de una cosa, de la cual verás la experiencia cuando te cuente los sucesos de mi vida; y es que los cuentos unos encierran y tienen la gracia en ellos mismos, otros en el modo de contarlos (quiero decir que algunos hay que, aunque se cuenten sin preámbulos y ornamentos de palabras, dan contento); otros hay que es menester vestirlos de palabras, y con demostraciones del rostro y de las manos, y con mudar la voz, se hacen algo de nonada, y de flojos y desmayados se vuelven agudos y gustosos; y no se te olvide este advertimiento, para aprovecharte dél en lo que te queda por decir.

BERGANZA.—Yo lo haré así, si pudiere y si me da lugar la grande tentación que tengo de hablar; aunque me parece que con grandísima dificultad me podré ir a la mano.

CIPIÓN.—Vete a la lengua, que en ella consisten los mayores daños de la humana vida.

BERGANZA.—«Digo, pues, que mi amo me enseñó a llevar una espuerta en la boca y a defenderla de quien quitármela quisiese. Enseñóme también la casa de su amiga, y con esto se escusó la venida de su criada al Matadero, porque yo le llevaba las madrugadas lo que él había hurtado las noches. Y un día que, entre dos luces, iba yo diligente a llevarle la porción, oí que me llamaban por mi nombre desde una ventana; alcé los ojos y vi una moza hermosa en estremo; detúveme un poco, y ella bajó a la puerta de la calle, y me tornó a llamar. Lleguéme a ella, como si fuera a ver lo que me quería, que no fue otra cosa que quitarme lo que llevaba en la cesta y ponerme en su lugar un chapín viejo. Entonces dije entre mí: "La carne se ha ido a la carne". Díjome la moza, en habiéndome quitado la carne: "Andad Gavilán, o

take from the dead animals, which they mutilate and pollard as if they were willows or grapevines. But nothing amazed me more, or seemed worse to me, than seeing those butchers kill a man just as easily as a cow: for the merest trifle, in one-two-three, they stick a yellow-handled knife into a person's belly as if they were slaughtering a bull. It's a marvel if a day goes by without fights and wounds or sometimes deaths; they all boast of being brave, and even have a touch of the thug; there isn't one who doesn't have a protector at the town hall or main law court, whom they've won over with beef loins and tongues. In short, I've heard a clever man say that the king still had three things to conquer in Seville: the Calle de la Caza, the Costanilla, and the slaughterhouse.

SCIPIO: If, my friend Berganza, you're going to dwell as long as you just have on the nature of the masters you've served and the defects in their professions, we'll have to ask heaven to grant us the power of speech for at least a year, and I even fear that, at the rate you're going, you won't get halfway through your story. And I want to point one thing out to you which you'll notice when I tell you the events of *my* life: that the charm of some tales is natural and intrinsic, while in others it lies in the way they're told (I mean that some give pleasure even without preambles and carefully chosen words); there are others which must be clothed in fine words; facial expressions, hand gestures, and modulation of the voice make something out of nothing, and convert the tales from flabby and wilted into lively and pleasurable; don't forget this advice, but make use of it as you continue your narration.

BERGANZA: I will if I can and if I'm not prevented by my great temptation to speak; though I believe it will be very hard for me to restrain myself.

SCIPIO: Watch out for your tongue, because it can cause the greatest harm in human life.

BERGANZA: Well, I'll go on to say that my master taught me to carry a basket in my mouth and defend it against anyone who wanted to take it. He also taught me the way to his mistress's house, thereby making it unnecessary for her servant girl to come to the slaughterhouse, because early every morning I would take to her whatever he had stolen the night before. And one day, at first light, when I was diligently on my way to take her her portion, I heard someone call me by name from a window; I looked up and saw an extremely beautiful young woman; I halted for a while, and she came down to the street door and called me again. I went over to her, to see what she wanted of me, which was nothing else than to take away what I had in the basket and substitute an old chopine for it. Then I said to myself: "The flesh has gone to the flesh." After taking the

como os llamáis, y decid a Nicolás el Romo, vuestro amo, que no se fíe de animales, y que del lobo un pelo, y ése de la espuerta". Bien pudiera yo volver a quitar lo que me quitó, pero no quise, por no poner mi boca jifera y sucia en aquellas manos limpias y blancas.»

CIPIÓN.—Hiciste muy bien, por ser prerrogativa de la hermosura que siempre se le tenga respecto.

BERGANZA.—«Así lo hice yo; y así, me volví a mi amo sin la porción y con el chapín. Parecióle que volví presto, vio el chapín, imaginó la burla, sacó uno de cachas y tiróme una puñalada que, a no desviarme, nunca tú oyeras ahora este cuento, ni aun otros muchos que pienso contarte. Puse pies en polvorosa, y, tomando el camino en las manos y en los pies, por detrás de San Bernardo, me fui por aquellos campos de Dios adonde la fortuna quisiese llevarme.

»Aquella noche dormí al cielo abierto, y otro día me deparó la suerte un hato o rebaño de ovejas y carneros. Así como le vi, creí que había hallado en él el centro de mi reposo, pareciéndome ser propio y natural oficio de los perros guardar ganado, que es obra donde se encierra una virtud grande; como es amparar y defender de los poderosos y soberbios los humildes y los que poco pueden. Apenas me hubo visto uno de tres pastores que el ganado guardaban, cuando diciendo "¡To, to!" me llamó; y yo, que otra cosa no deseaba, me llegué a él, bajando la cabeza y meneando la cola. Trújome la mano por el lomo, abrióme la boca, escupióme en ella, miróme las presas, conoció mi edad, y dijo a otros pastores que yo tenía todas las señales de ser perro de casta. Llegló a este instante el señor del ganado sobre una yegua rucia a la jineta, con lanza y adarga: que más parecía atajador de la costa que señor de ganado. Preguntó al pastor: "¿Qué perro es éste, que tiene señales de ser bueno?" "Bien lo puede vuesa merced creer —respondió el pastor—, que yo le he cotejado bien y no hay señal en él que no muestre y prometa que ha de ser un gran perro. Agora se llegó aquí y no sé cúyo sea, aunque sé que no es de los rebaños de la redonda". "Pues así es —respondió el señor—, ponle luego el collar de Leoncillo, el perro que se murió, y denle la ración que a los demás, y acaríciale, porque tome cariño al hato y se quede en él". En diciendo esto, se fue; y el pastor me puso luego al cuello unas carlancas llenas de puntas de acero, habiéndome dado primero en un dornajo gran cantidad de sopas en leche. Y, asimismo, me puso nombre, y me llamó Barcino.

meat, the girl said: "Go, Gavilán,[1] or whatever your name is, and tell Snub-nosed Nicolás, your master, not to put his trust in animals: 'All you can get from the wolf is one hair, and that hair from the basket.'"[2] I could easily have recovered what she had taken, but I refrained, to avoid putting my filthy slaughterhouse mouth on those clean white hands.

SCIPIO: You were very right to do so, for it's a prerogative of beauty always to be respected.

BERGANZA: And so I did; and so I returned to my master without the meat and with the chopine. He thought I was back too soon, he saw the chopine, he realized the trick, he took out his yellow-handle, and aimed such a thrust at me that, if I hadn't swerved aside, you wouldn't be hearing this story now, or many others I intend telling you. I hit the road and, trusting to my speed, left behind the suburb of San Bernardo and lit out for whichever of God's countrysides fortune wanted to take me to.

That night I slept outdoors, and the next day fate sent me a group or flock of ewes and rams. As soon as I saw it, I felt I had found my peace of mind, considering it a dog's proper and natural task to guard livestock, a job entailing the great virtue of protecting and defending the humble and weak against the powerful and haughty. The moment I was seen by one of the three shepherds watching the flock, he called me over with a "Toh, toh!" And I, who wanted nothing better, went up to him, lowering my head and wagging my tail. He passed his hand over my back, opened my mouth and spat into it,[3] looked at my canines and gauged my age, and told the other shepherds that I showed every sign of being a purebread dog. Just then the owner of the flock arrived on a gray mare, fitted with short stirrups. Carrying a lance and shield, he resembled a military scout of the coastline rather than a sheep owner. He asked the shepherd: "What dog is this which shows signs of being a good one?" "Your worship may well believe it," the shepherd replied, "because I've given him a good inspection and every sign on him shows and promises that he'll become a first-rate dog. He just got here and I don't know whose he is, though I do know he doesn't come from any flock around here." "That being the case," the owner replied, "put the collar of Lion Cub, the dog that died, on him right away, and give him the same food allowance as the rest, and treat him well so he'll get to like the flock and stay with it." With these words, he departed; and the shepherd then placed around my neck a strong collar with steel spikes, having first given me a large quantity of milksops in a bowl. And likewise he gave me a name, calling me Rusty.

---

1. Sparrow hawk. 2. The actual proverb ends "from his forehead." 3. To avoid the evil eye, or being bitten.

»Vime harto y contento con el segundo amo y con el nuevo oficio; mostréme solícito y diligente en la guarda del rebaño, sin apartarme dél sino las siestas, que me iba a pasarlas o ya a la sombra de algún árbol, o de algún ribazo o peña, o a la de alguna mata, a la margen de algún arroyo de los muchos que por allí corrían. Y estas horas de mi sosiego no las pasaba ociosas, porque en ellas ocupaba la memoria en acordarme de muchas cosas, especialmente en la vida que había tenido en el Matadero, y en la que tenía mi amo y todos los como él, que están sujetos a cumplir los gustos impertinentes de sus amigas.»

¡Oh, qué de cosas te pudiera decir ahora de las que aprendí en la escuela de aquella jifera dama de mi amo! Pero habrélas de callar, porque no me tengas por largo y por murmurador.

CIPIÓN.—Por haber oído decir que dijo un gran poeta de los antiguos que era difícil cosa el no escribir sátiras, consentiré que murmures un poco de luz y no de sangre; quiero decir que señales y no hieras ni des mate a ninguno en cosa señalada: que no es buena la murmuración, aunque haga reír a muchos, si mata a uno; y si puedes agradar sin ella, te tendré por muy discreto.

BERGANZA.—Yo tomaré tu consejo, y esperaré con gran deseo que llegue el tiempo en que me cuentes tus sucesos; que de quien tan bien sabe conocer y enmendar los defetos que tengo en contar los míos, bien se puede esperar que contará los suyos de manera que enseñen y deleiten a un mismo punto.

«Pero, anudando el roto hilo de mi cuento, digo que en aquel silencio y soledad de mis siestas, entre otras cosas, consideraba que no debía de ser verdad lo que había oído contar de la vida de los pastores; a lo menos, de aquellos que la dama de mi amo leía en unos libros cuando yo iba a su casa, que todos trataban de pastores y pastoras, diciendo que se les pasaba toda la vida cantando y tañendo con gaitas, zampoñas, rabeles y chirumbelas, y con otros instrumentos extraordinarios. Deteníame a oírla leer, y leía cómo el pastor de Anfriso cantaba estremada y divinamente, alabando a la sin par Belisarda, sin haber en todos los montes de Arcadia árbol en cuyo tronco no se hubiese sentado a cantar, desde que salía el sol en los brazos de la Aurora hasta que se ponía en los de Tetis; y aun después de haber tendido la negra noche por la faz de la tierra sus negras y escuras alas, él no cesaba de sus bien cantadas y mejor lloradas quejas. No se le quedaba entre renglones el pastor Elicio, más enamorado que atrevido, de quien decía

I found myself well fed and contented with my second master and new job; I displayed care and diligence in guarding the flock, leaving it only at siesta time, which I'd spend in the shade of some tree, or of some embankment, boulder, or bush, on the brink of some one of the many brooks that flowed in the area. And I didn't spend those hours of rest idly; I called upon my memory at such times to remember many things, especially the life I had led in the slaughterhouse and the life led by my first master and all those like him, who are compelled to gratify the peevish wishes of their mistresses.

Oh, all the things I could tell you now about the ones I learned in the school of that butcher's moll of my master's! But I must pass them over in silence, so you won't find me a longwinded narrator and a slanderer.

SCIPIO: Because I've heard that a great poet of antiquity[4] said it was hard to keep from writing satires, I'll allow you to grumble a little in a moderate way, without drawing blood; I mean, I'll allow you to put your stamp on a person without wounding him or annihilating him by what you point out; because backbiting is wrong (though it may make many laugh) if it kills someone; and if you can be pleasing without it, I'll consider you very wise.

BERGANZA: I'll take your advice, and wait most expectantly for the time to come for you to tell me *your* life; for someone so well able to recognize and correct my faults in telling mine can surely be expected to tell his in such a way that it gives profit and pleasure at the same time.

But, to pick up the dropped thread of my story, I say that in that silence and solitude of my siestas, it occurred to me, among other things, that what I had heard tell about the life of shepherds couldn't be true; at least, as regards the ones my first master's lady used to read about in some books when I visited her house; they were all about shepherds and shepherdesses, telling how they spent their whole life singing and playing on bagpipes, panpipes, rebecs, and shawms, and other unusual instruments. I used to wait there listening to her reading aloud, and she'd read about how the shepherd Anfriso[5] sang superbly and divinely in praise of the matchless Belisarda, there being no tree in the forests of Arcadia against a trunk of which he hadn't sat down to sing, from the time that the sun rose in the arms of Aurora until it set in those of Thetis; and even after black night had spread its dark, black wings over the face of the earth, he ceased not from his well-sung and better-wept complaints. She didn't fail to mention the shepherd Elicio, more loving than bold, of whom she said that, at-

---

4. Juvenal. 5. The characters who follow appear in 16th-century Spanish pastoral novels by Lope, Cervantes, Gálvez, and Montemayor.

que, sin atender a sus amores ni a su ganado, se entraba en los cuidados ajenos. Decía también que el gran pastor de Fílida, único pintor de un retrato, había sido más confiado que dichoso. De los desmayos de Sireno y arrepentimiento de Diana decía que daba gracias a Dios y a la sabia Felicia, que con su agua encantada deshizo aquella máquina de enredos y aclaró aquel laberinto de dificultades. Acordábame de otros muchos libros que deste jaez la había oído leer, pero no eran dignos de traerlos a la memoria.»

CIPIÓN.—Aprovechándote vas, Berganza, de mi aviso: murmura, pica y pasa, y sea tu intención limpia, aunque la lengua no lo parezca.

BERGANZA.—En estas materias nunca tropieza la lengua si no cae primero la intención; pero si acaso por descuido o por malicia murmurare, responderé a quien me reprehendiere lo que respondió Mauleón, poeta tonto y académico de burla de la Academia de los Imitadores, a uno que le preguntó que qué quería decir *Deum de Deo*; y respondió que «dé donde diere».

CIPIÓN.—Ésa fue respuesta de un simple; pero tú, si eres discreto o lo quieres ser, nunca has de decir cosa de que debas dar disculpa. Di adelante.

BERGANZA.—«Digo que todos los pensamientos que he dicho, y muchos más, me causaron ver los diferentes tratos y ejercicios que mis pastores, y todos los demás de aquella marina, tenían de aquellos que había oído leer que tenían los pastores de los libros; porque si los míos cantaban, no eran canciones acordadas y bien compuestas, sino un "Cata el lobo dó va, Juanica" y otras cosas semejantes; y esto no al son de chirumbelas, rabeles o gaitas, sino al que hacía el dar un cayado con otro o al de algunas tejuelas puestas entre los dedos; y no con voces delicadas, sonoras y admirables, sino con voces roncas, que, solas o juntas, parecía, no que cantaban, sino que gritaban o gruñían. Lo más del día se les pasaba espulgándose o remendando sus abarcas; ni entre ellos se nombraban Amarilis, Fílidas, Galateas y Dianas, ni había Lisardos, Lausos, Jacintos ni Riselos; todos eran Antones, Domingos, Pablos o Llorentes; por donde vine a entender lo que pienso que deben de creer todos: que todos aquellos libros son cosas soñadas y bien escritas para entretenimiento de los ociosos, y no verdad alguna; que, a serlo, entre mis pastores hubiera alguna reliquia de aquella felicísima vida, y de aquellos amenos prados, espaciosas selvas, sagrados montes, hermosos jardines, arroyos claros y cristalinas fuentes, y de aquellos tan honestos cuanto bien declarados re-

tending neither to his love affair nor his flock, he concerned himself with other people's worries. She also said that the great shepherd who loved Phyllis, wonderful painter of a word portrait of her, had been more trusting than fortunate. Concerning the distresses of Sireno and the repentance of Diana, she said she thanked God and the wisewoman Felicia, with her enchanted water, for untangling that web of deceit and illuminating that maze of difficulties. I remembered many other books of that sort which I had heard her read, but they weren't worth recalling to memory.

SCIPIO: You're making use of my advice, Berganza: grumble, sting, and pass on, and let your intentions be pure, even if your tongue doesn't seem to be so.

BERGANZA: On such subjects one's tongue never stumbles unless one's intentions fall down first; but if by chance I should grumble out of heedlessness or ill will, I'll reply to whoever reprimands me what Mauleón, a foolish poet and a mock academician of the Academy of Imitators of Italian Academies, replied to someone who asked him what *Deum de Deo*[6] meant that it meant: "Give when you're given."

SCIPIO: That was a simpleton's reply; but you, if you're wise or want to be, should never say anything you need to apologize for. Continue.

BERGANZA: As I was saying, all those thoughts I mentioned, and many others, led me to see how different the dealings and occupations of my shepherds, and all the rest on that coast, were from those of the shepherds in the books I had heard her read. Because if mine sang, they sang not tuneful, well-written songs, but things like "Watch where the wolf goes, Juanica" and suchlike pieces; and not to the sound of shawms, rebecs, or bagpipes, but to that made by knocking two crooks together or rattling pieces of tile in their fingers; and not in delicate, resonant, and lovely voices, but in hoarse voices which, solo or joined, made it sound not like singing, but yelling or growling. They spent most of the day hunting for lice or patching their sandals; nor were there any women among them named Amaryllis, Phyllis, Galatea, or Diana; nor was there any Lisardo, Lauso, Jacinto, or Riselo; they were all either Antón, Domingo, Pablo, or Llorente; so that I came to realize what I think everyone should believe: that all those books are imaginary things, well written for the entertainment of the idle, and not at all true; because, if they were, there would have been some trace among my shepherds of that most blissful life, of those pleasant meadows, spacious woods, sacred forests, lovely gardens, clear streams, and crystal fountains, and of those expressions of love, as decent as they were well-worded, and of that swooning of a shepherd

6. "God from God"; from the Credo.

quiebros, y de aquel desmayarse aquí el pastor, allí la pastora, acullá resonar la zampoña del uno, acá el caramillo del otro.»

CIPIÓN.—Basta, Berganza; vuelve a tu senda y camina.

BERGANZA.—Agradézcotelo, Cipión amigo; porque si no me avisaras, de manera se me iba calentando la boca, que no parara hasta pintarte un libro entero destos que me tenían engañado; pero tiempo vendrá en que lo diga todo con mejores razones y con mejor discurso que ahora.

CIPIÓN.—Mírate a los pies y desharás la rueda, Berganza; quiero decir que mires que eres un animal que carece de razón, y si ahora muestras tener alguna, ya hemos averiguado entre los dos ser cosa sobrenatural y jamás vista.

BERGANZA.—Eso fuera ansí si yo estuviera en mi primera ignorancia; mas ahora que me ha venido a la memoria lo que te había de haber dicho al principio de nuestra plática, no sólo no me maravillo de lo que hablo, pero espántome de lo que dejo de hablar.

CIPIÓN.—Pues ¿ahora no puedes decir lo que ahora se te acuerda?

BERGANZA.—Es una cierta historia que me pasó con una grande hechicera, discípula de la Camacha de Montilla.

CIPIÓN.—Digo que me la cuentes antes que pases más adelante en el cuento de tu vida.

BERGANZA.—Eso no haré yo, por cierto, hasta su tiempo: ten paciencia y escucha por su orden mis sucesos, que así te darán más gusto, si ya no te fatiga querer saber los medios antes de los principios.

CIPIÓN.—Sé breve, y cuenta lo que quisieres y como quisieres.

BERGANZA.—«Digo, pues, que yo me hallaba bien con el oficio de guardar ganado, por parecerme que comía el pan de mi sudor y trabajo, y que la ociosidad, raíz y madre de todos los vicios, no tenía que ver conmigo, a causa que si los días holgaba, las noches no dormía, dándonos asaltos a menudo y tocándonos a arma los lobos; y, apenas me habían dicho los pastores "¡al lobo, Barcino!", cuando acudía, primero que los otros perros, a la parte que me señalaban que estaba el lobo: corría los valles, escudriñaba los montes, desentrañaba las selvas, saltaba barrancos, cruzaba caminos, y a la mañana volvía al hato, sin haber hallado lobo ni rastro dél, anhelando, cansado, hecho pedazos y los pies abiertos de los garranchos; y hallaba en el hato, o ya una oveja muerta, o un carnero degollado y medio comido del lobo. Desesperábame de ver de cuán poco servía mi mucho cuidado y dili-

here, a shepherdess there, the sound of someone's panpipe over yonder, and of someone else's fife over here."

SCIPIO: Enough, Berganza; return to your path and walk down it.

BERGANZA: I thank you, friend Scipio; because if you hadn't admonished me, my mouth was getting so warm that I wouldn't have stopped until I had dictated a whole book to you on the subject of the ones that had disappointed me; but there'll come a time when I'll tell it all in better words, and better arranged, than now.

SCIPIO: "Look at your ugly feet, peacock, and you won't flash your tail." I mean, Berganza, that you should remember you're an animal devoid of reason, and if you now show that you have some, we've already ascertained between the two of us that it's something supernatural and unheard-of.

BERGANZA: That would be so if I were still in my original ignorance; but now that I've recalled what I should have told you at the beginning of our conversation, I not only fail to be surprised that I can speak: I'm astounded at what I omit to say.

SCIPIO: Well, can't you say now what you now remember?

BERGANZA: It's a certain story that befell me with a great sorceress, a disciple of La Camacha of Montilla.[7]

SCIPIO: I say you should tell it to me before you go any further with the story of your life.

BERGANZA: I won't, surely, till the right time arrives: be patient and listen to my adventures in sequence; that way, you'll enjoy them more, unless you're dead set on hearing the middle of things before the beginning.

SCIPIO: Be brief, and tell me what you want and how you want.

BERGANZA: Well, then, as I said, I was contented with my job of guarding the flock, because I felt as if I were eating my bread by the sweat of my brow and my work, and that I had no truck with idleness, that root and mother of all the vices; because if I relaxed during the day, I didn't sleep at night, since wolves frequently attacked us and sounded our alarm. The moment the shepherds called "After the wolf, Rusty!" I would come running before the other dogs in the direction where they indicated that the wolf was located; I'd run through the valleys, scrutinize the forests, scour the woods, leap ravines, crisscross roads, and in the morning I'd return to the flock without having found a wolf or a trace of one, panting, tired out, a wreck, my feet pierced by twigs; and in the flock I'd find a dead ewe, or a ram slaughtered and half eaten by the wolf. I was in despair to see how little good my great care and diligence did. The owner

7. In Córdoba province.

gencia. Venía el señor del ganado; salían los pastores a recebirle con las pieles de la res muerta; culpaba a los pastores por negligentes, y mandaba castigar a los perros por perezosos: llovían sobre nosotros palos, y sobre ellos reprehensiones; y así, viéndome un día castigado sin culpa, y que mi cuidado, ligereza y braveza no eran de provecho para coger el lobo, determiné de mudar estilo, no desviándome a buscarle, como tenía de costumbre, lejos del rebaño, sino estarme junto a él; que, pues el lobo allí venía, allí sería más cierta la presa.

»Cada semana nos tocaban a rebato, y en una escurísima noche tuve yo vista para ver los lobos, de quien era imposible que el ganado se guardase. Agachéme detrás de una mata, pasaron los perros, mis compañeros, adelante, y desde allí oteé, y vi que dos pastores asieron de un carnero de los mejores del aprisco, y le mataron de manera que verdaderamente pareció a la mañana que había sido su verdugo el lobo. Pasméme, quedé suspenso cuando vi que los pastores eran los lobos y que despedazaban el ganado los mismos que le habían de guardar. Al punto, hacían saber a su amo la presa del lobo, dábanle el pellejo y parte de la carne, y comíanse ellos lo más y lo mejor. Volvía a reñirles el señor, y volvía también el castigo de los perros. No había lobos, menguaba el rebaño; quisiera yo descubrillo, hallábame mudo. Todo lo cual me traía lleno de admiración y de congoja. "¡Válame Dios! —decía entre mí—, ¿quién podrá remediar esta maldad? ¿Quién será poderoso a dar a entender que la defensa ofende, que las centinelas duermen, que la confianza roba y el que os guarda os mata?"»

CIPIÓN.—Y decías muy bien, Berganza, porque no hay mayor ni más sotil ladrón que el doméstico, y así, mueren muchos más de los confiados que de los recatados; pero el daño está en que es imposible que puedan pasar bien las gentes en el mundo si no se fía y se confía. Mas quédese aquí esto, que no quiero que parezcamos predicadores. Pasa adelante.

BERGANZA.—«Paso adelante, y digo que determiné dejar aquel oficio, aunque parecía tan bueno, y escoger otro donde por hacerle bien, ya que no fuese remunerado, no fuese castigado. Volvíme a Sevilla, y entré a servir a un mercader muy rico.»

CIPIÓN.—¿Qué modo tenías para entrar con amo? Porque, según lo que se usa, con gran dificultad el día de hoy halla un hombre de bien señor a quien servir. Muy diferentes son los señores de la tierra del Señor del cielo: aquéllos, para recebir un criado, primero le espulgan el linaje, examinan la habilidad, le marcan la apostura, y aun quieren saber los vestidos que tiene; pero, para entrar a servir a Dios, el más

of the flock would come; the shepherds would go out to meet him with the skin of the dead animal; he'd blame the shepherds for their negligence and order the dogs to be punished for their laziness; we were showered with blows, and reprimands on top of that; and so, finding myself punished one day for no fault of mine, and seeing that my concern, my speed, and my bravery were of no use in catching the wolf, I decided to change my methods: I wouldn't run off to look for him far from the flock, as had been my wont, but I'd stay near it; since the wolf came there, his capture would be surer there.

Every week we had an alarm, and one very dark night my eyes were good enough to see the wolves which it was impossible to guard the sheep against. I hunched down behind a bush, my fellow dogs rushed ahead past me, and, watching from there, I saw two shepherds seize one of the best rams in the fold and kill it in such a way that it really looked in the morning as if the wolf had been its executioner. I was shocked and dumbfounded when I saw that the shepherds were the wolves and that the very men who were to guard the sheep were the ones mangling them. At once they'd inform their master of the wolf's depredations, give him the skin and part of the meat, and eat most of it, the best of it, themselves. The owner would bawl them out again, and the dogs would be punished again. There were no wolves, the flock was dwindling; I wanted to unmask them, but found myself speechless. All this filled me with wonder and sorrow. "God help me!" I'd say to myself. "Who can cure this evil? Who will have the power to inform the owner that the defenders are on the offensive, the sentinels are asleep, the trustees are thieves, and the sheep's guardians are killing them?"

SCIPIO: And you were quite right, Berganza, because there's no greater or subtler thief than the insider; thus, many more trusting people die than cautious ones; yet the harm is in the impossibility for people to be happy in this world without mutual trust and confidence. But let that rest here, because I don't want us to resemble preachers. Continue.

BERGANZA: I continue, saying that I decided to leave that job, though it seemed so good, and to choose another which, if I did it well but wasn't compensated, at least I wouldn't be punished for. I returned to Seville, and entered the service of a very rich merchant.

SCIPIO: What method did you use to find a master? Because, as things are nowadays, it's very hard for a decent person to find a master to serve. The lords of the earth are very different from the Lord of heaven: they, before taking on a servant, delve into his ancestry, test his skills, study his appearance, and even want to know what clothes he owns; whereas, to enter God's service, the poorest man is the richest, and the humblest is

pobre es más rico; el más humilde, de mejor linaje; y, con sólo que se disponga con limpieza de corazón a querer servirle, luego le manda poner en el libro de sus gajes, señalándoselos tan aventajados que, de muchos y de grandes, apenas pueden caber en su deseo.

BERGANZA.—Todo eso es predicar, Cipión amigo.

CIPIÓN.—Así me lo parece a mí, y así, callo.

BERGANZA.—A lo que me preguntaste del orden que tenía para entrar con amo, digo que ya tú sabes que la humildad es la basa y fundamento de todas virtudes, y que sin ella no hay alguna que lo sea. Ella allana inconvenientes, vence dificultades, y es un medio que siempre a gloriosos fines nos conduce; de los enemigos hace amigos, templa la cólera de los airados y menoscaba la arrogancia de los soberbios; es madre de la modestia y hermana de la templanza; en fin, con ella no pueden atravesar triunfo que les sea de provecho los vicios, porque en su blandura y mansedumbre se embotan y despuntan las flechas de los pecados.

«Désta, pues, me aprovechaba yo cuando quería entrar a servir en alguna casa, habiendo primero considerado y mirado muy bien ser casa que pudiese mantener y donde pudiese entrar un perro grande. Luego arrimábame a la puerta, y cuando, a mi parecer, entraba algún forastero, le ladraba, y cuando venía el señor bajaba la cabeza y, moviendo la cola, me iba a él, y con la lengua le limpiaba los zapatos. Si me echaban a palos, sufríalos, y con la misma mansedumbre volvía a hacer halagos al que me apaleaba, que ninguno segundaba, viendo mi porfía y mi noble término. Desta manera, a dos porfías me quedaba en casa: servía bien, queríanme luego bien, y nadie me despidió, si no era que yo me despidiese, o, por mejor decir, me fuese; y tal vez hallé amo que éste fuera el día que yo estuviera en su casa, si la contraria suerte no me hubiera perseguido.»

CIPIÓN.—De la misma manera que has contado entraba yo con los amos que tuve, y parece que nos leímos los pensamientos.

BERGANZA.—Como en esas cosas nos hemos encontrado, si no me engaño, y yo te las diré a su tiempo, como tengo prometido; y ahora escucha lo que me sucedió después que dejé el ganado en poder de aquellos perdidos.

«Volvíme a Sevilla, como dije, que es amparo de pobres y refugio de desechados, que en su grandeza no sólo caben los pequeños, pero no se echan de ver los grandes. Arriméme a la puerta de una gran casa de un mercader, hice mis acostumbradas diligencias, y a pocos lances me quedé en ella. Recibiéronme para tenerme atado detrás de la puerta de día y suelto de noche; servía con gran cuidado y diligencia; ladraba

the one with the finest family background; and if you merely prepare to serve him with a pure heart, he immediately has you entered on his payroll, destining such good wages to you, so abundant and great, that they exceed your wishes.

BERGANZA: All this is preaching, friend Scipio.

SCIPIO: I think so, too, so I'll keep quiet.

BERGANZA: In answer to your question about how I applied as a servant, I reply: you already know that humility is the basis and foundation of all virtues, and without it no virtue really is one. It does away with disadvantages, it overcomes difficulties, and is a means that always leads us to a glorious end; it makes friends of enemies, tempers the wrath of the angry, and abates the haughtiness of the proud; it's the mother of modesty and sister of temperance; in short, the vices can't place an obstacle against it useful to themselves, because the arrows of sin are blunted and dulled by humility's softness and meekness.

Well, it was humility I made use of when applying for service in any house, having first considered and carefully observed that it was a house where a large dog could be nourished if he joined the staff. Then I'd lean against the door and when someone who looked like a stranger to me tried to get in, I'd bark, and when the owner came I'd lower my head and go up to him, wagging my tail, and clean his shoes with my tongue. If I was beaten, I endured it, and with the same meekness I fawned again on the man beating me; no one did it a second time, in view of my persistence and noble nature. And so, after being persistent twice, I stayed in the house; I served well, I was immediately liked, and no one showed me the door, unless I showed myself out or, rather, took off; and at times I found so good a master that I'd still be in his house today, had not bad luck pursued me.

SCIPIO: In the same manner you've related, I, too, entered my various services, as if we had read each other's minds.

BERGANZA: Our natures are congenial in such things, if I'm not mistaken, things I'll tell you about when the time comes; but now listen to what befell me after leaving the flock in the clutches of those scoundrels.

I returned to Seville, as I said, that bulwark of the poor and refuge of outcasts, for in its magnitude not only do small folk have plenty of room, but even great folk are lost to sight. I leaned against the door of a merchant's great house, put my usual ploys into action, and before long I was taken in. Having accepted me, they kept me tied behind the door in the daytime and released me at night; I served with great care and diligence;

a los forasteros y gruñía a los que no eran muy conocidos; no dormía de noche, visitando los corrales, subiendo a los terrados, hecho universal centinela de la mía y de las casas ajenas. Agradóse tanto mi amo de mi buen servicio, que mandó que me tratasen bien y me diesen ración de pan y los huesos que se levantasen o arrojasen de su mesa, con las sobras de la cocina, a lo que yo me mostraba agradecido, dando infinitos saltos cuando veía a mi amo, especialmente cuando venía de fuera; que eran tantas las muestras de regocijo que daba y tantos los saltos, que mi amo ordenó que me desatasen y me dejasen andar suelto de día y de noche. Como me vi suelto, corrí a él, rodeéle todo, sin osar llegarle con las manos, acordándome de la fábula de Isopo, cuando aquel asno, tan asno que quiso hacer a su señor las mismas caricias que le hacía una perrilla regalada suya, que le granjearon ser molido a palos. Parecióme que en esta fábula se nos dio a entender que las gracias y donaires de algunos no están bien en otros.»

Apode el truhán, juegue de manos y voltee el histrión, rebuzne el pícaro, imite el canto de los pájaros y los diversos gestos y acciones de los animales y los hombres el hombre bajo que se hubiere dado a ello, y no lo quiera hacer el hombre principal, a quien ninguna habilidad déstas le puede dar crédito ni nombre honroso.

CIPIÓN.—Basta; adelante, Berganza, que ya estás entendido.

BERGANZA.—¡Ojalá que como tú me entiendes me entendiesen aquellos por quien lo digo; que no sé qué tengo de buen natural, que me pesa infinito cuando veo que un caballero se hace chocarrero y se precia que sabe jugar los cubiletes y las agallas, y que no hay quien como él sepa bailar la chacona! Un caballero conozco yo que se alababa que, a ruegos de un sacristán, había cortado de papel treinta y dos florones para poner en un monumento sobre paños negros, y destas cortaduras hizo tanto caudal, que así llevaba a sus amigos a verlas como si los llevara a ver las banderas y despojos de enemigos que sobre la sepultura de sus padres y abuelos estaban puestas.

«Este mercader, pues, tenía dos hijos, el uno de doce y el otro de hasta catorce años, los cuales estudiaban gramática en el estudio de la Compañía de Jesús; iban con autoridad, con ayo y con pajes, que les llevaban los libros y aquel que llaman *vademécum*. El verlos ir con tanto aparato, en sillas si hacía sol, en coche si llovía, me hizo considerar y reparar en la mucha llaneza con que su padre iba a la Lonja a negociar sus negocios, porque no llevaba otro criado que un negro, y algunas veces se desmandaba a ir en un machuelo aun no bien aderezado.»

CIPIÓN.—Has de saber, Berganza, que es costumbre y condición de

I'd bark at strangers and growl at people I didn't know very well; at night I didn't sleep, but inspected the yards and ascended to the flat roofs, becoming the universal sentinel of my house and others. My master was so pleased with my good service that he gave orders that I be treated well and fed on bread and on the bones taken or flung away from his table, together with the kitchen scraps; for this I used to show my gratitude by leaping up infinite times when I saw my master, especially when he was coming from outdoors; and I'd give so many indications of joy, and I'd jump so much, that my master ordered me untied, free to walk around day and night. Finding myself untied, I ran up to him and danced around him, but I didn't venture to touch him with my front paws, remembering the Aesop fable in which that donkey was such a donkey that he wanted to caress his master the way a pampered lapdog of his did, and was thoroughly thrashed for his efforts. It seemed to me that that fable taught us that the airs and graces of some people are unbecoming in others.

Let the jester invent nicknames, let the clown juggle and turn somersaults, let rascals bray, let that base man given to such things imitate birdsongs, and the various expressions of animals and men, but let it not be attempted by a decent man, to whom none of those talents can lend repute or an honorable name!

SCIPIO: Enough! Continue, Berganza, for you've been understood.

BERGANZA: I wish that, just as I'm understood by you, I were understood by those I have in mind; I have some bit of natural goodness in me, so that I'm infinitely grieved to see a gentleman telling blue jokes and priding himself on his ability to play the shell game or dance the chaconne better than anyone else! I know a gentleman who boasted that, at the request of a sacristan, he had cut out thirty-two paper flowers to place on a tomb over black draperies, and he made such a to-do over those cutouts that he brought his friends to see them as if bringing them to see the banners and spoils of enemies displayed above the tomb of his parents and grandparents.

Well, this merchant had two sons, one of twelve and one of about fourteen, who were studying Latin at the Jesuit school; they'd go there ostentatiously, with their private tutor and with pages who carried their books and that portfolio called a vademecum. To see them going with such pomp, in sedan chairs if it was sunny, in a carriage if it rained, made me ponder and observe the great simplicity with which their father used to go to the Chamber of Commerce to transact his business; *he* wouldn't have any servant but an African man, and only a few times would he go so far as to ride a young mule that wasn't even well adorned.

SCIPIO: I'd have you know, Berganza, that it's the manner and custom

los mercaderes de Sevilla, y aun de las otras ciudades, mostrar su autoridad y riqueza, no en sus personas, sino en las de sus hijos; porque los mercaderes son mayores en su sombra que en sí mismos. Y, como ellos por maravilla atienden a otra cosa que a sus tratos y contratos, trátanse modestamente; y, como la ambición y la riqueza muere por manifestarse, revienta por sus hijos, y así los tratan y autorizan como si fuesen hijos de algún príncipe; y algunos hay que les procuran títulos, y ponerles en el pecho la marca que tanto distingue la gente principal de la plebeya.

BERGANZA.—Ambición es, pero ambición generosa, la de aquel que pretende mejorar su estado sin perjuicio de tercero.

CIPIÓN.—Pocas o ninguna vez se cumple con la ambición que no sea con daño de tercero.

BERGANZA.—Ya hemos dicho que no hemos de murmurar.

CIPIÓN.—Sí, que yo no murmuro de nadie.

BERGANZA.—Ahora acabo de confirmar por verdad lo que muchas veces he oído decir. Acaba un maldiciente murmurador de echar a perder diez linajes y de caluniar veinte buenos, y si alguno le reprehende por lo que ha dicho, responde que él no ha dicho nada, y que si ha dicho algo, no lo ha dicho por tanto, y que si pensara que alguno se había de agraviar, no lo dijera. A la fe, Cipión, mucho ha de saber, y muy sobre los estribos ha de andar el que quisiere sustentar dos horas de conversación sin tocar los límites de la murmuración; porque yo veo en mí que, con ser un animal, como soy, a cuatro razones que digo, me acuden palabras a la lengua como mosquitos al vino, y todas maliciosas y murmurantes; por lo cual vuelvo a decir lo que otra vez he dicho: que el hacer y decir mal lo heredamos de nuestros primeros padres y lo mamamos en la leche. Vese claro en que, apenas ha sacado el niño el brazo de las fajas, cuando levanta la mano con muestras de querer vengarse de quien, a su parecer, le ofende; y casi la primera palabra articulada que habla es llamar puta a su ama o a su madre.

CIPIÓN.—Así es verdad, y yo confieso mi yerro y quiero que me le perdones, pues te he perdonado tantos. Echemos pelillos a la mar, como dicen los muchachos, y no murmuremos de aquí adelante; y sigue tu cuento, que le dejaste en la autoridad con que los hijos del mercader tu amo iban al estudio de la Compañía de Jesús.

BERGANZA.—A Él me encomiendo en todo acontecimiento; y, aunque el dejar de murmurar lo tengo por dificultoso, pienso usar de un remedio que oí decir que usaba un gran jurador, el cual, arrepen-

of the merchants in Seville, and even other cities, to display their pomp and wealth not in themselves but in their children; because merchants are greater in the shadow they cast than in themselves. And since they rarely attend to anything but their deals and contracts, they don't spend much money on themselves; but since ambition and wealth are just dying to make themselves known, they burst forth in the children, who are treated and indulged as if they were the children of some prince; and some merchants even procure titles for them, placing those emblems on their breast which so distinguish lordly folk from commoners.

BERGANZA: That is ambition, but a noble ambition, which strives to better its standing with no harm to others.

SCIPIO: Ambition is seldom or never satisfied without harm to others.

BERGANZA: We've agreed to avoid backbiting.

SCIPIO: Yes, and I'm not grumbling at anyone.

BERGANZA: Now I finally find that what I've often heard is completely true. A slanderous backbiter has just ruined ten noble families and calumniated twenty good men, and if someone reproaches him for what he said, he replies that he has said nothing, and that if he *has* said something, he didn't mean anything by it, and that, if he had imagined anyone would be offended by it, he wouldn't have said it. Honestly, Scipio, you've got to be very wise and very cautious if you want to keep up a two hours' conversation without bordering on backbiting; for I see it in myself: though an animal, as I am, whenever I string a few sentences together, words come to my tongue like gnats to wine, and all of them malicious and slanderous words; so that I repeat what I said earlier:[8] that we inherit evil deeds and words from our ancestors and imbibe them with our mothers' milk. This is clearly seen when a baby who has just taken his arm out of his swaddling clothes raises it as if to try and take revenge on someone he thinks has offended him; and almost the first clear word he speaks is when he calls his wet nurse or mother "whore."

SCIPIO: It's true, and I admit my mistake and beg your pardon for it, since I've pardoned you for so many. Let's "make up," as children say, and let's avoid backbiting from here on; continue your story, which you left off when you mentioned how ostentatiously the sons of your master the merchant used to go to the school of the Company of Jesus.

BERGANZA: To Jesus I commend myself on all occasions. Though I find it hard to cease backbiting, I intend to use a remedy which I've heard was used by a great swearer of oaths; repentant for his bad habit, whenever

8. It was Scipio who said it.

tido de su mala costumbre, cada vez que después de su arrepentimiento juraba, se daba un pellizco en el brazo, o besaba la tierra, en pena de su culpa; pero, con todo esto, juraba. Así yo, cada vez que fuere contra el precepto que me has dado de que no murmure y contra la intención que tengo de no murmurar, me morderé el pico de la lengua de modo que me duela y me acuerde de mi culpa para no volver a ella.

CIPIÓN.—Tal es ese remedio, que si usas dél, espero que te has de morder tantas veces que has de quedar sin lengua, y así, quedarás imposibilitado de murmurar.

BERGANZA.—A lo menos, yo haré de mi parte mis diligencias, y supla las faltas el cielo.

«Y así, digo que los hijos de mi amo se dejaron un día un cartapacio en el patio, donde yo a la sazón estaba; y, como estaba enseñado a llevar la esportilla del jifero mi amo, así del *vademécum* y fuime tras ellos, con intención de no soltalle hasta el estudio. Sucedióme todo como lo deseaba: que mis amos, que me vieron venir con el *vademécum* en la boca, asido sotilmente de las cintas, mandaron a un paje me le quitase; mas yo no lo consentí ni le solté hasta que entré en el aula con él, cosa que causó risa a todos los estudiantes. Lleguéme al mayor de mis amos, y, a mi parecer, con mucha crianza se le puse en las manos, y quedéme sentado en cuclillas a la puerta del aula, mirando de hito en hito al maestro que en la cátedra leía. No sé qué tiene la virtud, que, con alcanzárseme a mí tan poco o nada della, luego recibí gusto de ver el amor, el término, la solicitud y la industria con que aquellos benditos padres y maestros enseñaban a aquellos niños, enderezando las tiernas varas de su juventud, porque no torciesen ni tomasen mal siniestro en el camino de la virtud, que juntamente con las letras les mostraban. Consideraba cómo los reñían con suavidad, los castigaban con misericordia, los animaban con ejemplos, los incitaban con premios y los sobrellevaban con cordura; y, finalmente, cómo les pintaban la fealdad y horror de los vicios y les dibujaban la hermosura de las virtudes, para que, aborrecidos ellos y amadas ellas, consiguiesen el fin para que fueron criados.»

CIPIÓN.—Muy bien dices, Berganza; porque yo he oído decir desa bendita gente que para repúblicos del mundo no los hay tan prudentes en todo él, y para guiadores y adalides del camino del cielo, pocos les llegan. Son espejos donde se mira la honestidad, la católica dotrina, la singular prudencia, y, finalmente, la humildad profunda, basa sobre quien se levanta todo el edificio de la bienaventuranza.

BERGANZA.—Todo es así como lo dices.

he swore after becoming repentant, he'd pinch his arm, or kiss the ground, as a penalty for his failing: but, despite all this, he'd swear. And so, every time I contravene the admonition you've given me not to backbite, and my own intention not to do so, I'll bite the tip of my tongue, so it hurts, and I'll remember my failing and won't relapse.

SCIPIO: It's such a remedy that, if you use it, I expect you to bite yourself so often that you'll be left tongueless and thus incapable of backbiting.

BERGANZA: At least, for my part I'll be careful, and may heaven make up for my failings!

Well, then, I go on: One day my master's sons left a portfolio in the patio, where I happened to be; and, having been trained to carry the basket of my master the butcher, I grasped the vademecum and went after them, resolved not to let go of it until I arrived at the school. Everything turned out as I wished: my young masters, seeing me coming with the vademecum in my mouth, lightly gripped by the straps, ordered a page to take it from me; but I didn't let him, and I didn't release it until I entered the classroom with it, which made all the pupils laugh. I went up to the elder of my masters and with great delicacy, to my mind, I placed it in his hands; then I remained seated on my haunches at the classroom door, staring at the teacher who was lecturing from the chair. I don't know what power virtue has, but, having so small a share of it, or none at all, I nevertheless immediately took pleasure in seeing the love, good nature, care, and skill with which those blessed priests and teachers instructed those boys, straightening the tender shoots of their youth so they wouldn't get twisted or acquire bad habits on the path of virtue, which they taught them along with their letters. I observed how gently they reprimanded them, how mercifully they punished them, how they encouraged them with good examples, incited them with prizes, and uplifted them with wisdom; lastly, how they depicted to them the ugliness and horror of the vices and portrayed to them the beauty of the virtues, so that, abhorring the former and loving the latter, they could attain the goal for which they had been created.

SCIPIO: You put it very well, Berganza; for I've heard it said of those blessed people that, as lovers of the public welfare, no one else in the whole world is so thoughtful, and, as guides and leaders on the road to heaven, few come up to them. They're mirrors that reflect honesty, Catholic doctrine, unusual prudence, and, lastly, profound humility, the basis on which the entire edifice of felicity is raised.

BERGANZA: It's just as you say.

«Y, siguiendo mi historia, digo que mis amos gustaron de que les llevase siempre el *vademécum*, lo que hice de muy buena voluntad; con lo cual tenía una vida de rey, y aun mejor, porque era descansada, a causa que los estudiantes dieron en burlarse conmigo, y domestiquéme con ellos de tal manera, que me metían la mano en la boca y los más chiquillos subían sobre mí. Arrojaban los bonetes o sombreros, y yo se los volvía a la mano limpiamente y con muestras de grande regocijo. Dieron en darme de comer cuanto ellos podían, y gustaban de ver que, cuando me daban nueces o avellanas, las partía como mona, dejando las cáscaras y comiendo lo tierno. Tal hubo que, por hacer prueba de mi habilidad, me trujo en un pañuelo gran cantidad de ensalada, la cual comí como si fuera persona. Era tiempo de invierno, cuando campean en Sevilla los molletes y mantequillas, de quien era tan bien servido, que más de dos Antonios se empeñaron o vendieron para que yo almorzase. Finalmente, yo pasaba una vida de estudiante sin hambre y sin sarna, que es lo más que se puede encarecer para decir que era buena; porque si la sarna y la hambre no fuesen tan unas con los estudiantes, en las vidas no habría otra de más gusto y pasatiempo, porque corren parejas en ella la virtud y el gusto, y se pasa la mocedad aprendiendo y holgándose.

»Desta gloria y desta quietud me vino a quitar una señora que, a mi parecer, llaman por ahí razón de estado; que, cuando con ella se cumple, se ha de descumplir con otras razones muchas. Es el caso que aquellos señores maestros les pareció que la media hora que hay de lición a lición la ocupaban los estudiantes, no en repasar las liciones, sino en holgarse conmigo; y así, ordenaron a mis amos que no me llevasen más al estudio. Obedecieron, volviéronme a casa y a la antigua guarda de la puerta, y, sin acordarse señor el viejo de la merced que me había hecho de que de día y de noche anduviese suelto, volví a entregar el cuello a la cadena y el cuerpo a una esterilla que detrás de la puerta me pusieron.»

¡Ay, amigo Cipión, si supieses cuán dura cosa es de sufrir el pasar de un estado felice a un desdichado! Mira: cuando las miserias y desdichas tienen larga la corriente y son continuas, o se acaban presto, con la muerte, o la continuación dellas hace un hábito y costumbre en padecellas, que suele en su mayor rigor servir de alivio; mas, cuando de la suerte desdichada y calamitosa, sin pensarlo y de improviso, se sale a gozar de otra suerte próspera, venturosa y alegre, y de allí a poco

To continue my history: it pleased my masters for me to carry their vademecum always, which I did very gladly; thereby I led a royal life, or even better, because it was easy, since the pupils began enjoying themselves with me, and I became so tame with them that they'd put their hand in my mouth and the littlest ones would ride me. They'd throw their bonnets or hats and I'd return them to their hands, clean, displaying great joy. They began to feed me as much as they could, and when they gave me walnuts or hazelnuts, they enjoyed seeing me crack them open like a monkey, leaving the shells and eating the kernels. One boy, to test my skill, brought me a lot of salad in a handkerchief, and I ate it as if I were a human being. It was wintertime, when Seville abounds with bread rolls and butter, with which I was so well supplied that more than two Latin grammars[9] were pawned or sold to provide lunches for me. In short, I led a student's life without hunger or mange, which is the highest possible praise to express that it was a good life; because, if mange and hunger weren't so closely associated with students, no other life would be more pleasurable and entertaining, seeing that, in it, virtue and enjoyment are coupled and one's youth is spent in learning and fun.

I was taken from this glory and quietude by a "lady" who I think is here called reason of state; when "her" dictates are followed, many other kinds of reason have to be discarded. What happened is that those teachers decided that the half hour between lessons was being used by the pupils not to review their lessons, but to fool around with me; so they ordered my masters not to bring me to school any more. They obeyed, they returned me to the house and my former guard duty at the door, and, my adult master not recalling the favor he had done me of allowing me to go about loose day and night, I once more surrendered my neck to the chain and my body to a small mat they laid for me behind the door.

Oh, friend Scipio, if you only knew how hard it is for an unfortunate person to endure the passing of a happy condition! Just see: when wretchedness and misfortune have a broad current and are continuous, either they end quickly, in death, or else their continuance creates a constancy and habit in undergoing them which generally acts as a relief to even their greatest harshness; but when you emerge suddenly and unexpectedly from an unhappy, disastrous lot into the enjoyment of another one that's prosperous, fortunate, and merry, and shortly thereafter go

9. Called *Antonios* in the Spanish text because they were written by Antonio de Nebrija (published 1481).

se vuelve a padecer la suerte primera y a los primeros trabajos y desdichas, es un dolor tan riguroso que si no acaba la vida, es por atormentarla más viviendo.

«Digo, en fin, que volví a mi ración perruna y a los huesos que una negra de casa me arrojaba, y aun éstos me dezmaban dos gatos romanos: que, como sueltos y ligeros, érales fácil quitarme lo que no caía debajo del distrito que alcanzaba mi cadena.»

Cipión hermano, así el cielo te conceda el bien que deseas, que, sin que te enfades, me dejes ahora filosofar un poco; porque si dejase de decir las cosas que en este instante me han venido a la memoria de aquellas que entonces me ocurrieron, me parece que no sería mi historia cabal ni de fruto alguno.

CIPIÓN.—Advierte, Berganza, no sea tentación del demonio esa gana de filosofar que dices te ha venido, porque no tiene la murmuración mejor velo para paliar y encubrir su maldad disoluta que darse a entender el murmurador que todo cuanto dice son sentencias de filósofos, y que el decir mal es reprehensión y el descubrir los defetos ajenos buen celo. Y no hay vida de ningún murmurante que, si la consideras y escudriñas, no la halles llena de vicios y de insolencias. Y debajo de saber esto, filosofea ahora cuanto quisieres.

BERGANZA.—Seguro puedes estar, Cipión, de que más murmure, porque así lo tengo prosupuesto.

«Es, pues, el caso, que como me estaba todo el día ocioso y la ociosidad sea madre de los pensamientos, di en repasar por la memoria algunos latines que me quedaron el ella de muchos que oí cuando fui con mis amos al estudio, con que, a mi parecer, me hallé algo más mejorado de entendimiento, y determiné, como si hablar supiera, aprovecharme dellos en las ocasiones que se me ofreciesen; pero en manera diferente de la que se suelen aprovechar algunos ignorantes.»

Hay algunos romancistas que en las conversaciones disparan de cuando en cuando con algún latín breve y compendioso, dando a entender a los que no lo entienden que son grandes latinos, y apenas saben declinar un nombre ni conjugar un verbo.

CIPIÓN.—Por menor daño tengo ése que el que hacen los que verdaderamente saben latín, de los cuales hay algunos tan imprudentes que, hablando con un zapatero o con un sastre, arrojan latines como agua.

BERGANZA.—Deso podremos inferir que tanto peca el que dice latines delante de quien los ignora, como el que los dice ignorándolos.

CIPIÓN.—Pues otra cosa puedes advertir, y es que hay algunos que no les escusa el ser latinos de ser asnos.

back to suffering the earlier lot and the former labors and misfortunes, it's so harsh a sorrow that, if it doesn't end your life, it's only to torment you more as you go on living.

In short: I returned to my dog's rations and the bones that an African servant woman threw me; and even those were decimated for me by two striped cats: since they were untied and fleetfooted, it was easy for them to take away from me whatever lay beyond the area my chain could reach.

Brother Scipio (so may heaven grant you the good things you desire!), without getting angry, let me now philosophize a little; because, if I neglected to say the things which I have just recalled among those which occurred to me then, I don't think my history would be complete or at all profitable.

SCIPIO: Make sure, Berganza, that this urge to philosophize which you say has come upon you isn't a temptation of the devil's, because backbiting has no better veil to palliate and conceal its dissolute wickedness than when the backbiter makes out that everything he says is philosophers' dicta, and that slander is a reprimand, and the uncovering of others' faults is laudable zeal. And there's no life of any slanderer which, well observed and scrutinized, won't be found to be full of vice and insolence. Keeping this in mind, now philosophize to your heart's content.

BERGANZA: You can be sure, Scipio, that I will no longer backbite, for I've resolved not to.

Well, the case is that, since I was idle all day and idleness is the mother of musing, I started to review in my memory some Latin sayings which remained there out of the many I had heard when at school with my young masters; in my opinion, they had improved my mind somewhat, and I resolved, as if I knew how to speak, to make use of them on any occasion that offered; but not in the way in which some ignorant people are wont to use them.

There are some people who know only Spanish, but in their conversation occasionally spit out some brief, concise bit of Latin, letting on to those who don't understand that they're great Latinists, though they can scarcely decline a noun or conjugate a verb.

SCIPIO: I consider that less harmful than what people do who really know Latin, some of whom are so thoughtless that, when speaking to a cobbler or a tailor, they pour out Latin like water.

BERGANZA: From this we may deduce that the man who speaks Latin to someone who doesn't know it is as much at fault as the man who speaks it while himself ignorant of it.

SCIPIO: Then you can observe another thing, which is that there are some whose knowledge of Latin doesn't prevent them from being fools.

BERGANZA.—Pues ¿quién lo duda? La razón está clara, pues cuando en tiempo de los romanos hablaban todos latín, como lengua materna suya, algún majadero habría entre ellos, a quien no escusaría el hablar latín dejar de ser necio.

CIPIÓN.—Para saber callar en romance y hablar en latín, discreción es menester, hermano Berganza.

BERGANZA.—Así es, porque tan bien se puede decir una necedad en latín como en romance, y yo he visto letrados tontos, y gramáticos pesados, y romancistas vareteados con sus listas de latín, que con mucha facilidad pueden enfadar al mundo, no una sino muchas veces.

CIPIÓN.—Dejemos esto, y comienza a decir tus filosofías.

BERGANZA.—Ya las he dicho: éstas son que acaba de decir.

CIPIÓN.—¿Cuáles?

BERGANZA.—Éstas de los latines y romances, que yo comencé y tú acabaste.

CIPIÓN.—¿Al murmurar llamas filosofar? ¡Así va ello! Canoniza, canoniza, Berganza, a la maldita plaga de la murmuración, y dale el nombre que quisieres, que ella dará a nosotros el de cínicos, que quiere decir perros murmuradores; y por tu vida que calles ya y sigas tu historia.

BERGANZA.—¿Cómo la tengo de seguir si callo?

CIPIÓN.—Quiero decir que la sigas de golpe, sin que la hagas que parezca pulpo, según la vas añadiendo colas.

BERGANZA.—Habla con propiedad: que no se llaman colas las del pulpo.

CIPIÓN.—Ése es el error que tuvo el que dijo que no era torpedad ni vicio nombrar las cosas por sus propios nombres, como si no fuese mejor, ya que sea forzoso nombrarlas, decirlas por circunloquios y rodeos que templen la asquerosidad que causa el oírlas por sus mismos nombres. Las honestas palabras dan indicio de la honestidad del que las pronuncia o las escribe.

BERGANZA.—Quiero creerte; «y digo que, no contenta mi fortuna de haberme quitado de mis estudios y de la vida que en ellos pasaba, tan regocijada y compuesta, y haberme puesto atraillado tras de una puerta, y de haber trocado la liberalidad de los estudiantes en la mezquinidad de la negra, ordenó de sobresaltarme en lo que ya por quietud y descanso tenía.»

Mira, Cipión, ten por cierto y averiguado, como yo lo tengo, que al desdichado las desdichas le buscan y le hallan, aunque se esconda en los últimos rincones de la tierra.

«Dígolo porque la negra de casa estaba enamorada de un negro, asimismo esclavo de casa, el cual negro dormía en el zaguán, que es

BERGANZA: Who doubts it? The reason is clear: when in Roman times everybody spoke Latin as their mother tongue, there must have been some ninnies among them, whose Latin speech wouldn't have prevented them from being stupid.

SCIPIO: To know how to keep quiet in Spanish and talk in Latin, wisdom is needed, brother Berganza.

BERGANZA: Right, because it's just as easy to say foolish things in Latin as in Spanish, and I've seen educated men who were stupid, and Latinists who were tedious, and Spanish speakers whose speech was interlarded with Latin; and they can very readily irritate the world, not once but many times.

SCIPIO: Let's drop this; start to pronounce your philosophy.

BERGANZA: I already have; it's what I've just said.

SCIPIO: What?

BERGANZA: All that about Latin and Spanish speakers, which I began and you finished.

SCIPIO: You call slander philosophy? That's the limit! Canonize it, Berganza, canonize the cursed plague of backbiting, and give it any name you like, because it will give *us* the name of cynics, which means grumbling dogs; on your life, be quiet now and continue your history.

BERGANZA: How can I if I keep still?

SCIPIO: I mean, continue it once and for all, and don't make it resemble an octopus by adding so many tails to it.

BERGANZA: Speak correctly: the arms of an octopus aren't called tails.

SCIPIO: That's the mistake made by the man who said that it wasn't folly or vice to call things by their right name, as if it weren't better, once it's necessary to name them, to do so in roundabout circumlocutions which can temper the disgust caused by hearing their right names. Decent words indicate the decency of the man who pronounces or writes them.

BERGANZA: I'm willing to believe you. But, to go on: My fortune, not content with having removed me from my studies and the life I was leading in them, such a happy, calm life, or with having tied me up behind a door, or with having replaced the pupils' generosity with the African woman's stinginess, ordained that I should be shaken out of that remainder of peace and rest that I still thought I possessed.

See, Scipio, be sure and certain of it, as I am: misfortunes seek out and find an unfortunate man even if he hides in the remotest corners of the earth.

I say this because the African woman in the household was in love with an African man, likewise a slave in the house; this man slept in the en-

entre la puerta de la calle y la de en medio, detrás de la cual yo estaba; y no se podían juntar sino de noche, y para esto habían hurtado o contrahecho las llaves; y así, las más de las noches bajaba la negra, y tapándome la boca con algún pedazo de carne o queso, abría al negro, con quien se daba buen tiempo, facilitándolo mi silencio, y a costa de muchas cosas que la negra hurtaba. Algunos días me estragaron la conciencia las dádivas de la negra, pareciéndome que sin ellas se me apretarían las ijadas y daría de mastín en galgo. Pero, en efeto, llevado de mi buen natural, quise responder a lo que a mi amo debía, pues tiraba sus gajes y comía su pan, como lo deben hacer no sólo los perros honrados, a quien se les da renombre de agradecidos, sino todos aquellos que sirven.»

CIPIÓN.—Esto sí, Berganza, quiero queu pase por filosofía, porque son razones que consisten en buena verdad y en buen entendimiento; y adelante y no hagas soga, por no decir cola, de tu historia.

BERGANZA.—Primero te quiero rogar me digas, si es que lo sabes, qué quiere decir *filosofía;* que, aunque yo la nombro, no sé lo que es; sólo me doy a entender que es cosa buena.

CIPIÓN.—Con brevedad te la diré. Este nombre se compone de dos nombres griegos, que son *filos* y *sofía; filos* quiere decir amor, y *sofía,* la ciencia; así que *filosofía* significa «amor de la ciencia», y *filósofo,* «amador de la ciencia».

BERGANZA.—Mucho sabes, Cipión. ¿Quién diablos te enseñó a ti nombres griegos?

CIPIÓN.—Verdaderamente, Berganza, que eres simple, pues desto haces caso; porque éstas son cosas que las saben los niños de la escuela, y también hay quien presuma saber la lengua griega sin saberla, como la latina ignorándola.

BERGANZA.—Eso es lo que yo digo, y quisiera que a estos tales los pusieran en una prensa, y a fuerza de vueltas les sacaran el jugo de lo que saben, porque no anduviesen engañando el mundo con el oropel de sus gregüescos rotos y sus latines falsos, como hacen los portugueses con los negros de Guinea.

CIPIÓN.—Ahora sí, Berganza, que te puedes morder la lengua, y tarazármela yo, porque todo cuanto decimos es murmurar.

BERGANZA.—Sí, que no estoy obligado a hacer lo que he oído decir que hizo uno llamado Corondas, tirio, el cual puso ley que ninguno entrase en el ayuntamiento de su ciudad con armas, so pena de la vida. Descuidóse desto, y otro día entró en el cabildo ceñida la espada; ad-

tranceway, between the street door and the inner door behind which I was stationed; and they could meet only at night, for which purpose they had stolen or counterfeited the keys; and so, most nights the woman came downstairs and, shutting my mouth with some piece of meat or cheese, let the man in and had a good time with him, aided by my silence, at the cost of many things the woman stole. Some days the woman's gifts corrupted my conscience, since I thought that without them my flanks would be shriveled and I'd look like a greyhound instead of a mastiff. But, after all, inspired by the goodness natural to me, I tried to live up to my duty to my master (since I was drawing his wages and eating his bread), as not only honorable dogs should do, which are renowned for their gratitude, but every kind of servant.

SCIPIO: *That,* Berganza, I'll admit is philosophy, because those words are truthful and show a good understanding; move forward and don't drag needless elements into your story.

BERGANZA: First I want to ask you to tell me, if you know, what the word philosophy means; for, although I use the word, I don't know what the thing is; I merely take it that it's something good.

SCIPIO: I'll tell you briefly. The word is composed of two Greek nouns, *philos* and *sophia*. *Philos* means love; and *sophia,* knowledge;[10] so that philosophy means love of knowledge; and philosopher, lover of knowledge.

BERGANZA: You know a lot, Scipio. Who the hell taught you Greek nouns?

SCIPIO: Honestly, Berganza, you're simple if you make much of that; because those are things known by schoolboys, and there are also people who claim to know Greek when they don't, just as in the case of Latin.

BERGANZA: That's what I say, and I'd like such people to be put in a press, and the press turned till it squeezes the juice of their learning out of them, so they don't go around deceiving the world with the tinsel of their tattered Greek breeches and their fake Latin, as the Portuguese deceive the Africans in Guinea.

SCIPIO: *Now,* Berganza, you can bite your tongue, and I can chew up mine, because all we've been doing is grumbling.

BERGANZA: Yes, because I'm not obliged to do what I've heard that a Tyrian man named Corondas did;[11] having issued a decree that no one should enter the assembly of his city bearing arms, on penalty of death, he forgot about it. The next day he entered the city hall wearing a sword;

10. Actually, "friend" and "wisdom." 11. Actually Charondas of Thurium.

virtiéronselo y, acordándose de la pena por él puesta, al momento desenvainó su espada y se pasó con ella el pecho, y fue el primero que puso y quebrantó la ley y pagó la pena. Lo que yo dije no fue poner ley, sino prometer que me mordería la lengua cuando murmurase; pero ahora no van las cosas por el tenor y rigor de las antiguas: hoy se hace una ley y mañana se rompe, y quizá conviene que así sea. Ahora promete uno de enmendarse de sus vicios, y de allí a un momento cae en otros mayores. Una cosa es alabar la disciplina y otra el darse con ella, y, en efeto, del dicho al hecho hay gran trecho. Muérdase el diablo, que yo no quiero morderme ni hacer finezas detrás de una estera, donde de nadie soy visto que pueda alabar mi honrosa determinación.

CIPIÓN.—Según eso, Berganza, si tú fueras persona, fueras hipócrita, y todas las obras que hicieras fueran aparentes, fingidas y falsas, cubiertas con la capa de la virtud, sólo porque te alabaran, como todos los hipócritas hacen.

BERGANZA.—No sé lo que entonces hiciera; esto sé que quiero hacer ahora: que es no morderme, quedándome tantas cosas por decir, que no sé cómo ni cuándo podré acabarlas; y más, estando temeroso que al salir del sol nos hemos de quedar a escuras, faltándonos la habla.

CIPIÓN.—Mejor lo hará el cielo. Sigue tu historia y no te desvíes del camino carretero con impertinentes digresiones; y así, por larga que sea, la acabarás presto.

BERGANZA.—«Digo, pues, que, habiendo visto la insolencia, ladronicio y deshonestidad de los negros, determiné, como buen criado, estorbarlo, por los mejores medios que pudiese; y pude tan bien, que salí con mi intento. Bajaba la negra, como has oído, a refocilarse con el negro, fiada en que me enmudecían los pedazos de carne, pan o queso que me arrojaba . . .»

¡Mucho pueden las dádivas, Cipión!

CIPIÓN.—Mucho. No te diviertas, pasa adelante.

BERGANZA.—Acuérdome que cuando estudiaba oí decir al precetor un refrán latino, que ellos llaman adagio, que decía: *Habet bovem in lingua.*

CIPIÓN.—¡Oh, que en hora mala hayáis encajado vuestro latín! ¿Tan presto se te ha olvidado lo que poco ha dijimos contra los que entremeten latines en las conversaciones de romance?

BERGANZA.—Este latín viene aquí de molde; que has de saber que los atenienses usaban, entre otras, de una moneda sellada con la figura de un buey, y cuando algún juez dejaba de decir o hacer lo que era

when this was pointed out to him, he remembered the penalty he himself had set, and he immediately drew his sword and pierced his breast with it, becoming the first man to issue the decree, violate it, and pay the penalty. What I said wasn't the issuing of a decree, but a promise to bite my tongue if I grumbled; but nowadays matters aren't taken as strictly and rigorously as in antiquity: a law is made today and broken tomorrow, and perhaps it's right that it should be so. Now a person promises to mend his ways, and a moment later commits other offenses that are worse. It's one thing to praise discipline and another to confront punishment,[12] and, in fact, it's a long way between the word and the deed. Let the devil bite himself, because I don't want to bite myself or do fine deeds while lying on a mat where no one can see me and praise my honorable resolve.

SCIPIO: To judge by that, Berganza, if you were human you'd be a hypocrite, and all your actions would be specious, feigned, and false, cloaked with the mantle of virtue, solely to get yourself praised, like all hypocrites.

BERGANZA: I don't know what I'd do in that case; I know I want to do this now: not to bite myself, because I still have so much to tell that I don't know how or when I'll manage to finish; especially since I'm afraid that at sunrise we'll be left in the dark; that is, we won't be able to speak.

SCIPIO: Heaven will look after that. Continue your story and don't get off the high road with inopportune digressions; that way, however long your story is, you'll get through it speedily.

BERGANZA: Well, to continue: having observed the insolence, thievery, and indecency of those Africans, I determined, as a good servant, to prevent it as best I could; and I was so good at it that I accomplished what I intended. The woman used to come down, as you've heard, to have fun with the man, confident that the pieces of meat, bread, or cheese that she threw to me would keep me quiet . . .

Gifts have great powers, Scipio!

SCIPIO: Great. Don't digress, continue.

BERGANZA: I recall that when in school I heard the lecturer quote a Latin saying, which they call an adage, that went: *Habet bovem in lingua*, "There's an ox on his tongue."

SCIPIO: Oh, how inopportunely you've shoved in your Latin! Have you forgotten so soon what we were just saying about those who insert Latin into their Spanish conversation?

BERGANZA: This quotation fits in perfectly here; for I'll have you know that, in their coinage, the Athenians used a coin stamped with the image of an ox, and whenever some judge said or did anything that was contrary

12. *Disciplina* also means "whip."

razón y justicia, por estar cohechado, decían: «Este tiene el buey en la lengua».

CIPIÓN.—La aplicación falta.

BERGANZA.—¿No está bien clara, si las dádivas de la negra me tuvieron muchos días mudo, que ni quería ni osaba ladrarla cuando bajaba a verse con su negro enamorado? Por lo que vuelvo a decir que pueden mucho las dádivas.

CIPIÓN.—Ya te he respondido que pueden mucho, y si no fuera por no hacer ahora una larga digresión, con mil ejemplos probara lo mucho que las dádivas pueden; mas quizá lo diré, si el cielo me concede tiempo, lugar y habla para contarte mi vida.

BERGANZA.—Dios te dé lo que deseas, y escucha.

«Finalmente, mi buena intención rompió por las malas dádivas de la negra; a la cual, bajando una noche muy escura a su acostumbrado pasatiempo, arremetí sin ladrar, porque no se alborotasen los de casa, y en un instante le hice pedazos toda la camisa y le arranqué un pedazo de muslo: burla que fue bastante a tenerla de veras más de ocho días en la cama, fingiendo para con sus amos no sé qué enfermedad. Sanó, volvió otra noche, y yo volví a la pelea con mi perra, y, sin morderla, la arañé todo el cuerpo como si la hubiera cardado como manta. Nuestras batallas eran a la sorda, de las cuales salía siempre vencedor, y la negra, malparada y peor contenta. Pero sus enojos se parecían bien en mi pelo y en mi salud: alzóseme con la ración y los huesos, y los míos poco a poco iban señalando los nudos del espinazo. Con todo esto, aunque me quitaron el comer, no me pudieron quitar el ladrar. Pero la negra, por acabarme de una vez, me trujo una esponja frita con manteca; conocí la maldad; vi que era peor que comer zarazas, porque a quien la come se le hincha el estómago y no sale dél sin llevarse tras sí la vida. Y, pareciéndome ser imposible guardarme de las asechanzas de tan indignados enemigos, acordé de poner tierra en medio, quitándomeles delante de los ojos.

»Halléme un día suelto, y sin decir adiós a ninguno de casa, me puse en la calle, y a menos de cien pasos me deparó la suerte al alguacil que dije al principio de mi historia, que era grande amigo de mi amo Nicolás el Romo; el cual, apenas me hubo visto, cuando me conoció y me llamó por mi nombre; también le conocí yo, y, al llamarme, me llegué a él con mis acostumbradas ceremonias y caricias. Asióme del cuello y dijo a dos corchetes suyos: "Éste es famoso perro de ayuda, que fue de un grande amigo mío; llevémosle a casa". Holgáronse los corchetes, y dijeron que si era de ayuda a todos sería

to reason and justice, because he had been bribed, they said: "He's got the ox on his tongue."

SCIPIO: I don't see how it applies.

BERGANZA: Isn't it quite clear that, if the African woman's gifts shut my mouth for many days, I neither wished nor dared to bark at her when she came down to meet her lover? Therefore, I repeat that gifts have great power.

SCIPIO: I've already agreed that they have, and if it weren't that I don't want to make a long digression here, I'd prove by a thousand examples how powerful gifts are; but perhaps I'll still tell you that, if heaven grants me the time, opportunity, and faculty of speech to tell you *my* life.

BERGANZA: May God grant your wish! Listen:

Finally my good resolve overcame the woman's gifts; one very dark night, when she came down for her customary pleasures, I attacked her without barking, so as not to disturb the family, and in an instant I tore her whole nightgown to shreds and bit off a piece of her thigh: a jest which sufficed to keep her in bed for over a week for real, while she told her masters she had some kind of illness. She recovered and returned another night, and I returned to the fray with that slave bitch; without biting her, I scratched up her whole body as if I had been carding wool. Our battles were noiseless, and I won them all, the woman being left in bad shape and worse humor. But her vexation let itself be clearly seen in my coat and my general health: she took away my food and bones, and my own bones gradually became conspicuous, such as my vertebrae. Nevertheless, though my food was taken away, my bark couldn't be. But, to finish me off once and for all, the woman brought me a sponge fried in lard; I recognized her wicked purpose, and saw that it would be worse than eating dog-killing food with poison or ground glass in it; because if you eat a sponge your stomach swells up and you can't evacuate it without losing your life. Since it seemed impossible to protect myself against the stratagems of such indignant enemies, I decided to put space between us and remove myself from their sight.

Finding myself untied one day, without saying good-bye to anyone in the house, I ran into the street, and in less than a hundred paces fate placed in my path the constable I mentioned early in my story, that close friend of my first master, Snub-nosed Nicolás; as soon as he saw me, he recognized me and called me by name; I recognized him as well and, being called, I went up to him with my usual ceremonies and fawning. He seized me by the neck and said to his assistants: "This is the famous watchdog that belonged to a close friend of mine; let's take him home." His assistants were glad and said that, being trained, I'd be of use to them

de provecho. Quisieron asirme para llevarme, y mi amo dijo que no era menester asirme, que yo me iría, porque le conocía.

»Háseme olvidado decirte que las carlancas con puntas de acero que saqué cuando me desgarré y ausenté del ganado me las quitó un gitano en una venta, y ya en Sevilla andaba sin ellas; pero el alguacil me puso un collar tachonado todo de latón morisco.»

Considera, Cipión, ahora esta rueda variable de la fortuna mía: ayer me vi estudiante y hoy me vees corchete.

CIPIÓN.—Así va el mundo, y no hay para qué te pongas ahora a esagerar los vaivenes de fortuna, como si hubiera mucha diferencia de ser mozo de un jifero a serlo de un corchete. No puedo sufrir ni llevar en paciencia oír las quejas que dan de la fortuna algunos hombres que la mayor que tuvieron fue tener premisas y esperanzas de llegar a ser escuderos. ¡Con qué maldiciones la maldicen! ¡Con cuántos improperios la deshonran! Y no por más de que porque piense el que los oye que de alta, próspera y buena ventura han venido a la desdichada y baja en que los miran.

BERGANZA.—Tienes razón; «y has de saber que este alguacil tenía amistad con un escribano, con quien se acompañaba; estaban los dos amancebados con dos mujercillas, no de poco más a menos, sino de menos en todo; verdad es que tenían algo de buenas caras, pero mucho de desenfado y de taimería putesca. Éstas les servían de red y de anzuelo para pescar en seco, en esta forma: vestíanse de suerte que por la pinta descubrían la figura, y a tiro de arcabuz mostraban ser damas de la vida libre; andaban siempre a caza de estranjeros, y, cuando llegaba la vendeja a Cádiz y a Sevilla, llegaba la huella de su ganancia, no quedando bretón con quien no embistiesen; y, en cayendo el grasiento con alguna destas limpias, avisaban al alguacil y al escribano adónde y a qué posada iban, y, en estando juntos, les daban asalto y los prendían por amancebados; pero nunca los llevaban a la cárcel, a causa que los estranjeros siempre redimían la vejación con dineros.

»Sucedió, pues, que la Colindres, que así se llamaba la amiga del alguacil, pescó un bretón unto y bisunto; concertó con él cena y noche en su posada; dio el cañuto a su amigo; y, apenas se habían desnudado, cuando el alguacil, el escribano, dos corchetes y yo dimos con ellos. Alborotáronse los amantes; esageró el alguacil el delito; mandóles vestir a toda priesa para llevarlos a la cárcel; afligióse el bretón; terció, movido de caridad, el escribano, y a puros ruegos redujo la pena a solos cien reales. Pidió el bretón unos follados de camuza que había puesto en una silla a los pies de la cama, donde tenía dineros para

all. They wanted to take hold of me to lead me away, but my new master said it wasn't necessary; I'd come along because I knew him.

I forgot to tell you that the steel-spiked collar I took along when I lit out and took leave of the sheep had been taken off by a Gypsy at an inn, and in Seville I hadn't been wearing any; but the constable put a studded collar on me that was all of Moorish brass.

Now, Scipio, contemplate that turning wheel of my fortune: yesterday I was a student and today you see me a constable's assistant.

SCIPIO: That's how the world goes, and you have no call now to exaggerate the vicissitudes of fortune, as if there were a lot of difference between serving a butcher and serving a constable. I can't abide, or patiently hear, the complaints about fortune uttered by some people whose greatest fortune was to have indications and hopes of becoming a gentleman's attendant. How fiercely they curse it! What dishonorable insults they heap upon it! And merely so that their listeners will think that it was from a high, prosperous, fine estate that they have fallen into the unhappy, low one they are seen to be in.

BERGANZA: You're right. To continue: this constable was friends with a lawyer, whom he went around with; each of them had a prostitute mistress who was not "merely so-so," but "no good at all." To be honest, their faces were fairly nice, but they were very wanton and shrewd, as whores are. These women served them as a net and hook for fishing on dry land, in this manner: they'd doll themselves up in such a way that their warpaint revealed their true nature, and at the distance of a harquebus shot you could see they were ladies of the evening; they constantly hunted for foreigners and, when the autumn commodities fair came to Cádiz and Seville, the trail of their profits showed up, and there was no foreigner they didn't accost; and when a well-heeled customer hired one of these clean girls, they'd inform the constable and the lawyer where they were going and to which inn; when the pair was together, they'd raid the room and arrest them for indecency; but they'd never take them to jail, because the foreigners always bought themselves off with money.

Well, it came about that La Colindres (that was the name of the constable's girl) hooked an extremely rich foreigner and arranged to have supper with him and spend the night in his room; she tipped off her friend, and as soon as the pair had their clothes off, the constable, two of his assistants, the lawyer, and I burst in. The lovers were upset; the constable exaggerated the gravity of the crime; he ordered them to dress posthaste so he could take them to jail; the foreigner was in distress; the lawyer, out of humanity, intervened and by urgent requests got the penalty reduced to only a hundred reales. The foreigner asked for a pair of pleated chamois

pagar su libertad, y no parecieron los follados, ni podían parecer; porque, así como yo entré en el aposento, llegó a mis narices un olor de tocino que me consoló todo; descubríle con el olfato, y halléle en una faldriquera de los follados. Digo que hallé en ella un pedazo de jamón famoso, y, por gozarle y poderle sacar sin rumor, saqué los follados a la calle, y allí me entregué en el jamón a toda mi voluntad, y cuando volví al aposento hallé que el bretón daba voces diciendo en lenguaje adúltero y bastardo, aunque se entendía, que le volviesen sus calzas, que en ellas tenía cincuenta *escuti d'oro in oro*. Imaginó el escribano o que la Colindres o los corchetes se los habían robado; el alguacil pensó lo mismo; llamólos aparte, no confesó ninguno, y diéronse al diablo todos. Viendo yo lo que pasaba, volví a la calle donde había dejado los follados, para volverlos, pues a mí no me aprovechaba nada el dinero; no los hallé, porque ya algún venturoso que pasó se los había llevado. Como el alguacil vio que el bretón no tenía dinero para el cohecho, se desesperaba, y pensó sacar de la huéspeda de casa lo que el bretón no tenía; llamóla, y vino medio desnuda, y como oyó las voces y quejas del bretón, y a la Colindres desnuda y llorando, al alguacil en cólera y al escribano enojado y a los corchetes despabilando lo que hallaban en el aposento, no le plugo mucho. Mandó el alguacil que se cubriese y se viniese con él a la cárcel, porque consentía en su casa hombres y mujeres de mal vivir. ¡Aquí fue ello! Aquí sí que fue cuando se aumentaron las voces y creció la confusión; porque dijo la huéspeda: "Señor alguacil y señor escribano, no conmigo tretas, que entrevo toda costura; no conmigo dijes ni poleos: callen la boca y váyanse con Dios; si no, por mi santiguada que arroje el bodegón por la ventana y que saque a plaza toda la chirinola desta historia; que bien conozco a la señora Colindres y sé que ha muchos meses que es su cobertor el señor alguacil; y no hagan que me aclare más, sino vuélvase el dinero a este señor, y quedemos todos por buenos; porque yo soy mujer honrada y tengo un marido con su carta de ejecutoria, y con *a perpenan rei de memoria,* con sus colgaderos de plomo, Dios sea loado, y hago este oficio muy limpiamente y sin daño de barras. El arancel tengo clavado donde todo el mundo le vea; y no conmigo cuentos, que, por Dios, que sé despolvorearme. ¡Bonita soy yo para que por mi orden entren mujeres con los huéspedes! Ellos tienen las llaves de sus aposentos, y yo no soy quince, que tengo de ver tras siete paredes".

breeches he had placed on a chair at the foot of the bed; in them he had money to buy his release. But the breeches were not to be found, nor could they be; because as soon as I entered the room, a highly gratifying smell of pork reached my nose; I detected it by scent, finding it in a pocket of those breeches. To be specific, I found there a piece of wonderful ham and, to be able to take it out noiselessly and enjoy it, I dragged the breeches into the street, where I lit into the ham to my heart's content. When I returned to the room, I found the foreigner yelling in a Spanish that was an incorrect pidgin, but still comprehensible, for his breeches to be returned because they contained fifty "escuti" in solid gold. The lawyer thought they had been stolen by La Colindres or the constable's men, and so did the constable; he called them over to one side, but no one confessed, and everyone was furious. Seeing what was going on, I returned to the street, where I had left the breeches, meaning to return them, since the money was of no use to me; but I didn't find them because some lucky passerby had already carried them off. When the constable saw that the foreigner had no money for the bribe, he fell into despair, and decided to get from the hostess of the inn what the foreigner didn't have; he called her, and she came half naked; when she heard the lamenting cries of the foreigner and saw La Colindres naked and weeping, the constable in a rage, the lawyer angry, and the constable's men pilfering whatever they found in the room, she was greatly displeased. The constable ordered her to get dressed and come to jail with him, because she allowed indecent men and women in her establishment. That was the limit! That was when voices were raised and the confusion grew worse. Because the hostess said: "Constable, lawyer, no tricks with me, because I catch on to every dodge; no threats or showing off with me: shut up and go your way, or else, by my blessed soul, I'll make a real stink and make your whole scheme public. I'm very familiar with Señora Colindres and I know that the constable has been her protector for many months; don't make me speak more plainly, but give this gentleman his money back, and let's all remain friends; because I'm an honorable woman and I've got a husband with a patent of nobility, with *a perpenan rei de memoria*[13] and the hanging lead seals on it, God be praised, and I ply this trade very decently with no harm to others. I've got the regulations nailed up where everyone can see them; so no tall stories with me because, by God, I know how to protect myself. Is it my doing if women come in with my guests? They've got the keys to their rooms, and I don't have eyes like a 'quinx' so I can see through seven walls!"

---

13. An ignorant error for *ad perpetuam rei memoriam* ("in perpetual recollection of the matter"), a legal formula.

»Pasmados quedaron mis amos de haber oído la arenga de la huéspeda y de ver cómo les leía la historia de sus vidas; pero, como vieron que no tenían de quién sacar dinero si della no, porfiaban en llevarla a la cárcel. Quejábase ella al cielo de la sinrazón y justicia que la hacían, estando su marido ausente y siendo tan principal hidalgo. El bretón bramaba por sus cincuenta *escuti*. Los corchetes porfiaban que ellos no habían visto los follados, ni Dios permitiese lo tal. El escribano, por lo callado, insistía al alguacil que mirase los vestidos de la Colindres, que le daba sospecha que ella debía de tener los cincuenta *escuti*, por tener de costumbre visitar los escondrijos y faldriqueras de aquellos que con ella se envolvían. Ella decía que el bretón estaba borracho y que debía de mentir en lo del dinero. En efeto, todo era confusión, gritos y juramentos, sin llevar modo de apaciguarse, ni se apaciguaran si al instante no entrara en el aposento el teniente de asistente, que, viniendo a visitar aquella posada, las voces le llevaron adonde era la grita. Preguntó la causa de aquellas voces; la huéspeda se la dio muy por menudo: dijo quién era la ninfa Colindres, que ya estaba vestida; publicó la pública amistad suya y del alguacil; echó en la calle sus tretas y modo de robar; disculpóse a sí misma de que con su consentimiento jamás había entrado en su casa mujer de mala sospecha; canonizóse por santa y a su marido por un bendito, y dio voces a una moza que fuese corriendo y trujese de un cofre la carta ejecutoria de su marido, para que la viese el señor tiniente, diciéndole que por ella echaría de ver que mujer de tan honrado marido no podía hacer cosa mala; y que si tenía aquel oficio de casa de camas, era a no poder más; que Dios sabía lo que le pesaba, y si quisiera ella tener alguna renta y pan cuotidiano para pasar la vida, que tener aquel ejercicio. El teniente, enfadado de su mucho hablar y presumir de ejecutoria, le dijo: "Hermana camera, yo quiero creer que vuestro marido tiene carta de hidalguía con que vos me confeséis que es hidalgo mesonero". "Y con mucha honra —respondió la huéspeda—. Y ¿qué linaje hay en el mundo, por bueno que sea, que no tenga algún dime y direte?" "Lo que yo os digo, hermana, es que os cubráis, que habéis de venir a la cárcel". La cual nueva dio con ella en el suelo; arañóse el rostro; alzó el grito; pero, con todo eso, el teniente, demasiadamente severo, los llevó a todos a la cárcel; conviene a saber: al bretón, a la Colindres y a la huéspeda. Después supe que el bretón perdió sus cincuenta *escuti*, y más diez, en que le condenaron en las costas; la huéspeda pagó otro tanto, y la Colindres salió libre por la puerta afuera. Y el mismo día que la soltaron pescó a un marinero, que pagó por el bretón, con el mismo embuste del soplo; porque veas, Cipión, cuántos y cuán grandes inconvenientes nacieron de mi golosina.»

My masters were amazed to hear the hostess's harangue and to see how she spouted their life stories; but, finding that she was the only one they could squeeze money out of, they insisted on taking her to jail. She complained to heaven about the unfairness and injustice they were doing her, in the absence of her husband, who was such a distinguished nobleman. The foreigner kept roaring for his fifty "escuti." The constable's men insisted that they hadn't seen the breeches, God forbid. The lawyer quietly urged the constable to search the clothes of La Colindres, whom he suspected of having the fifty "escuti," because she had the habit of examining the hiding places and pockets of the men who took up with her. She kept saying that the foreigner was drunk and must be lying about the money. In fact, all was confusion, shouting, and swearing, with no signs of calming down; nor would they have calmed down if the deputy of the chief city magistrate hadn't come into the room just then; while he was inspecting that inn, the sound of voices led him to where the shouting was. He asked the reason for that yelling, and the hostess told him every detail: she told him who the prostitute Colindres was (she was now dressed); she revealed her notorious romance with the constable; she made public their ploys and way of stealing; she absolved herself from all blame for ever allowing a woman of ill repute to enter her house; she canonized herself as a saint and beatified her husband as a "blessed," and she yelled to a servant girl to run and bring her husband's patent of nobility from a chest, so the deputy could see it, telling him that he would thereby realize that the wife of so honorable a husband couldn't commit a crime, and that if she plied that trade of innkeeper, it was because she couldn't help it; God knew how it irked her and how much she'd prefer having some fixed income, and daily bread to live on, to following that trade. The deputy, irritated by her long speech and claims to nobility, said: "My good hostess, I'm willing to believe that your husband has a patent of nobility if you admit to me that he's an innkeeping nobleman." "And very respected," the hostess replied. "What ancestry is there in the world, as good as it as, that doesn't have something debatable about it?" "What I tell you, ma'am, is to get dressed, because you must come to jail." This news floored her; she scratched her face, she raised a yell, but all the same the excessively strict deputy took them all to jail: that is, the foreigner, La Colindres, and the hostess. I learned afterward that the foreigner lost his fifty "escuti" and ten more, because he had to pay the costs; the hostess paid the same amount, while La Colindres walked out the door a free woman. And the very day she was released she hooked a sailor who compensated for the foreigner when that same blackmail trick was employed; so you can see, Scipio, how much serious trouble was caused by my gluttony.

CIPIÓN.—Mejor dijeras de la bellaquería de tu amo.

BERGANZA.—Pues escucha, que aun más adelante tiraban la barra, puesto que me pesa de decir mal de alguaciles y de escribanos.

CIPIÓN.—Sí, que decir mal de uno no es decirlo de todos; sí, que muchos y muy muchos escribanos hay buenos, fieles y legales, y amigos de hacer placer sin daño de tercero; sí, que no todos entretienen los pleitos, ni avisan a las partes, ni todos llevan más de sus derechos, ni todos van buscando e inquiriendo las vidas ajenas para ponerlas en tela de juicio, ni todos se aúnan con el juez para «háceme la barba y hacerte he el copete», ni todos los alguaciles se conciertan con los vagamundos y fulleros, ni tienen todos las amigas de tu amo para sus embustes. Muchos y muy muchos hay hidalgos por naturaleza y de hidalgas condiciones; muchos no son arrojados, insolentes, ni mal criados, ni rateros, como los que andan por los mesones midiendo las espadas a los estranjeros, y, hallándolas un pelo más de la marca, destruyen a sus dueños. Sí, que no todos como prenden sueltan, y son jueces y abogados cuando quieren.

BERGANZA.—«Más alto picaba mi amo; otro camino era el suyo; presumía de valiente y de hacer prisiones famosas; sustentaba la valentía sin peligro de su persona, pero a costa de su bolsa. Un día acometió en la Puerta de Jerez él solo a seis famosos rufianes, sin que yo le pudiese ayudar en nada, porque llevaba con un freno de cordel impedida la boca (que así me traía de día, y de noche me le quitaba). Quedé maravillado de ver su atrevimiento, su brío y su denuedo; así se entraba y salía por las seis espadas de los rufos como si fueran varas de mimbre; era cosa maravillosa ver la ligereza con que acometía, las estocadas que tiraba, los reparos, la cuenta, el ojo alerta porque no le tomasen las espaldas. Finalmente, él quedó en mi opinión y en la de todos cuantos la pendencia miraron y supieron por un nuevo Rodamonte, habiendo llevado a sus enemigos desde la Puerta de Jerez hasta los mármoles del Colegio de Mase Rodrigo, que hay más de cien pasos. Dejóles encerrados, y volvió a coger los trofeos de la batalla, que fueron tres vainas, y luego se las fue a mostrar al asistente, que, si mal no me acuerdo, lo era entonces el licenciado Sarmiento de Valladares, famoso por la destruición de La Sauceda. Miraban a mi amo por las calles do pasaba, señalándole con el dedo, como si dijeran: "Aquél es el valiente que se atrevió a reñir solo con la flor de los bravos de la Andalucía". En dar vueltas a la ciudad, para dejarse ver, se pasó lo que quedaba del día,

SCIPIO: You should rather say: by your master's villainy.

BERGANZA: Listen, then, because they became even more daring, though I don't like badmouthing constables and lawyers.

SCIPIO: But badmouthing *one* isn't the same as badmouthing *all*; for there are many, very many lawyers who are good, loyal, and law-abiding, eager to give pleasure with no harm to others; not all of them delay trials, give advice to both parties at law, or receive more than their due fee; not all investigate and delve into other people's lives in order to call them into question; not all collude with the judge in a "you scratch my back, I'll scratch yours" arrangement; nor do all constables make deals with vagabonds and sharpsters, nor do all have mistresses like your master's to abet them in confidence games. There are many, very many, who are noblemen by nature, with noble behavior; many are not inconsiderate, insolent, or rude, or petty thieves like the ones who hang around inns measuring foreigners' swords and, finding them a hair longer than the law permits, ruining their owners. Not all of them release you as readily as they arrest you, or play the judge or attorney whenever they want.

BERGANZA. My master was aiming higher; he had a loftier goal: he boasted of bravery, of making flashy arrests, and he maintained that reputation without danger to his person, but at financial expense. One day at the Puerta de Jerez he attacked six notorious thugs singlehanded, without my being able to help him at all, because my mouth was restrained with a cord muzzle (which I always wore by day; it was taken off at night). I was amazed at his daring, energy, and courage; he wove in and out of the thugs' six swords as if they were osier rods; it was wonderful to see the speed of his attacks, the thrusts he made, his parries, his care and alertness in protecting his back. In short, he remained in my opinion, and that of all who saw or heard of the fight, as a new Rodomonte,[14] having driven his enemies from the Puerta de Jerez all the way to the marble-clad Colegio de Mase Rodrigo, over a hundred paces away. He left them shut in and returned to gather up the trophies of the battle—six scabbards—which he then went to show to the chief magistrate, who, if I remember correctly, was then the graduate Sarmiento de Valladares,[15] famous for the destruction of La Sauceda.[16] People gazed at my master when he went down the street, as if to say: "That's the hero bold enough to fight alone with the flower of Andalusian bravos." He spent the rest of the day walking around town to let himself be seen, and night found us in Triana, on a street next to the Powder Mill; my master,

14. A daredevil in Italian Renaissance heroic-epic poems. 15. This places the incident in 1589 or 1590. 16. A den of thieves.

y la noche nos halló en Triana, en una calle junto al Molino de la Pólvora; y, habiendo mi amo avizorado (como en la jácara se dice) si alguien le veía, se entró en una casa, y yo tras él, y hallamos en un patio a todos los jayanes de la pendencia, sin capas ni espadas, y todos desabrochados; y uno, que debía de ser el huésped, tenía un gran jarro de vino en la una mano y en la otra una copa grande de taberna, la cual, colmándola de vino generoso y espumante, brindaba a toda la compañía. Apenas hubieron visto a mi amo, cuando todos se fueron a él con los brazos abiertos, y todos le brindaron, y él hizo la razón a todos, y aun la hiciera a otros tantos si le fuera algo en ello, por ser de condición afable y amigo de no enfadar a nadie por pocas cosas.»

Quererte yo contar ahora lo que allí se trató, la cena que cenaron, las peleas que se contaron, los hurtos que se refirieron, las damas que de su trato se calificaron y las que se reprobaron, las alabanzas que los unos a los otros se dieron, los bravos ausentes que se nombraron, la destreza que allí se puso en su punto, levantándose en mitad de la cena a poner en prática las tretas que se les ofrecían, esgrimiendo con las manos, los vocablos tan exquisitos de que usaban; y, finalmente, el talle de la persona del huésped, a quien todos respetaban como a señor y padre, sería meterme en un laberinto donde no me fuese posible salir cuando quisiese.

«Finalmente, vine a entender con toda certeza que el dueño de la casa, a quien llamaban Monipodio, era encubridor de ladrones y pala de rufianes, y que la gran pendencia de mi amo había sido primero concertada con ellos, con las circunstancias del retirarse y de dejar las vainas, las cuales pagó mi amo allí, luego, de contado, con todo cuanto Monipodio dijo que había costado la cena, que se concluyó casi al amanecer, con mucho gusto de todos. Y fue su postre dar soplo a mi amo de un rufián forastero que, nuevo y flamante, había llegado a la ciudad; debía de ser más valiente que ellos, y de envidia le soplaron. Prendióle mi amo la siguiente noche, desnudo en la cama: que si vestido estuviera, yo vi en su talle que no se dejara prender tan a mansalva. Con esta prisión que sobrevino sobre la pendencia, creció la fama de mi cobarde, que lo era mi amo más que una liebre, y a fuerza de meriendas y tragos sustentaba la fama de ser valiente, y todo cuanto con su oficio y con sus inteligencias granjeaba se le iba y desaguaba por la canal de la valentía.

»Pero ten paciencia, y escucha ahora un cuento que le sucedió, sin añadir ni quitar de la verdad una tilde. Dos ladrones hurtaron en Antequera un caballo muy bueno; trujéronle a Sevilla, y para venderle sin peligro usaron de un ardid que, a mi parecer, tiene del agudo y del discreto. Fuéronse a posar a posadas diferentes, y el uno se fue a la justicia y pidió por una petición que Pedro de Losada le debía cua-

having kept an eye peeled (as is said in thieves' jargon) to avoid being spotted, entered a house and I followed; in a patio we found all the thugs who had been in the fight, without capes or swords, and all with their clothes undone. One, who must have been the host, held a big jug of wine in one hand and a big tavern goblet in the other; filling this with heady, foaming wine, he toasted the whole gathering. As soon as they saw my master, they all came up to him with open arms and toasted him; he replied to every toast, and would even have done so to the same number again if called upon, being affable by nature and eager not to anger anyone over trifles.

If I now wanted to tell you what went on there, the supper they ate, the fights they recounted, the thefts they mentioned, the ladies they praised or blamed for their way of life, the praise they showered on one another, the absent bravos they referred to, the fencing skills they brought to perfection there, as they got up in the middle of supper to try out the feints that occurred to them, fencing with their hands, the very choice terms they used, and lastly the appearance of their host, whom everyone looked up to as a master and father, I'd get lost in a maze that I couldn't get out of when I wanted to.

Finally, I realized fully that the owner of the house, whom they called Monipodio, was a protector of thieves and a leader of thugs, and that my master's great fight had been prearranged with them, with instructions for them to retreat and leave behind their scabbards, which my master at once paid for there in cash, along with all that Monipodio said the supper had cost; the meal ended when it was nearly dawn, to everyone's great satisfaction. As dessert, my master was tipped off about a thug who was a stranger in town, brand new, and had just arrived; he must have been braver than the others, so that they ratted on him out of envy. My master arrested him the following night when he was in bed naked; I saw from his appearance that, if he had been dressed, he wouldn't have let himself be taken so easily. That arrest, following right after the fight, augmented my cowardly master's fame (he was more timorous than a hare), and by dint of meals and drinks he maintained his repute as a hero, all the money he gained by his position and spy service being squandered and washed away down the channel of false heroism.

But have patience, and now hear of something that befell him, all true with not a jot added or subtracted. Two thieves stole a very good horse in Antequera; they brought it to Seville, and to sell it without danger they used a ruse I find witty and clever. They went to lodge at different inns, then one went to the police and laid a claim that Pedro de Losada owed him four hundred reales which he had borrowed, as shown by a signed

trocientos reales prestados, como parecía por una cédula firmada de su nombre, de la cual hacía presentación. Mandó el tiniente que el tal Losada reconociese la cédula, y que si la reconociese, le sacasen prendas de la cantidad o le pusiesen en la cárcel; tocó hacer esta diligencia a mi amo y al escribano su amigo; llevóles el ladrón a la posada del otro, y al punto reconoció su firma y confesó la deuda, y señaló por prenda de la ejecución el caballo, el cual visto por mi amo, le creció el ojo, y le marcó por suyo si acaso se vendiese. Dio el ladrón por pasados los términos de la ley, y el caballo se puso en venta y se remató en quinientos reales en un tercero que mi amo echó de manga para que se le comprase. Valía el caballo tanto y medio más de lo que dieron por él. Pero, como el bien del vendedor estaba en la brevedad de la venta, a la primer postura remató su mercaduría. Cobró el un ladrón la deuda que no le debían, y el otro la carta de pago que no había menester, y mi amo se quedó con el caballo, que para él fue peor que el Seyano lo fue para sus dueños. Mondaron luego la haza los ladrones, y, de allí a dos días, después de haber trastejado mi amo las guarniciones y otras faltas del caballo, pareció sobre él en la plaza de San Francisco, más hueco y pomposo que aldeano vestido de fiesta. Diéronle mil parabienes de la buena compra, afirmándole que valía ciento y cincuenta ducados como un huevo un maravedí; y él, volteando y revolviendo el caballo, representaba su tragedia en el teatro de la referida plaza. Y, estando en sus caracoles y rodeos, llegaron dos hombres de buen talle y de mejor ropaje, y el uno dijo: "¡Vive Dios, que éste es Piedehierro, mi caballo, que ha pocos días que me le hurtaron en Antequera!" Todos los que venían con él, que eran cuatro criados, dijeron que así era la verdad: que aquél era Piedehierro, el caballo que le habían hurtado. Pasmóse mi amo, querellóse el dueño, hubo pruebas, y fueron las que hizo el dueño tan buenas, que salió la sentencia en su favor y mi amo fue desposeído del caballo. Súpose la burla y la industria de los ladrones, que por manos e intervención de la misma justicia vendieron lo que habían hurtado, y casi todos se holgaban de que la codicia de mi amo le hubiese rompido el saco.

»Y no paró en esto su desgracia; que aquella noche, saliendo a rondar el mismo asistente, por haberle dado noticia que hacia los barrios de San Julián andaban ladrones, al pasar de una encrucijada, vieron pasar un hombre corriendo, y dijo a este punto el asistente, asiéndome por el collar y zuzándome: "¡Al ladrón, Gavilán! ¡Ea, Gavilán, hijo, al

I.O.U. which he submitted as evidence. The deputy chief magistrate gave orders that this Losada should acknowledge the note and, if he did so, pledges were to be taken from him for that amount or he was to be jailed; the assignment was given to my master and his friend the lawyer; the thief led them to the other's inn; the fellow immediately acknowledged his signature and admitted the debt, indicating as a pledge the horse, which, as soon as my master saw it, he set his heart on, and determined it should be his if by chance it were sold. The thief said the legal deadline was past, and the horse was placed on sale and auctioned off at five hundred reales to a third party in cahoots with my master to buy it. The horse was worth more than twice what was given for him. But since it was to the seller's advantage to sell him off quickly, he accepted the first bid for his merchandise. One thief recouped a debt that wasn't owed to him, and the other the receipt that he didn't need, and my master kept the horse, which did him more harm than Seius's did to its owners.[17] The thieves immediately departed with their gains and, two days later, after my master had bought new trappings and taken care of the horse's other needs, he turned up riding him on the Plaza de San Francisco, more vain and pompous than a villager dressed for a holiday. He received a thousand congratulations on his good purchase, and the assurance that the horse was worth a hundred fifty ducats if it was worth a cent; and he, turning the horse around and around, played out his tragedy with the above-mentioned square for a stage. While he was performing his caracoles and circuits, two men of good build land even better attire arrived, one of whom said: "My God, that's my horse Ironhoof, which was stolen from me in Antequera a few days ago!" All the men with him, four servants, said it was true: it was Ironhoof, the horse that had been stolen. My master was dumbfounded, the owner lodged a complaint, proof was brought forward, and the owner's evidence was so solid that judgment was given in his favor and the horse was taken from my master. People learned of the dodge and the craftiness of the thieves, who at the hands, and by the intervention, of the law itself had sold what they had stolen; almost everyone was glad that my master's covetousness had made his sack burst.

But this wasn't the end of his misfortunes; that night, when the chief magistrate himself went out to make the rounds, having received word that thieves were roaming around the San Julián neighborhood, as he and his men passed a crossroads they saw a man running by; at once the magistrate, seizing me by the collar and egging me on, said: "Get the thief,

17. In ancient Rome, Cnaeus Seius's horse brought disaster on a number of successive owners.

ladrón, al ladrón!" Yo, a quien ya tenían cansado las maldades de mi amo, por cumplir lo que el señor asistente me mandaba sin discrepar en nada, arremetí con mi propio amo, y sin que pudiese valerse, di con él en el suelo; y si no me le quitaran, yo hiciera a más de a cuatro vengados; quitáronme con mucha pesadumbre de entrambos. Quisieran los corchetes castigarme, y aun matarme a palos, y lo hicieran si el asistente no les dijera: "No le toque nadie, que el perro hizo lo que yo le mandé".

»Entendióse la malicia, y yo, sin despedirme de nadie, por un agujero de la muralla salí al campo, y antes que amaneciese me puse en Mairena, que es un lugar que está cuatro leguas de Sevilla. Quiso mi buena suerte que hallé allí una compañía de soldados que, según oí decir, se iban a embarcar a Cartagena. Estaban en ella cuatro rufianes de los amigos de mi amo, y el atambor era uno que había sido corchete y gran chocarrero, como lo suelen ser los más atambores. Conociéronme todos y todos me hablaron; y así, me preguntaban por mi amo como si les hubiera de responder; pero el que más afición me mostró fue el atambor, y así, determiné de acomodarme con él, si él quisiese, y seguir aquella jornada, aunque me llevase a Italia o a Flandes; porque me parece a mí, y aun a ti te debe parecer lo mismo, que, puesto que dice el refrán "quien necio es en su villa, necio es en Castilla", el andar tierras y comunicar con diversas gentes hace a los hombres discretos.»

Cipión.—Es eso tan verdad, que me acuerdo haber oído decir a un amo que tuve de bonísimo ingenio que al famoso griego llamado Ulises le dieron renombre de prudente por sólo haber andado muchas tierras y comunicado con diversas gentes y varias naciones; y así, alabo la intención que tuviste de irte donde te llevasen.

Berganza.—«Es, pues, el caso que el atambor, por tener con qué mostrar más sus chacorrerías, comenzó a enseñarme a bailar al son del atambor y a hacer otras monerías, tan ajenas de poder aprenderlas otro perro que no fuera yo como las oirás cuando te las diga.

»Por acabarse el distrito de la comisión, se marchaba poco a poco; no había comisario que nos limitase; el capitán era mozo, pero muy buen caballero y gran cristiano; el alférez no hacía muchos meses que había dejado la Corte y el tinelo; el sargento era matrero y sagaz y grande arriero de compañías, desde donde se levantan hasta el embarcadero. Iba la compañía llena de rufianes churrulleros, los cuales hacían algunas insolencias por los lugares do pasábamos, que redundaban en maldecir a quien no lo merecía. Infelicidad es del buen

Gavilán! Go on, Gavilán my boy, after the thief, after the thief!" I, already fed up with my master's misdeeds, to comply fully with the magistrate's orders attacked my own master; he couldn't help being knocked to the ground, and if they hadn't pulled me off him, I'd have avenged a great number of people; but I was pulled off, to the great sorrow of both parties. The constable's men wanted to punish me, and even cudgel me to death, and they would have if the magistrate hadn't said: "No one touch the dog, because he was following my orders!"

My ill will[18] was recognized and, without saying good-bye to anyone, I ran into the countryside through a hole in the city wall and before dawn was in Mairena, a hamlet four leagues from Seville. As my good luck would have it, I there found a troop of soldiers who, from what I heard, were on their way to take ship at Cartagena. Among them were four thugs who had been my master's friends; the drummer had been one of his assistants, a great joker as most drummers usually are. They all recognized me and talked to me, asking me about my master as if I could reply; but the one who seemed fondest of me was the drummer, so I decided to play up to him, if he wanted, and go on their journey, even if it took me to Italy or Flanders; because it's my opinion, and surely even yours as well, that, even though the proverb says "A fool at home: a fool wherever you roam," traveling and meeting different people makes men wise.

SCIPIO: That's so true that I recall hearing a master of mine, a very clever man, say that the famous Greek called Ulysses was renowned for his prudence merely because he had visited many lands and met different people in various countries; therefore I praise your decision to go wherever they took you.

BERGANZA: Well, the fact is that the drummer, in order to have a wider scope for displaying his clowning, began teaching me to dance to the sound of the drum and to do other tricks, as hard to learn for any dog but me as you'll realize when I describe them to you.

Because we had passed beyond the range of commissary supplies, we were making frequent short marches; there was no quartermaster officer to restrict us. Our captain was young, but a very fine gentleman and good Christian; our lieutenant had left Madrid and his family home only a few months earlier; our sergeant was a smart, wise man, great at marshaling troops from their recruitment to their embarkation. Our troop was full of showoff thugs who committed some offenses in the hamlets we passed through, which led to people cursing those who didn't deserve it. It's an unfortunate concomitant of being a good ruler to the blamed by some of

18. Or: "My master's villainy."

príncipe ser culpado de sus súbditos por la culpa de sus súbditos, a causa que los unos son verdugos de los otros, sin culpa del señor; pues, aunque quiera y lo procure no puede remediar estos daños, porque todas o las más cosas de la guerra traen consigo aspereza, riguridad y desconveniencia.

»En fin, en menos de quince días, con mi buen ingenio y con la diligencia que puso el que había escogido por patrón, supe saltar por el Rey de Francia y a no saltar por la mala tabernera. Enseñóme a hacer corvetas como caballo napolitano y a andar a la redonda como mula de atahona, con otras cosas que, si yo no tuviera cuenta en no adelantarme a mostrarlas, pusiera en duda si era algún demonio en figura de perro el que las hacía. Púsome nombre del "perro sabio", y no habíamos llegado al alojamiento cuando, tocando su atambor, andaba por todo el lugar pregonando que todas las personas que quisiesen venir a ver las maravillosas gracias y habilidades del perro sabio en tal casa o en tal hospital las mostraban, a ocho o a cuatro maravedís, según era el pueblo grande o chico. Con estos encarecimientos no quedaba persona en todo el lugar que no me fuese a ver, y ninguno había que no saliese admirado y contento de haberme visto. Triunfaba mi amo con la mucha ganancia, y sustentaba seis camaradas como unos reyes. La codicia y la envidia despertó en los rufianes voluntad de hurtarme, y andaban buscando ocasión para ello: que esto del ganar de comer holgando tiene muchos aficionados y golosos; por esto hay tantos titereros en España, tantos que muestran retablos, tantos que venden alfileres y coplas, que todo su caudal, aunque le vendiesen todo, no llega a poderse sustentar un día; y, con esto, los unos y los otros no salen de los bodegones y tabernas en todo el año; por do me doy a entender que de otra parte que de la de sus oficios sale la corriente de sus borracheras. Toda esta gente es vagamunda, inútil y sin provecho; esponjas del vino y gorgojos del pan.»

CIPIÓN.—No más, Berganza; no volvamos a lo pasado: sigue, que se va la noche, y no querría que al salir del sol quedásemos a la sombra del silencio.

BERGANZA.—Tenle y escucha.

«Como sea cosa fácil añadir a lo ya inventado, viendo mi amo cuán bien sabía imitar el corcel napolitano, hízome unas cubiertas de guadamací y una silla pequeña, que me acomodó en las espaldas, y sobre ella puso una figura liviana de un hombre con una lancilla de correr sortija, y enseñóme a correr derechamente a una sortija que entre dos palos ponía; y el día que había de correrla pregonaba que aquel día corría sortija el perro sabio y hacía otras nuevas y nunca vis-

your subjects for the deeds of other subjects; because the former are tormented by the latter, and their lord isn't to blame: though he wants to and tries, he can't remedy that harm, since everything or almost everything concerning war brings with it harshness, rigor, and disadvantage.

Finally, in less than two weeks, what with my intelligence and the persistence of the man I had chosen as my boss, I knew how to jump when he said it was "for the king of France" and to hold still when it was "for the bad tavern hostess." He taught me to curvet like a Neapolitan horse and walk in a circle like a grainmill mule, along with other things which, if I hadn't been careful not to be pushy in demonstrating them, might have made it uncertain whether it wasn't some devil in the shape of a dog that was doing them. He dubbed me "the learned dog," and we hadn't reached our quarters when, playing his drum, he would march all around the hamlet we were in announcing that whoever wanted to come and see the wonderful arts and skills of the learned dog could do so in such-and-such a house or hospice, at eight or four maravedis admission, depending on whether the village was big or small. Hearing that spiel, no one in the hamlet failed to come to see me, and no one failed to come out amazed and happy for having done so. My master reveled in his big profits, and supported six buddies in royal fashion. Greed and envy aroused the wish to steal me in the thugs, who kept seeking an opportunity; because the prospect of earning one's bread in idleness is attractive and appealing to many; that's why there are so many puppeteers in Spain, so many people who set up portable stages, so many who sell pins and songsheets, their whole stock, even if they sold it all, being insufficient to feed them for a day; and yet none of these people are out of cookshops and taverns all year long; from which I gather that the source of their drunken jags rises from something other than their professions. All this tribe are vagabonds, useless and unprofitable to others: sponges of wine and weevils of bread.

SCIPIO: Stop, Berganza; let's not retread old ground: continue, because the night is passing, and I wouldn't want us to be left in the darkness of silence when the sun comes up.

BERGANZA: Keep silent yourself, and listen.

Since it's easy to add to what has already been invented, when my master saw how well I could imitate a Neapolitan steed, he made some printed-leather coverings and a little saddle for me, which he adjusted on my back, and on top of that he placed a lightweight figure of a man bearing a miniature lance for tilting at the ring; and he taught me to run directly at a ring he placed between two sticks; and on the day I was to run he announced that that day the learned dog would tilt at the ring and do

tas galanterías, las cuales de mi santiscario, como dicen, las hacía por no sacar mentiroso a mi amo.

»Llegamos, pues, por nuestras jornadas contadas a Montilla, villa del famoso y gran cristiano Marqués de Priego, señor de la casa de Aguilar y de Montilla. Alojaron a mi amo, porque él lo procuró, en un hospital; echó luego el ordinario bando, y, como ya la fama se había adelantado a llevar las nuevas de las habilidades y gracias del perro sabio, en menos de una hora se llenó el patio de gente. Alegróse mi amo viendo que la cosecha iba de guilla, y mostróse aquel día chacorrero en demasía. Lo primero en que comenzaba la fiesta era en los saltos que yo daba por un aro de cedazo, que parecía de cuba: conjurábame por las ordinarias preguntas, y cuando él bajaba una varilla de membrillo que en la mano tenía, era señal del salto; y cuando la tenía alta, de que me estuviese quedo. El primer conjuro deste día (memorable entre todos los de mi vida) fue decirme: "Ea, Gavilán amigo, salta por aquel viejo verde que tú conoces que se escabecha las barbas; y si no quieres, salta por la pompa y el aparato de doña Pimpinela de Plafagonia, que fue compañera de la moza gallega que servía en Valdeastillas. ¿No te cuadra el conjuro, hijo Gavilán? Pues salta por el bachiller Pasillas, que se firma licenciado sin tener grado alguno. ¡Oh, perezoso estás! ¿Por qué no saltas? Pero ya entiendo y alcanzo tus marrullerías: ahora salta por el licor de Esquivias, famoso al par del de Ciudad Real, San Martín y Ribadavia". Bajó la varilla y salté yo, y noté sus malicias y malas entrañas.

»Volvióse luego al pueblo y en voz alta dijo: "No piense vuesa merced, senado valeroso, que es cosa de burla lo que este perro sabe: veinte y cuatro piezas le tengo enseñadas que por la menor dellas volaría un gavilán; quiero decir que por ver la menor se pueden caminar treinta leguas. Sabe bailar la zarabanda y chacona mejor que su inventora misma; bébese una azumbre de vino sin dejar gota; entona un *sol fa mi re* tan bien como un sacristán; todas estas cosas, y otras muchas que me quedan por decir, las irán viendo vuesas mercedes en los días que estuviere aquí la compañía; y por ahora dé otro salto nuestro sabio, y luego entraremos en lo grueso". Con esto suspendió el auditorio, que había llamado senado, y les encendió el deseo de no dejar de ver todo lo que yo sabía.

»Volvióse a mí mi amo y dijo: "Volved, hijo Gavilán, y con gentil agilidad y destreza deshaced los saltos que habéis hecho; pero ha de ser

other new, never-before-seen stunts, which I performed out of my own head, as the saying is, so as not to make a liar of my master.

Well, on our short marches we arrived in Montilla, the town of the famous good Christian the Marquess de Priego, head of the house of Aguilar and Montilla. At his own request, my master was billeted in an overnight hospice; he immediately made his usual proclamation and, since our reputation had preceded us, bringing news of the skills and arts of the learned dog, in less than an hour the courtyard was full of people. My master rejoiced to see that bumper crop, and clowned around to excess that day. The first number on that festive occasion was my jumping through the hoop of a strainer, which looked like a barrel hoop; he gave me the usual commands: when he lowered an osier twig he held in his hand, it was the signal to jump; when he held it in the air, I was to hold still. In his first spiel on that day (which was the most memorable of my life) he said: "All right, friend Gavilán, jump for that boyish old man who, as you know, dyes his beard; if you don't want to, jump for the pomp and finery of Doña Pimpinela of 'Plaphagonia,' who was the companion of the young Galician woman who was a servant in Valdeastillas. Doesn't my patter sit well with you, Gavilán? Then jump for the bachelor of arts Pasillas, who calls himself a graduate but has no degree. Oh, you're lazy! Why don't you jump? But now I understand, and I catch on to your artful dodges: now jump for the wine of Esquivias, as famous as that of Ciudad Real, San Martín, and Ribadavia." He lowered the twig and I jumped, taking note of his malice and evil nature.

Then he turned to the audience and said aloud: "My dear public, don't imagine that this dog's knowledge is a mere trifle: I've taught him twenty-four items[19] for the least of which a sparrow hawk would fly; that is, to see the slightest of them you can travel thirty leagues. He can dance the saraband and chaconne better than the lady who invented them; he can drink a half gallon of wine without leaving a drop; he can sing a *sol fa mi re* as well as a sacristan; all these things, and many more I could still mention, you will be seeing, ladies and gentlemen, during the days our troop remains here; but for now let our learned fellow give another jump, and then we'll get to the main event." Thereby he riveted the attention of the audience, which he had called his public, inflaming their desire to see every last thing I knew how to do.

My master turned back to me and said: "Come again, Gavilán my boy, and with fine agility and dexterity outdo[20] the jumps you've already made;

19. There is probably a word play here on two meanings of *pieza:* a piece, and a hunter's quarry or "bag." 20. Possibly: "reverse."

a devoción de la famosa hechicera que dicen que hubo en este lugar". Apenas hubo dicho esto, cuando alzó la voz la hospitalera, que era una vieja, al parecer, de más de sesenta años, diciendo: "¡Bellaco, charlatán, embaidor y hijo de puta, aquí no hay hechicera alguna! Si lo decís por la Camacha, ya ella pagó su pecado, y está donde Dios se sabe; si lo decís por mí, chacorrero, ni yo soy ni he sido hechicera en mi vida; y si he tenido fama de haberlo sido, merced a los testigos falsos, y a la ley del encaje, y al juez arrojadizo y mal informado, ya sabe todo el mundo la vida que hago en penitencia, no de los hechizos que no hice, sino de otros muchos pecados: otros que como pecadora he cometido. Así que, socarrón tamborilero, salid del hospital; si no, por vida de mi santiguada que os haga salir más que de paso". Y, con esto, comenzó a dar tantos gritos y a decir tantas y tan atropelladas injurias a mi amo, que le puso en confusión y sobresalto; finalmente, no dejó que pasase adelante la fiesta en ningún modo. No le pesó a mi amo del alboroto, porque se quedó con los dineros y aplazó para otro día y en otro hospital lo que en aquél había faltado. Fuese la gente maldiciendo a la vieja, añadiendo al nombre de hechicera el de bruja, y el de barbuda sobre vieja. Con todo esto, nos quedamos en el hospital aquella noche; y, encontrándome la vieja en el corral solo, me dijo: "¿Eres tú, hijo Montiel? ¿Eres tú, por ventura, hijo?" Alcé la cabeza y miréla muy de espacio; lo cual visto por ella, con lágrimas en los ojos se vino a mí y me echó los brazos al cuello, y si la dejara, me besara en la boca; peru tuve asco y no lo consentí.»

CIPIÓN.—Bien hiciste, porque no es regalo, sino tormento, el besar ni dejar besarse de una vieja.

BERGANZA.—Esto que ahora te quiero contar te lo había de haber dicho al principio de mi cuento, y así escusáramos la admiración que nos causó el vernos con habla.

«Porque has de saber que la vieja me dijo: "Hijo Montiel, vente tras mí y sabrás mi aposento, y procura que esta noche nos veamos a solas en él, que yo dejaré abierta la puerta; y sabe que tengo muchas cosas que decirte de tu vida y para tu provecho". Bajé yo la cabeza en señal de obedecerla, por lo cual ella se acabó de enterar en que yo era el perro Montiel que buscaba, según después me lo dijo. Quedé atónito y confuso, esperando la noche, por ver en lo que paraba aquel misterio, o prodigio, de haberme hablado la vieja; y, como había oído llamarla de hechicera, esperaba de su vista y habla grandes cosas. Llegóse, en fin, el punto de verme con ella en su aposento, que era escuro, estrecho y bajo, y solamente claro con la débil luz de un candil de barro que en él estaba; atizóle la vieja, y sentóse sobre una arquilla,

but this time dedicate them to the famous sorceress said to have lived in this hamlet." The moment he said that, the voice of the hospice matron, an old woman who seemed to be over sixty, was raised, saying: "Villain, charlatan, faker, and whoreson, there's no sorceress here! If you mean La Camacha, she has already paid for her sin and is where God knows; if you mean me, buffoon, I am not and have never been a sorceress in my life; and if people have said I was, thanks to false witnesses, and to a judge making up the law in his head—an impetuous, ill-informed judge—by now the whole world knows the life of penance that I lead, not for sorcery, which I never did, but for many other sins, others that I committed as a sinner. And so, sly drummer boy, leave this hospice; if not, by my blessed soul I'll make you leave, and not at a walking pace!" Thereupon she began to utter such cries and to heap so many confused insults on my master that she confounded and alarmed him; in short, she absolutely refused to let the show go on. My master didn't mind the uproar, because he kept the money and postponed the rest of the performance until another day, at another hospice. The people left, cursing the old woman, and calling her witch on top of sorceress, and bearded lady on top of old lady. Nevertheless, we remained in the hospice that night; finding me alone in the yard, the old woman said: "Is it you, young Montiel? Is it by chance you, son?" I raised my head and looked at her long and hard; noticing this, she came up to me with tears in her eyes and threw her arms around my neck; if I had let her, she'd have kissed me on the mouth; but I was disgusted, and didn't allow it.

SCIPIO: You were right, because it's not a treat but a torture to kiss or be kissed by an old woman.

BERGANZA: What I now wish to tell you, I should have mentioned at the beginning of my story; that way we would have avoided being amazed at finding ourselves able to speak.

Because I'll have you know that the old woman said: "Young Montiel, come with me and you'll learn which is my room. Then try to meet me there alone tonight, for I'll leave the door unlocked; know that I have many things to tell you about your life, to your advantage." I lowered my head as a sign that I'd obey her, whereupon she was firmly convinced that I was the dog Montiel she had been looking for, as she told me later. I remained astonished and confused, waiting for nightfall, to see what would come of that mystery, or marvel, of that old woman's speaking to me; and, since I had heard her called a sorceress, I expected great things from seeing and hearing her. Finally the time for me to join her in her room arrived; it was a dark, narrow, low room, illuminated only by the weak light of a clay lamp that hung there; the old woman stirred up its flame and sat

y llegóme junto a sí, y, sin hablar palabra, me volvió a abrazar, y yo volví a tener cuenta con que no me besase. Lo primero que me dijo fue:

»"Bien esperaba yo en el cielo que, antes que estos mis ojos se cerrasen con el último sueño, te había de ver, hijo mío; y, ya que te he visto, venga la muerte y lléveme desta cansada vida. Has de saber, hijo, que en esta villa vivió la más famosa hechicera que hubo en el mundo, a quien llamaron la Camacha de Montilla; fue tan única en su oficio, que las Eritos, las Circes, las Medeas, de quien he oído decir que están las historias llenas, no la igualaron. Ella congelaba las nubes cuando quería, cubriendo con ellas la faz del sol, y cuando se le antojaba, volvía sereno el más turbado cielo; traía los hombres en un instante de lejas tierras, remediaba maravillosamente las doncellas que habían tenido algún descuido en guardar su entereza, cubría a las viudas de modo que con honestidad fuesen deshonestas, descasaba las casadas y casaba las que ella quería. Por diciembre tenía rosas frescas en su jardín y por enero segaba trigo. Esto de hacer nacer berros en una artesa era lo menos que ella hacía, ni el hacer ver en un espejo, o en la uña de una criatura, los vivos o los muertos que le pedían que mostrase. Tuvo fama que convertía los hombres en animales, y que se había servido de un sacristán seis años, en forma de asno, real y verdaderamente, lo que yo nunca he podido alcanzar cómo se haga, porque lo que se dice de aquellas antiguas magas, que convertían los hombres en bestias, dicen los que más saben que no era otra cosa sino que ellas, con su mucha hermosura y con sus halagos, atraían los hombres de manera a que las quisiesen bien, y los sujetaban de suerte, sirviéndose dellos en todo cuanto querían, que parecían bestias. Pero en ti, hijo mío, la experiencia me muestra lo contrario: que sé que eres persona racional y te veo en semejanza de perro, si ya no es que esto se hace con aquella ciencia que llaman tropelía, que hace parecer una cosa por otra. Sea lo que fuere, lo que me pesa es que yo ni tu madre, que fuimos discípulas de la buena Camacha, nunca llegamos a saber tanto como ella; y no por falta de ingenio, ni de habilidad, ni de ánimo, que antes nos sobraba que faltaba, sino por sobra de su malicia, que nunca quiso enseñarnos las cosas mayores, porque las reservaba para ella.

»"Tu madre, hijo, se llamó la Montiela, que después de la Camacha fue famosa; yo me llamo la Cañizares, si ya no tan sabia como las dos, a lo menos de tan buenos deseos como cualquiera dellas. Verdad es que el ánimo que tu madre tenía de hacer y entrar en un cerco y encerrarse en él con una legión de demonios, no le hacía ventaja la

down on a little chest; drawing me close but not speaking a word, she embraced me again, and once more I took care that she shouldn't kiss me. The first thing she said to me was:

"I kept hoping to heaven that, before these eyes of mine closed in their final sleep, I might see you, son; and now that I have, let death come and take me from this weary life! You should know, son, that in this town there lived the most famous sorceress of all time, called La Camacha of Montilla; she was so exceptional in her line that the Erichthos, Circes, and Medeas, whom I've heard that history books are full of, never equaled her. She could gather the clouds together whenever she wished, making them cover the face of the sun, and whenever it took her fancy she'd make the most troubled sky clear again; in an instant she brought men from distant lands, and performed marvelous cures on young women who had been a little careless guarding their virginity; she'd look after widows so that they could be dishonorable while seeming honorable, she'd unmarry married women and marry off any that she wished. In December she'd have fresh roses in her garden, and she'd reap wheat in January. The art of making watercress grow from a trough was the least of her accomplishments; likewise, making people see in a mirror, or reflected from a baby's fingernail, any living or dead person they asked her to show them. She was reputed to be able to change people into animals, and to have made use of a sacristan for six years in the shape of a donkey, really and truly, something I've never been able to find the way of, because the most learned people say that the ancient sorceresses' reputation for changing men into beasts merely meant that with their great beauty and allurements they attracted men and made them love them, and subjected them in such a way that they could use them however they liked, and they thus resembled animals. But in your case, son, experience shows me the opposite: I know you're a human being endowed with reason and I find you in the semblance of a dog, unless this has been done by that art known as sleight of hand, which makes one thing look like another. Whatever it is, what grieves me is that neither I nor your mother, both pupils of good Camacha, never came to know as much as she did; and not from a lack of brains, skill, or courage, which we had too much of rather than too little, but through her exceeding ill will, for she always refused to teach us the greater things, reserving them for herself.

"Your mother, my boy, was called La Montiela, and she was second in fame to La Camacha; my name is La Cañizares, and if I'm not as learned as those two, at least my wishes are as strong as those of either of them. It's true that your mother's courage in drawing a circle and entering it, enclosing herself along with a legion of devils, couldn't be matched by La

misma Camacha. Yo fui siempre algo medrosilla; con conjurar media legión me contentaba, pero, con paz sea dicho de entrambas, en esto de conficionar las unturas con que las brujas nos untamos, a ninguna de las dos diera ventaja, ni la daré a cuantas hoy siguen y guardan nuestras reglas. Que has de saber, hijo, que como yo he visto y veo que la vida, que corre sobre las ligeras alas del tiempo, se acaba, he querido dejar todos los vicios de la hechicería, en que estaba engolfada muchos años había, y sólo me he quedado con la curiosidad de ser bruja, que es un vicio dificultosísimo de dejar. Tu madre hizo lo mismo: de muchos vicios se apartó, muchas buenas obras hizo en esta vida, pero al fin murió bruja; y no murió de enfermedad alguna, sino de dolor de que supo que la Camacha, su maestra, de envidia que la tuvo porque se le iba subiendo a las barbas en saber tanto como ella (o por otra pendenzuela de celos, que nunca pude averiguar), estando tu madre preñada y llegándose la hora del parto, fue su comadre la Camacha, la cual recibió en sus manos lo que tu madre parió, y mostróle que había parido dos perritos; y, así como los vio, dijo: '¡Aquí hay maldad, aquí hay bellaquería!' 'Pero, hermana Montiela, tu amiga soy; yo encubriré este parto, y atiende tú a estar sana, y haz cuenta que esta tu desgracia queda sepultada en el mismo silencio; no te dé pena alguna este suceso, que ya sabes tú que puedo yo saber que si no es con Rodríguez, el ganapán tu amigo, días ha que no tratas con otro; así que, este perruno parto de otra parte viene y algún misterio contiene.' Admiradas quedamos tu madre y yo, que me hallé presente a todo, del estraño suceso. La Camacha se fue y se llevó los cachorros; yo me quedé con tu madre para asistir a su regalo, la cual no podía creer lo que le había sucedido.

»"Llegóse el fin de la Camacha, y, estando en la última hora de su vida, llamó a tu madre y le dijo como ella había convertido a sus hijos en perros por cierto enojo que con ella tuvo; pero que no tuviese pena, que ellos volverían a su ser cuando menos lo pensasen; mas que no podía ser primero que ellos por sus mismos ojos viesen lo siguiente:

> Volverán en su forma verdadera
> cuando vieren con presta diligencia
> derribar los soberbios levantados,
> y alzar a los humildes abatidos,
> con poderosa mano para hacello.

»"Esto dijo la Camacha a tu madre al tiempo de su muerte, como ya te he dicho. Tomólo tu madre por escrito y de memoria, y yo lo fijé en la mía para si sucediese tiempo de poderlo decir a alguno de

Camacha herself. I was always a bit timorous; I was contented to conjure up half a legion, but, may they both rest in peace, in the matter of preparing those ointments we witches smear ourselves with, I believe I outshone both of them, as well as all those who follow and keep our rules today. For I'll have you know, son, that having seen and seeing that life, which passes on the light wings of time, is drawing to a close, I have decided to leave behind all the vices of sorcery in which I was immersed many years ago, remaining with only the desire to be a witch, a vice that's very hard to drop. Your mother did the same: she gave up many vices and performed many good works in this life, but at the end she died a witch; and she didn't die of any illness, but of her sorrow at learning what her teacher La Camacha had done. Envying your mother because she was becoming her rival in the extent of her knowledge (or because of some other jealous quarrel—I could never find out), La Camacha, when your mother was pregnant and ready to give birth, was her midwife and received your mother's offspring in her hands, then showed her she had given birth to two puppies. As soon as your mother saw them, she said: 'There's evil here, there's mischief here!' 'But, sister Montiela, I'm your friend; I shall keep this birth secret; you attend to getting well and consider this misfortune of yours buried in total silence; let this event cause you no grief, since you know that I know very well that, except for Rodríguez, your friend the porter, you haven't had any truck with another man for ages; so that this dog-birth comes from elsewhere and conceals some mystery.' Your mother and I (because I was present that whole time) were both astonished at the odd event. La Camacha left, taking away the puppies; I stayed with your mother to see to her comforts, and she couldn't believe what had happened to her.

"La Camacha's life ended, and in her last hour she summoned your mother and told her she had changed her sons into dogs because of a certain grudge against her; but she was not to worry, because they would regain their true form when they least expected it; but this couldn't happen before they had seen the following with their own eyes:

> They will return to their true shape
> when they see, with swift diligence,
> the lofty proud laid low,
> and the downtrodden humble exalted,
> by a hand with the power to do this.

"That's what La Camacha told your mother on her deathbed, as I said. Your mother took it down in writing and committed it to memory, and I fixed it in mine in case the time should ever come when I could tell it to

vosotros; y, para poder conoceros, a todos los perros que veo de tu color los llamo con el nombre de tu madre, no por pensar que los perros han de saber el nombre, sino por ver si respondían a ser llamados tan diferentemente como se llaman los otros perros. Y esta tarde, como te vi hacer tantas cosas y que te llaman el *perro sabio,* y también como alzaste la cabeza a mirarme cuando te llamé en el corral, he creído que tú eres hijo de la Montiela, a quien con grandísimo gusto doy noticia de tus sucesos y del modo con que has de cobrar tu forma primera; el cual modo quisiera yo que fuera tan fácil como el que se dice de Apuleyo en *El asno de oro,* que consistía en sólo comer una rosa. Pero éste tuyo va fundado en acciones ajenas y no en tu diligencia. Lo que has de hacer, hijo, es encomendarte a Dios allá en tu corazón, y espera que éstas, que no quiero llamarlas profecías, sino adivinanzas, han de suceder presto y prósperamente; que, pues la buena de la Camacha las dijo, sucederán sin duda alguna, y tú y tu hermano, si es vivo, os veréis como deseáis.

»"De lo que a mí me pesa es que estoy tan cerca de mi acabamiento, que no tendré lugar de verlo. Muchas veces he querido preguntar a mi cabrón qué fin tendrá vuestro suceso, pero no me he atrevido, porque nunca a lo que le preguntamos responde a derechas, sino con razones torcidas y de muchos sentidos. Así que, a este nuestro amo y señor no hay que preguntarle nada, porque con una verdad mezcla mil mentiras; y, a lo que yo he colegido de sus respuestas, él no sabe nada de lo por venir ciertamente, sino por conjeturas. Con todo esto, nos trae tan engañadas a las que somos brujas, que, con hacernos mil burlas, no le podemos dejar. Vamos a verle muy lejos de aquí, a un gran campo, donde nos juntamos infinidad de gente, brujos y brujas, y allí nos da de comer desabridamente, y pasan otras cosas que en verdad y en Dios y en mi ánima que no me atrevo a contarlas, según son sucias y asquerosas, y no quiero ofender tus castas orejas. Hay opinión que no vamos a estos convites sino con la fantasía, en la cual nos representa el demonio las imágenes de todas aquellas cosas que después contamos que nos han sucedido. Otros dicen que no, sino que verdaderamente vamos en cuerpo y en ánima; y entrambas opiniones tengo para mí que son verdaderas, puesto que nosotras no sabemos cuándo vamos de una o de otra manera, porque todo lo que nos pasa en la fantasía es tan intensamente, que no hay diferenciarlo de cuando vamos real y verdaderamente. Algunas experiencias desto han hecho los señores inquisidores con algunas de nosotras que han tenido presas, y pienso que han hallado ser verdad lo que digo.

»"Quisiera yo, hijo, apartarme deste pecado, y para ello he hecho mis diligencias: heme acogido a ser hospitalera; curo a los pobres, y algunos

either of you; and, to be able to recognize you, I call all the dogs of your color I see, naming your mother, not because I think the dogs will know the name, but to see if they respond to being called so differently from the way other dogs are. And this afternoon, seeing you do so many tricks and hearing you called the learned dog, and also seeing how you raised your head to look at me when I called to you in the yard, I was sure you are a son of La Montiela; and with the greatest pleasure I now inform you of your story and what you must do to regain your original shape; I wish the task were as easy as the one reported of Apuleius in *The Golden Ass*, which consisted merely of eating a rose. But this task of yours depends on the actions of others, not on your own industry. What you must do, son, is to commend yourself to God down deep in your heart and have hopes that these—I won't call them prophecies, but divinations—will come true quickly and beneficially; for, since the good Camacha pronounced them, they will undoubtedly come true, and you and your brother, if he's alive, will meet, as you both desire.

"What grieves me is that I'm so close to my end that I won't have the opportunity to see that. I've often wanted to ask my he-goat how your story will turn out, but I've never dared to, because he never answers our questions directly, but with twisted, very ambivalent words. So that it doesn't pay to ask that lord and master of ours anything, because he mingles one truth with a thousand lies; and from what I've gathered from his replies, he knows nothing of the future for a certainty, but only by conjecture. All the same, he has us witches so deceived that, even if he plays a thousand tricks on us, we can't abandon him. We go to see him very far from here, on a big field where an infinity of people assemble, warlocks and witches; there he gives us bad-tasting food to eat, and other things go on which, by truth, God, and my soul, I don't dare relate, they're so filthy and disgusting, and I don't want to offend your chaste ears. Some people think we travel to those feasts only in our imagination, in which the devil shows us the images of all those things we later say really befell us. Others disagree, saying that we truly go in body and spirit; personally, I think both opinions are correct, although we ourselves don't know when we're going in one way or the other, because everything that occurs in our imagination does so so intensely that we can't tell it apart from a real and true journey. The lord inquisitors have heard some things of the sort from some of us whom they held prisoner, and I think they've found what I said to be true.

"Son, I'd like to put aside this sin, and I've made efforts in that direction: I've resorted to hospice keeping; I tend the poor, and some who

se mueren que me dan a mí la vida con lo que me mandan o con lo que se les queda entre los remiendos, por el cuidado que yo tengo de espulgarlos los vestidos. Rezo poco y en público, murmuro mucho y en secreto. Vame mejor con ser hipócrita que con ser pecadora declarada: las apariencias de mis buenas obras presentes van borrando en la memoria de los que me conocen las malas obras pasadas. En efeto, la santidad fingida no hace daño a ningún tercero, sino al que la usa. Mira, hijo Montiel, este consejo te doy: que seas bueno en todo cuanto pudieres; y si has de ser malo, procura no parecerlo en todo cuanto pudieres. Bruja soy, no te lo niego; bruja y hechicera fue tu madre, que tampoco te lo pueda negar; pero las buenas apariencias de las dos podían acreditarnos en todo el mundo. Tres días antes que muriese, habíamos estado las dos en un valle de los Montes Perineos en una gran gira, y, con todo eso, cuando murió fue con tal sosiego y reposo, que si no fueron algunos visajes que hizo un cuarto de hora antes que rindiese el alma, no parecía sino que estaba en aquélla como en un tálamo de flores. Llevaba atravesados en el corazón sus dos hijos, y nunca quiso, aun en el artículo de la muerte, perdonar a la Camacha: tal era ella de entera y firme en sus cosas. Yo le cerré los ojos y fui con ella hasta la sepultura; allí la dejé para no verla más, aunque no tengo perdida la esperanza de verla antes que me muera, porque se ha dicho por el lugar que la han visto algunas personas andar por los cimenterios y encrucijadas en diferentes figuras, y quizá alguna vez la toparé yo, y le preguntaré si manda que haga alguna cosa en descargo de su conciencia".

»Cada cosa destas que la vieja me decía en alabanza de la que decía ser mi madre, era una lanzada que me atravesaba el corazón, y quisiera arremeter a ella y hacerla pedazos entre los dientes; y si lo dejé de hacer, fue porque no le tomase la muerte en tan mal estado. Finalmente, me dijo que aquella noche pensaba untarse para ir a uno de sus usados convites, y que cuando allá estuviese pensaba preguntar a su dueño algo de lo que estaba por sucederme. Quisiérale yo preguntar qué unturas eran aquellas que decía, y parece que me leyó el deseo, pues respondió a mi intención como si se lo hubiera preguntado, pues dijo:

»"Este ungüento con que las brujas nos untamos es compuesto de jugos de yerbas en todo estremo fríos, y no es, como dice el vulgo, hecho con la sangre de los niños que ahogamos. Aquí pudieras también preguntarme qué gusto o provecho saca el demonio de hacernos matar las criaturas tiernas, pues sabe que, estando bautizadas, como inocentes y sin pecado, se van al cielo, y él recibe pena particular con cada alma cristiana que se le escapa; a lo que no te sabré responder otra cosa sino lo que dice el refrán: 'que tal hay que se quiebra dos ojos porque su ene-

die give me life with what they bequeath to me or what they leave behind in their patched clothes, because I take good care to rummage through them. My few prayers I say in public, my many detractions I utter privately. I do better by being a hypocrite than by being a declared sinner: the outward show of my present good works erase my past evil deeds from the memories of those who know me. Indeed, feigned piety harms no third party, only the one who practices it. Look, young Montiel, I give you this advice: be good in every way you can, and if you must be bad, try to conceal it as much as you can. I'm a witch, I don't deny it; your mother was a witch and a sorceress, which I can't deny, either; but our good outsides were able to raise our repute with everyone. Three days before she died, the two of us had been in a valley of the Pyrenees at a large sabbath, but all the same, when she died it was with such calm and repose that, except for a few grimaces she made fifteen minutes before giving up the ghost, she appeared at that hour to be lying on a bed of roses. The fate of her two sons had transfixed her heart, and not even on the point of death would she ever forgive La Camacha, she was so firm and solid in her doings. I closed her eyes and followed her to her grave; there I left her, never to see her again, though I haven't lost hopes of seeing her before I die, because it's been said around town that some people have seen her walking through cemeteries and past crossroads in various guises, and perhaps I, too, will run into her sometime and ask her whether she wants anything done to unburden her conscience."

Each of those things the old woman told me in praise of the woman she said was my mother was a spear thrust piercing my heart, and I wanted to attack her and tear her to pieces with my teeth; and if I refrained, it was so that death wouldn't take her in such an evil state. Finally, she told me that she intended to smear herself that night to go to one of her usual feasts, and that when she was there she intended to ask her master something about my future. I wanted to ask her what those ointments were that she spoke of, and she seemed to have read my mind, because she replied to my thoughts as if I had uttered them, saying:

"This ointment with which we witches smear ourselves is made up of extremely cold juices of herbs, and not, as vulgar people say, made with the blood of children we throttle. You might also now ask me what pleasure or profit the devil derives from making us kill tender babes, since he knows that, being baptized, innocent, and without sin, they go to heaven, and he feels a special pain whenever any Christian soul escapes him. All I could answer is what the proverb says: 'Some people put out both their eyes to make their enemy put out one.' He may also enjoy the

migo se quiebre uno'; y por la pesadumbre que da a sus padres matándoles les hijos, que es la mayor que se puede imaginar. Y lo que más le importa es hacer que nosotras cometamos a cada paso tan cruel y perverso pecado; y todo esto lo permite Dios por nuestros pecados, que sin su permisión yo he visto por experiencia que no puede ofender el diablo a uno hormiga; y es tan verdad esto que, rogándole yo una vez que destruyese una viña de un mi enemigo, me respondió que ni aun tocar a una hoja della no podía, porque Dios no quería; por lo cual podrás venir a entender, cuando seas hombre, que todas las desgracias que vienen a las gentes, a los reinos, a las ciudades y a los pueblos: las muertes repentinas, los naufragios, las caídas, en fin, todos los males que llaman de daño, vienen de la mano del Altísimo y de su voluntad permitente; y los daños y males que llaman de culpa vienen y se causan por nosotros mismos. Dios es impecable, de do se infiere que nosotros somos autores del pecado, formándole en la intención, en la palabra y en la obra; todo permitiéndolo Dios, por nuestros pecados, como ya he dicho.

»"Dirás tú ahora, hijo, si es que acaso me entiendes, que quién me hizo a mí teóloga, y aun quizá dirás entre ti: '¡Cuerpo de tal con la puta vieja! ¿Por qué no deja de ser bruja, pues sabe tanto, y se vuelve a Dios, pues sabe que está más prompto a perdonar pecados que a permitirlos?' A esto te respondo, como si me lo preguntaras, que la costumbre del vicio se vuelve en naturaleza; y éste de ser brujas se convierte en sangre y carne, y en medio de su ardor, que es mucho, trae un frío que pone en el alma, tal que la resfría y entorpece aun en la fe, de donde nace un olvido de sí misma, y ni se acuerda de los temores con que Dios la amenaza ni de la gloria con que la convida; y, en efeto, como es pecado de carne y de deleites, es fuerza que amortigüe todos los sentidos, y los embelese y absorte, sin dejarlos usar sus oficios como deben; y así, quedando el alma inútil, floja y desmazalada, no puede levantar la consideración siquiera a tener algún buen pensamiento; y así, dejándose estar sumida en la profunda sima de su miseria, no quiere alzar la mano a la de Dios, que se la está dando, por sola su misericordia, para que se levante. Yo tengo una destas almas que te he pintado: todo lo veo y todo lo entiendo, y como el deleite me tiene echados grillos a la voluntad, siempre he sido y seré mala.

»"Pero dejemos esto y volvamos a lo de las unturas; y digo que son tan frías, que nos privan de todos los sentidos en untándonos con ellas, y quedamos tendidas y desnudas en el suelo, y entonces dicen que en la fantasía pasamos todo aquello que nos parece pasar verdaderamente. Otras veces, acabadas de untar, a nuestro parecer, mudamos forma, y convertidas en gallos, lechuzas o cuervos, vamos al lugar

grief he causes the parents by killing their children, the greatest grief imaginable. But what he most desires is for us to commit such a cruel, perverse sin frequently. And God allows this to happen because of our sins, for I've seen by experience that without God's permission the devil can't hurt an ant. This is so true that, when I once asked him to destroy a vineyard belonging to an enemy of mine, he replied that he couldn't touch even a leaf of it, because God didn't want him to; thereby you may come to understand, when you're a man, that every misfortune that befalls nations, realms, cities, and towns—sudden death, shipwrecks, landslides; in short, all the ills called acts of God—come from the hand of the Highest and from his will which permits this; whereas the harm and evil called crimes come from, and are caused by, us. God cannot sin, from which it can be deduced that we are the authors of sin, forming it in our thoughts, words, and deeds, God permitting all this because of our sins, as I said.

"At this point, son, you'll ask, if perhaps you understand me, who made me a theologian, and you may even wonder to yourself: 'Damn this old whore! Why doesn't she give up being a witch if she knows so much, and turn back to God, since she knows he's readier to forgive sins than to permit them?' To which I reply, as if you had asked, that the habit of vice becomes second nature, and this vice of being a witch becomes our flesh and blood; in the midst of its very great heat it brings such a coldness to the soul that it chills it and makes it sluggish even in its faith; this gives rise to a self-forgetfulness, and the soul fails to recall the terrors with which God threatens it, and the glory with which he allures it; in fact, since this is a sin of the flesh and a sin of delectation, it necessarily deadens all the senses, casting a spell on them and suspending their activity, so that they can't function as they should; thus, the soul remaining useless, flaccid, and decomposed, it can't even raise its sights to harboring some good thought, and, letting itself sink into the deep abyss of its wretchedness, it refuses to raise its hand to God's, who is holding out *his,* out of sheer mercy, to raise it up. I have one of those souls I've described: I see and understand everything, but since carnal pleasure has fettered my will, I always have been and always will be bad.

"But let's drop this subject and return to that of the ointments; as I said, they're so cold that they bereave us of all our senses when we smear them on, and we remain stretched out naked on the floor; and then they say we experience in our imagination all that seems to be really happening to us. Other times, after putting on the ointment, we feel that we're changing shape and that, turned into roosters, owls, or ravens, we go to the place

donde nuestro dueño nos espera, y allí cobramos nuestra primera forma y gozamos de los deleites que te dejo de decir, por ser tales, que la memoria se escandaliza en acordarse dellos, y así, la lengua huye de contarlos; y, con todo esto, soy bruja, y cubro con la capa de la hipocresía todas mis muchas faltas. Verdad es que si algunos me estiman y honrad por buena, no faltan muchos que me dicen, no dos dedos del oído, el nombre de las fiestas, que es el que les imprimió la furia de un juez colérico que en los tiempos pasados tuvo que ver conmigo y con tu madre, depositando su ira en las manos de un verdugo que, por no estar sobornado, usó de toda su plena potestad y rigor con nuestras espaldas. Pero esto ya pasó, y todas las cosas se pasan; las memorias se acaban, las vidas no vuelven, las lenguas se cansan, los sucesos nuevos hacen olvidar los pasados. Hospitalera soy, buenas muestras doy de mi proceder, buenos ratos me dan mis unturas, no soy tan vieja que no pueda vivir un año, puesto que tengo setenta y cinco; y, ya que no pueda ayunar, por la edad, ni rezar, por los váguidos, ni andar romerías, por la flaqueza de mis piernas, ni dar limosna, porque soy pobre, ni pensar en bien, porque soy amiga de murmurar, y para haberlo de hacer es forzoso pensarlo primero, así que siempre mis pensamientos han de ser malos, con todo esto, sé que Dios es bueno y misericordioso y que Él sabe lo que ha de ser de mí, y basta; y quédese aquí esta plática, que verdaderamente me entristece. Ven, hijo, y verásme untar, que todos los duelos con pan son buenos, el buen día, meterle en casa, pues mientras se ríe no se llora; quiero decir que, aunque los gustos que nos da el demonio son aparentes y falsos, todavía nos parecen gustos, y el deleite mucho mayor es imaginado que gozado, aunque en los verdaderos gustos debe de ser al contrario".

»Levantóse, en diciendo esta larga arenga, y, tomando el candil, se entró en otro aposentillo más estrecho; seguíla, combatido de mil varios pensamientos y admirado de lo que había oído y de lo que esperaba ver. Colgó la Cañizares el candil de la pared y con mucha priesa se desnudó hasta la camisa; y, sacando de un rincón una olla vidriada, metió en ella la mano, y, murmurando entre dientes, se untó desde los pies a la cabeza, que tenía sin toca. Antes que se acabase de untar me dijo que, ora se quedase su cuerpo en aquel aposento sin sentido, ora desapareciese dél, que no me espantase, ni dejase de aguardar allí hasta la mañana, porque sabría las nuevas de lo que me quedaba por pasar hasta ser hombre. Díjele bajando la cabeza que sí haría, y con esto acabó su untura y se tendió en el suelo como muerta. Llegué mi boca a la suya y vi que no respiraba poco ni mucho.»

where our master is awaiting us, and there we regain our original shape and enjoy the delights which I shall omit telling you about, because they're such that our memory is shocked at recalling them, and so the tongue avoids relating them. Despite all this, I'm a witch, and I cover all my many faults with the cloak of hypocrisy. It's true that, if some people esteem me and honor me as a good woman, there are many who tell me, and right in my ear, exactly what they think of me. This animus was implanted in them by the fury of a choleric judge who had dealings with me and your mother long ago, depositing his wrath in the hands of a torturer who, because no one paid him a bribe, used all his plenary powers and rigor on our backs. But that was in the past, and all things pass; memories give out, lives don't return, tongues grow weary, new events make people forget past ones. I'm a hospice matron, I show evidence of good management, my ointments provide me with good times, I'm not so old that I can't live another year, though I'm seventy-five; and though I can no longer fast because of my age, or pray because of my dizzy spells, or go on pilgrimages because of the weakness in my legs, or give alms because of my poverty, or have good thoughts because of my fondness for backbiting (and in order to do good one must first think good thoughts, so that my thoughts must always be evil)—nevertheless, I know that God is good and merciful, and that he knows what's to become of me, and that's enough. Let this conversation end here, because truly it saddens me. Come, son, and you'll see me smear myself, because 'with bread, all sorrows are bearable' and 'make hay while the sun shines,' because 'while you're laughing, you're not crying'; I mean: even though the pleasures the devil gives us are illusory and false, still they seem like pleasures to us, and pleasure is much greater imagined than enjoyed, though with true pleasures the opposite must be the case."

Finishing this long speech, she stood up, took the lamp, and entered another little room that was even more cramped; I followed her, assailed by a thousand different thoughts and amazed by what I had heard and what I expected to see. La Cañizares hung up the lamp on the wall and very quickly stripped to her chemise; taking a glazed earthenware pot from a corner, she put her hand into it and, muttering between her teeth, smeared herself from her bare head to her feet. Before she finished, she told me that, whether her body remained senseless in that room or vanished from it, I was not to be frightened or cease to wait till morning, because then she'd know what I still had to do to become a man. Lowering my head, I promised to do so; then she was all smeared, and she stretched out on the floor like a corpse. I put my mouth up to hers and found that she wasn't breathing at all.

Una verdad te quiero confesar, Cipión amigo: que me dio gran temor verme encerrado en aquel estrecho aposento con aquella figura delante, la cual te la pintaré como mejor supiere.

«Ella era larga de más de siete pies; toda era notomía de huesos, cubiertos con una piel negra, vellosa y curtida; con la barriga, que era de badana, se cubría las partes deshonestas, y aun le colgaba hasta la mitad de los muslos; las tetas semejaban dos vejigas de vaca secas y arrugadas; denegridos los labios, traspillados los dientes, la nariz corva y entablada, desencasados los ojos, la cabeza desgreñada, la mejillas chupadas, angosta la garganta y los pechos sumidos; finalmente, toda era flaca y endemoniada. Púseme de espacio a mirarla y apriesa comenzó a apoderarse de mí el miedo, considerando la mala visión de su cuerpo y la peor ocupación de su alma. Quise morderla, por ver si volvía en sí, y no hallé parte en toda ella que el asco no me lo estorbase; pero, con todo esto, la así de un carcaño y la saqué arrastrando al patio; mas ni por esto dio muestras de tener sentido. Allí, con mirar el cielo y verme en parte ancha, se me quitó el temor; a lo menos, se templó de manera que tuve ánimo de esperar a ver en lo que paraba la ida y vuelta de aquella mala hembra, y lo que me contaba de mis sucesos. En esto me preguntaba yo a mí mismo: "¿quién hizo a esta mala vieja tan discreta y tan mala? ¿De dónde sabe ella cuáles son males de daño y cuáles de culpa? ¿Cómo entiende y habla tanto de Dios, y obra tanto del diablo? ¿Cómo peca tan de malicia, no escusándose con ignorancia?"

»En estas consideraciones se pasó la noche y se vino el día, que nos halló a los dos en mitad del patio: ella no vuelta en sí y a mí junto a ella, en cuclillas, atento, mirando su espantosa y fea catadura. Acudió la gente del hospital, y, viendo aquel retablo, unos decían: "Ya la bendita Cañizares es muerta; mirad cuán disfigurada y flaca la tenía la penitencia"; otros, más considerados, la tomaron el pulso, y vieron que le tenía, y que no era muerta, por do se dieron a entender que estaba en éxtasis y arrobada, de puro buena. Otros hubo que dijeron: "Esta puta vieja sin duda debe de ser bruja, y debe de estar untada; que nunca los santos hacen tan deshonestos arrobos, y hasta ahora, entre los que la conocemos, más fama tiene de bruja que de santa". Curiosos hubo que se llegaron a hincarle alfileres por las carnes, desde la punta hasta la cabeza: ni por eso recordaba la dormilona, ni volvió en sí hasta las siete

I want to admit one thing to you, friend Scipio: I was terrified to find myself shut up in that cramped room with that figure before me, which I'll now describe as best I can.

She was over seven *pies*[21] tall; she was cadaverously bony, and her skin was black, hairy, and weatherbeaten; her flabby belly hung down over her shameful parts, and even halfway down her thighs; her teats resembled two dry, wrinkled cow's bladders; her lips were blackish, her teeth were very close together, her nose was hooked and bent to one side,[22] her eyes were bulging, her hair was disheveled, her cheeks were emaciated, her throat was narrow, and her bosom was sunken in; in short, she was completely feeble and possessed by a devil. I remained looking at her for some time, and fear soon began to take hold of me, in view of the bad appearance of her body and the even worse nature of her soul. I wanted to bite her, to see whether she'd come to, but I couldn't find any part of her where disgust didn't prevent me; nevertheless, I seized her by one heel and dragged her out to the patio; but, even so, she showed no sign of feeling anything. There, seeing the sky and finding myself in an open space, I stopped being afraid; or at least, my fear was moderated, so that I got the courage to wait and see how that evil woman's return trip would turn out, and what she'd tell me about my life. Meanwhile I asked myself: "Who made this evil old woman so clever and so bad? How does she know which disasters are acts of God and which are human crimes? How can she understand and speak so much about God, and do so much of the devil's work? How can she sin with such ill will, without the excuse of ignorance?"

In such ponderings the night went by and day came, finding the two of us in the center of the patio: her not yet recovered and me beside her, on my haunches, attentive, looking at her ugly, frightful form. The hospice people came up and, viewing that scene, some said: "The blessed Cañizares is now dead; just see how disfigured and weak her penance made her." Others, more thoughtful, felt her pulse and, finding she had one and wasn't dead, imagined that she was in an ecstatic rapture, being so good. Others said: "No doubt this old whore is a witch, smeared with ointment, because holy people never fall into such indecent raptures, and up to now we who know her have considered her to be more of a witch than a saint." There were inquisitive people who came and stuck pins in her flesh, from point to head, but not even that revived the heavy sleeper, nor did she come to until about seven; then, feeling herself riddled with

---

21. The *pie* ("foot") has varied with time and place; even the modern Castilian 11-inch *pie* may be too long for this situation. 22. "Bent to one side" is a conjecture based on other meanings of *entablado*; another translator has "square," on what warrant I can't tell.

del día; y, como se sintió acribada de los alfileres, y mordida de los carcañares, y magullada del arrastramiento fuera de su aposento, y a vista de tantos ojos que la estaban mirando, creyó, y creyó la verdad, que yo había sido el autor de su deshonra; y así, arremetió a mí, y, echándome ambas manos a la garganta, procuraba ahogarme diciendo: "¡Oh bellaco, desagradecido, ignorante y malicioso! ¿Y es éste el pago que merecen las buenas obras que a tu madre hice y de las que te pensaba hacer a ti?" Yo, que me vi en peligro de perder la vida entre las uñas de aquella fiera arpía, sacudíme, y, asiéndole de las luengas faldas de su vientre, la zamarreé y arrastré por todo el patio; ella daba voces que la librasen de los dientes de aquel maligno espíritu.

»Con estas razones de la mala vieja, creyeron los más que yo debía de ser algún demonio de los que tienen ojeriza continua con los buenos cristianos, y unos acudieron a echarme agua bendita, otros no osaban llegar a quitarme, otros daban voces que me conjurasen; la vieja gruñía, yo apretaba los dientes, crecía la confusión, y mi amo, que ya había llegado al ruido, se desesperaba oyendo decir que yo era demonio. Otros, que no sabían de exorcismos, acudieron a tres o cuatro garrotes, con los cuales comenzaron a santiguarme los lomos; escocióme la burla, solté la vieja, y en tres saltos me puse en la calle, y en pocos más salí de la villa, perseguido de una infinidad de muchachos, que iban a grandes voces diciendo: "¡Apártense que rabia el perro sabio!"; otros decían: "¡No rabia, sino que es demonio en figura de perro!" Con este molimiento, a campana herida salí del pueblo, siguiéndome muchos que indubitablemente creyeron que era demonio, así por las cosas que me habían visto hacer como por las palabras que la vieja dijo cuando despertó de su maldito sueño.

»Dime tanta priesa a huir y a quitarme delante de sus ojos, que creyeron que me había desparecido como demonio: en seis horas anduve doce leguas, y llegué a un rancho de gitanos que estaba en un campo junto a Granada. Allí me reparé un poco, porque algunos de los gitanos me conocieron por el perro sabio, y con no pequeño gozo me acogieron y escondieron en una cueva, porque no me hallasen si fuese buscado; con intención, a lo que después entendí, de ganar conmigo como lo hacía el atambor mi amo. Veinte días estuve con ellos, en los cuales supe y noté su vida y costumbres, que por ser notables es forzoso que te las cuente.»

CIPIÓN.—Antes, Berganza, que pases adelante, es bien que reparemos en lo que te dijo la bruja, y averigüemos si puede ser verdad la grande mentira a quien das crédito. Mira, Berganza, grandísimo disparate sería creer que la Camacha mudase los hombres en bestias y que el sacristán

pinpricks, bitten at the heels, and bruised by being dragged out of her room, and seeing all those eyes gazing at her, she realized, and realized correctly, that I had been the cause of her dishonor; and so she attacked me and, gripping my throat with both hands, tried to choke me, saying: "Oh, you ungrateful, ignorant, malicious villain! Is this the reward due to the good things I did for your mother and intended to do for you?" I, seeing myself in danger of losing my life between the claws of that fierce harpy, worked myself loose and, seizing her by the long folds of her belly, I shook her to and fro and dragged her all over the patio, while she shouted to be delivered from the fangs of that evil spirit.

At those words of the bad old woman, most of the bystanders believed I must be one of those devils who bear constant hatred toward good Christians, and some ran up and splashed holy water onto me, others didn't dare come close and pull me off her, and others shouted that I should be exorcised; the old woman was grunting, I was biting down hard, the confusion grew, and my master, who had already arrived on hearing the noise, fell into despair on hearing them say I was a devil. Others, who knew nothing of exorcisms, resorted to three or four cudgels, with which they began to belabor my back; the joke annoyed me, I let go of the old woman, and in three bounds I was in the street, and in just a few more I was out of the town, pursued by a mob of boys who shouted as they came: "Move away, because the learned dog is rabid!" Others said: "He's not rabid, he's the devil in the shape of a dog!" After taking that hiding, I left town like a bat out of hell, followed by many who surely believed I was a devil, not only because of the tricks they had seen me perform, but also because of the words the old woman had spoken on awakening from her accursed slumber.

I was in such a rush to escape and get out of their sight that they thought I had vanished like a devil: in six hours I ran twelve leagues, reaching a Gypsy camp located in a field near Granada. There I recovered somewhat, because some of the Gypsies recognized me as the learned dog, and with no little joy welcomed me and hid me in a cave so I wouldn't be found if looked for; from what I heard afterwards, they intended to make money with me as my master the drummer had. I stayed with them for three weeks, during which time I learned and noted their life style and ways, which are so remarkable I must tell you about them.

SCIPIO: Before you proceed, Berganza, we ought to dwell on what the witch told you and ascertain whether that great lie which you believe can be true. Look, Berganza, it would be enormous folly to believe that La Camacha changed men into beasts and that the sacristan turned donkey

en forma de jumento la serviese los años que dicen que la sirvió. Todas estas cosas y las semejantes son embelecos, mentiras y apariencias del demonio; y si a nosotros nos parece ahora que tenemos algún entendimiento y razón, pues hablamos siendo verdaderamente perros, o estando en su figura, ya hemos dicho que éste es caso portentoso y jamás visto, y que, aunque le tocamos con las manos, no le habemos de dar crédito hasta tanto que el suceso dél nos muestre lo que conviene que creamos. ¿Quiéreslo ver más claro? Considera en cuán vanas cosas y en cuán tontos puntos dijo la Camacha que consistía nuestra restauración; y aquellas que a ti te deben parecer profecías no son sino palabras de consejas o cuentos de viejas, como aquellos del caballo sin cabeza y de la varilla de virtudes, con que se entretienen al fuego las dilatadas noches del invierno; porque, a ser otra cosa, ya estaban cumplidas, si no es que sus palabras se han de tomar en un sentido que he oído decir se llama alegórico, el cual sentido no quiere decir lo que la letra suena, sino otra cosa que, aunque diferente, le haga semejanza; y así, decir:

> Volverán a su forma verdadera
> cuando vieren con presta diligencia
> derribar los soberbios levantados,
> y alzar a los humildes abatidos,
> por mano poderosa para hacello,

tomándolo en el sentido que he dicho, paréceme que quiere decir que cobraremos nuestra forma cuando viéremos que los que ayer estaban en la cumbre de la rueda de la fortuna, hoy están hollados y abatidos a los pies de la desgracia, y tenidos en poco de aquellos que más los estimaban; y, asimismo, cuando viéremos que otros que no ha dos horas que no tenían deste mundo otra parte que servir en él de número que acrecentase el de las gentes, y ahora están tan encumbrados sobre la buena dicha que los perdemos de vista; y si primero no parecían por pequeños y encogidos, ahora no los podemos alcanzar por grandes y levantados. Y si en esto consistiera volver nosotros a la forma que dices, ya lo hemos visto y lo vemos a cada paso; por do me doy a entender que no en el sentido alegórico, sino en el literal, se han de tomar los versos de la Camacha; ni tampoco en éste consiste nuestro remedio, pues muchas veces hemos visto lo que dicen y nos estamos tan perros como vees; así que, la Camacha fue burladora falsa, y la Cañizares embustera, y la Montiela tonta, maliciosa y bellaca, con perdón sea dicho, si acaso es nuestra madre de entrambos, o tuya, que yo no la quiero tener por madre. Digo, pues, que el verdadero sentido es un juego de bolos, donde con presta diligencia derriban los que están en pie y vuelven a alzar los caídos, y esto por la mano de quien lo puede hacer. Mira, pues,

served her for as long as they say. All these and similar things are deceptions, lies, or illusions caused by the devil; and if it now seems to us that we possess some human intelligence and reason, since we're speaking though we're really dogs, or in the form of dogs, we've already said that this is a portentous, unheard-of case, and that, palpable as it may seem to us, we mustn't believe it until its outcome shows us what we ought to believe. Do you want to see this more clearly? Consider how vain the things were, and how foolish the terms, on which La Camacha said our restoration depended; what must seem to you to be prophesies are merely fragments of fables or old wives' tales, like the stories about the headless horse and the magic wand, with which people amuse themselves by the fireside on long winter nights; because otherwise they would already have come true, unless her words are to be taken in a sense that I've heard is called allegorical; that kind of sense doesn't mean what's literally said, but something else which, though different, is similar. So, take the stanza:

They will return to their true shape
when they see, with swift diligence,
the lofty proud laid low,
and the downtrodden humble exalted,
by a hand with the power to do this.

If you take it in the sense I mentioned, I think it means that we'll regain our shape when we see that those who yesterday were atop the wheel of fortune are today trodden down and stamped on by the feet of misfortune, and held in low regard by those who most esteemed them; and, likewise, when we see that others, who not two hours ago had no share in this world but to help fill up the number of its population, are now mounted so high on good fortune that we can no longer see them; and, if formerly they were invisible because they were so small and shrunken, now we can't reach them because they're great and exalted. And if this were what was involved in our returning to the shape you mention, we've already seen it and we see it constantly; therefore I gather that La Camacha's verses are to be taken not in the allegorical sense, but literally; nor does this provide our remedy, either, because we've often seen what they say, but we're obviously still dogs. So that La Camacha was a false deceiver, and La Cañizares a con woman, and La Montiela foolish, malicious, and crooked, begging her pardon in case she's our mother, or yours, because I don't want her for a mother. So I say that the real meaning is a game of ninepins, in which with swift diligence the ones standing are knocked down and the fallen ones raised again, by the hand of someone who can do it. So consider whether in the course of our life we haven't seen peo-

si en el discurso de nuestra vida habremos visto jugar a los bolos, y si hemos visto por esto haber vuelto a ser hombres, si es que lo somos.

BERGANZA.—Digo que tienes razón, Cipión hermano, y que eres más discreto de lo que pensaba; y de lo que has dicho vengo a pensar y creer que todo lo que hasta aquí hemos pasado y lo que estamos pasando es sueño, y que somos perros; pero no por esto dejemos de gozar deste bien de la habla que tenemos y de la excelencia tan grande de tener discurso humano todo el tiempo que pudiéremos; y así, no te canse el oírme contar lo que me pasó con los gitanos que me escondieron en la cueva.

CIPIÓN.—De buena gana te escucho, por obligarte a que me escuches cuando te cuente, si el cielo fuere servido, los sucesos de mi vida.

BERGANZA.—«La que tuve con los gitanoso fue considerar en aquel tiempo sus muchas malicias, sus embaimientos y embustes, los hurtos en que se ejercitan, así gitanas como gitanos, desde el punto casi que salen de las mantillas y saben andar. ¿Vees la multitud que hay dellos esparcida por España? Pues todos se conocen y tienen noticia los unos de los otros, y trasiegan y trasponen los hurtos déstos en aquéllos y los de aquéllos en éstos. Dan la obediencia, mejor que a su rey, a uno que llaman *Conde,* al cual, y a todos los que dél suceden, tienen el sobrenombre de Maldonado; y no porque vengan del apellido deste noble linaje, sino porque un paje de un caballero deste nombre se enamoró de una gitana, la cual no le quiso conceder su amor si no se hacía gitano y la tomaba por mujer. Hízolo así el paje, y agradó tanto a los demás gitanos, que le alzaron por señor y le dieron la obediencia; y, como en señal de vasallaje, le acuden con parte de los hurtos que hacen, como sean de importancia.

»Ocúpanse, por dar color a su ociosidad, en labrar cosas de hierro, haciendo instrumentos con que facilitan sus hurtos; y así, los verás siempre traer a vender por las calles tenazas, barrenas, martillos; y ellas, trébedes y badiles. Todas ellas son parteras, y en esto llevan ventaja a las nuestras, porque sin costa ni aderentes sacan sus partos a luz, y lavan las criaturas con agua fría en naciendo; y, desde que nacen hasta que mueren, se curten y muestran a sufrir las inclemencias y rigores del cielo; y así, verás que todos son alentados, volteadores, corredores y bailadores. Cásanse siempre entre ellos, porque no salgan sus malas costumbres a ser conocidas de otros; ellas guardan el decoro a sus maridos, y pocas hay que les ofendan con otros que no sean de su generación. Cuando piden limosna, más la sacan con invenciones y chocarrerías que con devociones; y, a título que no hay quien se fíe dellas, no sirven y dan en ser holgazanas. Y pocas o ninguna vez he visto, si mal no me acuerdo, ninguna gitana a pie de altar comulgando, puesto que muchas veces he entrado en las iglesias.

ple play ninepins, and whether we've therefore turned back into human beings, if we are human.

BERGANZA: I say you're right, brother Scipio, and wiser than I thought; from what you've said I now think and believe that all our experiences so far and right now are a dream, and that we're dogs; but let's not for that reason cease to enjoy this gift of speech we have and the great benefit of discoursing like people as long as we can; thus, don't get weary of hearing me tell you what I experienced with the Gypsies who hid me in the cave.

SCIPIO: I hear you gladly, in order to oblige you to listen to me when it's my turn to narrate the events of my life, if heaven so wishes.

BERGANZA: My life with the Gypsies at that time was to observe their many wickednesses, frauds, and deceptions, the thefts they practice, both the women and the men, almost from the time they step out of baby clothes and learn how to walk. Do you see how many of them are disseminated all over Spain? Well, they all know one another and have news of one another, and they "decant" and transport the things they steal from here to there, and vice versa. They pay obedience, more than to their king, to a man they call "count"; on him, and all his successors, they bestow the surname Maldonado, not because they come of that noble family, but because a page of a gentleman of that name fell in love with a Gypsy woman, who wouldn't grant him her love unless he became a Gypsy and married her. The page did this, pleasing the other Gypsies so well that they made him their lord and paid homage to him; and, as if in token of vassalage, they give him a part of what they steal, if it's sizeable enough.

To lend an air of credibility to their idleness, they work at fashioning iron objects, making tools to make their robbing easier; so you'll always find the men in the streets hawking tongs, augers, and hammers, and the women selling trivets and fire shovels. The women are all midwives and thereby have the advantage over ours, because they give birth without expense or helpers, and wash the babies in cold water when they're born; from the day they're born to the day they die, they're suntanned and show they can endure the inclemencies and rigors of the weather; thus you'll find all of them high-spirited, acrobatic, good runners and dancers. They always marry among themselves, so their evil ways don't become known to others; the women preserve their chastity, and very few betray their husbands with other men not of their race. When they seek charity, they get it more by made-up stories and coarse jokes than by piety; and on the pretext that nobody trusts them, their women don't go out to service, but are given to idleness. And, if I remember correctly, never, or very seldom, have I seen any Gypsy woman taking Communion at an altar, although I've frequently gone into churches.

»Son sus pensamientos imaginar cómo han de engañar y dónde han de hurtar; confieren sus hurtos y el modo que tuvieron en hacellos; y así, un día contó un gitano delante de mí a otros un engaño y hurto que un día había hecho a un labrador, y fue que el gitano tenía un asno rabón, y en el pedazo de la cola que tenía sin cerdas le ingirió otra peluda, que parecía ser suya natural. Sacóle al mercado, comprósele un labrador por diez ducados, y, en habiéndosele vendido y cobrado el dinero, le dijo que si quería comprarle otro asno hermano del mismo, y tan bueno como el que llevaba, que se le vendería por más buen precio. Respondióle el labrador que fuese por él y le trujese, que él se le compraría, y que en tanto que volviese llevaría el comprado a su posada. Fuese el labrador, siguióle el gitano, y sea como sea, el gitano tuvo maña de hurtar al labrador el asno que le había vendido, y al mismo instante le quitó la cola postiza y quedó con la suya pelada. Mudóle la albarda y jáquima, y atrevióse a ir a buscar al labrador para que se le comprase, y hallóle antes que hubiese echado menos el asno primero, y a pocos lances compró el segundo. Fuésele a pagar a la posada, donde halló menos la bestia a la bestia; y, aunque lo era mucho, sospechó que el gitano se le había hurtado, y no quería pagarle. Acudió el gitano por testigos, y trujo a los que habían cobrado la alcabala del primer jumento, y juraron que el gitano había vendido al labrador un asno con una cola muy larga y muy diferente del asno segundo que vendía. A todo esto se halló presente un alguacil, que hizo las partes del gitano con tantas veras, que el labrador hubo de pagar el asno dos veces. Otros muchos hurtos contaron, y todos, o los más, de bestias, en quien son ellos graduados y en lo que más se ejercitan. Finalmente, ella es mala gente, y, aunque muchos y muy prudentes jueces han salido contra ellos, no por eso se enmiendan.

»A cabo de veinte días, me quisieron llevar a Murcia; pasé por Granada, donde ya estaba el capitán, cuyo atambor era mi amo. Como los gitanos lo supieron, me encerraron en un aposento del mesón donde vivían; oíles decir la causa, no me pareció bien el viaje que llevaban, y así, determiné soltarme, como lo hice. Y, saliéndome de Granada, di en una huerta de un morisco, que me acogió de buena voluntad, y yo quedé con mejor, pareciéndome que no me querría para más de para guardarle la huerta: oficio, a mi cuenta, de menos trabajo que el de guardar ganado. Y, como no había allí altercar sobre tanto más cuanto al salario, fue cosa fácil hallar el morisco criado a quien mandar y yo amo a quien servir. Estuve con él más de un mes, no por el gusto de la vida que tenía, sino por el que me daba saber la de mi amo, y por ella la de todos cuantos moriscos viven en España.»

Their thoughts are schemes as to how to cozen and where to rob; they confer about their thefts and their methods in committing them; thus, one day in my presence one Gypsy described to others a ruse, involving robbery, that he had once played on a peasant: the Gypsy had a donkey with a bobbed tail; onto the stump of tail, which was hairless, he attached a full, hairy one, which looked natural. He took it to market, where it was purchased by that peasant for ten ducats; having sold it and received the money, the Gypsy told him that if he wanted to buy another donkey from him, the brother of that one, and just as good as the one he now had, he'd sell it to him at a better price. The peasant, in reply, told him to fetch and bring it; he'd buy it. While awaiting his return, he'd take the one he had bought to his inn. The peasant departed, the Gypsy followed him, and, however it was, the Gypsy managed to steal from the peasant the donkey he had sold him; immediately he removed his false tail, leaving him with his hairless stump. He changed his packsaddle and halter, and had the nerve to look for the peasant and have him buy it. He found him before he had discovered the first donkey was missing, and before very long he bought the second. He went to the inn to pay him, and there that dumb animal found the animal gone; but, though he was very dumb, he suspected that the Gypsy had stolen it, and refused to pay him. The Gypsy went to get witnesses, bringing those who had received a cut on the first donkey; they swore that the Gypsy had sold the peasant a donkey with a very long tail, not at all like the second donkey he was selling. Present at the whole proceeding was a constable, who took the Gypsy's side so earnestly that the peasant had to pay for the donkey twice. They narrated many other thefts, all or most of them of animals, at which they're past masters, and which they practice most. In short, they're bad people and, even though many prudent judges have come out against them, that doesn't make them mend their ways.

After three weeks they wanted to take me to Murcia; I passed through Granada, where the captain, my master the drummer's commanding officer, then was. When the Gypsies found that out, they locked me up in a room of the inn where they were staying; I heard them state the reason, and the journey they were making didn't sound good to me; so I decided to get free, and I did. Leaving Granada, I came across the orchard of a baptized Moor, who welcomed me gladly; I was even gladder to stay, reflecting that he wouldn't want me to do more than guard the garden, a job I considered less laborious than guarding sheep. And since there was no occasion to bicker in detail over my pay, it was easy for the Moor to find a servant to give orders and for me to find a master to serve. I stayed with him over a month, not out of liking for the life I led, but for my pleasure in learning about my master's, and thereby the life of all the baptized Moors living in Spain.

¡Oh cuántas y cuáles cosas te pudiera decir, Cipión amigo, desta morisca canalla, si no temiera no poderlas dar fin en dos semanas! Y si las hubiera de particularizar, no acabara en dos meses; mas, en efeto, habré de decir algo; y así, oye en general lo que yo vi y noté en particular desta buena gente.

«Por maravilla se hallará entre tantos uno que crea derechamente en la sagrada ley cristiana; todo su intento es acuñar y guardar dinero acuñado, y para conseguirle trabajan y no comen; en entrando el real en su poder, como no sea sencillo, le condenan a cárcel perpetua y a escuridad eterna; de modo que, ganando siempre y gastando nunca, llegan y amontonan la mayor cantidad de dinero que hay en España. Ellos son su hucha, su polilla, sus picazas y sus comadrejas; todo lo llegan, todo lo esconden y todo lo tragan. Considérese que ellos son muchos y que cada día ganan y esconden, poco o mucho, y que una calentura lenta acaba la vida como la de un tabardillo; y, como van creciendo, se van aumentando los escondedores, que crecen y han de crecer en infinito, como la experiencia lo muestra. Entre ellos no hay castidad, ni entran en religión ellos ni ellas: todos se casan, todos multiplican, porque el vivir sobriamente aumenta las causas de la generación. No los consume la guerra, ni ejercicio que demasiadamente los trabaje; róbannos a pie quedo, y con los frutos de nuestras heredades, que nos revenden, se hacen ricos. No tienen criados, porque todos lo son de sí mismos; no gastan con sus hijos en los estudios, porque su ciencia no es otra que la del robarnos. De los doce hijos de Jacob que he oído decir que entraron en Egipto, cuando los sacó Moisés de aquel cautiverio, salieron seiscientos mil varones, sin niños y mujeres. De aquí se podrá inferir lo que multiplicarán las déstos, que, sin comparación, son en mayor número.»

Cipión.—Buscado se ha remedio para todos los daños que has apuntado y bosquejado en sombra, que bien sé que son más y mayores los que callas que los que cuentas, y hasta ahora no se ha dado con el que conviene; pero celadores prudentísimos tiene nuestra república que, considerando que España cría y tiene en su seno tantas víboras como moriscos, ayudados de Dios, hallarán a tanto daño cierta, presta y segura salida. Di adelante.

Berganza.—«Como mi amo era mezquino, como lo son todos los de su casta, sustentábame con pan de mijo y con algunas sobras de zahínas, común sustento suyo; pero esta miseria me ayudó a llevar el cielo por un modo tan estraño como el que ahora oirás.

»Cada mañana, juntamente con el alba, amanecía sentado al pie de un granado, de muchos que en la huerta había, un mancebo, al parecer estudiante, vestido de bayeta, no tan negra ni tan peluda que no pareciese

Oh, how many things I could tell you, Scipio, and what things, about that Moorish rabble, if I weren't afraid of being unable to finish in two weeks! If I had to spell them all out, I wouldn't finish in two months; but I *do* have to tell you something; so hear in a nutshell what I observed and noted in great detail about those fine people.

It would be a miracle to find among their great number even one who believes truly in the holy Christian religion; all their aim is to make money and keep it once they've made it; to acquire it, they work and they don't eat; if a coin falls into their hands, and isn't of short weight, they condemn it to perpetual imprisonment and eternal darkness; so that, always earning and never spending, they gather together and heap up the greatest quantity of money in Spain. They are her moneybox, her moths, her magpies, and her weasels; they accumulate, hide, and consume everything. Just consider that they are numerous and that every day they gain and hide a little or a lot, and that a slow fever kills as surely as a raging spotted fever; and as they increase, so do the hoarders of money, who increase and must increase to infinity, as experience shows. Among them there is no chastity, nor do either the men or the women enter into religion: they all marry and multiply, because a sober life increases the causes of fertility. They're not worn down by war or any other pursuit that taxes their strength excessively; they rob us without effort, and grow rich on the fruits of our inheritance, which they sell back to us. They don't keep servants because each of them is his own servant. They don't spend money on schooling their children because their scholarship is merely to rob us. The twelve sons of Jacob who I've heard entered Egypt had increased, by the time Moses released the Hebrews from that captivity, to six hundred thousand adults males, not counting the women and children. From this you can deduce how these men's wives will multiply, since there are incomparably more of them.

SCIPIO: A remedy has been sought for all the ills you've pointed out and sketched roughly, and I'm well aware that the ones you haven't mentioned are greater and more numerous than the ones you have, but up to now the right one hasn't been found; yet our nation possesses very wise and zealous men who, observing that Spain breeds in her bosom so many vipers like these Moors, will, with God's aid, find a sure, swift, and safe cure for so serious a disease. Continue.

BERGANZA: My master, being stingy, like all of his race, fed me with millet bread and leftover fritters (a usual food of theirs), but heaven helped me endure that misery in the strange way you will now hear.

Every morning at dawn, a young man would show up seated at the foot of one of the many pomegranate trees in the orchard; seemingly a student, he was clad in baize that wasn't so black and fuzzy that it

parda y tundida. Ocupábase en escribir en un cartapacio, y de cuando en cuando se daba palmadas en la frente y se mordía las uñas, estando mirando al cielo; y otras veces se ponía tan imaginativo, que no movía pie ni mano, ni aun las pestañas: tal era su embelesamiento. Una vez me llegué junto a él, sin que me echase de ver; oíle murmurar entre dientes, y al cabo de un buen espacio dio una gran voz, diciendo: "¡Vive el Señor, que es la mejor octava que he hecho en todos los días de mi vida!" Y, escribiendo apriesa en su cartapacio, daba muestras de gran contento; todo lo cual me dio a entender que el desdichado era poeta. Hícele mis acostumbradas caricias, por asegurarle de mi mansedumbre; echéme a sus pies, y él, con esta seguridad, prosiguió en sus pensamientos y tornó a rascarse la cabeza y a sus arrobos, y a volver a escribir lo que había pensado. Estando en esto, entró en la huerta otro mancebo, galán y bien aderezado, con unos papeles en la mano, en los cuales de cuando en cuando leía. Llegó donde estaba el primero y díjole: "¿Habéis acabado la primera jornada?" "Ahora le di fin —respondió el poeta—, la más gallardamente que imaginarse puede". "¿De qué manera?", preguntó el segundo. "Désta —respondió el primero—: Sale Su Santidad del Papa vestido de pontifical, con doce cardenales, todos vestidos de morado, porque cuando sucedió el caso que cuenta la historia de mi comedia era tiempo de *mutatio caparum*, en el cual los cardenales no se visten de rojo, sino de morado; y así, en todas maneras conviene, para guardar la propiedad, que estos mis cardenales salgan de morado; y éste es un punto que hace mucho al caso para la comedia; y a buen seguro dieran en él, y así hacen a cada paso mil impertinencias y disparates. Yo no he podido errar en esto, porque he leído todo el ceremonial romano, por sólo acertar en estos vestidos". "Pues ¿de dónde queréis vos —replicó el otro— que tenga mi autor vestidos morados para doce cardenales?" "Pues si me quita uno tan sólo —respondió el poeta—, así le daré yo mi comedia como volar. ¡Cuerpo de tal! ¿Esta apariencia tan grandiosa se ha de perder? Imaginad vos desde aquí lo que parecerá en un teatro un Sumo Pontífice con doce graves cardenales y con otros ministros de acompañamiento que forzosamente han de traer consigo. ¡Vive el cielo, que sea uno de los mayores y más altos espectáculos que se haya visto en comedia, aunque sea la del *Ramillete de Daraja*!"

»Aquí acabé de entender que el uno era poeta y el otro comediante. El comediante aconsejó al poeta que cercenase algo de los cardenales, si no quería imposibilitar al autor el hacer la comedia. A lo que dijo el poeta que le agradeciesen que no había puesto todo el cónclave que se halló junto al acto memorable que pretendía traer a la memoria de las gentes en su felicísima comedia. Rióse el recitante y dejóle en su ocupación por irse a la suya, que era estudiar un papel de una comedia nueva. El poeta, después de haber escrito algunas coplas de su

didn't look gray and shorn. He'd be busy writing in a portfolio, and every so often he'd slap his forehead and bite his nails while gazing at the sky; other times he'd get so lost in thought that he didn't stir hand or foot, or even his eyelashes, he was so spellbound. Once I went right up to him and he didn't notice me; I heard him muttering softly; after a long while he shouted out loud: "Thank God, this is the best eight-line stanza I've ever composed!" And, writing quickly in his portfolio, he showed signs of great contentment; all this made me realize that the unhappy fellow was a poet. I fawned on him, as was my practice, to assure him I was tame; I stretched out at his feet and he, now assured, pursued his thoughts and resumed his head scratching and his raptures, and again wrote down what he had conceived. At this point, another young man, elegant and well dressed, entered the orchard holding some papers, which he consulted every so often. He went up to the first man and said: "Have you finished the first act?" "Yes, just now," the poet replied, "and as gracefully as could be wished." "How does it end?" the second man asked. "Like this," the first man replied. "His Holiness the Pope enters in his pontifical robes, with twelve cardinals all dressed in violet, because the moment when my play takes place is the time of the Easter Sunday *mutatio caparum*, when the cardinals wear not red, but violet; and so, it's altogether proper, to be accurate, for these cardinals of mine to enter in violet; and this is a point of great importance to the play; careless people would surely bungle it, because so very many nonsensical mistakes are always made. I couldn't be wrong on this point, because I've read the entire Roman ceremonial merely to be accurate about these robes." "But," the other man retorted, "where do you expect my manager to get violet robes for twelve cardinals?" "Well, if he reduces them by even one," the poet replied, "I wouldn't give him my play any more than I can fly. Damn! Is such a great stage effect to be lost? Imagine right now how it will look on stage with the High Pontiff, twelve grave cardinals, and the other accompanying servants they must have with them. By God, it will be one of the greatest and loftiest spectacles ever seen in the theater, even outdoing *Daraja's Nosegay!*"

By now I was sure that one of them was a poet and the other, an actor. The actor advised the poet to trim away some of the cardinals, if he didn't want to make it impossible for the manager to put on the play. To which the poet replied that they should be grateful to him for not having introduced the entire conclave which was assembled on the memorable occasion he hoped to recall to people's minds in his most felicitous play. The performer laughed and left him at his occupation to return to his own, which was to study his role in a new play. After the poet had written

magnífica comedia, con mucho sosiego y espacio sacó de la faldriquera algunos mendrugos de pan y obra de veinte pasas, que, a mi parecer, entiendo que se las conté, y aun estoy en duda si eran tantas, porque juntamente con ellas hacían bulto ciertas migajas de pan que las acompañaban. Sopló y apartó las migajas, y una a una se comió las pasas y los palillos, porque no le vi arrojar ninguno, ayudándolas con los mendrugos, que morados con la borra de la faldriquera, parecían mohosos, y eran tan duros de condición que, aunque él procuró enternecerlos, paseándolos por la boca una y muchas veces, no fue posible moverlos de su terquedad; todo lo cual redundó en mi provecho, porque me los arrojó, diciendo: "¡To, to! Toma, que buen provecho te hagan". "¡Mirad —dije entre mí— qué néctar o ambrosía me da este poeta, de los que ellos dicen que se mantienen los dioses y su Apolo allá en el cielo!" En fin, por la mayor parte, grande es la miseria de los poetas, pero mayor era mi necesidad, pues me obligó a comer lo que él desechaba. En tanto que duró la composición de su comedia, no dejó de venir a la huerta ni a mí me faltaron mendrugos, porque los repartía conmigo con mucha liberalidad, y luego nos íbamos a la noria, donde, yo de bruces y él con un cangilón, satisfacíamos la sed como unos monarcas. Pero faltó el poeta y sobró en mí la hambre tanto, que determiné dejar al morisco y entrarme en la ciudad a buscar ventura, que la halla el que se muda.

»Al entrar de la ciudad vi que salía del famoso monasterio de San Jerónimo mi poeta, que como me vio se vino a mí con los brazos abiertos, y yo me fui a él con nuevas muestras de regocijo por haberle hallado. Luego al instante comenzó a desembaular pedazos de pan, más tiernos de los que solía llevar a la huerta, y a entregarlos a mis dientes sin repasarlos por los suyos: merced que con nuevo gusto satisfizo mi hambre. Los tiernos mendrugos, y el haber visto salir a mi poeta del monasterio dicho, me pusieron en sospecha de que tenía las musas vergonzantes, como otros muchos las tienen.

»Encaminóse a la ciudad, y yo le seguí con determinación de tenerle por amo si él quisiese, imaginando que de las sobras de su castillo se podía mantener mi real; porque no hay mayor ni mejor bolsa que la de la caridad, cuyas liberales manos jamás están pobres; y así, no estoy bien con aquel refrán que dice: "Más da el duro que el desnudo", como si el duro y avaro diese algo, como lo da el liberal desnudo, que, en efeto, da el buen deseo cuando más no tiene. De lance en lance, paramos en la casa de un autor de comedias que, a lo que me acuerdo, se llamaba Angulo el Malo, . . . de otro Angulo, no autor, sino representante, el más gracioso que entonces tuvieron y ahora tienen las comedias. Juntóse toda la compañía a oír la comedia

a few stanzas of his magnificent play, he very calmly and slowly drew from his pocket some broken bread and about twenty raisins, which I truly believe he counted, though I doubt whether there were that many, because their bulk was increased by the bread crumbs that came out with them. He blew away the crumbs, and ate the raisins one by one along with their stems, because I didn't see him throw any away, helping them down with the hunks of bread, which, turned violet by the lining of the pocket, looked moldy and were so tough by nature that, even though he tried to tenderize them by chewing them several times, it was impossible to overcome their stubbornness. All this redounded to my advantage, because he tossed them to me, saying: "Here, here! Take them and may they do you good!" "Look," I said to myself, "what nectar or ambrosia is given to me by this poet, food that his crew say nourishes the gods and their Apollo up in the sky!" In short, on the whole the poverty of poets is great, but my need was greater, since it compelled me to eat what he was rejecting. All the time he was working on his play, he kept coming to the orchard and I was supplied with broken bread, because he'd share it with me very generously; then we'd go to the waterwheel, where, I on my belly and he using a bucket on the wheel, we'd quench our thirst like a pair of kings. But the poet no longer came, and my hunger grew so excessive that I decided to leave the Moor and enter the city in quest of good fortune, which is found by the man who moves around from place to place.

On entering the city I saw my poet leaving the famous monastery of Saint Jerome; as soon as he saw me, he came to me with open arms, and I went up to him with new demonstrations of joy at having found him. At once he began to fish out pieces of bread, softer than those he had usually brought to the orchard, and to yield them to my teeth without chewing them with his own: a favor that stilled my hunger with a new pleasure. The soft hunks of bread, and my having seen my poet leaving the monastery I mentioned, led me to suspect that his Muse lived on charity, as is the case with many other poets.

He headed into town, and I followed him, resolved to have him for a master if he wished, thinking that "the leftovers from his castle could feed my camp"; because there's no bigger or better purse than that of charity, whose generous hands are never poor; therefore I don't hold with the proverb that says "Even a miser gives more than a pauper"—as if a stingy miser ever gave away anything, as a generous pauper does, because, in fact, a well-intentioned man gives when he is most penniless. Going on our errands, we stopped at the house of a theatrical manager called, if I remember correctly, Angulo the Bad, to distinguish him from another Angulo who was not a manager, but an actor, the funniest on the stage then or now. The entire troupe assembled to hear my master (for so I al-

de mi amo, que ya por tal le tenía; y, a la mitad de la jornada primera, uno a uno y dos a dos, se fueron saliendo todos, excepto el autor y yo, que servíamos de oyentes. La comedia era tal, que, con ser yo un asno en esto de la poesía, me pareció que la había compuesto el mismo Satanás, para total ruina y perdición del mismo poeta, que ya iba tragando saliva, viendo la soledad en que el auditorio le había dejado; y no era mucho, si el alma, présaga, le decía allá dentro la desgracia que le estaba amenazando, que fue volver todos los recitantes, que pasaban de doce, y, sin hablar palabra, asieron de mi poeta, y si no fuera porque la autoridad del autor, llena de ruegos y voces, se puso de por medio, sin duda le mantearan. Quedé yo del caso pasmado; el autor, desabrido; los farsantes, alegres, y el poeta, mohíno; el cual, con mucha paciencia, aunque algo torcido el rostro, tomó su comedia, y, encerrándosela en el seno, medio murmurando, dijo: "No es bien echar las margaritas a los puercos". Y con esto se fue con mucho sosiego.

»Yo, de corrido, ni pude ni quise seguirle; y acertélo, a causa que el autor me hizo tantas caricias que me obligaron a que con él me quedase, y en menos de un mes salí grande entremesista y gran farsante de figuras mudas. Pusiéronme un freno de orillos y enseñáronme a que arremetiese en el teatro a quien ellos querían; de modo que, como los entremeses solían acabar por la mayor parte en palos, en la compañía de mi amo acababan en zuzarme, y yo derribaba y atropellaba a todos, con que daba que reír a los ignorantes y mucha ganancia a mi dueño.»

¡Oh Cipión, quién te pudiera contar lo que vi en ésta y en otras dos compañías de comediantes en que anduve! Mas, por no ser posible reducirlo a narración sucinta y breve, lo habré de dejar para otro día, si es que ha de haber otro día en que nos comuniquemos. ¿Vees cuán larga ha sido mi plática? ¿Vees mis muchos y diversos sucesos? ¿Consideras mis caminos y mis amos tantos? Pues todo lo que has oído es nada, comparado a lo que te pudiera contar de lo que noté, averigüé y vi desta gente: su proceder, su vida, sus costumbres, sus ejercicios, su trabajo, su ociosidad, su ignorancia y su agudeza, con otras infinitas cosas: unas para decirse al oído y otras para aclamallas en público, y todas para hacer memoria dellas y para desengaño de muchos que idolatran en figuras fingidas y en bellezas de artificio y de transformación.

Cipión.—Bien se me trasluce, Berganza, el largo campo que se te descubría para dilatar tu plática, y soy de parecer que la dejes para cuento particular y para sosiego no sobresaltado.

Berganza.—Sea así, y escucha.

ready considered him) read his play aloud; but halfway through the first act they all gradually left, in ones or twos, except the manager and me, who served as audience. The play was of such a sort that, even though I'm an ignoramus when it comes to poetry, I thought it had been written by Satan himself, for the total ruin and destruction of the poet, who was now swallowing his saliva, as he viewed the solitude in which his listeners had left him; and it wouldn't be surprising if his prophetic soul was inwardly warning him of the misfortune threatening him, which was that all the actors, more than twelve people, returned and, without a word, seized my poet; if the authority of the manager, with many implorations and shouts, hadn't intervened, they would surely have tossed him in a blanket. I was astonished at the event; the manager, disgruntled; the actors, cheerful; and the poet, glum; with great patience, though his features were a bit distorted, he picked up his script, stored it away in his shirtfront, and said in a half mutter: "It doesn't do to cast one's pearls before swine." Thereupon he left very calmly.

I was so embarrassed that I couldn't and didn't want to follow him; and my decision was correct, because the manager treated me so kindly that I was obliged to stay with him, and in less than a month I appeared as a great performer in interludes and a great pantomimist. They put a selvage muzzle on me and taught me to attack on stage anyone they designated; so that, whereas most interludes generally end with a beating, in my master's troupe they ended by egging me on, and I would knock over and trample on everybody, making the ignorant laugh and bringing in a lot of money for my owner.

Oh, Scipio, I wish I could tell you all I saw in that troupe and two others I was a member of! But, since it's impossible to reduce it to a succinct, brief narrative, I must leave it for another day, if there will be another day on which we can communicate. See how long my story has been? See all the different things that have happened to me? Have you observed all my journeys and various masters? Well, everything you've heard is nothing compared to what I could tell you about what I noted, ascertained, and saw among those folk: their proceedings, their life, their ways, their practices, their work, their leisure time, their ignorance, and their sharp-wittedness, with an infinity of other things, some to be whispered in the ear and others to be proclaimed in public, but all to make a record of in order to disenchant many people who idolize feigned personalities and the beauties of artifice and transformation.

SCIPIO: I have a good notion, Berganza, of the wide field that was opened to you to lengthen your account, and I think you should leave it for a separate narration when we're at leisure and won't be disturbed.

BERGANZA: Be it so! Listen:

«Con una compañía llegué a esta ciudad de Valladolid, donde en un entremés me dieron una herida que me llegó casi al fin de la vida; no pude vengarme, por estar enfrenado entonces, y después, a sangre fría, no quise: que la venganza pensada arguye crueldad y mal ánimo. Cansóme aquel ejercicio, no por ser trabajo, sino porque veía en él cosas que juntamente pedían enmienda y castigo; y, como a mí estaba más el sentillo que el remediallo, acordé de no verlo; y así, me acogí a sagrado, como hacen aquellos que dejan los vicios cuando no pueden ejercitallos, aunque más vale tarde que nunca. Digo, pues, que, viéndote una noche llevar la linterna con el buen cristiano Mahudes, te consideré contento y justa y santamente ocupado; y lleno de buena envidia quise seguir tus pasos, y con esta loable intención me puse delante de Mahudes, que luego me eligió para tu compañero y me trujo a este hospital. Lo que en él me ha sucedido no es tan poco que no haya menester espacio para contallo, especialmente lo que oí a cuatro enfermos que la suerte y la necesidad trujo a este hospital, y a estar todos cuatro juntos en cuatro camas apareadas.»

Perdóname, porque el cuento es breve y no sufre dilación, y viene aquí de molde.

CIPIÓN.—Sí perdono. Concluye, que, a lo que creo, no debe de estar lejos el día.

BERGANZA.—«Digo que en las cuatro camas que están al cabo desta enfermería, en la una estaba un alquimista, en la otra un poeta, en la otra un matemático y en la otra uno de los que llaman arbitristas.»

CIPIÓN.—Ya me acuerdo haber visto a esa buena gente.

BERGANZA.—«Digo, pues, que una siesta de las del verano pasado, estando cerradas las ventanas y yo cogiendo el aire debajo de la cama del uno dellos, el poeta se comenzó a quejar lastimosamente de su fortuna, y, preguntándole el matemático de qué se quejaba, respondió que de su corta suerte. "¿Cómo, y no será razón que me queje —prosiguió—, que, habiendo yo guardado lo que Horacio manda en su *Poética,* que no salga a luz la obra que, después de compuesta, no hayan pasado diez años por ella, y que tenga yo una de veinte años de ocupación y doce de pasante, grande en el sujeto, admirable y nueva en la invención, grave en el verso, entretenida en los episodios, maravillosa en la división, porque el principio responde al medio y al fin, de manera que constituyen el poema alto, sonoro, heroico, deleitable y sustancioso; y que, con todo esto, no hallo un príncipe a quien diri-

In one troupe I arrived at this city of Valladolid, where in one interlude I received a wound that nearly cost me my life; I couldn't avenge myself, being muzzled at the time; later on, in cold blood, I no longer wanted to; because a premeditated revenge is a sign of cruelty and a bad heart. I got tired of that profession, not because it was hard work but because I found in it things that called for amendment and punishment at the same time. Since it was more my place to feel this than to remedy it, I decided to avoid seeing it; and so I ran away from the problem, as people do who abandon their vices when they can no longer commit them—though it's better late than never. Well, I mean that, seeing you one night carrying the lantern along with the good Christian Mahudes, I deemed that you were contented and occupied in a proper, holy way; filled with a good kind of envy, I decided to follow in your path, and with that praiseworthy purpose I appeared before Mahudes, who immediately chose me for your companion and brought me to this hospital. What has happened to me here isn't so brief that it wouldn't take time to tell it, especially the conversation I heard among four patients whom fate and need had brought to this hospital and had brought together in one row of four beds.

Forgive me, because the tale is brief and can't be expanded, and it fits right in with what we've been saying.

SCIPIO: Yes, I forgive you. Finish, because, as I believe, daylight can't be far off.

BERGANZA: Well, in the four beds at the far end of this infirmary there were an alchemist, a poet, a mathematician, and one of those men called economic experts.[23]

SCIPIO: I recall having seen those elegant characters.

BERGANZA: Well, during one siesta this past summer, when the windows were closed and I was taking the air beneath one of their beds, the poet began to complain pitifully of his fortune; when the mathematician asked him what he was complaining about, he said it was about his bad luck. "What? Don't I have cause to complain?" he continued. "Though I've followed Horace's rule in his *Ars poetica*, not to publish a piece of writing until ten years[24] after it's been composed, and I've got one that's been a master for twenty years and a journeyman for twelve, great in its subject matter, admirable and new in its inventiveness, serious in its versification, entertaining in its digressions, and marvelous in its structure, since its beginning matches its middle and its end, so that, taken together, they constitute a lofty, musical, heroic, delightful, and substantial poem,

23. An *arbitrista* recommended financial or political plans for the good of the nation. The English equivalent in Defoe's day was "projector." The term "promoter" used in an earlier translation doesn't convey the right feeling. 24. Horace specifies nine years.

girle? Príncipe, digo, que sea inteligente, liberal y magnánimo. ¡Mísera edad y depravado siglo nuestro!" "¿De qué trata el libro?", preguntó el alquimista. Respondió el poeta: "Trata de lo que dejó de escribir el Arzobispo Turpín del Rey Artús de Inglaterra, con otro suplemento de la *Historia de la demanda del Santo Brial,* y todo en verso heroico, parte en octavas y parte en verso suelto; pero todo esdrújulamente, digo en esdrújulos de nombres sustantivos, sin admitir verbo alguno". "A mí —respondió el alquimista— poco se me entiende de poesía; y así, no sabré poner en su punto la desgracia de que vuesa merced se queja, puesto que, aunque fuera mayor, no se igualaba a la mía, que es que, por faltarme instrumento, o un príncipe que me apoye y me dé a la mano los requisitos que la ciencia de la alquimia pide, no estoy ahora manando en oro y con más riquezas que los Midas, que los Crasos y Cresos." "¿Ha hecho vuesa merced —dijo a esta sazón el matemático—, señor alquimista, la experiencia de sacar plata de otros metales?" "Yo —respondió el alquimista— no la he sacado hasta agora, pero realmente sé que se saca, y a mí no me faltan dos meses para acabar la piedra filosofal, con que se puede hacer plata y oro de las mismas piedras". "Bien han exagerado vuesas mercedes sus desgracias —dijo a esta sazón el matemático—; pero, al fin, el uno tiene libro que dirigir y el otro está en potencia propincua de sacar la piedra filosofal; mas ¿qué diré yo de la mía, que es tan sola que no tiene donde arrimarse? Veinte y dos años ha que ando tras hallar el punto fijo, y aquí lo dejo y allí lo tomo; y, pareciéndome que ya lo he hallado y que no se me puede escapar en ninguna manera, cuando no me cato, me hallo tan lejos dél, que me admiro. Lo mismo me acaece con la cuadratura del círculo: que he llegado tan al remate de hallarla, que no sé ni puedo pensar cómo no la tengo ya en la faldriquera; y así, es mi pena semejable a las de Tántalo, que está cerca del fruto y muere de hambre, y propincuo al agua y perece de sed. Por momentos pienso dar en la coyuntura de la verdad, y por minutos me hallo tan lejos della, que vuelvo a subir el monte que acabé de bajar, con el canto de mi trabajo a cuestas, como otro nuevo Sísifo".

»Había hasta este punto guardado silencio el arbitrista, y aquí le rompió diciendo: "Cuatro quejosos tales que lo pueden ser del Gran Turco ha juntado en este hospital la pobreza, y reniego yo de oficios y ejercicios que ni entretienen ni dan de comer a sus dueños. Yo, señores, soy arbitrista, y he dado a Su Majestad en diferentes tiempos

nevertheless I can't find a prince to dedicate it to. I mean, a prince who's intelligent, generous, and magnanimous. What a wretched age and depraved era we live in!" "What's the book about?" the alchemist asked. The poet replied: "It treats of things that Archbishop Turpin omitted to write about King Arthur of England, with another supplement to the *History of the Quest for the Holy Braille,* and all in heroic verse, partly in eight-line stanzas and partly in black verse; but all ending in proparoxytones, I mean in proparoxytone nouns, never a verb." "I," the alchemist replied, "understand little about poetry, so I can't properly appreciate the misfortune your worship complains of, though, even if it were greater, it wouldn't equal mine, which is that, for lack of equipment, or a prince to support me and supply me with the tools which the science of alchemy demands, I am not now swimming in gold and more riches than a Midas, Crassus, or Croesus ever owned." At that point, the mathematician asked: "Alchemist, has your worship ever had the experience of turning other metals into silver?" The alchemist replied: "I haven't done so yet, but I really know it can be done, and I need less than two months to achieve the philosophers' stone, with which one can make silver and gold from ordinary stones." "Your worships have greatly exaggerated your misfortunes," the mathematician then said, "but, after all, one of you has a book to dedicate and the other is on the verge of acquiring the philosophers' stone; yet, what shall I say about *mine,* which is so special it has nothing to lean on? It's twenty-two years now that I've been trying to find the 'fixed point,'[25] which keeps eluding me; after I think I've found it and it can't possibly get away from me, at the least expected moment I find myself so far from it that I'm amazed. The same thing happens to me with the squaring of the circle: I've come so close to finding it that I don't know and can't imagine how come I don't already have it in my pocket; and so my torment resembles those of Tantalus, who's near the fruit and starving to death, and next to the water and dying of thirst. Continually I think I've hit upon the truth, and constantly I find myself so far from it that I once again climb the mountain that I've just descended, with the boulder of my labors on my back, like some new Sisyphus."

Up to then the economist had remained quiet, but now he broke his silence, saying: "Poverty has joined together in this hospital four whiners who might just as well be complaining about the Sultan of Turkey, and I renounce those professions and trades which don't maintain or feed their practitioners. I, gentlemen, am an economic expert, and at different

25. There are indications that this refers to ascertaining longitude at sea; the "fixed point" in physics (relating to temperature) and in math (relating to transformations) are surely too recent, and need not have been sought for avidly, whereas there definitely once were "longitude-hunters."

muchos y diferentes arbitrios, todos en provecho suyo y sin daño del reino; y ahora tengo hecho un memorial donde le suplico me señale persona con quien comunique un nuevo arbitrio que tengo: tal, que ha de ser la total restauración de sus empeños; pero, por lo que me ha sucedido con otros memoriales, entiendo que éste también ha de parar en el carnero. Mas, porque vuesas mercedes no me tengan por mentecapto, aunque mi arbitrio quede desde este punto público, le quiero decir, que es éste: Hase de pedir en Cortes que todos los vasallos de Su Majestad, desde edad de catorce a sesenta años, sean obligados a ayunar una vez en el mes a pan y agua, y esto ha de ser el día que se escogiere y señalare, y que todo el gasto que en otros condumios de fruta, carne y pescado, vino, huevos y legumbres que han de gastar aquel día, se reduzga a dinero y se dé a Su Majestad, sin defraudalle un ardite, so cargo de juramento; y con esto, en veinte años queda libre de socaliñas y desempeñado. Porque si se hace la cuenta, como yo la tengo hecha, bien hay en España más de tres millones de personas de la dicha edad, fuera de los enfermos, más viejos o más muchachos, y ninguno déstos dejará de gastar, y esto contado al menorete, cada día real y medio; y yo quiero que sea no más de un real, que no puede ser menos, aunque coma alholvas. Pues ¿paréceles a vuesas mercedes que sería barro tener cada mes tres millones de reales como ahechados? Y esto antes sería provecho que daño a los ayunantes, porque con el ayuno agradarían al cielo y servirían a su rey; y tal podría ayunar que le fuese conveniente para su salud. Éste es arbitrio limpio de polvo y de paja, y podríase coger por parroquias, sin costa de comisarios, que destruyen la república". Riyéronse todos del arbitrio y del arbitrante, y él también se riyó de sus disparates; y yo quedé admirado de haberlos oído y de ver que, por la mayor parte, los de semejantes humores venían a morir en los hospitales.»

CIPIÓN.—Tienes razón, Berganza. Mira si te queda más que decir.

BERGANZA.—Dos cosas no más, con que daré fin a mi plática, que ya me parece que viene el día.

«Yendo una noche mi mayor a pedir limosna en casa del corregidor desta ciudad, que es un gran caballero y muy gran cristiano, hallámosle solo; y parecióme a mí tomar ocasión de aquella soledad para decirle ciertos advertimientos que había oído decir a un viejo enfermo deste hospital, acerca de cómo se podía remediar la perdición tan notoria de las mozas vagamundas, que por no servir dan en malas, y tan malas, que pueblan los veranos todos los hospitales de los perdidos que las siguen: plaga intolerable y que pedía presto y eficaz remedio. Digo que, queriendo decírselo, alcé la voz, pensando que tenía habla, y en lugar de pronunciar razones concertadas ladré con tanta priesa y con

times I've laid before His Majesty many different projects, all to his advantage and of no danger to the kingdom; now I've written a petition begging him to indicate to me a person whom I can inform about a new project of mine, one so fine that it will mean the complete liquidation of his debts; but, from the experiences I've had with other petitions, I realize that this one, too, will end up in potter's field. But, so that you gentlemen won't think I'm a lunatic, even though it means making my scheme public at once, I want to describe it: It must be decreed in Parliament that all subjects of His Majesty between the ages of fourteen and sixty be compelled to fast on bread and water once a month, on a chosen, designated day, and that all the money they would have spent that day on other food, such as fruit, meat, fish, wine, and vegetables be given to His Majesty, without defrauding him of a cent, under oath; thereby, in twenty years he won't have to resort to underhanded fiscal policies, and he'll be out of debt. Because if you do the arithmetic, as I have, there are surely over three million people in Spain between those ages, not counting sick people or those older or younger, and none of them could fail to spend at least one and a half reales daily; and it's all right if it's only one real, because it can't be less, even if they eat wild plants. Well, do your worships think it would be chicken feed to have a clear three million reales every month? And for the fasters this would be an advantage rather than a detriment, because by fasting they'd please heaven and serve their king; and for some of them it would improve their health. This is a proposal with no dust or straw on it, and the money could be collected by parishes without the expense of revenue officers, who ruin the country." Everyone laughed at the proposal and its proposer, and he himself laughed at his nonsense; and I was amazed at having heard them and at seeing that most people of similar humors died in charity hospitals.

SCIPIO: You're right, Berganza. Do you have any more to tell?

BERGANZA: Two things only, with which I'll end my discourse, because I now think day is coming.

One night, when my master went seeking alms in the house of the civil governor of this city, who is a grand knight and a very good Christian, we found him alone; and I thought it right to take advantage of that and report to him certain admonitions I had heard from an elderly patient in this hospital, about ways to prevent the ruin, so well known, of young female vagabonds who get into mischief because they don't work, and such bad mischief that in summer they people every hospital with the good-for-nothings who pursue them; an intolerable plague which called for a swift, effective remedy. As I say, I wanted to repeat this to him, and I raised my voice, thinking I could speak, but instead of uttering con-

tan levantado tono que, enfadado el corregidor, dio voces a sus criados que me echasen de la sala a palos; y un lacayo que acudió a la voz de su señor, que fuera mejor que por entonces estuviera sordo, asió de una cantimplora de cobre que le vino a la mano, y diómela tal en mis costillas, que hasta ahora guardo las reliquias de aquellos golpes.»

CIPIÓN.—Y ¿quéjaste deso, Berganza?

BERGANZA.—Pues ¿no me tengo de quejar, si hasta ahora me duele, como he dicho, y si me parece que no merecía tal castigo mi buena intención?

CIPIÓN.—Mira, Berganza, nadie se ha de meter donde no le llaman, ni ha de querer usar del oficio que por ningún caso le toca. Y has de considerar que nunca el consejo del pobre, por bueno que sea, fue admitido, ni el pobre humilde ha de tener presumpción de aconsejar a los grandes y a los que piensan que se lo saben todo. La sabiduría en el pobre está asombrada; que la necesidad y miseria son las sombras y nubes que la escurecen, y si acaso se descubre, la juzgan por tontedad y la tratan con menosprecio.

BERGANZA.—Tienes razón, y, escarmentando en mi cabeza, de aquí adelante seguiré tus consejos.

«Entré asimismo otra noche en casa de una señora principal, la cual tenía en los brazos una perrilla destas que llaman de falda, tan pequeña, que la pudiera esconder en el seno; la cual, cuando me vio, saltó de los brazos de su señora y arremetió a mí ladrando, y con tan gran denuedo, que no paró hasta morderme de una pierna. Volvíla a mirar con respecto y con enojo, y dije entre mí: "Si yo os cogiera, animalejo ruin, en la calle, o no hiciera caso de vos o os hiciera pedazos entre los dientes". Consideré en ella que hasta los cobardes y de poco ánimo son atrevidos e insolentes cuando son favorecidos, y se adelantan a ofender a los que valen más que ellos.»

CIPIÓN.—Una muestra y señal desa verdad que dices nos dan algunos hombrecillos que a la sombra de sus amos se atreven a ser insolentes; y si acaso la muerte o otro accidente de fortuna derriba el árbol donde se arriman, luego se descubre y manifiesta su poco valor; porque, en efeto, no son de más quilates sus prendas que los que les dan sus dueños y valedores. La virtud y el buen entendimiento siempre es una y siempre es uno: desnudo o vestido, solo o acompañado. Bien es verdad que puede padecer acerca de la estimación de las gentes, mas no en la realidad verdadera de lo que merece y vale. Y, con esto, pongamos fin a esta plática, que la luz que entra por estos resquicios muestra que es muy entrado el día, y esta noche que viene, si no nos ha dejado este grande beneficio de la habla, será la mía, para contarte mi vida.

BERGANZA.—Sea ansí, y mira que acudas a este mismo puesto.

nected discourse I barked so quickly and in such loud tones that the governor got angry and shouted to his servants to drive me from the room with a beating; and a footman who responded to his master's call (better if he had been deaf at the time!) seized a copper siphon that was handy and struck me so hard on the ribs with it that I still bear the marks of those blows.

SCIPIO: And you complain of that, Berganza?

BERGANZA: Well, shouldn't I, if it still hurts, as I said, and I don't think my good intentions deserved such a punishment?

SCIPIO: Look, Berganza, nobody should butt in when he's not asked, or should want to ply a trade that in no way applies to him. And you ought to reflect that, good as it might be, a poor man's advice has never been taken, nor should a humble pauper presume to counsel the great and those who think they know everything. Wisdom in the poor is under a cloud, because need and poverty are the shadows and clouds that darken it, and if by chance it's uncovered, people consider it folly and treat it with disdain.

BERGANZA: You're right, and, learning this lesson in my head, from now on I'll follow your advice.

Likewise, on another night I entered the house of a distinguished lady who was holding in her arms one of those little female dogs called lapdogs, so small that she could hide it in her bodice; when it saw me, it leaped out of its mistress's arms and attacked me, barking, and so courageously that it didn't stop before it had bitten me on the leg. I turned to gaze on it with both respect and annoyance, and I said to myself: "If I caught you on the street, wretched little beast, either I'd pay no attention to you or I'd rip you to shreds with my teeth." I reflected, on thinking about that dog, that even low-spirited cowards are bold and insolent when they're protected, and then offer to insult those worthier than they.

SCIPIO: A sign and token of the truth that you express is afforded to us by certain puny little men who, with the backing of their masters, dare to be insolent; and if by chance death or another accident of fortune topples the tree they lean on, their lack of worth is instantly revealed and made manifest; because in fact their gold is only of the degree of purity that their masters and protectors assign to it. Virtue is always the same, as is intelligence: naked or dressed, alone or accompanied. It's true that it may suffer in people's estimation, but not in the true reality of its worth and value. And herewith let us bring this conversation to a close, because the light shining in through these cracks indicates that day has long since broken. This coming night, if we haven't been deprived of this great benefit of speech, will be mine, to tell you *my* life.

BERGANZA: So be it, and be sure to come to this very place.

A CATALOG OF SELECTED
DOVER BOOKS
IN ALL FIELDS OF INTEREST

THE CLARINET AND CLARINET PLAYING, David Pino. Lively, comprehensive work features suggestions about technique, musicianship, and musical interpretation, as well as guidelines for teaching, making your own reeds, and preparing for public performance. Includes an intriguing look at clarinet history. "A godsend," *The Clarinet*, Journal of the International Clarinet Society. Appendixes. 7 illus. 320pp. 5⅜ x 8½. 0-486-40270-3

HOLLYWOOD GLAMOR PORTRAITS, John Kobal (ed.). 145 photos from 1926-49. Harlow, Gable, Bogart, Bacall; 94 stars in all. Full background on photographers, technical aspects. 160pp. 8⅜ x 11¼. 0-486-23352-9

THE RAVEN AND OTHER FAVORITE POEMS, Edgar Allan Poe. Over 40 of the author's most memorable poems: "The Bells," "Ulalume," "Israfel," "To Helen," "The Conqueror Worm," "Eldorado," "Annabel Lee," many more. Alphabetic lists of titles and first lines. 64pp. 5³⁄₁₆ x 8¼. 0-486-26685-0

PERSONAL MEMOIRS OF U. S. GRANT, Ulysses Simpson Grant. Intelligent, deeply moving firsthand account of Civil War campaigns, considered by many the finest military memoirs ever written. Includes letters, historic photographs, maps and more. 528pp. 6⅛ x 9¼. 0-486-28587-1

ANCIENT EGYPTIAN MATERIALS AND INDUSTRIES, A. Lucas and J. Harris. Fascinating, comprehensive, thoroughly documented text describes this ancient civilization's vast resources and the processes that incorporated them in daily life, including the use of animal products, building materials, cosmetics, perfumes and incense, fibers, glazed ware, glass and its manufacture, materials used in the mummification process, and much more. 544pp. 6⅛ x 9¼. (Available in U.S. only.) 0-486-40446-3

RUSSIAN STORIES/RUSSKIE RASSKAZY: A Dual-Language Book, edited by Gleb Struve. Twelve tales by such masters as Chekhov, Tolstoy, Dostoevsky, Pushkin, others. Excellent word-for-word English translations on facing pages, plus teaching and study aids, Russian/English vocabulary, biographical/critical introductions, more. 416pp. 5⅜ x 8½. 0-486-26244-8

PHILADELPHIA THEN AND NOW: 60 Sites Photographed in the Past and Present, Kenneth Finkel and Susan Oyama. Rare photographs of City Hall, Logan Square, Independence Hall, Betsy Ross House, other landmarks juxtaposed with contemporary views. Captures changing face of historic city. Introduction. Captions. 128pp. 8¼ x 11. 0-486-25790-8

NORTH AMERICAN INDIAN LIFE: Customs and Traditions of 23 Tribes, Elsie Clews Parsons (ed.). 27 fictionalized essays by noted anthropologists examine religion, customs, government, additional facets of life among the Winnebago, Crow, Zuni, Eskimo, other tribes. 480pp. 6⅛ x 9¼. 0-486-27377-6

TECHNICAL MANUAL AND DICTIONARY OF CLASSICAL BALLET, Gail Grant. Defines, explains, comments on steps, movements, poses and concepts. 15-page pictorial section. Basic book for student, viewer. 127pp. 5⅜ x 8½. 0-486-21843-0

THE MALE AND FEMALE FIGURE IN MOTION: 60 Classic Photographic Sequences, Eadweard Muybridge. 60 true-action photographs of men and women walking, running, climbing, bending, turning, etc., reproduced from rare 19th-century masterpiece. vi + 121pp. 9 x 12. 0-486-24745-7

PSYCHOLOGY OF MUSIC, Carl E. Seashore. Classic work discusses music as a medium from psychological viewpoint. Clear treatment of physical acoustics, auditory apparatus, sound perception, development of musical skills, nature of musical feeling, host of other topics. 88 figures. 408pp. 5⅜ x 8½. 0-486-21851-1

LIFE IN ANCIENT EGYPT, Adolf Erman. Fullest, most thorough, detailed older account with much not in more recent books, domestic life, religion, magic, medicine, commerce, much more. Many illustrations reproduce tomb paintings, carvings, hieroglyphs, etc. 597pp. 5⅜ x 8½. 0-486-22632-8

SUNDIALS, Their Theory and Construction, Albert Waugh. Far and away the best, most thorough coverage of ideas, mathematics concerned, types, construction, adjusting anywhere. Simple, nontechnical treatment allows even children to build several of these dials. Over 100 illustrations. 230pp. 5⅜ x 8½. 0-486-22947-5

THEORETICAL HYDRODYNAMICS, L. M. Milne-Thomson. Classic exposition of the mathematical theory of fluid motion, applicable to both hydrodynamics and aerodynamics. Over 600 exercises. 768pp. 6⅛ x 9¼. 0-486-68970-0

OLD-TIME VIGNETTES IN FULL COLOR, Carol Belanger Grafton (ed.). Over 390 charming, often sentimental illustrations, selected from archives of Victorian graphics–pretty women posing, children playing, food, flowers, kittens and puppies, smiling cherubs, birds and butterflies, much more. All copyright-free. 48pp. 9¼ x 12¼. 0-486-27269-9

PERSPECTIVE FOR ARTISTS, Rex Vicat Cole. Depth, perspective of sky and sea, shadows, much more, not usually covered. 391 diagrams, 81 reproductions of drawings and paintings. 279pp. 5⅜ x 8½. 0-486-22487-2

DRAWING THE LIVING FIGURE, Joseph Sheppard. Innovative approach to artistic anatomy focuses on specifics of surface anatomy, rather than muscles and bones. Over 170 drawings of live models in front, back and side views, and in widely varying poses. Accompanying diagrams. 177 illustrations. Introduction. Index. 144pp. 8⅜ x11¼. 0-486-26723-7

GOTHIC AND OLD ENGLISH ALPHABETS: 100 Complete Fonts, Dan X. Solo. Add power, elegance to posters, signs, other graphics with 100 stunning copyright-free alphabets: Blackstone, Dolbey, Germania, 97 more–including many lower-case, numerals, punctuation marks. 104pp. 8⅛ x 11. 0-486-24695-7

THE BOOK OF WOOD CARVING, Charles Marshall Sayers. Finest book for beginners discusses fundamentals and offers 34 designs. "Absolutely first rate . . . well thought out and well executed."–E. J. Tangerman. 118pp. 7¾ x 10⅝. 0-486-23654-4

ILLUSTRATED CATALOG OF CIVIL WAR MILITARY GOODS: Union Army Weapons, Insignia, Uniform Accessories, and Other Equipment, Schuyler, Hartley, and Graham. Rare, profusely illustrated 1846 catalog includes Union Army uniform and dress regulations, arms and ammunition, coats, insignia, flags, swords, rifles, etc. 226 illustrations. 160pp. 9 x 12. 0-486-24939-5

WOMEN'S FASHIONS OF THE EARLY 1900s: An Unabridged Republication of "New York Fashions, 1909," National Cloak & Suit Co. Rare catalog of mail-order fashions documents women's and children's clothing styles shortly after the turn of the century. Captions offer full descriptions, prices. Invaluable resource for fashion, costume historians. Approximately 725 illustrations. 128pp. 8⅜ x 11¼. 0-486-27276-1

HOW TO DO BEADWORK, Mary White. Fundamental book on craft from simple projects to five-bead chains and woven works. 106 illustrations. 142pp. 5⅜ x 8.
0-486-20697-1

THE 1912 AND 1915 GUSTAV STICKLEY FURNITURE CATALOGS, Gustav Stickley. With over 200 detailed illustrations and descriptions, these two catalogs are essential reading and reference materials and identification guides for Stickley furniture. Captions cite materials, dimensions and prices. 112pp. 6½ x 9¼. 0-486-26676-1

EARLY AMERICAN LOCOMOTIVES, John H. White, Jr. Finest locomotive engravings from early 19th century: historical (1804–74), main-line (after 1870), special, foreign, etc. 147 plates. 142pp. 11⅜ x 8¼. 0-486-22772-3

LITTLE BOOK OF EARLY AMERICAN CRAFTS AND TRADES, Peter Stockham (ed.). 1807 children's book explains crafts and trades: baker, hatter, cooper, potter, and many others. 23 copperplate illustrations. 140pp. 4⅝ x 6.
0-486-23336-7

VICTORIAN FASHIONS AND COSTUMES FROM HARPER'S BAZAR, 1867–1898, Stella Blum (ed.). Day costumes, evening wear, sports clothes, shoes, hats, other accessories in over 1,000 detailed engravings. 320pp. 9⅜ x 12¼.
0-486-22990-4

THE LONG ISLAND RAIL ROAD IN EARLY PHOTOGRAPHS, Ron Ziel. Over 220 rare photos, informative text document origin (1844) and development of rail service on Long Island. Vintage views of early trains, locomotives, stations, passengers, crews, much more. Captions. 8⅞ x 11¾. 0-486-26301-0

VOYAGE OF THE LIBERDADE, Joshua Slocum. Great 19th-century mariner's thrilling, first-hand account of the wreck of his ship off South America, the 35-foot boat he built from the wreckage, and its remarkable voyage home. 128pp. 5⅜ x 8½.
0-486-40022-0

TEN BOOKS ON ARCHITECTURE, Vitruvius. The most important book ever written on architecture. Early Roman aesthetics, technology, classical orders, site selection, all other aspects. Morgan translation. 331pp. 5⅜ x 8½. 0-486-20645-9

THE HUMAN FIGURE IN MOTION, Eadweard Muybridge. More than 4,500 stopped-action photos, in action series, showing undraped men, women, children jumping, lying down, throwing, sitting, wrestling, carrying, etc. 390pp. 7⅞ x 10⅝.
0-486-20204-6 Clothbd.

TREES OF THE EASTERN AND CENTRAL UNITED STATES AND CANADA, William M. Harlow. Best one-volume guide to 140 trees. Full descriptions, woodlore, range, etc. Over 600 illustrations. Handy size. 288pp. 4½ x 6⅜. 0-486-20395-6

GROWING AND USING HERBS AND SPICES, Milo Miloradovich. Versatile handbook provides all the information needed for cultivation and use of all the herbs and spices available in North America. 4 illustrations. Index. Glossary. 236pp. 5⅜ x 8½.
0-486-25058-X

BIG BOOK OF MAZES AND LABYRINTHS, Walter Shepherd. 50 mazes and labyrinths in all–classical, solid, ripple, and more–in one great volume. Perfect inexpensive puzzler for clever youngsters. Full solutions. 112pp. 8⅛ x 11. 0-486-22951-3

PIANO TUNING, J. Cree Fischer. Clearest, best book for beginner, amateur. Simple repairs, raising dropped notes, tuning by easy method of flattened fifths. No previous skills needed. 4 illustrations. 201pp. 5⅜ x 8½. 0-486-23267-0

DRIED FLOWERS: How to Prepare Them, Sarah Whitlock and Martha Rankin. Complete instructions on how to use silica gel, meal and borax, perlite aggregate, sand and borax, glycerine and water to create attractive permanent flower arrangements. 12 illustrations. 32pp. 5⅜ x 8½. 0-486-21802-3

EASY-TO-MAKE BIRD FEEDERS FOR WOODWORKERS, Scott D. Campbell. Detailed, simple-to-use guide for designing, constructing, caring for and using feeders. Text, illustrations for 12 classic and contemporary designs. 96pp. 5⅜ x 8½. 0-486-25847-5

THE COMPLETE BOOK OF BIRDHOUSE CONSTRUCTION FOR WOODWORKERS, Scott D. Campbell. Detailed instructions, illustrations, tables. Also data on bird habitat and instinct patterns. Bibliography. 3 tables. 63 illustrations in 15 figures. 48pp. 5¼ x 8½. 0-486-24407-5

SCOTTISH WONDER TALES FROM MYTH AND LEGEND, Donald A. Mackenzie. 16 lively tales tell of giants rumbling down mountainsides, of a magic wand that turns stone pillars into warriors, of gods and goddesses, evil hags, powerful forces and more. 240pp. 5⅜ x 8½. 0-486-29677-6

THE HISTORY OF UNDERCLOTHES, C. Willett Cunnington and Phyllis Cunnington. Fascinating, well-documented survey covering six centuries of English undergarments, enhanced with over 100 illustrations: 12th-century laced-up bodice, footed long drawers (1795), 19th-century bustles, 19th-century corsets for men, Victorian "bust improvers," much more. 272pp. 5⅜ x 8¼. 0-486-27124-2

ARTS AND CRAFTS FURNITURE: The Complete Brooks Catalog of 1912, Brooks Manufacturing Co. Photos and detailed descriptions of more than 150 now very collectible furniture designs from the Arts and Crafts movement depict davenports, settees, buffets, desks, tables, chairs, bedsteads, dressers and more, all built of solid, quarter-sawed oak. Invaluable for students and enthusiasts of antiques, Americana and the decorative arts. 80pp. 6½ x 9¼. 0-486-27471-3

WILBUR AND ORVILLE: A Biography of the Wright Brothers, Fred Howard. Definitive, crisply written study tells the full story of the brothers' lives and work. A vividly written biography, unparalleled in scope and color, that also captures the spirit of an extraordinary era. 560pp. 6⅛ x 9¼. 0-486-40297-5

THE ARTS OF THE SAILOR: Knotting, Splicing and Ropework, Hervey Garrett Smith. Indispensable shipboard reference covers tools, basic knots and useful hitches; handsewing and canvas work, more. Over 100 illustrations. Delightful reading for sea lovers. 256pp. 5⅜ x 8½. 0-486-26440-8

FRANK LLOYD WRIGHT'S FALLINGWATER: The House and Its History, Second, Revised Edition, Donald Hoffmann. A total revision–both in text and illustrations–of the standard document on Fallingwater, the boldest, most personal architectural statement of Wright's mature years, updated with valuable new material from the recently opened Frank Lloyd Wright Archives. "Fascinating"–*The New York Times*. 116 illustrations. 128pp. 9¼ x 10¾. 0-486-27430-6

PHOTOGRAPHIC SKETCHBOOK OF THE CIVIL WAR, Alexander Gardner. 100 photos taken on field during the Civil War. Famous shots of Manassas Harper's Ferry, Lincoln, Richmond, slave pens, etc. 244pp. 10⅝ x 8¼. 0-486-22731-6

FIVE ACRES AND INDEPENDENCE, Maurice G. Kains. Great back-to-the-land classic explains basics of self-sufficient farming. The one book to get. 95 illustrations. 397pp. 5⅜ x 8½. 0-486-20974-1

A MODERN HERBAL, Margaret Grieve. Much the fullest, most exact, most useful compilation of herbal material. Gigantic alphabetical encyclopedia, from aconite to zedoary, gives botanical information, medical properties, folklore, economic uses, much else. Indispensable to serious reader. 161 illustrations. 888pp. 6½ x 9¼. 2-vol. set. (Available in U.S. only.) Vol. I: 0-486-22798-7 Vol. II: 0-486-22799-5

HIDDEN TREASURE MAZE BOOK, Dave Phillips. Solve 34 challenging mazes accompanied by heroic tales of adventure. Evil dragons, people-eating plants, blood-thirsty giants, many more dangerous adversaries lurk at every twist and turn. 34 mazes, stories, solutions. 48pp. 8¼ x 11. 0-486-24566-7

LETTERS OF W. A. MOZART, Wolfgang A. Mozart. Remarkable letters show bawdy wit, humor, imagination, musical insights, contemporary musical world; includes some letters from Leopold Mozart. 276pp. 5⅜ x 8½. 0-486-22859-2

BASIC PRINCIPLES OF CLASSICAL BALLET, Agrippina Vaganova. Great Russian theoretician, teacher explains methods for teaching classical ballet. 118 illustrations. 175pp. 5⅜ x 8½. 0-486-22036-2

THE JUMPING FROG, Mark Twain. Revenge edition. The original story of The Celebrated Jumping Frog of Calaveras County, a hapless French translation, and Twain's hilarious "retranslation" from the French. 12 illustrations. 66pp. 5⅜ x 8½. 0-486-22686-7

BEST REMEMBERED POEMS, Martin Gardner (ed.). The 126 poems in this superb collection of 19th- and 20th-century British and American verse range from Shelley's "To a Skylark" to the impassioned "Renascence" of Edna St. Vincent Millay and to Edward Lear's whimsical "The Owl and the Pussycat." 224pp. 5⅜ x 8½. 0-486-27165-X

COMPLETE SONNETS, William Shakespeare. Over 150 exquisite poems deal with love, friendship, the tyranny of time, beauty's evanescence, death and other themes in language of remarkable power, precision and beauty. Glossary of archaic terms. 80pp. 5$\frac{3}{16}$ x 8¼. 0-486-26686-9

HISTORIC HOMES OF THE AMERICAN PRESIDENTS, Second, Revised Edition, Irvin Haas. A traveler's guide to American Presidential homes, most open to the public, depicting and describing homes occupied by every American President from George Washington to George Bush. With visiting hours, admission charges, travel routes. 175 photographs. Index. 160pp. 8¼ x 11. 0-486-26751-2

THE WIT AND HUMOR OF OSCAR WILDE, Alvin Redman (ed.). More than 1,000 ripostes, paradoxes, wisecracks: Work is the curse of the drinking classes; I can resist everything except temptation; etc. 258pp. 5⅜ x 8½. 0-486-20602-5

SHAKESPEARE LEXICON AND QUOTATION DICTIONARY, Alexander Schmidt. Full definitions, locations, shades of meaning in every word in plays and poems. More than 50,000 exact quotations. 1,485pp. 6½ x 9¼. 2-vol. set. Vol. 1: 0-486-22726-X Vol. 2: 0-486-22727-8

SELECTED POEMS, Emily Dickinson. Over 100 best-known, best-loved poems by one of America's foremost poets, reprinted from authoritative early editions. No comparable edition at this price. Index of first lines. 64pp. 5$\frac{3}{16}$ x 8¼. 0-486-26466-1

THE INSIDIOUS DR. FU-MANCHU, Sax Rohmer. The first of the popular mystery series introduces a pair of English detectives to their archnemesis, the diabolical Dr. Fu-Manchu. Flavorful atmosphere, fast-paced action, and colorful characters enliven this classic of the genre. 208pp. 5$\frac{3}{16}$ x 8¼. 0-486-29898-1

CATALOG OF DOVER BOOKS